EMPLOYMENT RELATIONS
in the
UNITED STATES

EMPLOYMENT RELATIONS
in the
UNITED STATES
Law, Policy, and Practice

Raymond Hogler
Colorado State University

SAGE Publications
International Educational and Professional Publisher
Thousand Oaks ■ London ■ New Delhi

For information:

Sage Publications, Inc.
2455 Teller Road
Thousand Oaks, California 91320
E-mail: order@sagepub.com

Sage Publications Ltd.
6 Bonhill Street
London EC2A 4PU
United Kingdom

Sage Publications India Pvt. Ltd.
B-42, Panchsheel Enclave
Post Box 4109
New Delhi 110 017 India

Printed in the United States of America

Library of Congress Cataloging-in-Publication Data

Hogler, Raymond L.
Employment relations in the United States: Law, policy, and practice / by Raymond Hogler.
     p. cm.
Includes bibliographical references and index.
ISBN 1-4129-0414-5 (cloth)
ISBN 0-7619-2654-2 (pbk.)
     1. Labor laws and legislation—United States. 2. Industrial relations—United States. I. Title. KF3369. H643 2004
344′7301—dc22

                                        2003021149

This book is printed on acid-free paper.

03   04   05   06   10   9   8   7   6   5   4   3   2   1

Acquisitions Editor:	Al Bruckner
Editorial Assistant:	MaryAnn Vail
Production Editor:	Denise Santoyo
Copy Editor:	Toni Williams
Typesetter:	C&M Digitals (P) Ltd.
Indexer:	Juniee Oneida
Cover Designer:	Michelle Lee Kenny

Contents

Preface

L
ike most people in this country, my ancestors came from somewhere else. One grandfather, Jesse, emigrated from England. My father's father, Louis, left Austria in 1904 to avoid being conscripted for the empire's military adventures. Both of them eventually made their way west to settle in rural Colorado. They lived through the bad times of the Depression and the good times after World War II, raising families and making a contribution to their communities. But their experiences differed in crucial ways.

A self-employed builder and all-purpose entrepreneur, Jesse sometimes used the phrase "a job of work." He meant by that term an expenditure of labor over a discrete period of time and limited to a defined task. So, he might say, "I'm going to Dove Creek next week for a job of work." His usage reflected the traditional definition of the word *job*, and it implied a relatively transitory attachment to the relationship between him and whoever purchased his services. In his later years, Jesse lived a fairly marginal and peripatetic existence. He had no fixed address, no steady means of support, and little prospect of economic security. Independent and self-reliant, he migrated around the country to suit his means and inclination.

My grandfather Louis, in comparison, had a job as we now understand it—that is, regular employment—as a coal miner. He worked for the Oliver Coal Company in Somerset, Colorado, for many years. In August 1933, he and the other miners organized Local No. 6417 of the United Mine Workers of America (UMWA). The UMWA negotiated a contract with Oliver, and it continued in effect until the mine closed its operation. Louis enjoyed a long and comfortable retirement. He received a regular monthly pension check from the union, in addition to his social security payment. He had health insurance benefits that paid for medical care, and he owned a modest home. When he died, my grandmother continued to collect his pension.

This book deals with employment relations in the United States from a historical and institutional perspective. I start from the premise that the two cases above illustrate important points about work in this country. What distinguishes one story from the other is the nature of the employment contract. A self-employed person stands in a much different position to a buyer of labor than someone who is an employee. In the latter instance, a set of legal conditions attach to the relationship that are not necessarily part of the parties' explicit agreement. My coal-mining grandfather, for example, did not have to bargain for insurance to protect him against workplace injuries. When Colorado enacted a workers' compensation law, insurance coverage came automatically with employment. Nor did Louis individually negotiate with the coal company for the wages and the benefits in the collective bargaining agreement. All employees in the bargaining unit fell under the contract's coverage and had the same rights. Later, after the New Deal, Louis's union pension was supplemented by the federal pension program of Social Security.

To begin with, the book presents an overview of employment in the United States and sketches the thematic development used in the following chapters. Briefly, I characterize the cycles of employment relations in terms of dominant actors. From the end of the Civil War up to the beginning of the Depression and the election of Franklin D. Roosevelt in 1932, managers tended to exercise their prerogatives without interference from employees or the government. One consequence was protracted industrial conflict. As economic conditions worsened in the 1930s, the federal government began to intervene aggressively in labor relations. The result was laws protecting unions, establishing retirement and unemployment benefits, and setting a floor under wages and a ceiling over hours. In the 1960s, civil rights legislation emerged; gradually, individual employment rights overshadowed other aspects of employment. By the end of the twentieth century, union membership had declined from a peak of one-third of the nonagricultural workforce to just over 13 percent. With that decline, workers have experienced a steady erosion of wages and benefits over the past three decades. Presently, issues of health care coverage, retirement, and unemployment are taking on a greater urgency in the national discourse.

Employment in this country is closely connected to wealth, status, and security. For that reason, it is a subject of interest across a range of academic disciplines. My approach incorporates material from different specialties, and the notes to each chapter attempt to be complete and informative. Each chapter also contains a list of recommended readings and a set of questions for further inquiry. Those with an interest in a particular topic can find references for an extended consideration of the topic.

A number of individuals read portions of the book and offered helpful comments. Their suggestions helped to improve the book and I appreciate the thoughtfulness and attention of the reviewers, but at the end of the day, the job was mine.

CHAPTER 1

Contemporary Employment Relations in Historical Perspective

T he U.S. employment system has its origins in the arrival of European settlers to the new continent. The early colonists brought with them English traditions of labor, upon which they imposed variations suited to different conditions. One of those variations involved a form of contractual or indentured servitude by which an emigrant agreed to labor for a period of years in exchange for passage to the New World. Another variation was the "peculiar institution" of slavery, which enabled a buyer to purchase human labor power as a form of property. The practice of indentured servitude gradually fell into disfavor as population growth furnished a source of labor. Slavery, and its attendant regime of ownership rights, endured until the passage of the Thirteenth Amendment in 1865. It stamped U.S. society with characteristics that still resonate today; among them are the laws prohibiting race discrimination in employment that make up an important part of contemporary labor market regulation.[1]

With the rise of industrialization in the latter nineteenth century, U.S. workers began to organize national labor unions as a response to managerial control over employment. That effort met with limited success until the early twentieth century. As the country experienced world war and depression, unions became a more attractive means of conducting labor market transactions, and such leaders as John L. Lewis, Walter and Victor Reuther, and Jimmy Hoffa emerged as the new men of power in our political economy. For three decades after World War II, unions played a central role in setting terms of employment. Union membership and influence declined sharply in the 1980s, and a burgeoning scheme of governmental regulation emerged to protect the rights of individual employees. The scope and complexity of employment law now rival more traditional fields of legal study.

This book describes the historical context of employment relations in this country and offers an interpretation of the factors shaping its evolution. The system arose in part as a consequence of external forces, but it also followed a trajectory dictated by its internal dynamic. To illustrate with one notable example, the idea of participatory democracy makes up the cornerstone of our national culture. The grandest experiment in workplace democracy began in 1915, when John D. Rockefeller Jr. visited the state of Colorado and declared that capitalists, workers, and shareholders were all partners in the great economic venture of the Colorado Fuel & Iron Corporation and labor was therefore entitled to a voice in the affairs of the enterprise.[2] Rockefeller devised his industrial plan as a reaction to pressure from President Woodrow Wilson and vociferous public criticism after the labor conflict at Ludlow a year earlier. Eventually, Rockefeller's ideas led to the widespread use of company unions in the 1930s and prompted Senator Robert Wagner in 1935 to make them illegal under the federal collective bargaining law. Leading policy-makers and academics now question whether Wagner's views continue to be relevant to today's circumstances.[3] Without a proper historical appreciation of the topic, however, the debate over workplace democracy has little contemporary substance. The remainder of this chapter sketches the major themes and ideas developed over the course of the book.

The Start of a New Millennium

Beginning in the early 1990s, the U.S. economy embarked on an era of expansion and prosperity that lasted through the end of the decade. Stock prices climbed to a historic peak, reaching 11,722 on the Dow Jones Industrial Average in January 2000. The unemployment rate dropped from 7.8 percent in 1991 to 3.9 percent in September 2000. Inflation rates remained low, and productivity grew at an annual rate of 2.5 percent between 1995 and 2000. Workers in low and middle income levels experienced real wage gains for the first time since the early 1970s, and income differentials began to moderate. Recipients of public welfare entered the workforce, gaining a foothold in the labor market. In March 2001, the number of households below the poverty line fell to 11.3 percent, its lowest level since 1973. As employment grew, even unskilled workers found jobs that offered training and prospects of advancement. But the run of prosperity came to an end at the turn of the century.[4]

The destruction of the World Trade Center towers in September 2001 and the ensuing war against terrorism aggravated existing weaknesses in the economy and precipitated a recession persisting into the next year. The stock market reported a record numerical decline in late September. Following a brief period of recovery, disclosures of accounting irregularities in major firms such as Enron and WorldCom led to further market declines, and the Dow Jones index fell to 7,286 in October 2002.[5] The national unemployment rate rose to a four-year high of 6 percent in November 2002. As a response to threats of financial instability, the Federal Reserve continued to lower key interest rates until they reached levels of 1961.[6] Following significant Republican victories in the 2002 congressional elections, officials in the administration of President George W. Bush debated policy moves to stimulate the economy, including tax cuts for businesses and upper income families and investment incentives based on elimination of taxation of corporate dividends. Democratic members of Congress put forward their own proposals, one of which featured a payroll-tax holiday to provide financial relief to low income workers.[7] Those measures were designed to encourage business investment and consumer spending to avert a downward spiral that threatened the global economy.[8]

The outbreak of war against Iraq in early 2003 prompted a surge in stock prices and the index gained nearly 1,000 points in eight sessions, only to drop by one-third shortly thereafter.[9] As the costs of the conflict and reconstruction became more defined, domestic policies gave way to the international agenda. Congress appropriated $70 billion to the military effort, despite mounting concern over the effect of deficits on such domestic programs as Medicare, health care for uninsured individuals, schools, and aid to financially distressed state governments.[10] The airline industry, particularly affected by the conflict, requested substantial amounts of federal aid.[11] After the war officially ended in Iraq, unemployment remained at relatively high levels and reached a nine-year high of 6.4 percent in June 2003. Many discouraged workers stopped seeking work, raising the total number of unemployed to 3.82 million.[12] President Bush insisted that his tax cuts would act as a stimulus to create jobs. Democrats, meanwhile, continued to press for more federal aid for states and extended unemployment benefits.[13] Analysts vigorously debated the effects of the administration's economic policies on future budget deficits, interest rates, and growth.[14]

The idea that our federal government should play an active role in managing labor markets to promote social policy gained widespread acceptance in the New Deal era of the 1930s, when many of the programs originated that make up the foundations of modern workplace relations. Those changes were prompted by the crisis of the Great Depression. At the time of Franklin Delano Roosevelt's election in November 1932, more than one-quarter of the workforce was unemployed, capital investment had largely ceased, and the economy had steadily contracted since 1929. In response, Roosevelt and the New Deal Congress enacted legislation that profoundly altered the industrial environment, and the effects of those changes persist today. The major legislative components of the New Deal program included laws encouraging unions and collective bargaining, a system of retirement security, minimum wage and hour regulation, and unemployment insurance. Such innovations marked a radical break with existing law, which, with some rare exceptions, consisted of judicial common law doctrines formulated over the course of nearly two centuries. But government activism was then, and is now, politically controversial.[15]

In contrast to other industrialized nations, the U.S. pattern of employment regulation evolved sporadically and unsystematically. One important reason was the absence of a strong working-class political movement to promote aggressive state intervention in labor markets.[16] European countries adopted integrated approaches to regulation, driven in large part by powerful trade unions representing class interests, and, as a result, legal rules helped to stabilize compensation, working conditions, and living standards.[17] Today, labor market concerns remain embedded in discussions of political issues, such as the aims and objectives of the European Union as it expands its membership.[18] To understand the U.S. system, it is useful to examine some background about the United States' unique approach to employment and its relevance to public policy.[19]

Analyzing "Exceptionalism": Is the United States Different and Why?

The distinction between the labor relations system in the United States and its global competitors is sometimes described by the term *American exceptionalism*, which emphasizes the fact that U.S. workers do not make up a coherent group united by class sentiment and common goals.[20] The lack of a unified political force in this country has resulted in less social legislation to assist wage earners, such as guaranteed health insurance, paid parental leaves, and other kinds of mandated employment benefits. During the early twentieth century, scholars devoted increased attention to emerging trends in the relations between workers and employers. Writing in 1906, the German political economist Werner Sombart analyzed the U.S. trade union movement and pointed out that neither U.S. workers nor their leaders accepted the basic tenets of socialism. Indeed, Sombart said, "emotionally the American worker has a share in capitalism: I believe that he loves it."[21] He then went on to suggest a number of reasons why U.S. industrial relations were unique, including the attitudes of workers, the two-party system in U.S. politics, the relatively high material conditions of U.S. workers, and greater opportunities for upward and geographical mobility.

Early studies of U.S. labor were influenced by Sombart's views. Selig Perlman, in his classic book *Theory of the Labor Movement* (1928), echoed the notion that Americans were unique in their outlook and approach to labor organization. For Perlman, the crucial feature of labor was a *consciousness of scarcity of opportunity*. Such consciousness led to collective attempts to control and ration opportunities for work. Business, in contrast, was dominated by a *consciousness of unlimited opportunity* or abundance. Because U.S. workers historically enjoyed access to land and economic mobility, their social philosophy at first resembled that of the business entrepreneur. Only when the consciousness of abundance had been replaced by a *consciousness of job scarcity* did workers in this country create a stable labor movement. Even then, peculiarly U.S. conditions produced a relatively weak labor movement.

Perlman identified two main factors in the U.S. environment affecting trade union formation. One was the strength of the institution of private property, and the second was the lack of a *class consciousness* in U.S. labor. Vigorous trade unionism, Perlman said, was always "a campaign against the absolute rights of private property" because it circumscribed an employer's prerogatives in the workplace.

The absence of class consciousness in the United States could be attributed to a fluid economic system that offered social advancement, a political system giving most workers a right to vote, and ethnic and cultural diversity. As a result, Perlman believed, the U.S. labor movement was dominated by a *job consciousness* that had only a narrow objective of controlling wages and working conditions, rather than broad political reform.[22] The basic attitudes and beliefs that Sombart and Perlman identified are still used as explanatory factors in studies analyzing the low rates of union membership in the United States. According to a recent analysis, "American workers are less class conscious than their counterparts in almost all other developed countries." Thus, Americans have less inclination toward group action, such as unions, because we favor values of individualism and merit over collective action and social protections.[23]

Employers, likewise, demonstrate considerable hostility to unions in their workplaces. Indeed, the opposition of U.S. employers to unions "has always been more extreme than that of employers in other nations" and is an important factor in union decline.[24] When union membership fell by over 30 percent in the 1980s, influential scholars attributed the decline to increases in employer unfair labor practices and their effects on workers.[25] Such research prompted a debate about the role of unions in our economy and the effectiveness of U.S. labor laws; that controversy remains unsettled.[26] Subsequent chapters of this book examine the contributions of the union movement to creating stable employment conditions and the rise of a system of fringe benefits.

Negative views about unions are also prevalent in our judicial system, and adverse common law decisions in the nineteenth century forced labor leaders to focus on job-related matters and discouraged labor radicalism through outright legal repression.[27] One important rule was the principle of *employment at will,* which permitted employers to fire employees at any time for any reason. The rule has been qualified by various statutes and judicial exceptions, discussed later in the book, which created a patchwork of rights and duties that often results in litigation to resolve disputes. During the late nineteenth century, the U.S. Supreme Court rendered important decisions striking down both state and federal legislation attempting to limit employers' power in the workplace. The Court did not change its constitutional view of federal power over employment until 1937, when it upheld the constitutionality of the National Labor Relations (Wagner) Act. Since that time, the federal government has exercised its authority over most dimensions of employment, ranging from an employer's selection of workers through conditions on the job and mandatory benefits.

Studying Work

Because the U.S. employment system evolved through social practice, judicial doctrine, and statutory enactment, it has overlapping and contradictory features that extend across a number of intellectual disciplines. As employment became defined as a subject of study, scholars such as Perlman and his teacher at the University of

Wisconsin, John R. Commons, established the field of industrial relations in this country. In the *History of Labour in the United States,* Commons and his associates traced the "interaction of economic, industrial, and political conditions, with many varieties of individualistic, socialistic, and protectionist philosophies. The labour history of the country," Commons said, "is here treated as a part of its industrial and political history."[28] Commons, like Sombart, considered the "wide expanse of free land" in the United States to be an important explanatory factor in the development of industrial relations. He also argued that the market was the predominant economic force shaping employment relationships during the formative period of industrial development in the United States, thereby differentiating the U.S. experience from the European "class conflict" theory advanced by Marx and Engels.[29]

The interdisciplinary perspective adopted by Commons eventually split into two fairly distinct intellectual currents that are still apparent today. The personnel management school of industrial relations took root in the 1920s; it emphasized work environments, the social and psychological organization of work, and managerial leadership. Economists concentrated on forces external to the workplace and the conflicting interests of workers and employers. For personnel managers, unions hindered good workplace relations and made little positive contribution to employment. The economists, in contrast, believed that unions served a valuable social purpose by obtaining higher wages for workers through collective negotiations.[30] Over several decades, personnel management evolved into the area of human resource management and became linked with the field of organizational behavior.[31] Labor economics, likewise, changed direction in the 1960s and 1970s. Greater attention to individual behavior, markets, and competition was inconsistent with the collectivist model favored by traditional labor economists, particularly as union membership declined, and topics of interest to the early industrial relations specialists fell into neglect.[32] As a result, the integrated approach adopted by Commons gradually fragmented into more specialized areas of research featuring newer and more empirical methodologies, and industrial relations declined as a distinct academic field.

Over the past few years, however, scholarly contributions in the areas of history, political science, sociology, and law have demonstrated the need for an expanded view of workplace relations. Those studies examine the importance of workers' movements for our society as a whole and the institutions that shape those movements. A political scientist, for example, explored union decline within its historical context, attributing that decline to the relations between classes in this country.[33] A legal historian traced the relationship between organized labor and state activism to explain the ways in which regulation both constrains and encourages trade union activity.[34] Two labor economists described the positive impacts that unions can have on productivity and the importance of employee voice in the workplace.[35] Other studies provided insights into the historical development of labor markets in the United States,[36] the evolution of paternalistic corporate welfare policies as a political strategy,[37] and the impact of judicial lawmaking on trade union philosophy.[38] With the recent changes in the nature of employment, one

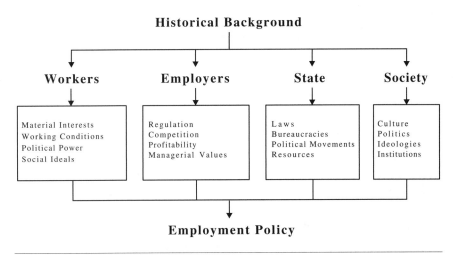

Figure 1.1   Employment Relations System

branch of sociological research argues that labor market conditions should be studied as part of our contemporary social life.[39] Figure 1.1 illustrates some of the complex forces underlying the employment system.

Renewed attention to the broader dimensions of employment and labor markets builds on the groundwork established nearly a century ago and emphasizes a historical perspective. Because of their interest in all aspects of the organization of commercial activity, Commons and other economists of his time were labeled as *institutionalists.* An influential contemporary movement has appropriated the label and describes itself as the *new institutional economics.* The theory begins with the general principle that institutions are recognized, established sets of practices, customs, and rules that govern the interactions among individuals; it departs from neoclassical assumptions about markets as the determinant of action by adopting a more realistic view of human nature in which passion matters as well as rationality.[40] When patterns of action become regulated and reproduced through some system of reward or sanction, they have become *institutionalized.*[41] Ronald Coase, a Nobel Prize winner in economics, began a revolution in economic thinking based on the insight that we cannot "really come to grips with how economies perform without putting at the foundation institutions and the way they affect economic performance."[42] Institutions, Coase said, are central to analysis because they determine the cost of economic transactions.

Coase's ideas, elaborated in a large body of subsequent research, have important implications for the dealings between employers and employees. Coase focused on the nature of the agreement between firms and workers and the ways in which such agreements had unique qualities. He described a firm as a system of relationships in which an entrepreneur controls the deployment of resources and exercises authority over employees. The firm exists because it can lower the transaction costs associated with hiring labor on the open market.[43] Coase's insights are a good starting point to begin a discussion of employment. They also illustrate why customary dealings between parties are an important supplement to regulations imposed by the state.

The Nature of Labor Contracts

In this country, a legal distinction is drawn between a market transaction and an employment relationship. The law differentiates for important purposes between an *independent contractor* and an *employee*. The independent contractor undertakes a market contract with a purchaser, but an employee enters into a relationship of legal status with an employer. In the first instance, the contractor agrees to furnish a set amount of work and is paid a price rather than a wage. The contractor performs work using his or her discretion in its conception and execution; the buyer exercises no direct control or supervision over the work. If either party is dissatisfied with the outcome of the transaction, he or she can attempt to recover damages for breach of contract. Those damages would compensate the injured party for losses that flowed from the wrongful act. If a painter used the wrong color of paint on a house, for example, the homeowner might recover the cost of repainting the house, but would not be entitled to damages for any emotional pain and suffering arising out of his or her neighbors' ridicule.

Employment relationships, in contrast, are actually agreements to enter into an ongoing commitment in which the employee submits to the direction and control of the employer over an indefinite period of time. That is, the employer directs the employee to report at a specified time and place, and the employer has authority to monitor the activities of the employee in doing the company's business to ensure that the employee works with sufficient effort. The employer's power over the worker is the threat of firing, and the employee's power over the employer is the threat of quitting. Because the relationship is one *at will*, it is not an enforceable contract in any meaningful sense.[44] If the employer does not realize at least as much value from the employee's labor as the employer pays in wages, the employer will eventually go out of business. On the other hand, the employee's labor may enable the employer to realize a surplus value over and above what the employer has paid the employee.

To further illustrate the point, we can describe two competing views of the wage–labor bargain. One conception relies on a theory of voluntary contractual exchange, and the other relies on a theory of hierarchical power. As a recent treatment of the subject notes, it is the difference between the ideas of neoclassical economics (or markets) and political economy (or hierarchies).[45] The basic principles of each approach have important consequences for the study of employment law because they can be used to support arguments about the level of government intervention in labor markets. Some degree of state involvement is always necessary to create and sustain the economic environment, but the extent to which the government should actually participate in fixing the terms of employment remains an area of fundamental disagreement between the two schools. For example, Federal Reserve Chairman Alan Greenspan, who is credited as the guiding genius of the 1990s economic expansion through his manipulation of interest rates, does not believe that the government should set a minimum wage for labor.[46]

The market model treats employment as a generic contractual exchange similar to a contract to buy a used car through the classified section of the newspaper. In that instance, both buyer and seller have enough bargaining power to deal with each other on a basis of rough equality. Neither party can coerce the other to make an agreement, but each party has a certain degree of dependence on the other because of mutual need. Presumably, the parties have the information, ability, and motivation to make the best possible bargain for themselves. The buyer could research the price of comparable cars and gain enough familiarity with automobiles to evaluate the particular vehicle based on its mileage, model, and overall condition. The seller knows the history of the car and its defects. Therefore, the end result will reflect all relevant factors such as the buyer's subjective tastes, market conditions, the uniqueness of the item, and the seller's financial need.[47]

Some economists propose that work is essentially the same. In this view, ordering an employee to do a specific task at work is no different than "telling a grocer to sell me this brand of tuna rather than that brand of bread." The reason for such a conclusion is that just as a consumer has no contractual obligation to buy goods from a particular supermarket, "neither the employee nor the employer is bound by any contractual obligations to continue their relationship."[48] Consequently, the employer's power over the employee consists of the same power that consumers exercise over sellers of products. The firm's owner is only the central agent who coordinates and renegotiates the efforts of the team members (employees) making up the organization. But if this conception fully explained how labor markets worked, there would be no need for companies. A person who wanted goods or services would simply buy them on an open market such as eBay, and employers would become merely contracting agents.[49]

A consideration of the new institutionalist ideas can be used to explain why firms are created and change in size. Coase addressed the problem by proposing the notion of transaction costs to explain the nature of economic organizations. He started from the proposition that decentralized contracting between individuals is theoretically sufficient to carry out productive activity. But because there are costs to making contracts, such as acquiring information and enforcing agreements, "firms will emerge to organize what would otherwise be market transactions whenever their costs were less than the costs of carrying out the transactions through the market. The limit to the size of the firm is set where its costs of organizing a transaction become equal to the cost of carrying it out through the market."[50] In other words, an entrepreneur will hire an employee when conditions make it difficult for the entrepreneur to obtain the same skills or services on the open market.

Another influential economist, Oliver Williamson, applied Coase's insights specifically to employment.[51] He identified several factors that make up transaction costs and create relational contracting in employment. Because humans lack complete information, Williamson said, they make choices based on "bounded rationality." Employers seek to pay as little as necessary for labor. Employees, in turn, try to shirk by giving less than their complete effort and must be monitored. Once an employer selects an individual from the pool of applicants, that individual begins to acquire knowledge about the employer's business operation and may learn special skills, thereby gaining what Williamson calls "asset specificity." Those circumstances lead to an indefinite, ongoing relationship that is negotiated as needed to continue the mutual commitment.

This model explains why employers and employees may have durable expectations about their relationship, even though it is one legally terminable at any time. Both parties exercise bargaining power in pursuit of their economic advantage. Employers compete with other firms for valuable employees, and competent employees can force companies to offer good wages, benefits, and working conditions by threatening to quit the firm. Logically, employers will have little incentive or opportunity to discriminate against workers except as it relates to their job performance, and laws are unnecessary to regulate decisions about hiring and firing. Therefore, the theory concludes, buyers and sellers of labor are best served by a legal regime that least interferes with their free and voluntary negotiations because it reflects their mutual interests, abilities, and preferences.

The second theoretical model, in contrast, sees employment in terms of coercion rather than consent. It draws on ideas of power and class to explain why some groups, such as women and racial minorities, appear to have lower incomes and less desirable jobs than white males. The starting point is Marx's insight that labor cannot be sold like other commodities because it depends on human effort. Marx noted that capitalists purchase only the potential labor power of a worker, not a fixed quantity of labor itself. Buyers and sellers of labor initially meet on equal terms in the market, where "freedom, equality, and the rights of man" prevail. But once the wage bargain is made, the capitalist exploits the worker in order to extract more value from the labor of the worker than the price the capitalist paid for it. In Marx's words, "the value of labor-power, and the value which that labor-power creates in the labor-process, are two entirely different magnitudes; and this difference of the two values was what the capitalist had in view when he was purchasing the labor-power."[52] Capitalist firms exist to exploit workers, not to be efficient. In short, firms must be profitable, but not necessarily productive.[53]

The political economy model emphasizes class divisions, power, and discriminatory labor markets. Workers and employers have conflicting, rather than cooperative, interests. Historically, the model's proponents point out, U.S. capitalists have acted to oppose and undermine workers' efforts to organize collectively and control the sale of their labor. Employers attacked unions and maintained class divisions between races and genders, which were reinforced by cultural patterns of discrimination.[54] As a result, social factors permeate the relations of employment, and employers use their power over workers for economic gain. It follows from this conception that political measures are needed to protect workers against the more extreme forms of exploitation.[55] Laws against discrimination based on race, gender, or disability, for example, serve as a needed corrective to capitalists' attempts to create and maintain pools of low-wage labor.

From either of the two basic conceptions of employment, it follows that some set of rules is necessary to make the system work. Markets depend on contracts, and contracts must be enforced through legal mechanisms that define rights of property and the obligations of the parties. For the new institutionalists, consequently, law and practice serve to enhance the voluntary transactions of workers and employers and reduce the costs of maintaining the economic relationship. In contrast, the political economists attempt to calculate the appropriate level of policy intervention needed to attain a balance of social welfare and economic output. Clearly, in any event, individuals acting alone cannot create the networks of binding obligation, macroeconomic guidance, and administrative apparatus necessary to sustain economic activity.

In short, political forces, managerial strategies, and workers' movements all play an important role in building employment relationships in the United States. The system evolved over time, and it can best be understood as a product of historical development; equally important, emerging policy choices will be simultaneously informed by and constrained by past developments. In her recent discussion of evolving workplace relations, Katherine Stone cogently assembles historical materials to advance proposals for systematic reform of the employment regime.[56] Such work demonstrates how U.S. industrial relations exhibit discernible trajectories over time and the importance of a scheme of periodization to analyze and guide change. What follows is a description of the chronological framework used here to explain the structure of employment relations and to suggest possible future directions.

An Overview of This Book

To begin with, from the 1880s through the 1920s, U.S. management exercised supremacy over workplace organization and conditions of labor. Workers challenged that dominance through political movements and overt conflict, but by the mid-1920s, managerial control was firmly entrenched. Firms adopted various strategies for dealing with labor, including both suppression and substitution. Suppression meant outright opposition and coercion of workers. Union substitution programs led to welfare capitalism and the rise of personnel policies. The Great Depression brought most of those efforts to an end. After the economic collapse of the 1930s, managerial power declined, and between the immediate postwar era and the 1970s, unions played a central role in determining employment policies. Collective bargaining, that is, set the standard for employment practices. Beginning in the mid-1970s, unions' ability to manage labor markets began to wane. At the same time, the state became more interventionist, establishing a regime of individual workplace rights enforceable through legal processes rather than contractual ones. Those general themes are summarized in Table 1.1 and developed in the subsequent discussion.

Table 1.1   A Conceptual Overview

Era	Time	Dominant Actor	Employment System	Specific Characteristics
Industrial management	1880s–1920s	Corporations	Employer prerogatives and discretion	Terms and conditions of work set by employers; legal regime based on liberty of contract and constitutional safeguards of property against state intervention
Collective bargaining	1930s–1970s	Labor unions	Labor market institutions and practices	Negotiated agreements; labor-management relations and stability; macroeconomic policies; private dispute resolution
Individual employment rights	1970s–2000s	Government	Protective legislation	Statutes and common law doctrines creating employee rights; litigation as a means of conflict resolution

Part I: The Era of Management, 1880–1935

This section begins with an overview of U.S. industrial development. Among other points, it summarizes economic growth after the Civil War, the emergence of various industrial sectors, and the rise of the corporation as a legal entity. The supplement to laws protecting individuals doing business within the corporate shell was the emerging law of labor markets—the contract for employment at will. This common law rule represented one of the most durable principles in the U.S. legal system. It assumed constitutional proportions in the early twentieth century, guaranteeing as a practical matter employers' complete discretion in matters of employment. By embedding the fundamental prerogative of hiring and firing in judicial doctrine, judges could shield employers from restrictive legislation and provide a ready weapon against collective action in the form of injunctions and other common law sanctions. Although the at-will rule now features an elaborate web of exceptions, it nonetheless remains the baseline principle of the U.S. employment system.[57]

A lack of legal rights did not discourage U.S. workers from making common cause with one another. After the Civil War, various workers' organizations sprang up in response to expanding economic activity. Those organizations offer important insights into the nature of unionism, its different manifestations, and their contemporary relevance. The Knights of Labor, for example, illustrates how a class-based form of organization attracted broad membership and political power during the 1880s and 1890s, eventually dying out as a result of ineffectual leadership. In contrast, the American Federation of Labor (AFL), established around the same time, began to thrive in the early twentieth century and now stands as the cornerstone of modern unionism. The International Workers of the World (IWW) offered a striking counterpoint to the narrow job-oriented perspective of the AFL. The IWW was a genuinely U.S. articulation of radical politics; its manifesto declared that the working classes and employing classes had nothing in common, and the goal of workers should be to overthrow the wage system. Once thought to have disappeared around 1917, the "Wobblies" currently solicit members on their Internet site.[58] The efforts of contemporary unions to rebuild their membership involve an exploration of their historical roots.

As workers' organizations began to challenge corporate power, there were numerous conflicts between labor and capital from the 1880s into the 1920s. Each incident illuminates a different aspect of the evolution of managerial power. After the 1881 Haymarket riot, for example, such ideas as the eight-hour day were discredited by association with foreign radicalism. Andrew Carnegie's defeat of steel workers at the Homestead strike in 1892 signified the struggle for control over industrial production. Two years later, the strike at the Pullman Company illustrated the power of the federal judiciary to impose legal sanctions against workers and imprison one of the most popular political figures in the country. The Ludlow massacre of 1914, which appeared to be a victory for labor, actually led to one of the most effective antiunion strategies ever devised by employers. At the end of World War I, an invigorated labor movement moved against U.S. Steel and was utterly crushed, making clear that employers could and would resist any encroachment on their authority.

Through such struggles, managerial power rose between 1890 and 1930 to its historical zenith in this country. The consolidation of power featured two vital modes, coercion and consent. During the 1920s, employers not only engaged in overt antiunionism, but also fashioned a system of welfare capitalism that formed the beginnings of modern human resource management; most of the contemporary techniques for dealing with employees originate from this period. To take just one example, the notion of *workplace justice* pervades the contemporary organizational literature. No modern system, however, compares in depth and sophistication to the employee representation plan developed in 1915 by John D. Rockefeller Jr. and Mackenzie King. The dampening of pro-union sentiment was complemented by an ideology indispensable to modern work organization—Frederick Taylor's dictum that managers conceived how work should be done and workers carried out that conception. Peter Drucker, the founder of contemporary management theory, called Taylor's writings on scientific management the most influential ideas since the Federalist papers. Taylorism, he said, formed the bedrock of U.S. work design, and its basics remain apparent everywhere in today's workplace.[59] The origin of workers' compensation systems shows how the interplay between law, politics, and economics led to a compromise on the issue of workplace injury that served the interests of employers as much as it benefited workers.

Part II: The Evolution of Collective Bargaining

During World War I, the federal government actively promoted collective bargaining practices in industries important to the war effort, and for the first time, employers confronted the concerted deployment of state power in matters of labor relations. Government policies had the desired effect and produced a marked increase in union membership density in the 1910s. Union growth posed a threat that employers promptly dealt with after the war ended. Employers signaled their hostility to collective bargaining at the 1919 Industrial Conference, and they put their program of union evisceration into action through the early 1920s. Despite that, federal labor policy had some lasting results, such as the Railway Labor Act (RLA). An examination of the origins, constitutionality, and current application of the RLA helps to underscore how specific circumstances can lead to seemingly incongruous political outcomes. We then summarize the growing economic crisis of the late 1920s and the conditions leading to Franklin Delano Roosevelt's election in 1932.

The New Deal began with passage of the National Industrial Recovery Act of 1933. Section 7(a) of that statute gave workers a right to organize unions and bargain collectively "through representatives of their own choosing." President Roosevelt approved the formation of an administrative body, the National Labor Board, to implement Section 7(a), and Senator Robert Wagner agreed to serve as chair of the new agency.[60] A few years later, Wagner's experiences on the board proved invaluable in drafting the National Labor Relations Act (NLRA). In addition to a collective bargaining law, the New Deal legislative agenda included pensions for retired workers, a minimum wage, and protections against loss of employment. Those laws—Social Security, fair labor standards, and unemployment insurance—are in effect today and have an important stabilizing effect on the economy by helping to sustain consumer purchasing power.

Between 1935 and 1945, U.S. unions organized workers in the core industrial sectors of the economy and became the driving force in labor markets. The Congress of Industrial Organizations (CIO), under the leadership of John L. Lewis, recruited some three million members in the first few years of its existence, and Lewis forced General Motors and U.S. Steel to deal with the CIO as representative of the corporations' employees. Particularly in steel, the labor agreement at U.S. Steel marked a historic breakthrough for trade unions. After defeats in 1892 and 1919, steelworkers brought the largest and most powerful corporation in the world to an agreement without a strike.[61] During World War II, labor entrenched its power in the workplace through the oversight of the National War Labor Board. The business community reacted to the rise of labor with a series of political initiatives during the war. Restrictive state laws foreshadowed developments in the federal law, which began with management's repudiation of wartime corporatism and culminated in the antiunion Taft-Hartley law of 1947.

Between 1947 and 1978, labor and management enjoyed a period of detente during which workers steadily improved their real earnings and obtained the various fringe benefits that now make up the customary employment package (holidays, vacations, retirement, and health insurance). The economic slump from the mid-1970s to the mid-1980s was characterized by high inflation, high unemployment, and declines in real wages for most U.S. workers. Beginning with the defeat of the union-sponsored Labor Reform Act of 1978, employers intensified their opposition to collective bargaining; as a result, union membership dropped by 30 percent from 1980 to 1990, a rate of decline comparable to that of 1920 to 1930.[62] There is presently no meaningful sign of recovery in the labor movement, and a well-known industrial relations expert has described current conditions as the "twilight" of collective bargaining.[63]

In part, unions are victims of their political success. Organized labor provided essential support for the growth of employment legislation from the mid-1960s through the early 1990s. As a result of expansive state involvement, many workers now believe—erroneously—that a comprehensive scheme of law covers all aspects of work, including separations from employment.[64] Law is not a complete substitute for the traditional union contract, however, because it lacks such crucial components as a just cause provision that obligates employers to provide convincing proof of cause for discipline and an effective disputes resolution procedure administered by workers' representatives. That complex pattern of rights and obligations is the topic addressed next.

Part III: Individual Employment Rights, 1960s–2000s

This part of the book surveys the major employment laws affecting today's workplace. Those laws can be analyzed according to their regulatory approach. The first category of employment law consists of limitations on managerial prerogatives with regard to hiring, firing, and terms of employment. This type of law identifies a specific class of workers, such as women or ethnic groups, and forbids employers from engaging in discriminatory treatment against them because of their status. In bringing legal claims under these statutes, the individual worker must prove that the employer took some adverse action against him or her and that the reason for that action fell within the statutory proscriptions. One exception to the procedure is when the employer has a policy that differentially affects a protected group; in that case, the employer may be required to show that the policy is based on business necessity. Consider, for example, an employer's hiring policy for ocean lifeguards that requires successful applicants to swim one mile in less than thirty minutes. Does this affect any particular group, and is it necessary to the job of being a lifeguard at a public beach? Other interesting and controversial applications of the nondiscrimination principle are the cases in which the employer intentionally favors a minority worker in order to further some organizational goal such as diversity. When white male managers at Ford Motor Company complained that the corporation created different categories of eligibility for promotions and deliberately excluded them from serious consideration, Ford decided to settle the case without litigation.[65]

The second regulatory approach, in contrast, does not single out employees by virtue of immutable characteristics. Instead, any employee who qualifies under the terms of the statute is entitled to its benefits. This category of law includes rights to a safe and healthy workplace, benefits for retirement and unemployment, minimum wages and overtime, family and medical leaves, and a continuation of health insurance coverage. As mentioned above, the basic elements of this dimension of employment law were enacted in the 1930s and have been added to since that time. The most recent example is the Family and Medical Leave Act (FMLA), adopted in 1993. Although the FMLA does not mandate any compensation, it does entitle employees to a period of leave with job retention rights. While most citizens might agree that discrimination against a group should be outlawed, affirmative grants of benefits are more controversial—recall Alan Greenspan's opposition to the minimum wage, mentioned earlier in this chapter. Similar reasoning about markets and individual responsibility and initiative apply here; if a worker wants to retire comfortably, for example, he or she arguably should set aside money toward that objective rather than relying on a state-mandated system such as Social Security.

A final topic covered in this chapter has to do with changing common law rules that create exceptions to the employment at will principle. Those exceptions constitute an important source of evolving rights for employees and a particularly troublesome area of law for employers. Broadly, the exceptions to the rule fall under either contract or tort doctrine. If the employer states in a handbook that employees will have job security and access to a grievance procedure, the employer may have created an obligation that negates the at-will principle. Likewise, the employer may terminate an employee under circumstances that make out a traditional tort claim, such as the infliction of emotional distress or libel. One of the most bizarre cases in this respect involved a male employee who was fired for telling a female coworker about a Seinfeld television episode featuring a name that rhymed with a female body part; he sued his employer and won several million dollars.[66] The case study at the end of Chapter 7 involves another highly publicized example of an exception to employment at will; it offers helpful insights into the judicial policies that led to various theories of litigation.

Part IV: Rebuilding the Employment Contract

Public policy drives debates about changes in the regulatory environment. Laws are designed to promote the well-being of all citizens and not merely the individual involved in a particular case. If laws fail to promote the intended policy, they should be changed. Employment laws have an important policy dimension because most Americans depend on work for basic needs of life. Contemporary policy issues in employment include the privatizing of retirement programs, expanding health and safety protections, raising the minimum wage, reforming labor law, making dispute procedures effective, and the growth of a contingent workforce. The various proposals to reform Social Security, for example, have serious implications for all citizens, regardless of age. Many younger workers, unfortunately, have little faith in the system and believe that they will never receive benefits. Such beliefs undermine the intergenerational compact on which Social Security is based, undermining as well the social fabric that sustains reciprocal obligations in our national community.[67]

Other significant policy questions have to do with our contemporary workplace institutions. According to recent surveys, U.S. workers would like more say about their jobs and their companies. Approximately one-third of all eligible workers indicate a desire to have union representation, about the density rate of the 1950s. If an effective voice at work is important to employees, then our policies about collective bargaining should be reexamined and made more effective. Works councils are a common feature in other industrialized countries, and they may offer an example for U.S. employment. Similarly, some nonunion employers now provide a system of arbitration to resolve workplace disputes. The U.S. Supreme Court has afforded those schemes some legitimacy, and they have advantages for both employers and employees.[68] The state of Montana in 1985 enacted a statutory process involving rights to challenge a discharge and incentives for the parties to arbitrate issues of termination.[69] Arguably, that approach would minimize the risks of litigation for employers and reduce the costs of protesting an employment decision for employees.

Whatever the specific subject matter, policy discussions about work invoke fundamental ideologies and beliefs. Linking laws and practices with a theoretical perspective helps to clarify the choices available to policymakers and the implications of those choices. A historical context also suggests the political limitations on workplace changes, regardless of their intellectual appeal. With rare exceptions, when U.S. employers concertedly oppose measures that otherwise enjoy popular support, such as protections against repetitive motion injuries, those measures fail.[70] As a result, employment policy depends on practical as well as theoretical factors.

The final chapter reviews the main themes of the book and offers some conclusions about work in the United States. This country continues to be an exception to the industrial model prevalent elsewhere in the world. The important difference lies in employing institutions, which lack any real degree of coordination and integration. U.S. workers must rely on a fragmented, incomplete, and enormously complicated set of rules and rights. At the level of national policy, employment relations has little explicit connection with social relations because we conceptualize work as a distinct sphere of endeavor. But work is one of the defining realms of modern life, and it touches on many dimensions of intellectual inquiry related to our well-being. Moreover, the policies affecting employment must be operationalized through explicit and implicit rules created by the main actors in the employment system. Those actors include the legal regime or the state, employing institutions in the form of corporations, the organized labor movement, and our communities. For purposes of background, the prominent features of each actor are described now.

The State and Its Agencies

The exertion of the state's coercive power—that is, law—depends on administrative procedures, legislative mandate, and judicial implementation. Historically, and with some justification, workers complained that law in the United States served the interests of property owners and employers rather than wage earners. A compelling articulation of the point is contained in the 1914 final report to the Commission on

Industrial Relations. This federal tribunal compiled a massive body of data about labor conditions in the United States just prior to World War I. The main author of the report, Basil Manley, observed,

> No testimony presented to the commission has left a deeper impression than the evidence that there exists among the workers an almost universal conviction that they, both as individuals and as a class, are denied justice in the enactment, adjudication, and administration of law, that the very instruments of democracy are often used to oppress them and to place obstacles in the way of their movement toward economic, industrial, and political freedom and justice.[71]

Our legal system contains features that make it particularly susceptible to the influence of lawyers, judges, litigants, and political factions. Some legal rules have democratic roots, but others, such as common law doctrines and Supreme Court decisions, appear to be autocratic ones dependent on the whims of judges. Administrative law developed at a relatively late date, and it is treated in the context of specific statutory provisions such as the National Labor Relations Act. For the moment, it is useful to summarize four main sources of law that directly bear on labor policy. Note that each successive level of law takes precedence over and supercedes the previous level.

Common Law

The common law consists of rules made by judges and applied to specific fact situations. A familiar application is the body of common law known as *torts,* which provides remedies for wrongful actions that injure another person. Take the widely publicized case of the woman in New Mexico who successfully sued McDonald's after she burned herself by spilling hot coffee into her lap. She claimed that McDonald's was negligent in serving her coffee that was unreasonably hot, and it was foreseeable that she might spill the coffee and injure herself. Therefore, McDonald's owed her a duty to take reasonable steps to prevent those injuries, either by lowering the coffee's temperature or by warning her of the danger of placing a paper cup filled with hot liquid between her legs. Many similar cases arise in connection with employment.

As noted earlier, the common law rule dating from the 1880s to the present was that employees could be fired at any time, for a good reason, a bad reason, or no reason. However, that rule began to change in the late twentieth century, and many courts have recognized some exceptions to the rule. Presently, there are a number of common law theories that give rise to employment litigation, and one publishing service compiles an entire collection of judicial decisions related to such litigation.[72] The case study at the end of Chapter 7 provides an interesting example of a suit against an employer for wrongful discharge. That case has become widely cited as an example of questionable judicial thinking about rights and duties in the workplace, in part because of its unusual fact situation. The explosion in employment litigation, according to one critic, has created a minefield for employers.[73] Where appropriate, this book discusses common law concepts relevant to labor markets.

Local and State Legislation

The founders of our constitutional form of government envisioned a political structure in which citizens exercised the greatest control over the governmental units that most affected them. Therefore, state and local governments had authority to enact a variety of routine rules for everyday conduct, such as making economic transactions, entering into domestic relationships, and protecting the public safety. Federal power was therefore limited to matters of national concern. Those matters included national defense, a postal system, and regulation of interstate commerce. When the federal government acts within its defined scope, it preempts any inconsistent state laws. But federal power must be tested against the principle of separate and distinct spheres of political influence. The Tenth Amendment to the U.S. Constitution summarizes the point nicely. It says, "The powers not delegated to the United States by the Constitution, nor prohibited by it to the States, are reserved to the States respectively, or to the people."

Until the New Deal, control over employment was almost exclusively relegated to the states. Prior to 1937, the Supreme Court made clear that the federal interests did not generally extend to labor relations and that doctrine remained in force for many years. The result was a decentralized pattern of employment law in which individual states hesitated to impose regulatory burdens on corporations that might discourage business investment, and workers faced serious political obstacles when they attempted to secure protective legislation. Coupled with the authority of judges to devise common law and constitutional employment rules, the legal regime substantially hampered workers' efforts at collective action and contributed to the growth of American exceptionalism. The system of workers' compensation, which consists entirely of state law and came into existence in the first two decades of the twentieth century, might seem anomalous. However, as demonstrated later, those laws protected employers as well as workers, and business supported the particular legislation.

At present, federal law provides a baseline of employment legislation, and other government entities can fill in or expand federal provisions. Some states and cities have supplemented minimum wage standards by establishing a living wage that exceeds the federal minimum; in Santa Fe, New Mexico, for example, the minimum hourly wage is $8.50 rather than $5.15.[74] Similarly, federal civil rights law protects only specified classes of individuals, and some other governmental entities go beyond those categories to protect against discrimination because of sexual orientation. A number of states have also created their own administrative machinery to enforce federal rights. Congress explicitly authorized states to handle civil rights complaints arising under federal legislation, and the two levels of government coordinate and share resources. A similar arrangement occurs under the Occupational Safety and Health Act, which ensures a workplace free from recognized health and safety hazards. The federal labor law of collective bargaining excludes public and agricultural workers from its coverage, and states are free to enact legislation for those groups. Such examples underscore the complexity of employment regulation under our particular political framework of dual authority.

Federal Legislation

As noted, the federal government in 1935 took a critical first step toward an expansive role in regulating employment when Congress enacted the National Labor Relations Act written by Senator Robert Wagner. In 1964, Congress passed the Civil Rights Act outlawing race and gender discrimination in various economic and social spheres. Title VII of that statute applies specifically to employment, and from its provisions, a complex and often confusing body of law has developed. The Occupational Safety and Health Act was passed in 1970 to give workers protection on the job. In 1989, the Supreme Court tried to modify Title VII by interpreting the law in unusual ways. Congress overturned the Court's rulings in the 1991 Civil Rights Act, which confirmed and strengthened protections against discriminatory treatment. During the administration of George H. W. Bush, Congress passed the 1990 Americans With Disabilities Act, designed to give persons with disabilities a fair chance to compete for jobs. President Bill Clinton supported the Family and Medical Leave Act of 1993; this law gives workers rights to time off to care for family matters or their own illness and to return to their jobs.

In addition to the statutes above, Congress has regulated pensions, working time and wages, unemployment insurance, and many other matters. Those laws are dealt with in detail later in this book. For now, it should be emphasized that the federal regulatory framework is a dynamic one subject to ongoing challenge and change. Even with the extent of current regulation, important areas of work remain relatively neglected. No federal rule generally covers the matter of employment termination, nor does it address such important issues as universal health care coverage, employee participation in managerial decisions, or paid time off. Compared with other nations, the United States leaves important aspects of employment to private contracting between employer and employee. The result, as in the case of health insurance coverage, is that market forces may fail to produce socially desirable outcomes.[75]

U.S. Constitution

Since *Marbury v. Madison* in 1801, the Supreme Court assumed the authority to interpret the federal constitution and to strike down any laws inconsistent with its provisions. To take a current employment problem, the Court has struggled for several decades with the question of affirmative action or reverse discrimination, which benefits a protected group and disadvantages ones not legally protected. One of its most recent forays into the area demonstrates the judicial ambivalence about such practices. In the case of *Adarand Constructors v. Pena*, a businessman named

Randy Pech challenged the federal government's program to encourage minority construction contractors. Because the government offered to subsidize qualified businesses, a minority company was awarded a contract for work even though Pech was the low bidder. The case reached the Supreme Court in 1995, and five members agreed that race discrimination in favor of minorities was only permissible where the government proved a "compelling state interest" and that its program was "narrowly tailored" to achieve its goals. Justice Scalia stated that the rule would outlaw reverse discrimination altogether because the government could "never have a compelling interest" in implementing a race-based benefit. To the majority's surprise, a federal appeals court upheld the government's modified program. Pech appealed again, and the Court took jurisdiction to conclusively dispense with the issue. This time, though, the case had become so factually complicated that the Court was forced in November 2001 to dismiss it without an opinion.[76] No doubt litigants will try again to overturn similar programs, even though the Court in 2003 approved the use of diversity in university admissions procedures.[77]

Another important limitation of power is that federal regulation of employment must be measured against the governments' legitimate constitutional authority to make laws that may impinge on state sovereignty. The Court recently held that Congress could not force state governments to comply with the requirements of the Age Discrimination in Employment Act, even though Congress intended to remove a state's immunity to suits. According to five members of the Court, the statute did not meet the standards necessary to constitutionally enact such laws.[78] Other opinions in the Court's recent cases reexamine basic principles of federal power and emphasize the role of states in dealing with employment issues.[79] To what extent the Court will continue its move back to an age of truncated federal power depends on future cases and the philosophical predilections of new appointees to the Court.

In addition to nullifying some legislation, the Constitution provides positive rights in the workplace when state action is involved. Thus, government workers have a right to publicly state their opinions on matters of public interest if it does not interfere with their work performance. They also have other rights, such as freedom from unreasonable searches, guarantees of procedural due process treatment if liberty or property interests are threatened, and protection against arbitrary workplace rules. If the employee is disciplined under circumstances that violate his or her rights, the employee will have a constitutional claim against the employer.[80] It needs repeating, however, that the Constitution does not protect workers in the private sector because the state action requirement is lacking. An employee at Microsoft has no protected legal right to criticize the company's management for engaging in monopolistic practices and could be dismissed without viable recourse for doing so.

Firms and Managers

Between the end of the Civil War and the beginning of World War I, U.S. industry emerged as the preeminent world power. Our economy shifted from an agricultural base to an industrial one, and the gross national product increased at an annual average rate of over 4 percent during that period. New industries such as machinery production, printing and publishing, and iron and steel displaced older economic activities. Technological innovation, improved managerial practices, and alternative energy sources such as coal contributed to rapid industrial growth. At the same time, corporations engaged in a wave of mergers and consolidation that produced increasingly larger firms.[81]

The reasons for corporate growth and structural change continue to interest researchers. One influential analysis of corporate structure argued that U.S. corporations evolved as a result of "conceptions of control," which allowed large firms to minimize threats to their profitability.[82] Those threats came from other business organizations or from regulation, such as antitrust laws. In response to crises in their external environment, companies developed strategies for new courses of action. Once leading firms chose a path for growth, smaller firms attempted to follow. A key element in corporate transformation was the state, which either permitted or prohibited specified courses of action for the corporation through devices such as restrictions on monopolies. The interpretation reinforces the idea that an understanding of employment relations requires consideration of the dynamic institutional framework in which economic activity takes place. It also refutes the notion that markets are the driving force behind corporate behavior. Individuals who controlled corporations were "well aware that markets were social constructions that revolved around systems of power, both private and public." Accordingly, "the rules of markets could be changed by powerful corporate actors and the government."[83]

A further component of corporate organization addresses the problem of the separation of ownership and control. A classic study by Adolf Berle Jr. and Gardiner Means traced the conflicts between managers who operated a firm and shareholders who invested in the firm.[84] Managers made important decisions about the firm's affairs and expended resources toward their objectives; sometimes, however, managers' goals conflicted with those of the owners. In late 2001, to illustrate, Hewlett-Packard's chief executive officer proposed a merger with Compaq to improve the competitive abilities of both companies. The major shareholders, members of the Hewlett and Packard families, opposed the move. The proposed merger, which eventually occurred, led to threats of resignations, litigation, and public controversy.[85] With regard to employment, the separation between ownership and control leads to important issues of responsibility and liability. For example, if a manager engages in sexual harassment of another employee, should the firm be financially liable for that activity? The Supreme Court provided an answer to that question in 1998, but its answer is not altogether satisfactory from a policy standpoint.[86]

Organized Labor

When two or more workers join together to deal with their employer, they engage in *concerted activity*. That term of art refers to a rudimentary form of unionism, and it has important implications for labor law and employment in general. All employers negotiate with their employees over terms and conditions of work; the crucial issue is whether the employer will deal with an individual employee and contract on that basis or whether it will be a collective endeavor in which a representative of the employees makes a bargain for everyone in the group. In the latter situation, employees have formed a union to advance their interests. Advocates of the free market model of employment argue that individual dealings are legitimate, but collective negotiations impose an inefficient monopoly on labor transactions.[87]

The combined American Federation of Labor and Congress of Industrial Organizations (AFL-CIO), which now formally represents the labor movement in the United States, has been in existence since 1955. Before that time, the AFL and the CIO were separate organizations with sometimes disparate and conflicting interests. The CIO, originally named the Committee for Industrial Organization, was formed in 1935 by John L. Lewis and others as a protest against the membership policies of the AFL. The AFL traces its origins to the Federation of Organized Trades and Labor Unions formed in 1881. In turn, the AFL was preceded by a number of earlier groups, such as the Knights of Labor, the National Trades Unions, and various craft organizations. Obviously, workers' organizations make up an enduring institution in this country.[88]

In the 1980s, unions experienced their worst losses in membership since the 1920s.[89] Major unions also engaged in several bitter and unsuccessful strikes that eroded unions' power to negotiate contracts which involved attempts to protect union standards of wages and benefits.[90] With the election of John Sweeney as head of the AFL-CIO in 1995, the labor movement devoted greater resources to organizing new bargaining units, but results have been mixed. In September 2001, the United Auto Workers attempted to unionize the Nissan plant in Smyrna, Tennessee. This drive was strategically crucial as an effort to increase penetration into the auto "transplants" owned by foreign manufacturers. Unfortunately for labor, workers voted to reject the UAW by a substantial margin.[91] In February 2003, the AFL-CIO executive council resolved to undertake an "unprecedented labor movement campaign" to bring representation rights to U.S. workplaces by committing greater resources to a three-pronged organizing effort.[92] The reasons for union decline are treated more fully in Chapter 5.

Community Institutions

Robert Putnam, a sociologist at Harvard, argued in a provocative 1993 article that Americans were participating less in communal activities and that our social institutions had steadily declined since the 1950s. That argument prompted considerable public debate, and in 2000, Putnam published a book-length study titled *Bowling Alone*.[93] Putnam documents in persuasive detail the ways in which our civic institutions have fallen into disrepair and neglect and our society is becoming one in which we pursue individual activities rather than collective endeavors. The book's title aptly captures the main thesis: although more people now bowl than ever before, fewer people belong to bowling teams. A number of negative consequences flow from declining participation, including worse schools, more violence, more jails, and more television. Unions, as one of the most enduring forms of collective action in this country, have an important role in communal endeavors.[94] That role is controversial, though, because unions are often depicted as oppressive institutions that make up a dark side of social capital.

Indeed, the debate over labor's place in the republic can be traced back to the Philadelphia Cordwainers Case of 1806, and many of the arguments in that case are relevant to today's political discourse.[95] For example, if unions bargain for higher wages, they actually might deprive some workers of employment; employers will not hire labor if the cost of labor exceeds the value of the product. Higher wages might also be a factor contributing to inflation, which harms all consumers. Further, critics point out that unions stifle individual initiative by emphasizing collective action. Union security clauses, which require membership in a union as a condition of the job, clearly infringe upon the free choice of individual workers. From this perspective, such union characteristics are incompatible with the important social goals of human autonomy and liberty. Citizens of Oklahoma voted in September 2001 to prohibit compulsory union membership in that state, and the debates about the proposed law reflected the underlying concerns about freedom, economic prosperity, and communal values.[96]

For such reasons, community attitudes toward workers' collective activities are sometimes ambivalent. The stated purpose of the federal labor law is to "encourage the process of collective bargaining." Assuming that goal remains viable, then the behavior of employers should be more effectively monitored to protect workers in their efforts to form unions. Conversely, as some scholars argue, perhaps unions should have no special legislative protections. At the end of the twentieth century, employees had an array of individual legal rights in the workplace. Those rights arguably supplant the need for group action. In any event, public policy choices must aim not only at economic ends but toward social considerations as well. By viewing the core of community as a collective endeavor based on obligation and responsibility, and not merely as a guarantor of economic freedom and a protector of property, we may appreciate the contributions of unions and their enhancement of democracy at the workplace. Bowling alone has its disadvantages.

Summary

The main ideas in this chapter are ones that carry on throughout the remainder of the book. They can be summarized briefly as follows:

- Relations between workers and employers in the United States differ from the relationships in other industrialized countries with which we compete economically. The term used to refer to the idea is *American exceptionalism*. Generally, it means that we do not have an organized working class political movement aimed at furthering the interests of a distinct economic group. The concept is still relevant to understanding work in this country because it provides a perspective on our political system.

- Institutions are central to the study of employment relations. New approaches to economic theory contribute to our knowledge of the way firms are organized, especially with regard to the indefinite, ongoing relationship that constitutes an employment contract. It is clear that institutions count, and they deserve attention as a means of sustaining basic expectations in the labor market. Most employees, for example, would be dissatisfied if their employer decided to end a practice of offering paid holidays.

- The study of employment relations is interdisciplinary in nature and includes such fields as psychology, sociology, history, law, political science, and economics. Contributions from those subject areas enrich our understanding of work in the United States.

- The content dealt with in this book has practical consequences for firms and for our political system. Case examples are a useful way to illustrate the effects of legal rules.

Further Analysis

1. When the World Trade Organization met in Seattle in late 1999, protesters mounted a highly publicized campaign of resistance to the activities of the organization. John Sweeney, head of the AFL-CIO, said that labor would not support any negotiations that failed to include labor and environmental standards. Do you think the U.S. labor movement should try to use its political influence to discourage global trade agreements? Should unions encourage civil disobedience to achieve their goals? If you don't think so, do you also disapprove of Martin Luther King Jr.'s advocacy of illegal sit-ins at segregated lunch counters in the South? What's the difference?

2. Having had some introduction to legal theory, you might consider an issue arising out of employment legislation. As noted, Congress passed Title VII of the Civil Rights Act in 1964 outlawing certain types of discrimination in employment. If a state wanted to enact a law prohibiting discrimination in employment because of sexual orientation, would it have a right to do so? (It would, and several states have done so. Why is that?) On the other hand, Colorado voters amended the state's constitution in 1992 to prohibit local laws, such as those in Denver and Aspen, that protected homosexuals from employment discrimination and both the Colorado and U.S. Supreme Courts ruled the amendment unconstitutional. If courts can reject the preferences of a majority of citizens, what role does judicial review play in a democratic system?[97]

3. Along related lines, sexual orientation is not a protected class under Title VII and it is specifically excluded from coverage under the Americans With Disabilities Act. Should it be made unlawful to discriminate against homosexuals under either law, both laws, or neither law? If it's clear to you that employers should not be allowed to discriminate against employees because of sexual orientation, why has Congress failed to prohibit it?

4. In your opinion, is the decline of unionism a good thing or a bad thing for this country? Would it be desirable if there were no trade unions in the United States?

5. The authors of a recent and highly regarded book on U.S. society argue "that only greater citizen participation in the large structures of the economy and the state will enable us to surmount the deepening problems of contemporary social life."[98] Assuming that statement to be accurate, would unions play any role in ensuring greater participation in "the large structures of the economy" or would you agree with Selig Perlman that unions are preoccupied with narrow job-related issues?

6. Consider the quotation from the 1914 Industrial Relations Commission setting forth the workers' view of the legal system. How could the *law* in this country be captured by the interests of any one group? Do you think workers were criticizing the legislative system or the judicial system? What is the function of each of those institutions with respect to law?

7. Is there too much or too little governmental regulation of employment at the present time? If too much, what specific legislation should be repealed? If too little, what protections do workers need that they do not now have? Do you think regulation impairs the efficiency of a firm? Then how do the highly regulated economies of the European Union compete so well against the United States, or do they?[99]

Suggested Readings

Albelda, Randy, Robert W. Drago, and Steven Shulman. *Unlevel Playing Fields: Understanding Wage Inequality and Discrimination.* Cambridge, MA: Economic Affairs Bureau, 2001.

Berg, Ivar, and Arne L. Kalleberg, eds. *Sourcebook of Labor Markets: Evolving Structures and Processes.* New York: Kluwer Academic/Plenum, 2000.

Bronfenbrenner, Kate, Sheldon Friedman, Richard W. Hurd, Rudolph A. Oswald, and Ronald L. Seeber. *Organizing to Win: New Research on Union Strategies.* Ithaca, NY: ILR Press, 1998.

Freeman, Richard, and James Medoff. *What Do Unions Do?* New York: Basic Books, 1984.

Kaufman, Bruce E., ed. *Government Regulation of the Employment Relationship.* Madison, WI: Industrial Relations Research Association, 1997.

Kochan, Thomas, Harry Katz, and Robert McKersie. *The Transformation of American Industrial Relations.* New York: Basic Books, 1986.

Mishel, Lawrence, Jared Bernstein, and John Schmitt. *The State of Working America, 2002–2003: An Economic Policy Institute Book.* Ithaca, NY: ILR Press, 2002.

Robertson, David B. *Capital, Labor, and State: The Battle for American Labor Markets From the Civil War to the New Deal.* Lanham, MD: Rowman & Littlefield, 2001.

Strauss, George, Daniel Gallagher, and Jack Fiorito, eds. *The State of the Unions.* Madison, WI: Industrial Relations Research Association, 1992.

Tomlins, Christopher. *The State and the Unions: Labor Relations, Law, and the Organized Labor Movement in America, 1880–1960.* Cambridge, UK: Cambridge University Press, 1985.

Endnotes

1. For treatments of the early period, see Philip S. Foner, *History of the Labor Movement in the United States, Vol. 1: From Colonial Times to the Founding of the American Federation of Labor* (New York: International, 1947); Richard Morris, *Government and Labor in Early America* (New York: Columbia University Press, 1946); Christopher Tomlins, *Law, Labor and Ideology in the Early American Republic* (Cambridge, UK: Cambridge University Press, 1993).

2. On Rockefeller and the development of employee participation generally, see Raymond Hogler and Guillermo Grenier, *Employee Participation and Labor Law in the American Workplace* (Westport, CT: Quorum, 1991).

3. Bruce E. Kaufman and Daphne Gottlieb Taras, eds., *Nonunion Employee Representation: History, Practice, and Policy* (Armonk, NY: M. E. Sharpe, 2000).

4. Jacob Schlesinger and Russell Gold, "Labor Lost: High-Employment Era Seems Over in Wake of Terrorist Attacks," *Wall Street Journal,* October 8, 2001, p. A1, col. 1. This article contains an excellent overview of economic developments before and after the events of September 11, 2001.

5. According to one analysis, the period between January 2000 and October 2002 "was the most wrenching bear market in stocks since the Great Depression." Investors lost close to $7 trillion in the collapse. E. S. Browning and Ianthe J. Dugan, "Aftermath of a Market Mania," *Wall Street Journal,* December 16, 2002, pp. C1, C13.

6. Greg Ip, "Federal Reserve Cuts Rates Half Point," *Wall Street Journal,* November 7, 2001, p. A2, col. 2.

7. John D. McKinnon, "White House Is Putting Together $300 Billion Stimulus Package," *Wall Street Journal,* December 9, 2002, pp. A1, A12. President Bush replaced two key economic advisers in December 2002. The crucial debate within the administration dealt with the issue of tax cuts and expanding deficits. Bob Davis and Jeanne Cummings, "Fight Brews Over New Tax Cuts," *Wall Street Journal,* December 10, 2002, p. A4. President Bush also announced his support for using federal funds to extend unemployment payments to workers who had exhausted their twenty-six weeks of benefits. Greg Hitt, "President Calls for Extending Unemployment Benefits," *Wall Street Journal,* December 16, 2002, p. A6.

8. Some predictions about global recession were particularly pessimistic. See, for example, "The Risks Are Worsening" and "How Far Down?," *The Economist,* October 20, 2001, pp. 12, 69.

9. Craig Karmin, "For Investors, Stock and Awe," *Wall Street Journal,* March 24, 2003, p. C1, col. 2.

10. One columnist, for example, offered the following criticisms of the president's neglect of domestic matters. "The Bush administration sounds the alarm for war and blows the trumpet for tax cuts, and Congress plunges ahead with the cuts in domestic programs that must inevitably follow. The voices of those who object are effectively silenced by the war propaganda and the fear of seeming unpatriotic." Bob Herbert, "Casualties at Home," *New York Times* (online), March 27, 2003.

11. Stephen Power and John D. McKinnon, "Government Rescue of Airlines May Come Slowly," *Wall Street Journal,* March 17, 2003, p. A3, col. 1.

12. Jon E. Hilsenrath, "Number of Jobless Hits 20-Year High as Claims Rise," *Wall Street Journal,* July 11, 2003, p. A2, col. 6.

13. "Another Bush, Another Jobless Recovery," *The Economist,* May 10, 2003, pp. 25–26. The tax cut formally amounted to $350 billion, but some reports indicated that the total package might amount to $810 billion and warned that the legislation "will likely provide a significant short-term boost to the tepid U.S. economy, but at a long-term cost." States, which

were experiencing their worst financial crisis since the 1930s, planned to raise taxes to meet budget demands. Greg Ip and John D. McKinnon, "Bush's Tax Cut: Victory—at a Cost," *Wall Street Journal,* May 23, 2003, p. A1. Congress extended unemployment benefits for unemployed workers who had exhausted twenty-six weeks of state benefits by providing an additional thirteen weeks of payments. Leigh Strope, *The Denver Post* [Associated Press], May 25, 2003, p. 11A.

14. Allan Sloan, "The Levitating Economy," *Newsweek,* July 7, 2003, pp. 35–36.

15. By the end of 2001, proposals for economic recovery appeared to be stalemated. According to one report, "Efforts to craft a stimulus plan for the U.S. economy collapsed this week because of a clash of ideologies, an explosive mix of personalities and a focus on next year's high-stakes election." Shailagh Murray and John D. McKinnon, "Never Mind—What Killed Stimulus?" *Wall Street Journal,* December 21, 2001, p. A1, col. 1. As the political debate sharpened again in early 2003, a well-known economist argued that the problem was not investment, but inequality. He pointed out, "According to the Census Bureau, the bottom 40 percent of American families earned 18 percent of the national income in 1970, but by 1998 they earned only 14 percent—and that figure could fall to 10 percent before too long." Robert J. Shiller, "Mind the Gap," *New York Times,* May 15, 2003.

16. Seymour Martin Lipset and Gary Marks, *It Didn't Happen Here: Why Socialism Failed in the United States* (New York: W. W. Norton, 2000).

17. Richard Freeman, ed., *Working Under Different Rules* (New York: Russell Sage, 1994). As an example, European workers typically receive six weeks of vacation annually and enjoy additional paid time off through government mandates; workers in the United States earn vacations at the discretion of employers. The trade-off for leisure time, however, may be lower productivity. Christopher Rhoads, "Clocking Out: Short Work Hours Undercut Europe in Economic Drive," *Wall Street Journal,* August 8, 2002, p. A1, col. 1.

18. See, for example, Linda Hantrais, *Social Policy in the European Union,* 2d ed. (New York: St. Martin's Press, 2000).

19. For a good illustration of comparative policy analysis, see Günther Schmid, Jacqueline O'Reilly, and Klaus Schömann, eds., *International Handbook of Labour Market Policy and Evaluation* (Cheltenham, UK: Edward Elgar, 1996). The editors define labor market policy "as the ensemble of all those policy interventions that are intended to directly improve the functioning of labour markets in achieving socially desired outcomes" (p. 8).

20. For a treatment of the historical context, see Kim Voss, *The Making of American Exceptionalism: The Knights of Labor and Class Formation in the Nineteenth Century* (Ithaca, NY: Cornell University Press, 1993).

21. Werner Sombart, *Why Is There No Socialism in the United States?* (White Plains, NY: International Arts and Sciences Press, 1976 [1906], ed. and trans. Patricia Hocking and C. T. Husbands), 20.

22. Selig Perlman, *A Theory of the Labor Movement* (New York: Augustus M. Kelley, 1949 [1928]), 7–8; 155–156; 165–168.

23. Seymour Martin Lipset and Ivan Katchanovski, "The Future of Private Sector Unions in the U.S.," *Journal of Labor Research* 22, no. 2 (2001): 239.

24. Sanford M. Jacoby, "American Exceptionalism Revisited: The Importance of Management," in *Masters to Managers: Historical and Comparative Perspectives on American Employers,* ed. Sanford M. Jacoby (New York: Columbia University Press, 1991), 174.

25. Paul Weiler, "Promises to Keep: Securing Workers' Rights to Self-Organization Under the NLRA," *Harvard Law Review* 96 (1983): 1769–1827.

26. For criticisms of the employer opposition thesis, see Leo Troy, *Beyond Unions and Collective Bargaining* (Armonk, NY: M. E. Sharpe, 1999). Troy argues that structural economic factors largely beyond the control of unions account for most of the membership decline.

27. William Forbath, *Law and the Shaping of the American Labor Movement* (Cambridge, MA: Harvard University Press, 1991).

28. John R. Commons et al., *History of Labour in the United States,* vol. 1 (New York: Macmillan, 1921), 3. For a summary of Commons' economic principles, see Bruce E. Kaufman, "Labor Markets and Employment Regulation: The View of the 'Old' Institutionalists," in *Government Regulation of the Employment Relationship,* ed. Bruce E. Kaufman (Madison, WI: Industrial Relations Research Association, 1997), 11–55.

29. For a concise summary of the point, see *History of Labour,* vol. 1, pp. 25–30.

30. The changes in industrial relations are described in Bruce E. Kaufman, *The Origins and Evolution of Industrial Relations in the United States* (Ithaca, NY: ILR Press, 1993).

31. One of the leading human resource management texts, for example, is written by an industrial/organizational psychologist. Wayne Cascio, *Managing Human Resources: Productivity, Quality of Work Life, Profits,* 5th ed. (Boston: Irwin/McGraw Hill, 1998).

32. Kaufman, *Origins,* pp. 103–135.

33. Michael Goldfield, *The Decline of Organized Labor in the United States* (Chicago: University of Chicago Press, 1987).

34. Christopher Tomlins, *The State and the Unions: Labor Relations, Law, and the Organized Labor Movement in America, 1880–1960* (Cambridge, UK: Cambridge University Press, 1985).

35. Richard Freeman and James Medoff, *What Do Unions Do?* (New York: Basic Books, 1984).

36. David M. Gordon, Richard Edwards, and Michael Reich, *Segmented Work, Divided Workers: The Historical Transformation of Labor in the United States* (Cambridge, UK: Cambridge University Press, 1982).

37. Neil Mitchell, *The Generous Corporation: A Political Analysis of Economic Power* (New Haven, CT: Yale University Press, 1989).

38. Forbath, *Law and the Shaping of the American Labor Movement.*

39. Ivar Berg and Arne L. Kalleberg, eds., *Sourcebook of Labor Markets: Evolving Structures and Processes* (New York: Kluwer Academic/Plenum, 2001).

40. Douglass North, who won the 1993 Nobel Prize in economics, described his disenchantment with neoclassical theory as follows: "Individual beliefs were obviously important to the choices people make, and only the extreme myopia of economists prevented them from understanding that ideas, ideologies, and prejudices mattered. Once you recognize that, you are forced to examine the rationality postulate critically." Douglass C. North, "Prologue," in *The Frontiers of the New Institutional Economics,* ed. John N. Drobak and John V. C. Nye (San Diego, CA: Academic Press, 1997), 3–12.

41. For a discussion of the new institutionalism in general, see Paul J. DiMaggio and Walter Powell, "Introduction," in *The New Institutionalism in Organizational Analysis,* ed. Walter W. Powell and Paul J. DiMaggio (Chicago: University of Chicago Press, 1991), 1–38. The definition here relies on Powell and DiMaggio's analysis and on Ronald Jepperson, "Institutions, Institutional Effects, and Institutionalism," in Powell and DiMaggio, *New Institutionalism,* 144–145.

42. Douglass C. North, "A Revolution in Economics," in *Institutions, Contracts, and Organizations: Perspectives From New Institutional Economics,* ed. Claude Menard (Cheltenham, UK: Edward Elgar, 2000), 37–41.

43. For a good collection of materials on this point, including a selection from Coase's seminal essay titled "The Nature of the Firm," see Louis Putterman, ed., *The Economic Nature of the Firm: A Reader* (Cambridge, UK: Cambridge University Press, 1986).

44. Historically, U.S. courts viewed a contract for labor as a contract *in its entirety.* If either party failed to fulfill his or her obligation, the other party could sue for a compensatory

remedy. For a detailed study of changes in judicial thinking, see James D. Schmidt, *Free to Work: Labor Law, Emancipation, and Reconstruction, 1815–1880* (Athens, GA: University of Georgia Press, 1998).

45. For a useful and concise recent treatment, see Randy Albelda, Robert Drago, and Steven Shulman, *Unlevel Playing Fields: Understanding Wage Inequality and Discrimination* (Cambridge, MA: Economic Affairs Bureau, 2001).

46. According to a report on the CBS television program *Sunday Morning,* "Federal Reserve Chairman Alan Greenspan told a congressional committee he'd like to get rid of [the minimum wage], saying, 'I'm not in favor of cutting anybody's earnings or preventing them from rising, but I am against them losing their jobs because of artificial government intervention, which is essentially what the minimum wage is.'" Online at www.cbsnews.com [visited December 19, 2001].

47. For a good overview of the negotiation process, see Roy Lewicki, David Saunders, and John Minton, *Essentials of Negotiation* (Boston: Irwin/McGraw Hill, 1997). The 2001 Nobel Prize in economics was awarded to three economists, one of whom explained how the market process protected itself against sellers of inferior cars, or lemons. George A. Ackerlof, "The Market for Lemons: Quality Uncertainty and the Market Mechanism," *Quarterly Journal of Economics* 84 (1970): 488–500.

48. Armen Alchian and Harold Demsetz, "Production, Information Costs, and Economic Organization," *American Economic Review* 62 (1972): 777–795, reprinted in Putterman, ed., *The Economic Nature of the Firm,* pp. 111–134.

49. In fact, some large U.S. firms in the nineteenth century used a form of inside contracting in which management made a deal with a gang boss about levels of production and compensation, and the foreman then hired his own workers to perform the work. See Dan Clawson, *Bureaucracy and the Labor Process: The Transformation of U.S. Industry, 1860–1920* (New York: Monthly Review Press, 1980).

50. Ronald Coase, *The Firm, the Market, and the Law* (Chicago: University of Chicago Press, 1988), 7. Coase published an article in 1938 setting out the basic idea, but his work became influential in the 1970s.

51. For an exposition of Williamson's main points, see Oliver Williamson, *The Economic Institutions of Capitalism* (New York: Free Press, 1975).

52. From *Capital,* vol. 1, reprinted in Robert C. Tucker, ed., *The Marx-Engels Reader,* 2d ed. (New York: Norton, 1978), 357.

53. Before its downfall in 2002, the Enron Corporation offered an example of how an agglomeration of financial assets could be handled in such a way as to generate substantial profits without actually producing anything of value.

54. The best development of this point is Gordon et al., *Segmented Work.*

55. A good articulation of this point is found in the preamble to the 1932 Norris-La Guardia Act, which states that under the economic conditions of the time, which were "developed with the aid of governmental authority for owners of property to organize in the corporate and other forms of ownership association, the individual unorganized worker is commonly helpless to exercise actual liberty of contract and to protect his freedom of labor, and thereby to obtain acceptable terms and conditions of employment."

56. Katherine V. W. Stone, "The New Psychological Contract: Implications of the Changing Workplace for Labor and Employment Law," *University of California Law Review* 48 (2001): 519–653.

57. For a recent case confirming the doctrine and upholding the employer's right to lay off employees, see *Baron v. Port Authority,* 2001 U.S. App. LEXIS 24353 (2d Cir. 2001).

58. Visit the IWW home page at www.iww.org. The site explains the IWW philosophy as follows: "The IWW is a union for all workers, a union dedicated to organizing on the job, in

our industries and in our communities both to win better conditions today and to build a world without bosses, a world in which production and distribution are organized by workers ourselves to meet the needs of the entire population, not merely a handful of exploiters."

59. For some important studies of Taylorism and its influence, see Harry Braverman, *Labor and Monopoly Capital: The Degradation of Work in the Twentieth Century* (New York: Monthly Review Press, 1974); Yehouda Shenhav, *Manufacturing Rationality: The Engineering Foundations of the Managerial Revolution* (New York: Oxford University Press, 1999).

60. Irving Bernstein, *The New Deal Collective Bargaining Policy* (Berkeley: University of California Press, 1950), 58.

61. Raymond L. Hogler, "Changing Forms of Workplace Representation: The United States Steel Corporation, 1933–1937," *Management Decision* 39 (2001): 488–496.

62. Marick Masters, *Unions at the Crossroads: Strategic Membership, Financial, and Political Perspectives* (Westport, CT: Quorum, 1997).

63. Leo Troy, *Beyond Unions and Collective Bargaining* (Armonk, NY: M. E. Sharpe, 1999).

64. Roger Freeman and Joel Rogers, *What Workers Want* (Ithaca, NY: ILR Press, 1999).

65. Norihiko Shirouzu, "Documents Suggest Ford Policies Kept White Males From Certain Promotions," *Wall Street Journal*, October 10, 2001, p. A4, col. 1–2.

66. The case made *Time* magazine. "It Was a Joke!" *Time*, July 28, 1997, p. 62. The woman's name, which Jerry could not remember, was Dolores.

67. For detailed information about the status of the social securities funds, see the 2002 trustees' report available at www.ssa.gov.

68. *Circuit City Stores, Inc. v. Saint Clair Adams*, 532 U.S. 105 (2001).

69. See Montana Code Ann., §§ 39-2-901 to 914 (1995).

70. That was the fate of the Occupational Safety and Health Administration's proposed standard dealing with musculoskeletal work disorders (MSWDs). It was enacted during the final months of the Clinton administration, and when George W. Bush assumed office, Congress declared by resolution that the standard was no longer in effect.

71. Basil M. Manly, "Report," *Final Report of the Commission on Industrial Relations*, vol. 1 (Washington, DC: Government Printing Office, 1916), 38–39.

72. Bureau of National Affairs, *Individual Employment Rights Reporter* (Washington, DC: Bureau of National Affairs Books) [The series consists of bound volumes and a loose-leaf supplement with regular updates].

73. Walter Olson, *The Excuse Factory: How Employment Law Is Paralyzing the American Workplace* (New York: Free Press, 1997).

74. Thom McGhee, "Minimum Wage Jumps in Santa Fe," *Denver Post*, March 17, 2003, p. 1C.

75. In 2002, health care costs were predicted to increase by 13 percent. Employers face the prospect of passing higher costs on to their employees or limiting benefits. As a result, experts anticipated that "the number of uninsured working Americans could reach 30% of the labor force by 2009," up from 23 percent in 1999. Ron Winslow, "Health Debate Emerges As Costs Rise Again," *Wall Street Journal*, December 17, 2001, p. A1, col. 5.

76. *Adarand Constructors, Inc. v. Mineta*, 122 Sup. Ct. 511 (2001).

77. A number of public interest groups monitor and challenge regulatory activity that impedes business. The Adarand case, for example, was litigated by the Mountain States Legal Foundation, which is supported by donors such as the Coors family. The foundation counts such notable figures as James Watt and Gail Norton (respectively, a former and current Secretary of the Interior) among its previous employees. For more information on the foundation, see www.mountainstateslegal.com. Opponents of affirmative action suffered a setback in June 2003 when the Supreme Court upheld a diversity program at the University of Michigan's law school. Justice O'Connor in the majority opinion held that racial diversity

can rise to a "compelling interest" justifying the use of racial criteria in education. June Kronholz, Robert Tomsho, Daniel Golden, and Robert S. Greenberger, "Race Matters: Court Preserves Affirmative Action," *Wall Street Journal*, June 24, 2003, p. A1, cols. 4–6.

78. *Kimel v. Florida Board of Regents*, 528 U.S. 62 (2000).

79. See, e.g., *Alden v. Maine*, 527 U.S. 706 (1999). This case deals with the application of the Fair Labor Standards Act to state employees. The majority and dissenting opinions provide an interesting debate about the political framework of this country and its founding.

80. See, for example, *Mount Healthy Board of Education v. Doyle*, 429 U.S. 274 (1977), which involved an employee's public statements disparaging school policies.

81. See generally Louis Galambos and Joseph Pratt, *The Rise of the Corporate Commonwealth: U.S. Business and Public Policy in the Twentieth Century* (New York: Basic Books, 1988); Gary M. Walton and Hugh Rockoff, *History of the American Economy*, 8th ed. (Fort Worth, TX: Dryden Press, 1998).

82. Neil Fligstein, *The Transformation of Corporate Control* (Cambridge, MA: Harvard University Press, 1990).

83. Fligstein, p. 302.

84. Adolf Berle Jr. and Gardiner C. Means, *The Modern Corporation and Private Property* (New York: Macmillan, 1933).

85. Molly Williams, "Walter Hewlett Let H-P Board Know Early He Opposed Compaq Deal, Says SEC Filing," *Wall Street Journal*, December 28, 2001, p. A3, cols. 1–3; Cesca Antonelli, "Co-founder Says Acquisition Battle Is Draining H-P," *Denver Post*, December 14, 2001, p. C4.

86. The Court ruled in *Faragher v. City of Boca Raton*, 524 U.S. 775 (1998), that an effective complaint procedure for dealing with sexual harassment might protect an employer against damage awards if the employee failed to use the procedure. For problems with the doctrine, see Raymond L. Hogler, Jennifer Frame, and George Thornton III, "Workplace Sexual Harassment Law: An Empirical Analysis of Organizational Justice and Legal Policy," *Journal of Managerial Issues* 14 (2002): 234–250.

87. For a polemical attack on unions from the neoclassical perspective, see Morgan O. Reynolds, *Making America Poorer: The Cost of Labor Law* (Washington, DC: Cato Institute, 1987).

88. For a readable historical treatment of working people, see Priscilla Murolo and A. B. Chitty, *From the Folks Who Brought You the Weekend: A Short, Illustrated History of Labor in the United States* (New York: New Press, 2001) (illustrations by Joe Sacco).

89. Masters, *Unions at the Crossroads*.

90. The strike at Pittson was documented in an episode of the television program *48 Hours*. Barbara Koppel produced a film about the Hormel strike titled *American Dream*, which won an Academy Award in the documentary category in 1990.

91. Jeffrey Ball, "Vote at Nissan Plant in Smyrna, Tenn. Is Key Union Test," *Wall Street Journal*, September 28, 2001, p. A4, col. 3. Roy Moore, "Nissan Workers Vote 2 to 1 Against UAW at Smyrna Plant," *Nashville Business Journal*, October 4, 2001. The story is available at the following site: http://nashville.bcentral.com/nashville/stories/2001/10/01/daily25.html.

92. For the text of the resolution, see Executive Council Actions, "An Unprecedented Labor Movement Campaign in Support of the Freedom of Workers to Choose a Voice at Work," February 26, 2003, at www.afl-cio.org.

93. Robert D. Putnam, *Bowling Alone: The Collapse and Revival of American Community* (New York: Simon & Schuster, 2000).

94. The role of communities in union movements is examined in Dan Cornfield, Holly McCammon, Darren McDaniel, and Dean Eatman, "In the Community or in the Union? The

Impact of Community Involvement on Nonunion Worker Attitudes About Unionizing," in *Organizing to Win: New Research on Union Strategies,* ed. Kate Bronfenbrenner, Sheldon Friedman, Richard W. Hurd, Rudolph A. Oswald, and Ronald L. Seeber (Ithaca, NY: ILR Press, 1998), 247–258.

95. For an analysis of the Philadelphia Cordwainers Case and its importance for the historical study of labor relations, see Raymond Hogler, "Law, Ideology, and Industrial Discipline: The Conspiracy Doctrine and the Rise of the Factory System," *Dickinson Law Review* 91 (1987): 697–745.

96. The supporters of the right to work law created an elaborate Web site to present their case. Organized labor made a sizeable financial commitment to the political campaign. The arguments are analyzed in Raymond L. Hogler and Robert LaJeunesse, "Oklahoma's Right to Work Initiative: Labor Policy and Political Ideology," *Labor Law Journal* 53 (2002): 109–121. For a response to that article, see Stan Greer and Charles W. Baird, "Reply to Hogler and LaJeunesse's 'Oklahoma's Right to Work Initiative: Labor Policy and Political Ideology,'" *Labor Law Journal* 54 (2003): 89–100.

97. The U.S. Supreme Court struck down the Colorado amendment in the case of *Romer v. Evans,* 517 U.S. 620 (1996). The majority, in an opinion by Justice Kennedy, noted, "It is not within our constitutional tradition to enact laws of this sort. Central both to the idea of the rule of law and to our own Constitution's guarantee of equal protection is the principle that government and each of its parts remain open on impartial terms to all who seek its assistance." Justices Scalia and Thomas and Chief Justice Rehnquist dissented. According to Scalia, "The Court has mistaken a Kulturkampf for a fit of spite." Colorado's law, he said, was not hostile to homosexuals but was merely an effort "to preserve traditional sexual mores against the efforts of a politically powerful minority to revise those mores through use of the laws." In his view, the amendment was "not only unimpeachable under any constitutional doctrine hitherto pronounced (hence the opinion's heavy reliance upon principles of right-eousness rather than judicial holdings); [but similar laws] have been specifically approved by the Congress of the United States and by this Court." To support his argument, Scalia cites a case in which the Court upheld a criminal conviction under Georgia's laws against sodomy. That decision was overturned in *Lawrence v. Texas,* 123 Sup. Ct. 2472 (June 26, 2003), which held that homosexuals have a protected constitutional right to engage in consensual sexual activity. Scalia wrote a dissenting opinion. Such issues illustrate some of the political impli-cations involved in civil rights legislation.

98. Robert N. Bellah et al., *The Good Society* (New York: Alfred A. Knopf, 1991), 6.

99. According to a report in a leading business magazine, Germany is threatened with economic stagnation created by excessive regulation and social protections for workers. "The Decline of Germany," *Business Week,* February 17, 2003, pp. 44–53.

PART I

The Era of Management, 1880–1935

CHAPTER 2

Industrial Expansion and the Foundations of Unionism

The labor problem was particularly acute in the early development of U.S. employment relations. To reiterate a point made in the previous chapter, employers devised creative responses to market conditions. One strategy was the complex, elaborate, and controversial system of slavery, with its highly nuanced legal and social apparatus. The second relied on the contractual bondage associated with indentured servitude. Until the mid-nineteenth century, those two forms of involuntary or "unfree" labor coexisted along with the voluntary employment contracts negotiated in open markets. The dissolution of relations of status—that is, of obligations imposed by state definition rather than by consent—eventually gave way to contractual rights and duties. Gradually, after slavery was abolished, the wage bargain became the prevailing type of relationship between workers and employers.[1] Direct state involvement consisted for the most part of common law doctrines governing employment transactions, which, in many instances, limited workers' rights to engage in collective dealings with their employers.[2] Massive immigration led to informal hiring networks through which workers and employers maintained a wage–labor exchange.[3] The origins of the modern trade union movement date from this period.

Between the end of the Civil War and the Great Depression, the United States emerged as the greatest industrial power in the world. That economic transformation was accomplished at a cost of considerable social turmoil. The modern corporation established itself as the prevalent form of economic organization in this country and acquired unsurpassed financial power. Workers responded to the growth of the corporations by militant unionism, political organization, and, in some instances, by violent resistance to perceived oppression. State control, and particularly judicial activism, was a crucial factor in the labor conflict. Organized labor eventually accepted a narrow, nonpolitical view of unions' role in advancing workers' interests, and the particular characteristics of the labor movement shaped its development into the twentieth century.

This chapter describes the evolution of corporations and unions in the period from 1865 to 1929. A significant part of that history involves mass movements of workers against the burgeoning economic might of employers. The labor struggles contain themes of radical politics, ethnic and cultural conflict, and the underlying aim of working class solidarity. Immediately after World War I, U.S. workers mounted one of the most sustained strike waves ever to occur in this country. Employers vigorously defended their prerogatives of control in the workplace, eventually reversing union expansion.[4] Their methods for doing so involve many modern techniques of personnel management.

The Rise of Corporations

The modern business corporation is a legal fiction designed to accommodate the emergent needs of a capitalist economy in the late nineteenth century. The essence of the corporate business entity is the limited liability it affords the shareholders, or owners, of the corporation's assets. Beginning in the 1880s, courts devised elaborate rules governing the creation and activity of corporations; the Supreme Court eventually attributed various rights to corporations, protecting them against deprivations of liberty and property and defining their assets very broadly to encompass such intangibles as goodwill. Out of those developments arose a legal environment that permitted investment of capital in exchange for a claim on corporate profits in the form of dividends.[5] The growth of large industrial corporations followed.

The first phase of U.S. industrial development took place in the railroads. As Alfred Chandler noted in his influential history of corporate growth, transportation and communications were "essential to high-volume production and distribution—the hallmark of large modern manufacturing or marketing enterprises."[6] With assistance from the federal government, the Union Pacific and the Central Pacific railroad companies completed a transcontinental line in May 1869. Railroads were among the largest economic activities of the time and needed large amounts of capital for the development of infrastructure. The Pennsylvania Railroad, for example, was in 1865 "the largest business enterprise in the world in terms of revenues, assets, and employees."[7] But rapid growth provided opportunities for graft and corruption. The federal government subsidized the railroads with grants of land for rights-of-way, and in conjunction with financing through issuance of stock, those subsidies allowed for considerable manipulation. During the Grant administration of the late 1860s, the financial firm of Credit Mobilier realized a $23 million cash profit on an investment of $10 million, and some members of Congress who voted for land grants were on the Union Pacific's board of directors.[8]

The growth of the railroads led to other important developments. First, in their efforts to evade destructive competition, rail lines entered into cooperative endeavors or *pools*. Through that device, they managed to impose control over prices in the industry and sometimes produce monopoly effects. As a result of variable and discriminatory rates, public sentiment led to governmental regulation in 1887. The Interstate Commerce Act, which created the Interstate Commerce Commission, was an early example of state intervention in a private commercial activity. Railway labor relations played an important part in the development of unions, and the earliest federal attempt at protective labor legislation occurred in the industry.[9] The first major strike of the post–Civil War period took place on the railroads in 1877.[10]

In manufacturing, economic growth was similarly pronounced. A useful comparison is between agriculture and manufacturing commodity production. Of total commodity output, agriculture represented 72 percent in 1839 as compared with 17 percent for manufacturing. In 1869, agriculture was 53 percent of that amount, while manufacturing was 33 percent and mining and construction together made up 14 percent. In 1899, the respective figures were 33 percent, 53 percent, and 14 percent.[11] The labor force grew from 11.1 million in 1860 to 37.5 million in 1910, increasing 3.4 times in size. By 1913, the United States was responsible for more than one-third of the industrial production in the world. New industries, such as printing and publishing, iron and steel, lumber, and malt liquor displaced such older industries as cotton goods, shoemaking, and woolen goods.[12]

As output increased, enterprises changed their organizational form to deal with the new business environment. Initially, employers sought to control business fluctuations through such simple devices as pooling, where each producer was accorded a certain market share or region. Pools were highly unstable, however, as the agreements were not legally enforceable, and in business downturns, many members failed to conform to the pooling arrangement. A succeeding form of combination was the trust, by which various companies gave shares of stock to trustees who operated the combine in the interests of the holders. Public opposition to the trusts, however, brought legal sanctions and an end to the trust form. The next and ultimately successful device was the holding company. The holding company permitted one business entity to own and control the shares of another company, thus allowing expansion. The expansion occurred both horizontally and vertically in two distinct phases.

In the horizontal phase of concentration, firms purchased their smaller competitors, thereby extending their geographic coverage. By concentrating a number of small entities into a large organization, businesses were able to stabilize prices and avoid the worst aspects of business cycles. Some examples of the horizontal mergers were the Standard Oil Company, the American Sugar Refining Company, and the United States Rubber Company. Generally, this phase took place between 1879 and 1893.

The sharp depression of 1893 halted economic expansion for several years, but thereafter merger activity resumed and reached a peak between 1899 and 1904. More than one-half of all U.S. manufacturing concerns were involved in mergers during this period. Typically, the mergers involved vertical integration, in which a firm acquired control over a related but not identical aspect of business. Andrew Carnegie, for example, owned coal and iron deposits. When Carnegie began to move into finished steel products, J. P. Morgan headed a financial group that bought out Carnegie and created the United States Steel Company, the largest corporation in the world at the time.[13]

Although one view suggests that large factories arose to take advantage of economies of scale, that explanation has several weaknesses. Many firms created during the merger era subsequently went out of business, so they hardly gained an economic advantage. Further, most of the increases in factory size took place before the 1890s. What more probably accounts for the merger activity is an attempt to reduce price competition.[14] The evolution of the U.S. corporation, in fact, can be traced primarily to the interplay between business and the state as firms tried to control uncertainty in the legal environment and destructive competition from rivals.[15] During the Progressive Era of 1904–1912, when reform coalitions wielded considerable political power, business was forced to fend off interference from the federal government. An important early instance of state interference in business activities came with the Sherman Act of 1890, which prohibited combinations in restraint of trade. Business was able to evade much of the impact of that law, but labor, as will be seen later in the chapter, was not.

Beginnings of Collective Organization

The U.S. working class responded to the rise of corporations with its own efforts at collective action. In some cases, such as the Knights of Labor, workers' organizations were broadly inclusive and directed toward political change rather than shop-floor action. Other groups were limited to persons in a particular occupation or industry, and they were oriented toward collective bargaining activities. Almost always, workers' movements were plagued by internal dissension, ethnic conflict, and employer hostility. A few organizations, including several national unions and the American Federation of Labor (AFL), still survive today, but most were short-lived. The National Typographers Union, founded in 1852, was the first national trade union formed in this country. In 1859, five other national organizations existed, and by 1939, there were a total of 194.[16]

Membership in labor organizations tended to fluctuate in the three decades between 1870 and 1900. As a percentage of industrial wage earners, trade union membership stood at 9.1 percent in 1870–1872 and then fell to 3.8 percent by 1880. It reached 5.0 percent in 1890 and 8.4 percent in 1900.[17] By 1910, membership density amounted to 10.9 percent of the nonagricultural workforce; that figure doubled over the next decade and reached 20.8 percent in 1920. The total number of union members for the latter date was 4,881,200.[18] Density declined from that peak until the organizing surge of the late 1930s.[19]

Again, immigration provided the most important source of labor for the expanding economy. In a five-year period between 1880 and 1885, for example, 2,855,000 immigrants arrived in this country. More than one-third were from

Table 2.1   Overview of Workers' Organizations, 1860s–1920s

Group	Occupational/Industrial Structure	Time Period
Knights of St. Crispin	Shoemakers	1860s–1872
National Labor Union	Federation of unions	1866–1872
Knights of Labor	All workers	1869–1890
American Federation of Labor	Federation of unions	1886–present
Industrial Workers of the World	All workers	1905–1917

Germany, with the remainder coming from Britain, Ireland, and Scandinavia. The numbers of manual wage earners increased by 301 percent from 1870 to 1910, while the total population of the country increased by 132 percent. Most workers were employed in construction, followed by metalworking, clothing, textiles, and mining.[20] The flood of immigrants came to an end with the outbreak of World War I, when rates of entry fell to five-decade lows.[21]

To begin with, we examine in further detail some of the more significant workers' organizations of the time. Not all of them were strictly trade unions, and some lasted only a few years; however, each contributed to the variety of organizational forms seized upon by workers to ensure their voice in the economic life of the country, and modern scholars often look to historical examples as a guide to contemporary issues confronting unions.[22] Table 2.1 provides an overview of those organizations. Each one illustrates a significant aspect of working class efforts to create a stable and coherent institution for collective action and merits further study for that reason.

Knights of Saint Crispin

In 1868, the shoemakers of Lynn, Massachusetts, organized a local of the Knights of St. Crispin and, shortly afterward, another local called the Daughters of St. Crispin. The local groups envisioned becoming a national organization made up of all workers in the shoe industry. Early studies of the Crispins, guided by the ideas of John Commons, portrayed the Crispins as a reactionary force opposing the introduction of new technology and the influx of new workers in the trade. The *green hands* interpretation, as it came to be known, is largely incorrect. Most members of the Crispins were actually factory workers, not skilled craftsmen who had spend a lifetime in the trade. Nor were the Crispins among the highly skilled factory elite or above average compared with other factory wage earners. The Crispins represented a cross section of the labor force employed in factories, and their main objective was resistance to the depredations of factory life. Encountering the regimentation of the factory, "they felt, in a word, proletarianized."[23]

The Knights of St. Crispin quickly became the largest trade union in the United States, enrolling between one-third and one-half of all male shoemakers in the country.[24] In early encounters with the shoe manufacturers, the Lynn Crispins successfully resisted wage cuts, achieved union recognition, and reached negotiated agreements with the employers. They were less fortunate in 1872, however, when the manufacturers declared a lockout and agreed among themselves not to enter into further agreements with the union.[25] Over the next several years, the Crispins declined in membership and influence, and other organizations gradually assumed more importance in the industry. The brief life of the Crispins nevertheless provided guidance and inspiration for future labor organizations. They illustrate, in the first instance, a union based on occupational concerns, rather than broad political and social interests. The next example falls into the latter kind of organization.

William Sylvis and the National Labor Union

Among the handful of unions at the end of the Civil War was the Iron Molders' International Union, founded in 1863 and headed by William Sylvis. An energetic leader, Sylvis established a cohesive organization that had substantial reserves to fund strike activities. Sylvis led his union in resisting the wage cuts imposed in the post–Civil War era, but employers decisively defeated Sylvis and other unionists. At the Iron Moulders' convention in 1868, Sylvis declared that the problem facing the union and U.S. workers generally was the wage system. He called for the establishment of workers' cooperative foundries, which could avoid the whole problem of strikes.[26]

In 1866, Sylvis joined with several other trade union leaders to form the National Labor Union (NLU). The NLU held congresses periodically until 1874, to which various unions sent delegates. Although primarily dedicated to politics rather than collective bargaining affairs, the NLU was nevertheless the first national institution representing the U.S. worker. Its 1866 program set forth basic ideas about labor in the United States. The platform called for laws establishing eight hours as the standard workday, for land reform and cooperatives, and for support of trade unions and collective bargaining practices. Last, the NLU urged that there should be no discrimination based on race, nationality, or religion. Rather, the NLU asserted, only one dividing line was of significance: "that which separates mankind into two great classes, the class that labors and the class that lives by others' labor."[27]

The NLU also supported trade unionism for female workers, and at the 1868 convention, the NLU recognized as delegates Susan B. Anthony, Elizabeth Cady Stanton, and two other women. Sylvis advocated equal civil rights for women, including rights to vote, run for office, and hold property. While the NLU membership did not agree with all aspects of the women's movement, it did promote wage equality through collective bargaining, and, in any event, the NLU vigorously and openly debated the basic issues of race and gender discrimination within the labor movement.

Sylvis eventually became preoccupied with the political dimensions of capitalism and devoted himself to the problem of currency reform. Sylvis believed that a national monetary system under federal control would resolve many difficulties facing workers at the time. Issuance of a paper currency, known as *greenbacks,* would provide low-interest capital to workers, farmers, and small entrepreneurs; by forming cooperative business ventures, workers could resist exploitation by bankers and wealthy capitalists. Such political adventures gradually weakened the relationship between the NLU and its trade union membership. As union support declined, political issues came to dominate the NLU, and its final convention in 1872 was devoted largely to currency reform and other legislative strategies.[28]

The NLU is noteworthy in several respects. First, it aimed for a national, inclusive presence by recruiting various occupational groups throughout the country. Second, the NLU demonstrates both the opportunities and the perils of political action. It was a progressive and socially active body, anticipating much of the legislative agenda that was enacted in the twentieth century such as protections based on race and gender. At the same time, working people may not always share common political beliefs and strategies, which can fragment efforts at solidarity. Precisely that issue arose in September 2002, when President George W. Bush appeared at a rally of the Brotherhood of Carpenters in an attempt to divide major unions from the influence of the national labor organization.[29]

Noble and Holy Order of the Knights of Labor

In December 1869, Uriah Stephens and other members of the Garment Cutters Association in Philadelphia dissolved their craft union and formed the Knights of Labor. Stephens was elected master workman, or head of the organization. The founders conducted their activities with the utmost secrecy and devised elaborate rituals. Stephens served as leader until 1879, when he was succeeded by Terence Powderly. Between 1869 and its decline in the late 1890s, the Knights grew from a small group of workers to one of the largest and most important workers' movements of the nineteenth century. At its peak in 1886, it had nearly 730,000 members.[30]

Although it began as a craft association, the General Assembly of 1878 drafted a constitution governing the formation of local units. The constitution required that three-fourths of the unit's membership consist of wage earners. Non-wage earners might thereafter be admitted, with the exception of lawyers, doctors, bankers, and liquor dealers; the prohibition was later modified to permit physicians to join, but the Knights added professional gamblers and stockbrokers to the list of excluded occupations. The Knights promoted a platform urging the development of "moral worth," guarantees of a greater share of wealth for workers, the establishment of cooperatives, and various specific legislative proposals, such as the abolition of child labor, the eight-hour workday, development of bureaus of labor statistics, and universal education.[31] The material below gives an idea of the Knights' objectives.

Rital of the Knights of Labor

[At the conclusion of the Knights' induction ceremony, the master workman was to read the following words to the candidate:]

In all the multifarious branches of trade, capital has its combinations, and whether intended or not, it crushes the manly hopes of labor and tramples poor humanity in the dust. We mean no conflict with legitimate enterprise, no antagonism to necessary capital, but men in their haste and greed, blinded by self interest, overlook the interests of others, and sometimes even violate the rights of those they deem helpless. We mean to uphold the dignity of labor, to affirm the nobility of all who live in accordance with the ordinance of God, "in the sweat of thy brow shalt thou eat bread." We mean to create a healthy public opinion on the subject of labor (the only creator of values or capital) and the justice of its receiving a full, just share of the values or capital it has created. We shall with all our strength, support laws made to harmonize the interests of labor and capital, for labor alone gives life and value to capital, and also those laws which tend to lighten the exhaustiveness of toil. We shall use every lawful and honorable means to procure and retain employ for one another, coupled with just and fair remuneration, and should accident or misfortune befall one of our number, render such aid as lies within our power to give, without inquiring as to his country or his creed; and without approving of general strikes among artisans, yet should it become justly necessary to enjoin an oppressor, we will protect and aid any of our number who thereby may suffer loss, and as opportunity offers, extend a helping hand to all branches of honorable toil.

Further Considerations About the Knights

1. Which of the ideas expressed in this passage do you agree with, if any? Which do you disagree with?
2. What appears to be the basic program of the Knights? In your opinion, is that program consistent with the principles of a "good" society?
3. What is the Knights' attitude toward strikes? If labor does not use the strike weapon against employers, how can labor obtain a "full, just share" of the wealth produced by industry?
4. What is the attitude of the Knights toward the legal system? Do you think the criminal conspiracy laws punishing a group of workers demanding a wage increase were the kinds of laws the Knights swore to uphold?

Powderly was elected president of the Knights in 1879, and under his leadership, the organization experienced both its greatest successes and its ultimate failure. Powderly quickly expanded the Knights' organizational base from the anthracite coal regions to a national confederation having considerable power in local politics.

In cities and towns across the United States, the Knights put forward candidates for local office, occasionally scoring important victories. The local assembly of Knights in Rutland, Vermont, for example, ran a slate of labor candidates in 1886 and took over the town's government. The Knights were also for a time a potent political force in such cities as Kansas City, Kansas; Richmond, Virginia; and Milwaukee, Wisconsin.[32]

Despite the Knights' preference for political action or negotiation over the strike weapon, their unprecedented surge in membership in 1886 was occasioned by a strike against one of the most powerful capitalists of the time, Jay Gould. Gould controlled the Southwestern railroad system, which included the Missouri Pacific, Wabash, and several other lines amounting to more than 10,000 miles of track. When Gould ordered a 10 percent wage reduction, the trainmen struck. Leaders of the Knights directed the stoppage and forced Gould to capitulate to a number of demands, including reinstatement of all strikers and guarantees of the rights of employees to belong to the Knights.[33] The Knights had achieved a major victory by forcing Gould to enter into "one of the first written contracts between a major American corporation and a national labor organization."[34] Membership in the Knights increased from around 100,000 members to more than 700,000 in July 1886. But the decline of the Knights was almost as rapid as its growth.

The relationship between the Knights and the established trade unions was always somewhat tenuous. While many craft workers joined the Knights and were an important part of the organization, the Knights' philosophy was not altogether compatible with the goals of trade unionism. As one leader of the Knights explained, the "essential difference" between the Knights and unions was that the former "contemplates a radical change in the existing industrial system, and labors to bring about that change, while Trades' Unions and other orders accept the industrial system as it is and endeavor to adapt themselves to it."[35] Although the Knights wished to transform the industrial system, they proposed to do so peacefully through education and political action; for that reason, Powderly tended to discourage strikes and to ignore requests for assistance from locals, even when those strikes were a last resort for the workers.

Another issue facing the Knights involved political strategies. The Haymarket affair of 1886, discussed later in this chapter, made labor issues a matter of national controversy, and Powderly faced a difficult choice in which groups to support. Eventually, Powderly chose to condemn the "revolutionists" held responsible for the Haymarket episode, and radicals charged Powderly with being a class traitor. Powderly also grew cautious in political affairs and counseled members to refrain from involvement in partisan politics. Such actions aroused great opposition within the Knights, and internal factionalism contributed to the demise of the organization. By 1890, the Knights had shrunk to approximately 100,000 members, and three years later, Powderly was removed from office. Thereafter, the organization gradually disintegrated.

The collapse of the organization contributed significantly to the failure of a broad working class political movement in this country; in fact, the Knights' demise "may have foreclosed important options for the American worker," thereby constraining the development of labor.[36] Despite its failures, the Knights was an impressive organization. In the first place, it demonstrated that the labor movement was a social and political force of significance. Second, the preoccupations of the Knights regarding workers and their role in industrial capitalism are far from resolved, as is the relationship between labor and the U.S. political system. The Knights' insistence on citizenship as a moral ideal, on the dignity of labor, and on democracy as a counterweight to capitalist power remains worthy of consideration.

The American Federation of Labor

One sign of the philosophical differences between the Knights and the trade unions was the Federation of Organized Trades and Labor Unions (FOTLU) convention held in Pittsburgh in 1881. Several trade unions were represented, including the Cigarmakers, whose delegate was Samuel Gompers. Over the next five years, the FOTLU held annual conventions, gradually moving toward a pure and simple kind of unionism that concentrated on industrial rather than political action and emphasized the autonomy of the craft units. In 1886, the FOTLU dissolved itself and was replaced by the American Federation of Labor, headed by Gompers. Although there were discussions between the Knights and the AFL, the two groups were unable to reconcile their differences over dual union membership.[37] By 1890, the AFL's membership was approximately equal to that of the Knights, and thereafter the AFL became the dominant labor organization in the United States for the next four decades.

As president of the AFL from 1886 until 1924, Gompers strongly influenced the development of the organization. In his youth, Gompers studied the work of Marx and became attracted to principles of socialism.[38] His early radicalism eventually gave way to a much narrower view of the role of labor organizations. One of the founding members of the FOTLU, Gompers was often enmeshed in disputes with the Knights of Labor over organizational jurisdiction. Gompers was a member and officer of Cigarmakers International Union (CMIU), Local 144, in New York City. There Gompers and Adolph Strasser implemented a system of high dues, high benefits, and strict union administrative controls modeled along the lines of British trade unions. While the system provided substantial protections for members, it had the effect of excluding unskilled, low wage workers from union affiliation. It also emphasized the financial dimension of union membership over the social and ideological ones.[39]

The split between the AFL and the Knights grew directly out of factionalism of the New York Cigarmakers. Radical elements within the CMIU refused to support the union's official choice in the 1882 state elections and broke off from the CMIU to form the Cigarmakers' Progressive Union. The Progressives eventually became associated with the Knights of Labor, District Assembly 49. As a result, there was continuous struggle between Gompers and the Knights regarding representation in the industry, and the schism between Powderly and Gompers was quite acrimonious at times.[40] Such conflict was instrumental in shaping Gompers's hostility toward industrial unions of unskilled labor and any incursions on the autonomy of the craft organizations.[41]

Gradually, Gompers and the AFL drifted away from socialist politics, adopting a "voluntarist" position toward labor relations that relied on agreements to provide workplace protections. He condemned radical groups such as the Industrial Workers of the World (IWW) and discouraged labor's alliance with either of the major political parties. Labor should be nonpartisan, rewarding its friends and punishing its enemies, whoever they might be. Similarly, workers were to better their wages and working conditions through trade union contracts and not through legislation. Even though Gompers supported laws limiting immigration and granting women's suffrage, he opposed laws fixing minimum wages and working hours for men; male adults, Gompers reasoned, should voluntarily protect themselves by choosing to participate in unions. By 1900, Gompers was convinced that it was essential to reach an accommodation with the large and powerful corporations; employers would tolerate unionism only "if it was confined mainly to the skilled trades, if it rejected militancy and radicalism, and if it was in general reasonable in its demands." In 1913, Gompers conceded that he no longer opposed capitalism but believed that workers should strive for its "fuller development and evolution."[42] But just as the AFL was consolidating its craft orientation and conservatism, the IWW took up the radical cause.

Rise and Fall and Rise of the "Wobblies," 1905–2002

Although a numerically small organization, the Industrial Workers of the World, or "Wobblies," as they were sometimes known, captured the imagination of U.S. workers and the unmitigated hostility of capitalists. The IWW held its founding convention in 1905, which was attended by some of the foremost labor leaders of the time. Among those present were Mary "Mother" Jones, Eugene Debs, William D. "Big Bill" Haywood, and the socialist theorist Daniel De Leon. The IWW advocated revolutionary opposition to capitalism and the abolition of the wage system through the establishment of "one big union" made up of all workers. As the 1908 preamble quoted below indicates, the Wobblies were radical and outspoken in their aims.

The Western Federation of Miners, led by Haywood, was instrumental in the formation of the IWW. Historians often trace the roots of the IWW to conditions in gold and silver mining in the American West.[43] But the strategies and tactics of the IWW were influenced by French syndicalism, which asserted that workers should control the means of production and should seize that control by force where necessary.[44] Toward that end, the Wobblies favored industrial unionism, which included all workers regardless of occupation, gender, or race. They disdained political action through the ballot box and urged *direct action* in the workplace. The weapons of direct action were general strikes, partial strikes, passive resistance, and sabotage. Sabotage, however, did not necessarily entail violence or destruction of property. The term, in fact, probably derives from a reference to inept or unskilled workers hired to replace French strikers. Those incompetent workers were typically associated with the countryside and wore wooden shoes or *sabots*; accordingly, sabotage is simply inferior, poorly done work. In any case, there is little evidence that the IWW engaged in the violent activities often attributed to the organization.[45]

Preamble to the IWW Constitution (1908)

The working class and the employing class have nothing in common. There can be no peace so long as hunger and want are found among millions of working people and the few, who make up the employing class, have all the good things of life.

Between these two classes a struggle must go on until the workers of the world organize as a class, take possession of the art and the machinery of production, and abolish the wage system.

We find that the centering of management of the industries into fewer and fewer hands makes the trade unions unable to cope with the ever growing power of the employing class. The trade unions foster a state of affairs which allows one set of workers to be pitted against another set of workers in the same industry, thereby helping defeat one another in wage wars. Moreover, the trade unions aid the employing class to mislead the workers into the belief that the working class have interests in common with their employers.

These conditions can be changed and the interest of the working class upheld only by an organization formed in such a way that all its members in any one industry, or in all industries if necessary, cease work whenever a strike or lockout is on in any department thereof, thus making an injury to one an injury to all.

Instead of the conservative motto, "A fair day's wage for a fair day's work," we must inscribe on our banner the revolutionary watchword, "Abolition of the wage system."

It is the historic mission of the working class to do away with capitalism. The army of production must be organized, not only for the every-day struggle with capitalists, but also to carry on production when capitalism shall have been overthrown. By organizing industrially we are forming the structure of the new society with the shell of the old.

More on the IWW

1. What is the attitude of the IWW toward the trade unions? Do you think Gompers was sympathetic to the aims of the IWW?
2. Do you agree or disagree with the notion that workers have interests in common with their employers? What interests are in common? What interests are conflicting?
3. How do the Wobblies propose to overthrow the capitalist class? As a theoretical proposition, would their strategy work? Should workers be permitted to engage in general strikes? How could they be prevented from doing so? Assume that a worker used a general strike to overthrow a despotic political leader and institute a democratic government—is that more legitimate than a general strike for higher wages?

Table 2.2   A Thematic Overview of Labor Conflict, 1880–1920

Event	Occupational Group	Major Themes
Haymarket Affair, 1886	All workers	Mass workers' movement; hours of work; labor radicalism; public opinion
Homestead Strike, 1892	Steel workers	Craft workers; employer strategies; private detective services; state military power
Pullman Strike, 1894	Railway workers	Welfare capitalism; industrial unionism; strikes and commerce; judicial power
Ludlow Massacre, 1914	Coal miners	Industrial violence; federal intervention in labor disputes; employee participation and antiunionism
U.S. Steel Strike, 1919	Steel workers	Corporate power; ethnic issues; structure of American labor movement

The IWW's radical philosophy continued the U.S. worker's confrontation with wage labor under capitalism. Although the Wobblies were ultimately unsuccessful in their revolutionary goals, they did originate a number of imaginative labor tactics, such as the sitdown strike and the partial strike. Moreover, their idealism has a particularly American quality and continues to enrich the study of labor history. The Wobblies have established an interesting site on the Web where they describe their philosophy and its relevance to the contemporary world of global capitalism.[46]

The foregoing description of workers' organizations gives some indication of the different principles around which unions formed into identifiable entities. Once organized, those entities inevitably confronted opposition to their aim of collective dealing with employers. Such opposition often manifested itself in convulsive struggles over the simple matter of recognition of the union. The next section describes the major battles between labor and management for dominance in setting the terms and conditions of the employment relation. After decades of conflict, management emerged as the clear victor in the contest between the movement for collective bargaining and employers' resistance to it.

Union Growth and Labor Conflict

A comprehensive encyclopedia of U.S. labor conflict describes some 254 major strikes in the United States, beginning with a mutiny of fishermen in 1636 and concluding with the Pittson Coal Company strike of 1989.[47] Obviously, labor conflict is an essential part of labor history, and that point is particularly true of the four decades between 1880 and 1920. A number of significant events took place during this time that indelibly stamped the U.S. labor movement. This section describes the more important strikes, beginning with the Haymarket incident in 1886 and concluding with the steel strike of 1919. Each strike illustrates significant dimensions of the labor movement and how employers dealt with labor. As we proceed, you should note certain emerging themes and their interrelationships as summarized in Table 2.2.

The Haymarket Affair, 1886

Limitations on the length of the workday had been a goal of U.S. labor for many years prior to 1886. The Knights of Labor, the Federation of Organized Trades and Labor Unions, and various socialist groups all supported the movement. With improving economic conditions in the 1880s, workers renewed their agitation for a shorter working day. This agitation culminated in the Haymarket affair in Chicago in 1886. The incident resulted in lasting damage to the movement for a shorter workday and brought disrepute to radical tendencies within the labor movement.

Several socialist groups united in 1876 to form the Workingmen's Party of the United States. Based on the tenets of European socialists and the influence of the International Workingmen's Association of 1870, the Workingmen's Party sponsored candidates in several local elections and ran a presidential candidate on the Socialist Labor Party ticket in 1880. Led by U.S.-born Albert Parsons and German immigrant August Spies, socialists in Chicago formed the Revolutionary Socialist Party in 1881. By 1886, their group dominated the Chicago labor movement.

Gompers and the FOTLU adopted a proposal in favor of the eight-hour day at their 1884 convention, and to achieve that goal, the FOTLU set May 1, 1886, as the date of a general strike. Powderly officially disapproved of the general strike concept, but many local groups of the Knights of Labor were attracted to the idea. In Chicago, Parsons, Spies, and other radicals organized the May 1 demonstration, and the two men addressed a gathering of 25,000 workers on April 25. Confronted by the impressive degree of working class solidarity, many employers, particularly in the meatpacking industry, had already granted the eight-hour day to employees.[48]

May 1 was a festive event for Chicago workers. Some 40,000 persons took part in the general strike to begin with, and that figure doubled over the next four days. Initially, the strike promised to be successful, but events on May 3 and 4 dramatically changed the nature of the event. For months, workers at the McCormick Harvester plant had been engaged in a work stoppage. Spies spoke to a group at the factory on May 3, and as strikebreakers left the plant, they were attacked. Police arrived on the scene, and in the ensuing conflict, the police shot and killed four people and wounded many others. Spies and Parsons issued a circular calling workers to arms and summoning them to a meeting the next day at Haymarket square.[49]

On May 4, the workers assembled at Haymarket for a peaceful meeting, which continued until late evening. Around 10:00 P.M., only a small number of demonstrators remained in the square. At that point, a detachment of police entered the area and commanded the crowd to disperse. Before they could do so, a bomb exploded, injuring several police officers. The police reacted by firing indiscriminately into the crowd; their shots not only killed and wounded a large number of civilians, but most probably resulted in the deaths of six of the seven police who died following the incident.

The event aroused national fury against the "anarchists" who perpetrated the bombing. Eight men, including Spies, Parsons, and other syndicalist leaders, were arrested and subsequently tried for the crime. Judge Joseph Gary presided over a trial that was so biased against the defendants that a commentator describes it as "one of the most unjust in the annals of American jurisprudence."[50] In the end, all eight defendants were convicted, even though there was no proof that any of them had actually thrown a bomb. The theory of the prosecution rested on the notion that a conspiracy was created when the defendants advocated terrorist acts through their speeches. The state appellate court upheld the convictions, and the U.S. Supreme Court refused to grant federal review.

Judge Gary sentenced seven defendants to death, but two sentences were commuted to life imprisonment. In 1892, John Altgeld was elected governor of Illinois, and he undertook an exhaustive review of the trial and Gary's behavior during the case. Altgeld pardoned the remaining defendants, stating that Gary had exhibited bias and prejudice against the defendants and denied them a fair trial. Moreover, Altgeld said that much of the evidence was "a pure fabrication" and that the police had suborned the testimony of many witnesses. Declaring the defendants innocent, Altgeld in his statement "showed that the court, the prosecution, and the jury had yielded to the hysteria promoted by the press and the police, and that the entire machinery of justice had been perverted to grossly unjust ends."[51]

One outcome of the Haymarket affair was to deal a serious blow to the radical impulse within the labor movement. Powderly condemned the acts of violence and sought to dissociate the Knights of Labor from any connection with the anarcho-syndicalists. Gompers, although personally more sympathetic to the defendants, deplored the teachings of the anarchists. Public opinion virulently denounced the "foreigners" who brought such alien ideas to the United States. When Altgeld issued the pardons, he was also strongly criticized in the press. Consequently, Haymarket brought radical ideas into disrepute for years, and it demonstrated the power of the media to influence public issues about labor.

The Homestead Steel Strike, 1892

In contrast to Haymarket, the Homestead strike was confined to a single employer, involved primarily skilled craft workers, and focused strictly on job-related issues. But it, too, ended in defeat for labor. The implications of Homestead have to do with the changing nature of workplace control, the power of capital to crush even a strong union, and the consequences of such defeats for labor.

By 1892, Andrew Carnegie had established his dominance in the steel industry. The Homestead Works, located near Pittsburgh on the Monongahela River, was the centerpiece of Carnegie's empire. It employed some 3,800 workers under the immediate control of general manager Henry Clay Frick. The Amalgamated Association of Iron and Steel Workers represented some 1,000 tonnage men whose wages were determined by the price Carnegie obtained for steel. The Amalgamated admitted only skilled workers to membership, but it nevertheless managed to unite unskilled employees behind the strike.

Deliberately seeking to undermine the union, Frick conducted negotiations for the 1892 contract in such a way as to force the Amalgamated into an impasse. He demanded reductions in wages and, for practical purposes, an end to the union's right to represent employees. Forced into an untenable position, the Amalgamated refused Frick's proposals. Frick constructed a large fence topped with barbed wire around the mill and informed the Amalgamated that it had until June 24 to accept the company's offer. When the union declined, Frick began shutting down the mills, and by June 30, the union was locked out. In the meantime, Frick had contacted the Pinkerton Agency and arranged for strikebreakers to be conducted into the works on barges.

The Pinkertons assembled on July 4 and sailed down the Ohio and Monongahela rivers toward Homestead. They were met with armed force, and following an intense battle with casualties on both sides, the Pinkertons surrendered. Union leaders escorted them through the town and released them, badly beaten, on the outskirts of Homestead. The company thereupon issued a press release declaring it would "never again recognize the Amalgamated Association or any other labor organization."[52]

Frick's next move was to appeal to the state for assistance. Governor Pattison eventually ordered 8,000 troops to the area. The strikers were faced with a dilemma: they were skilled craftsmen who prided themselves on their civic responsibilities and their status as homeowners and law-abiding citizens of the community. Their resistance to Frick and Carnegie was grounded on republican ideologies of civic duty and responsible conduct, and consistent with such principles, they could not oppose a legitimate government. "Thus, since Homestead's workers equated themselves with the American people and the actions of the state with their own goals, they were not willing to continue their resistance once the state government entered the confrontation. This led directly to their defeat."[53] Finally, in November, the union abandoned the strike and the workers returned under conditions dictated by Frick.

The defeat of the Amalgamated was extremely profitable for Carnegie. By 1910, the steel industry was nonunion in virtually all aspects. Managers were free to make labor decisions based only on minimizing costs and maximizing profits. The steelmaster "could with impunity manipulate the wage rate, step up the work, and extend the twelve-hour day and the seven-day week. The antiunion triumph completed economical steel manufacture."[54] Not until after World War I did unionism present a serious threat to the steel industry, when it was once again defeated.

Pullman and the Railway Strike, 1894

The U.S. economy entered another period of recession in 1893. This downturn was particularly severe, resulting in business failures and massive unemployment. Throughout the country, employers responded with wage cuts and other measures designed to cut production costs. Among workers so affected were those at the Pullman Company outside Chicago.

The Pullman Palace Car Company built elaborate sleeping cars for travel on the railroads. Founded by George Pullman in 1867, the company quickly eliminated any serious competition and serviced more than three-fourths of the U.S. railway mileage by 1894.[55] Pullman himself was widely regarded as a progressive, innovate employer. He built the town of Pullman to rent housing to his employees, and in many respects, it was a model community. It had excellent sanitary facilities, schools, and a public library, and city officials discouraged drinking and prostitution. Underneath the facade, however, life in Pullman was not ideal. Pullman expected his town to show a profit, and he charged prices for gas, water, and rent that were substantially higher than prices in surrounding communities. Moreover, the company followed the practice of issuing two checks to its workers, one for the amount of wages, and one for the amount of rent; the employee endorsed the rent check and promptly handed it back to the paymaster. Pullman also tried to control the political views of the town's inhabitants, instructing them on correct choices in local and national elections. Pullman's employees gradually came to resent his extreme paternalism.

The immediate origin of the strike was Pullman's order to reduce wages. The depression of 1893 substantially reduced Pullman's contracts for car construction, and he met competitive pressures by bidding at prices below the cost of building cars. To minimize his losses, Pullman cut workers' wages. Despite the wage reductions, Pullman refused to lower his rents, asserting that the rental business and the car construction business were separate. As a consequence, employees often had little income remaining after their rent payments. One skilled mechanic, for example, received a check for $9.07 for two weeks' work, but the company took $9.00 for rent.

Hard financial times, however, did not affect all equally. The Pullman managerial employees, including Pullman himself, maintained their salaries. The company had substantial assets in reserve and paid 8 percent dividends on its stock in the 1894 fiscal year and carried over a large cash surplus from the preceding year. According to one study, "Had the Pullman Corporation dipped but lightly into the $4,000,000 surplus of 1893 or had been willing to accept a somewhat smaller surplus for 1894, there would have been no need for the drastic wage reduction."[56] In desperation, employees organized and selected a grievance committee that met with Pullman on May 9. Pullman informed them that the company was in no position to grant a wage increase, nor would it reduce rents. He did assure members of the committee that there would not be any reprisals against them. The next day, however, three committeemen were discharged.

Many Pullman workers had become members of the American Railway Union (ARU), founded by Eugene Debs in June 1893. The ARU was an industrial union that accepted white members from all occupations on the railroad. Although a new organization, it numbered some 150,000 members at the time of the Pullman dispute. Debs and ARU officials believed that strikes generally ended badly for workers, and their approach favored arbitration or mediation of disputes rather than work stoppages. Debs was particularly reluctant to be drawn into a strike against Pullman, because it meant a battle against a powerful coalition of railroad operators.

The owners of rail lines operating from the Chicago area had formed a group known as the General Managers' Association (GMA). In 1894, it represented twenty-four lines and included some of the largest railroad companies in the world. The GMA typically dealt with a range of topics common to the industry, and it provided a common front for dealing with the ARU. Committee No. 2 of the GMA took responsibility for wage issues affecting the lines, and the membership agreed that the wage demands made on any operator would be referred to the committee for its recommendation. Should workers attempt a strike against the individual line, the combined resources of the GMA would be used to support the struck member.[57]

Pullman workers met on May 10 and voted to strike. The next day, fearing a lockout, the union walked out. Pullman closed his plant that evening "until further notice." Debs arrived in Pullman and delivered a scathing denunciation of George Pullman, calling his paternalism "the same as the interest of a slave holder in his human chattels." He told the workers, "You are striking to avert slavery and degradation."[58] At the ARU convention in June, Debs set a deadline of June 26 for the adjustment of the grievances. Thereafter, union members throughout the country would refuse to handle—or boycott—all Pullman railroad cars. The boycott began on June 27, and within a few days, had spread through the United States. It became apparent that the ARU was a powerful force on the railroads, and the GMA reacted accordingly.

Over the next several weeks, the GMA adopted strategies designed to annihilate the union. Any worker on any line who refused to handle a Pullman car was to be immediately discharged and barred from future employment on GMA lines. The GMA recruited strikebreakers from other railroads in the eastern United States and paid the cost of transporting new employees to Chicago. Another important strategy involved legal action against the ARU, primarily under federal laws protecting mail service and interstate commerce. The GMA's plan was to involve the U.S. government in the dispute and mold public opinion against the strike.

The U.S. Attorney General, Richard Olney, led the legal campaign against the ARU. His first step was to declare that any train carrying mail was, in its entirety, a mail train. Operators simply attached a Pullman car to trains with mail, and when strikers refused to handle the Pullman car, they were interfering with the U.S. mail. As Olney received reports of interrupted mail service, he procured warrants for the arrest of the offenders involved.

Next, Olney appointed a special federal attorney for the Chicago area and directed him to apply for an injunction under the Sherman Antitrust Act of 1890, which prohibited combinations in restraint of trade. Although Congress did not clearly intend the law to be applied against labor, the federal judiciary had so construed it on other occasions, and Olney obtained an injunction from the federal district court that forbid workers from attempting to induce by threats, coercion, or persuasion any refusal to work on the trains. Debs was subsequently charged with contempt for refusing to obey the injunction and sentenced to six months' imprisonment; the U.S. Supreme Court upheld the sentence.[59]

Attempting to enforce the court's injunction, federal marshals read the order to disperse to crowds of strikers, who generally disregarded it. Olney seized upon this civil disobedience as an excuse to call for federal troops and to authorize the swearing in of more federal deputies. By July 3, tension was so high that President

Grover Cleveland ordered a detachment of federal troops into Chicago over the objection of Illinois Governor John Altgeld. Federal troops also appeared in the communities of Los Angeles, California; Trinidad, Colorado; and Raton, New Mexico.[60] The presence of a massive armed force, Debs's arrest on July 10, and the failure of an anticipated general strike in Chicago all led to the defeat of the ARU.[61] By July 13, trains were operating on schedule and the rioting had stopped.

In the aftermath of the strike, Debs served a six months' contempt sentence at the prison in Woodstock, Illinois. He was also charged with the crime of conspiracy, and Clarence Darrow represented him at the trial. Darrow and Debs planned to use the trial to publicize the role of the GMA in instigating violence during the strike, but after a few days of trial, the prosecution abandoned the whole proceeding. Debs's imprisonment had a crucial effect on his political views, and he eventually adopted many socialist tenets. After his release from prison, Debs became an influential public figure. Over 100,000 people greeted him on his return to Chicago, and he delivered an impassioned speech urging political action to redeem the country from the grasp of corporate power.[62] Debs ran for president as a Socialist candidate in several national elections, and he received 6 percent of the popular vote in 1912.

The Pullman incident illustrates several themes. George Pullman exemplified the early welfare capitalist, who provided security and benefits for his workers so long as it was profitable; in the end, Pullman proved himself as ruthless in dealing with labor as Carnegie, Frick, and many other employers. Second, the federal government was a key player in the dispute. The federal injunction issued against the strikers was one of the most sweeping judicial orders ever conceived in this country, and federal troops enforced its terms. Third, the ARU was one of the earliest industrial unions, accepting skilled and unskilled alike into its ranks. The size and power of the ARU threatened railroad owners, who crushed it. Last, Debs is a noteworthy figure in American political life, and the strike helped to shape his beliefs about our society.

The Ludlow Massacre and the Coal Field Wars, 1914

After its founding in 1890, the United Mine Workers of America (UMWA) made repeated attempts to organize the coal fields in the western United States.[63] In September 1913, the UMWA commenced a strike against a group of mine operators. The Colorado Fuel and Iron Company, in which John D. Rockefeller Jr. owned a controlling interest, was the most powerful and influential of the mining concerns. Forced to abandon their company-owned housing at the mining camps, the miners established a number of tent colonies in the area; the largest, with some 10,000 inhabitants, was located between Trinidad and Walsenberg at a site called Ludlow.[64]

The strike continued throughout the winter of 1913–1914. Sporadic incidents of violence occurred during the period, and on April 14, a military detachment visited the Ludlow colony. The commanding officer demanded that the miners turn over a person believed to be in the camp. Louis Tikas, leader of the miners, refused to comply with the demand, and the soldiers took up positions outside the camp. A short time later, shooting commenced. The militia eventually overran the encampment and set fire to the tents. Two women and eleven children, who had taken shelter in a pit beneath one of the tents, died of suffocation, and Tikas himself was later killed by the soldiers. Their deaths led to an insurrection within the state of Colorado and outrage throughout the United States.[65] The incident also produced one of the most important industrial relations developments of this century.

As knowledge of the Ludlow incident spread across the nation, Rockefeller came under virulent personal attack. Rockefeller's biographer notes that "the name of Rockefeller was denounced from one end of the country to the other, and JDR Jr.'s assertion before the House committee [at an earlier date] that he would stand by the officers of the company at any expense was recalled with bitterness and recrimination."[66] Rockefeller resolved to take steps to protect the family name from further public embarrassment and commenced a two-part program of rehabilitation. The first step consisted of hiring a publicity agent named Ivy Lee to prepare and publish a series of bulletins setting forth the company's version of the Ludlow incident.

The second facet of Rockefeller's strategy was more complex and far-reaching. On August 1, 1914, Rockefeller wrote to Mackenzie King, formerly the Canadian Minister of Labor, and asked his assistance in resolving the strike. King responded with a scheme that would supplant unions on the one hand and, at the same time, enable Rockefeller to deal with their employees on a collective basis. It would also lead to one of the most important industrial relations developments of the century.

On September 5, 1914, President Wilson wrote to each of the coal operators, urging them to accept a three-year agreement, during the life of which the UMWA would neither demand recognition nor picket mine sites. The operators would in turn agree to comply with the mining laws of Colorado, to rehire any strikers who had not violated the law, and to provide a grievance procedure subject to final resolution by a commission appointed by the president. The UMWA, meeting in a special convention, accepted the plan; the operators rejected it as an interference with their right to manage their operations as *open shops* or nonunion workplaces.[67]

Shortly thereafter, Rockefeller undertook a publicity campaign that established his reputation as an authority in labor affairs and brought the idea of industrial democracy to national attention. On September 19, 1915, Rockefeller and King arrived unannounced in Trinidad, Colorado. They visited a number of mining camps and Rockefeller personally spoke to miners about their concerns.[68] The *New York Times* gave prominent coverage to the tour, and a particularly revealing feature story appeared in the *Times* on September 23. Rockefeller had visited a school in Trinidad, and a twelve-year-old girl whose father dug coal for Rockefeller explained how the children operated a store for the sale of school supplies. Prominently located on the front page of the *Times* was the following caption: "Miner's Child in Colorado Tells the Financier How to Make Money." The article related how the schoolgirl "walked to the front of the room, shook hands calmly with Mr. Rockefeller, and began her financial lesson." Rockefeller listened attentively.[69]

Through such coverage, the press created a favorable image of Rockefeller and publicized the idea of welfare capitalism generally. Rockefeller emphasized the political equality of all industrial citizens and asserted that no person—not even the world's richest man—was intrinsically superior to any other person in our democracy. The capitalist enterprise, Rockefeller asserted, was responsive to the needs of the individual American worker and was ideally suited to satisfy his or her needs. Accordingly, the relations between labor and capital were not adversarial; conflict arose from misunderstanding and a failure of trust. Rockefeller gave a speech in October 1915 that recapitulates the major themes of labor–management cooperation in the United States. Portions of that speech are set forth below.

John D. Rockefeller Jr. on Labor–Management Relations

I believe that the ultimate object of all activities in a republic should be the development of the manhood of its citizens; that such manhood can be developed to the fullest degree only under conditions of freedom for the individual, and that industrial enterprises can and should be conducted in accordance with these principles. I believe that a prime consideration in the carrying on of industry should be the well-being of the men and women engaged in it, and that the soundest industrial policy is that which has constantly in mind the welfare of the employe[e]s as well as the making of profits, and which, when the necessity arises, subordinates profits to welfare.

A business to be successful must not only provide to labor remunerative employment under proper working conditions, but it must also render useful service to the community and earn a fair return on the money invested. The adoption of any policy toward labor, however favorable it may seem, which results in the bankruptcy of the corporation and the discontinuance of its work, is as injurious to labor which is thrown out of employment, as it is to the public which loses the services of the enterprise, and to the stockholders whose capital is impaired.

I believe it to be the duty of every citizen to do all within his power to improve the conditions under which men work and live. I believe that that man renders the greatest social service who so co-operates in the organization of industry as to afford to the largest number of men the greatest opportunity for self-development, and the enjoyment by every man of those benefits which his own work adds to the wealth of civilization. In order to live, the wage-earner must sell his labor from day to day. Unless he can do this, the earnings from that day's labor are gone forever. Capital can defer its returns temporarily in the expectation of future profits, but labor cannot. If, therefore, fair wages and reasonable living conditions cannot otherwise be provided, dividends must be deferred or the industry abandoned. I believe that a corporation should be deemed to consist of its stockholders, directors, officers and employe[e]s; that the real interests of all are one, and that neither labor nor capital can permanently prosper unless the just rights of both are conserved.[70]

(Continued)

(Continued)

Some Questions About John D. Rockefeller Jr.

1. Do you agree with Rockefeller's statements? Do you think stockholders would willingly defer a dividend to give wage increases to employees or would the stockholder sell the company's stock and invest elsewhere? Under conditions of modern capitalism, is it accurate to call shareholders "owners" or are they just transient opportunists who have merely pecuniary interests in any enterprise?

2. Compare the ideal of civic virtue in this passage with the "artisanal republicanism" discussed in the material on the Knights of Labor or the National Labor Union. Are Rockefeller's sentiments similar to those of the labor radicals?

3. Rockefeller said that the Colorado Fuel and Iron Company's plan of industrial representation was based on a theory of common interest and cooperation. Would you agree that every member of an enterprise should have a formal, contractual right to participate in the decisions of the company? Would you support legislation giving employees such a right? Is that idea consistent with an employer's property right? Does any large modern corporation give employees a legal right to share in strategic decision making?

4. Some modern theories of corporate structure assert that the market should be the sole determinant of corporate behavior. How would this theory fit in with Rockefeller's notion that capital should defer its returns when necessary to provide a fair wage and reasonable working conditions?

The Ludlow incident and Rockefeller's creative response are landmarks in industrial relations theory and practice. The civil insurrection in Colorado was the subject of massive publicity, and labor was portrayed more sympathetically than in past disputes. President Wilson's intervention protected the interests of workers as well as those of employers, in distinct contrast to Cleveland's approach in the Pullman strike. Rockefeller's Industrial Plan marked an important step in labor relations. Positively, it offered a means by which workers could participate in the firm's activities, and while it was not the first program of industrial democracy, it was the best known of the time. Negatively, the representation plans discouraged workers from seeking outside union representation and eventually led to the company unions of the early 1930s. The theory of common interests is essential to labor–management cooperation and continues to be debated in the context of our labor law.[71]

The Strike at U.S. Steel, 1919

In 1901, J. P. Morgan and other financiers organized the U.S. Steel Corporation, creating the largest industrial concern in the world. U.S. Steel controlled more than

60 percent of the basic steel industry, including the former Carnegie properties. Judge Elbert E. Gary, who headed the company, was staunchly opposed to unionism in the industry. After the Homestead strike, the steel corporations had virtually eradicated the union presence, and within a few years, steelmakers enjoyed unchallenged dominance over labor. They used that power to impose twelve-hour working days on most employees, to reduce or maintain wages at levels they arbitrarily established, and to speed up work processes at their discretion. As summarized by John Fitch in his detailed survey completed in 1910, "A repressive regime that makes it impossible for men to protest against conditions that are inimical to their welfare serves now, and has served since the destruction of unionism, to keep the employers in the saddle."[72]

The economic and political conditions after World War I, which are considered more fully in the next chapter, led to an increase in union organizing activity. The steel industry, particularly, was an attractive target for the AFL. In August 1918, Gompers met with other labor leaders to establish a committee for the organization of iron and steel workers. The national committee selected William Z. Foster to lead the drive, and eventually twenty-four craft unions combined in the effort.[73] Workers responded enthusiastically to the drive, including the unskilled immigrants from Eastern Europe who had come to the United States in large numbers around the turn of the century. Among the most pressing grievances were declines in real wages, unemployment, and the long working hours. The organizing committee prepared a list of twelve demands that included rights of collective bargaining, overtime pay, abolition of company unions, and the eight-hour day. It presented the demands to Judge Gary on August 26, 1919, and he rejected them. The union established a strike deadline for September 22 and by the end of the month, almost 350,000 workers were involved in the stoppage.[74]

The steel companies initiated several strategies to defeat the strike. First, they encouraged the notion that the strike was caused by foreigners and Bolsheviks, whose aim was the overthrow of lawful government; the press eagerly publicized that point of view. Second, the companies distributed propaganda attesting that Foster and the IWW actually controlled the strike. Third, local officials flagrantly violated the strikers' civil rights to assemble and hold meetings. Fourth, through a network of spies and agents, the employers spread misinformation and ethnic and racial antagonisms. Gradually, the employers' tactics broke the momentum of the strike.

The Interchurch World Commission, a neutral observer of the strike, prepared a detailed report on the affair and forwarded it to President Wilson. The commission urged Wilson to take steps to ensure peaceful dealings between labor and capital in the industry; otherwise, renewed conflict "seems inevitable." The report concluded that conditions in the industry were largely fixed by U.S. Steel, which was controlled by a small group of financiers who set labor conditions without any practical knowledge of production. Most employees worked the twelve-hour day and the seven-day week. Over one-third of the employees earned less than the government's minimum subsistence wage, and 72 percent earned less than the standard set for minimum comfort level. The upper third of wage earners were largely skilled Americans and had disproportionately high wages, creating division and conflict among the workforce. As to corporate profits, the commission noted that in 1919, U.S. Steel had an undivided reserve of $493,048,202. Contrary to press reports, the commission said, the strike was a mass movement, and the "charges of Bolshevism or of industrial radicalism in the conduct of the strike were without foundation." The explanation for the defeat of the strike was the size of U.S. Steel, "together with the strength of its active opposition and the support accorded it by employers generally, by governmental agencies and by organs of public opinion."[75]

The defeat of the steel strike had important implications for labor. It signaled the beginning of an employer offensive against unions that significantly reduced their strength for the remainder of the 1920s. It also underscored the need for cohesive union organization in the conduct of strikes. The use of black strikebreakers pointed out the importance of racial integration within the labor movement. More positively for labor, the strike effort indicated that unskilled immigrant labor could be recruited into unions.[76] Nevertheless, the mighty U.S. Steel would not succumb to collective bargaining for nearly two more decades; but when it did so, not one worker was fired, not one hour of production was lost, and not one government official was involved.

From Conflict to Cooperation

The labor wars of the late nineteenth century offered lessons for management and policymakers. Lawmakers enacted measures to alleviate the more obvious problems in labor–management relations, and managers encountered environmental conditions that required more finesse than force. Political opposition to corporate power gradually mounted during the Progressive era of the early twentieth century, and public sentiment shifted toward protecting workers against the excesses of capitalist production. Combined with the shortage of labor during World War I, economics and politics led to substantial union membership gains. The next chapter begins with the effects of war on labor relations and then analyzes managerial strategies to deal with workplace issues. Those strategies included new ways of managing workers and administering a sophisticated regime of employment policies. As a result, the modern techniques of human resource management emerged in significant detail.

Summary

- Early labor organizations in this country took diverse forms and had diverse objectives. Out of the welter of contending groups, the American Federation of Labor emerged as the most successful union confederacy. It stamped the labor movement with indelible characteristics.
- Violent conflict is the distinguishing feature of labor relations between 1880 and 1920. Strikes were usually resolved by force, and employers usually had the most access to force.

- Important managerial techniques developed during the time. Welfare capitalism marks the beginnings of personnel management in U.S. firms; it was also a means of remaining nonunion.
- Legal rules played a crucial part in controlling workers' collective activities and shaping labor strategies. Employment at will gave employers substantial legal powers in the workplace.
- Constitutional doctrine prevented the federal government from enacting protective labor legislation. Injunctions were the device that judges used to outlaw certain labor tactics.
- In the early 1920s, employers mounted an offensive against unions. Union membership declined significantly over the decade. Wealth became more concentrated in the upper segments of the economic spectrum.

Further Analysis

1. What are some of the advantages of the corporate form of business? What are some explanations for the rise of large corporations in this country? Do you think corporations should be subject to more or less legislative control?

2. What in your opinion should be the relationship between organized labor and the political process? Which of the examples described in this chapter most closely fits your conception of how unions should adapt to political conditions?

3. What were the successes and failures of the Knights of Labor? Would an organization similar to the Knights succeed or fail in today's environment? How would an independent workers' party distinguish itself from the Democratic Party?

4. Consider the labor conflicts described in this chapter. In which instance do you think workers were more responsible for the violence? In which instance were employers? When was the use of force most justified? Least justified?

5. What are the positive aspects of welfare capitalism as a technique of labor relations? What are the negative aspects? Do you think it is still used today in the workplace?

6. Injunctions are a way to enforce the law. They were frequently used against workers, who just as frequently ignored them. In which of the following situations, if any, do you think it would be morally appropriate to break the law: (a) in protests led by Operation Rescue against abortion clinics; (b) in the protest/riot in Seattle in 1999; (c) in protests against the draft during the Vietnam war; (d) in the revolt against Great Britain led by the signers of the Declaration of Independence? What moral principle supports a distinction between any of the options?

7. Do you think comparisons between the 1920s and the 1980s have any validity? In what ways do those eras appear to be similar? How are they different? Will the 2000s be more like the 1980s or the 1990s?

8. Compare the idea of employee representation as advanced by Rockefeller with the idea of trade union representation held by Gompers. Which system is most advantageous to workers?

9. Assume, as some prominent academics do, that the law should be used to actively promote the economic goal of a free exchange of goods and services through contractual agreements. If labor is a commodity to be alienated or sold, why is prostitution illegal in most states? Should an individual be permitted to sell a kidney on eBay? What difference is there in the examples? According to news reports, the sale of spare body parts is common in some Third World countries.

Suggested Readings

Bernstein, Irving. *The Lean Years: A History of American Workers, 1920–1933.* Boston: Houghton Mifflin, 1960.

Brecher, Jeremy. *Strike!* Boston: South End Press, 1972.

Brody, David. *Labor in Crisis: The Steel Strike of 1919.* Philadelphia: J. B. Lippincott, 1965.

Chandler, Alfred. *The Visible Hand: The Managerial Revolution in American Business.* Cambridge, MA: Harvard University Press, 1977.

Dubofsky, Melvyn, and Warren Van Tine. *Labor Leaders in America.* Urbana: University of Illinois Press, 1987.

Filippelli, Ron, ed. *Labor Conflict in the United States: An Encyclopedia.* New York: Garland Press, 1991.

Foner, Philip. *History of the Labor Movement in the United States.* Vol. 1. New York: International Publishers, 1947.

Forbath, William. *Law and the Shaping of the American Labor Movement.* Cambridge, MA: Harvard University Press, 1991.

Hogler, Raymond, and Guillermo Grenier. *Employee Participation and Labor Law in the American Workplace.* New York: Quorum Books, 1992.

Lens, Sidney. *The Labor Wars: From the Molly Maguires to the Sitdowns.* Garden City, NY: Doubleday, 1973.

Lindsey, Almont. *The Pullman Strike.* 1942. Chicago: University of Chicago Press, 1964.

Montgomery, David. *The Fall of the House of Labor: The Workplace, the State, and American Labor Activism, 1865–1925.* Cambridge, UK: Cambridge University Press, 1987.

Ramirez, Bruno. *When Workers Fight: The Politics of Industrial Relations in the Progressive Era, 1898–1916.* Westport, CT: Greenwood Press, 1978.

Yellen, Samuel. *American Labor Struggles, 1877–1934.* 1936. New York: Monad Press, 1974.

Endnotes

1. The transformation from slavery to wage labor is described in James D. Schmidt, *Free to Work: Labor Law, Emancipation, and Reconstruction, 1815–1880* (Athens: University of Georgia Press, 1998).

2. For an excellent historical treatment of this period, see Christopher Tomlins, *Law, Labor, and Ideology in the Early American Republic* (Cambridge, UK: Cambridge University Press, 1993).

3. According to a recent historical treatment of labor market institutions, "During the late nineteenth century, close to one-quarter of gainfully employed workers were foreign born." Joshua L. Rosenbloom, *Looking for Work, Searching for Workers: American Labor Markets During Industrialization* (Cambridge, UK: Cambridge University Press, 2002), 18. This study is a valuable analysis of institutions and market dynamics.

4. An influential study of this period is David Montgomery, *Workers' Control in America: Studies in the History of Work, Technology, and Labor Struggles* (Cambridge, UK: Cambridge University Press, 1979).

5. Martin J. Sklar, *The Corporate Reconstruction of American Capitalism, 1890–1916: The Market, the Law, and Politics* (Cambridge, UK: Cambridge University Press, 1988), 43–53.

6. Alfred Chandler Jr., *The Visible Hand: The Managerial Revolution in American Business* (Cambridge, MA: Harvard University Press, 1977), 79.

7. Michael Best, *The New Competition: Institutions of Industrial Restructuring* (Cambridge, MA: Harvard University Press, 1990), 46.

8. Gary M. Walton and Hugh Rockoff, *History of the American Economy*, 6th ed. (New York: Harcourt Brace Jovanovich, 1990), 333.

9. See generally Gerald G. Eggert, *Railroad Labor Disputes: The Beginnings of Federal Strike Policy* (Ann Arbor: University of Michigan, 1967).

10. Railroad workers struck various lines across the country. See Philip Foner, *The Great Labor Uprising of 1877* (New York: Monad Press, 1977).

11. Robert Gallman, "Commodity Output, 1839–1899," in *Trends in the American Economy in the Nineteenth Century*, ed. National Bureau of Economic Research (Princeton, NJ: Princeton University Press, 1960), 26.

12. Walton and Rockoff, *History of the American Economy*, pp. 344–345.

13. Walton and Rockoff, *History of the American Economy*, pp. 356–362.

14. Anthony P. O'Brien, "Factory Size, Economies of Scale, and the Great Merger Wave of 1898–1902," *Journal of Economic History* 48 (1988): 639–649.

15. See Neil Fligstein, *The Transformation of Corporate Control* (Cambridge, MA: Harvard University Press, 1990), esp. 33–74; and also Morton Horwitz, "*Santa Clara* Revisited: The Development of Corporate Theory," *West Virginia Law Review* 88 (1985): 173–224.

16. Lloyd Ulman, *The Rise of the National Trade Union: The Development and Significance of Its Structure, Governing Institutions, and Economic Policies* (Cambridge, MA: Harvard University Press, 1955), 3–4.

17. Ulman, *Rise of the National Trade Union*, p. 19.

18. Leo Wolman, *The Growth of American Trade Unions, 1880–1923* (New York: National Bureau of Economic Research, 1924), 85.

19. In a recent analysis of union membership, Richard Freeman traces membership density from 1890 to 1995, and his figures differ from earlier studies. The general trends, however, remain the same. Richard B. Freeman, "Spurts in Union Growth: Defining Moments and Social Processes," in *The Defining Moment: The Great Depression and the American Economy in the Twentieth Century*, ed. Michael D. Bordo, Claudia Goldin, and Eugene N. White (Chicago: University of Chicago Press, 1998), 265–295.

20. David Montgomery, *The Fall of the House of Labor: The Workplace, the State, and American Labor Activism, 1865–1925* (Cambridge, UK: Cambridge University Press, 1987), 49–51.

21. Patterns fluctuated greatly from 1825 to 1935, but the greatest era of immigration in the country's history occurred in the decade of 1900–1910. Rosenbloom, *Looking for Work*, p. 6, Figure 1.1.

22. Hoyt Wheeler, a leading industrial relations expert, uses the Knights of Labor as a possible model for contemporary unions. See Hoyt N. Wheeler, *The Future of the American Labor Movement* (Cambridge, UK: Cambridge University Press, 2002).

23. Alan Dawley, *Class and Community: The Industrial Relation in Lynn* (Cambridge, MA: Harvard University Press, 1976), 143–148.

24. Dawley, *Class and Community,* p. 175.

25. Dawley, *Class and Community,* pp. 184–188.

26. David Montgomery, "William H. Sylvis," in *Labor Leaders in America,* ed. Melvyn Dubofsky and Warren Van Tine (Urbana: University of Illinois Press, 1987), 12.

27. Montgomery, "William H. Sylvis," p. 15.

28. On the politics of the National Labor Union, see David Montgomery, *Beyond Equality: Labor and the Radical Republicans* (New York: Alfred A. Knopf, 1967), 176–196.

29. Thomas B. Edsall, "Administration Courts Teamsters, Other Labor Groups," *Washington Post,* September 3, 2002.

30. The standard history of the formation and activities of the Knights is Norman Ware, *The Labor Movement in the United States, 1860–1895: A Study in Democracy* (New York: D. Appleton, 1929).

31. Ware, *Labor Movement,* Appendixes I and II.

32. Leon Fink, *Workingmen's Democracy: The Knights of Labor and American Politics* (Urbana: University of Illinois Press, 1983). For a biographical essay on Powderly, see Richard Oestreicher, "Terence V. Powderly, the Knights of Labor, and Artisinal Republicanism," in *Labor Leaders in America,* pp. 31–44.

33. Ware, *Labor Movement,* p. 143.

34. Oestreicher, "Terence Powderly," p. 47.

35. Quoted in Ware, *Labor Movement,* p. 181.

36. Kim Voss, *The Making of American Exceptionalism: The Knights of Labor and Class Formation in the Nineteenth Century* (Ithaca, NY: Cornell University Press, 1993), 231–232.

37. Ware, *Labor Movement,* pp. 280–298.

38. See Stuart Kaufman, *Samuel Gompers and the Origins of the American Federation of Labor, 1848–1896* (Westport, CT: Greenwood Press, 1973), 3–42.

39. John H. M. Laslett, "Samuel Gompers and the Rise of American Business Unionism," in *Labor Leaders in America,* pp. 73–75.

40. Kaufman, *Samuel Gompers,* p. 162.

41. Laslett, "Samuel Gompers," p. 79.

42. Laslett, "Samuel Gompers," pp. 82–84.

43. Melvyn Dubofsky, *We Shall Be All: A History of the Industrial Workers of the World* (Chicago: Quadrangle Books, 1969).

44. For a discussion of the French influences on the Wobblies, see Salvatore Salerno, *Red November Black November: Culture and Community in the Industrial Workers of the World* (Albany: State University of New York Press, 1989).

45. Joyce Kornbluh, *Rebel Voices: An I.W.W. Anthology* (Chicago: Charles H. Kerr, 1988), 37–38.

46. www.iww.org.

47. Ronald Filippelli, ed., *Labor Conflict in the United States: An Encyclopedia* (New York: Garland, 1990).

48. Sydney Lens, *The Labor Wars: From the Molly Macguires to the Sitdowns* (Garden City, NY: Doubleday, 1973), 59.

49. John R. Commons and Associates, *History of Labour in the United States,* vol. 2 (New York: MacMillan, 1936) [Selig Perlman, "Upheaval and Reorganisation"], 392–393.

50. Paul Avrich, *The Haymarket Tragedy* (Princeton, NJ: Princeton University Press, 1984), 262.

51. Avrich, *Haymarket Tragedy,* p. 423.

52. Quoted in Samuel Yellen, *American Labor Struggles, 1877–1934* (1936; reprint, New York: Monad Press, 1974), 87.

53. Linda Schneider, "The Citizen Striker: Workers' Ideology in the Homestead Strike of 1892," *Labor History* 23 (1982): 65.

54. David Brody, *Steelworkers in America: The Nonunion Era* (New York: Harper & Row, 1960), 78.

55. Almont Lindsey, *The Pullman Strike: The Story of a Unique Experiment and of a Great Labor Upheaval* (1942; reprint, Chicago: University of Chicago Press, 1964), 23.

56. Lindsey, *Pullman Strike,* p. 100.

57. Lindsey, *Pullman Strike,* pp. 114–118.

58. Lindsey, *Pullman Strike,* p. 124.

59. *In re Debs,* 158 U.S. 564 (1895).

60. Lindsey, *Pullman Strike,* p. 175.

61. Samuel Gompers came to Chicago and met with the Railway Brotherhoods, craft unions which were hostile to the ARU. Gompers declared that a general strike would be unwise, a position that Debs described as traitorous to the labor movement. Nick Salvatore, *Eugene V. Debs: Citizen and Socialist* (Urbana: University of Illinois Press, 1982), 136.

62. Salvatore, *Eugene V. Debs,* pp. 153–155).

63. For background to the strike, see Priscilla Long, *Where the Sun Never Shines: A History of America's Bloody Coal Industry* (New York: Paragon House, 1989), 172–271.

64. For studies of the strike, see Barron Beshoar, *Out of the Depths* (Denver: Colorado Labor Historical Committee, 1942) and George West, *Report on the Colorado Strike* (Washington, DC: Government Printing Office, 1915).

65. Long, *Where the Sun Never Shines,* pp. 295–298.

66. Raymond Fosdick, *John D. Rockefeller, Jr.: A Portrait* (New York: Harper & Brothers, 1953), 151.

67. West, *Report,* p. 98.

68. *Denver Post,* September 20, 1915, pp. 1, 3.

69. *New York Times,* September 23, 1915, p. 1.

70. John D. Rockefeller Jr., "To the People of Colorado," Address to Denver Chamber of Commerce, October 8, 1915.

71. See Raymond Hogler and Guillermo Grenier, *Employee Participation and Labor Law in the American Workplace* (New York: Quorum Books, 1992).

72. John Fitch, *The Steel Workers* (New York: Russell Sage Foundation, 1911), 206.

73. David Brody, *Labor in Crisis: The Steel Strike of 1919* (Philadelphia: J. B. Lippincott, 1965), 64–65.

74. Brody, *Labor in Crisis,* pp. 100–105.

75. Commission of Inquiry, Interchurch World Movement, *Report on the Steel Strike of 1919* (New York: Harcourt, Brace, and Howe, 1920), 10–15.

76. Yellen, *American Labor Struggles,* pp. 288–289.

CHAPTER 3

Managerial Control and the Beginnings of State Regulation

Economic conditions in the United States began to improve during the mid-1890s, and as firms prospered, labor unions increased in size. Between 1897 and 1921, membership in trade unions grew from 544,000 to 4,269,000; as a percentage of nonagricultural employment, density climbed from 4.03 to 17.4 percent.[1] With greater power and militancy, unions aggressively claimed an increased share of productive output until the 1920s, when adverse conditions halted union expansion. Firms continued to grow in size and scope, leading to reorganization of work processes and a consolidation of managerial control over production.[2] At the same time, a changing political environment encouraged public demands for more effective oversight of corporate activity. The diverse environmental forces evoked several coping strategies that employers used to counter union penetration, public approbation, and government regulation.

To begin with, managers focused more closely on modes of production inside their firms and exercised intensified supervision over the way in which work was done. One of the founders of modern management technique, Frederick Taylor, explained how operational processes could be designed to maximize output by motivating workers to give a "fair day's work" in exchange for a "fair day's pay." The genius of Taylor's system was that management determined both the amount of pay and the amount of work. Along with the rise of Taylorism, many leading firms instituted programs to benefit their employees by providing fringe benefits, recreational opportunities, and a system of employee participation. These programs of *welfare capitalism* made up an important component of labor market institutions before the New Deal and provided a foundation for personnel management. They incidentally helped to displace workers' desire for union representation.

Coincident with emerging theories and practices of management, judges created rules regulating employment contracts and workers' collective activities in ways that benefited employers. The most important common law rule held that employment was at will and could be terminated by either party at any time for any reason. The legal concept migrated into constitutional doctrine protecting rights of liberty and property, which meant that legislative impingements on the sale of labor contravened guarantees of due process and, therefore, failed to survive challenge in the Supreme Court. Together, the two prongs of judicial thinking insulated managerial prerogatives from individual legal challenges and from significant incursions at any level of government. Indeed, the American Federation of Labor's (AFL's) inability to engage in large-scale political action led to its fragmented and opportunistic approach to policy development.[3]

Even the unrestricted right to hire and fire, however, did not eliminate workers' resistance to unacceptable working conditions. Capitalists took a more favorable position toward the conservative AFL to minimize the appeal of radical unionism, and Samuel Gompers responded by joining in formal cooperative arrangements with employers. In 1900, an association of industrialists, public leaders, and labor representatives formed the National Civic Federation (NCF) to promote the peaceful resolution of industrial disputes. For the trade unionists, negotiated labor agreements offered a foundation for amicable relations, and the NCF actively promoted them.[4] But even as the NCF enjoyed some favorable results, many other employers undertook an organized revolt with the avowed objective of establishing the open, or nonunion, shop throughout the country.[5] The various trends in labor relations present a complex picture of labor market behavior in the early twentieth century. Many firms aimed to create stable and long-term relations with their workers, including relatively generous levels of benefits and compensation. Other companies openly deployed their power to eliminate any impediments to their authority.

This chapter begins with an overview of judicial developments affecting employment. Its main components are the doctrine of employment at will noted earlier and the use of judicial orders—injunctions—to protect employers' property rights against concerted worker activity. To deal with individual employees, management enjoyed substantial coercive power through hiring and firing. By recruiting the power of the judiciary to curtail the use of labor's economic weapons such as strikes and picketing, employers effectively defended against organizing efforts. With the implementation of management techniques to minimize worker discontent and turnover, welfare capitalism marked a turning point in the evolution of workplace relations. The powerful combination of legal coercion and managerial techniques reduced union density by one-half during the 1920s, and labor appeared utterly moribund on the eve of the Great Depression.

Judges and the Law of Employment Contracts

The common law rule of employment at will governed employment relationships in this country for more than a century. In its simplest form, the rule states that if the parties do not contract for a definite period of work, an employer has the right to discharge an employee at any time for a good reason, a bad reason, or no reason at all. The employee, likewise, has the right to quit his or her employment at any time. A number of consequences follow from that legal principle. First, the employer can modify any terms of employment at his or her discretion; employees cannot claim a breach of contract because no contract exists. Second, the employee has no basis to challenge a termination because the agreement to continue the employment is not binding. Third, because of the legal presumption, the employee has the burden of proving that employment is not at will. Even a promise of employment as long as the employee's service is satisfactory is not an enforceable commitment under basic common law principles. Note, too, that if the employer can fire at will, it logically follows that the employer can make any changes in the relationship at his or her discretion because a contract by definition cannot exist.

The historical origins of the rule have generated some controversy about when and why the principle found its way into our legal system. According to one line of research, the doctrine first appeared in U.S. law in 1877 in a treatise on the law of master and servants and erroneously construed existing legal principles.[6] In the middle of the nineteenth century, U.S. law regarding employment contracts was in a state of flux. English common law generally provided some degree of protection for both parties to the employment relationship through a presumption that, unless otherwise stated, employment was to be of one year's duration. In his *Commentaries,* the English jurist William Blackstone formulated the rule governing employment as follows:

> If the hiring be general, without any particular time limited, the law construes it to be a hiring for a year; upon a principle of natural equity, that the servant shall serve, and the master maintain him, throughout all the revolutions of the respective seasons, as well when there is work to be done as when there is not.[7]

Employment, then, was presumed to be for a fixed period of time. Employees could be lawfully terminated during the contract only when cause for discharge existed, and both parties had an obligation to give notice of intent to end the contract, which generally prevented action that would unduly disadvantage the other party.[8] Rejecting Blackstone's authority, some scholars have argued that employment contracts in this country never followed the English precedent of fixed-term employment; and the assertion that U.S. courts somehow deviated from an established rule simply ignores a clear body of law.[9]

Whether or not it was based on adequate precedent, Wood's "American" rule of hiring at will was widely followed by 1895.[10] The rule gave employers increased power in the employment relationship by removing any threat of challenge to employment decisions. One legal historian argued that the doctrine constituted the "ultimate guarantor of the capitalist's authority over the worker" and an effective device to preclude workers from gaining enforceable property interests in the enterprise.[11] Moreover, during the latter decades of the nineteenth century, it enabled the capitalist to shift the costs of a business cycle to the worker, who could simply be discharged in a period of economic contraction.[12] The underlying thrust of Wood's rule, on this view, was to allocate economic power. Another recent study summarizes the point underlying employment at will as follows: "Workers must be absolutely free to circulate in the labor market. Thus, labor would become a more movable commodity, sustaining capitalist development."[13] Put in modern terms, employers now cite the need for flexibility in maintaining levels of employment to compete in the global economy.

Policy arguments for and against the employment at will rule have hardly changed in a century. The leading common law case establishing the doctrine was *Payne v. Western & Atlantic R.R. Co.*, decided by the Tennessee Supreme Court in 1884.[14] The company threatened to discharge any employee who did business with a merchant named Payne. Payne sued, and the court addressed the issue of whether the railroad employees could be fired for disobeying the employer's order to boycott Payne. According to the majority opinion, employees had no legal claim for breach of their employment contracts because the contracts were for an indefinite term. If employment is terminable at will, neither party had grounds for complaint when the employment ended. In the majority's words,

> Men must be left, without interference to buy and sell where they please, and to discharge or retain employees at will for good cause or for no cause, or even for bad cause without thereby being guilty of an unlawful act *per se*. It is a right that an employee may exercise in the same way, to the same extent, for the same cause or want of cause as the employer.

That is, if the employee preferred to trade with a particular person, he could find employment elsewhere instead of the railroad.[15]

In a dissenting opinion, two judges set forth a view of employment that anticipated the reasoning of contemporary rulings. They pointed out that corporations should not have absolute control over their employees by exercising the right of discharge. Rather, the employer should be required to show some legitimate business justification for terminating any employee. The dissent said that corporations and individual workers did not stand on a footing of equality:

> In view of the immense development and large aggregations of capital in this favored country—a capital to be developed and aggregated within the life of the present generation more than a hundred fold—giving the command of immense numbers of employees, by such means as we have before us in this case, it is the demand of a sound public policy, for the future more especially, as well as now, that the use of this power should be restrained within legitimate boundaries.

Because employment had become crucial to the social order, public policy demanded that employers should be subjected to restraints in the use of their power. Employers' legitimate rights would not be infringed by a rule that served the public interest and would "only restrain wrong and prevent conduct that no sound judgment will approve as based on a sound morality."[16] Modern judicial thinking, as illustrated by the *Wagenseller* case in Chapter 7, adopts the same approach.

The rule articulated in *Payne* and elaborated in other numerous decisions was constitutionalized in the case of *Adair v. United States,* where the U.S. Supreme Court invalidated a federal statute affording railway workers a right to join and form labor unions. That statute, known as the Erdman Act, was a direct result of the Pullman strike and its deleterious impact on interstate rail transportation. Congress drafted an elaborate procedure for resolving labor disputes on railroads, and an important element of that legislation protected the right of workers to join a labor organization. Adair, a foreman for the Louisville & Nashville Railroad Company, fired a mechanic named O. B. Coppage because Coppage was a member of the Order of Locomotive Firemen. Coppage sued Adair and the railroad claiming his rights under the statute had been violated. The federal district court upheld the legislation, and a jury found Adair guilty of the offense.

Reversing the lower court, the Supreme Court ruled that the statute was repugnant to the due process clause of the Fifth Amendment.[17] The Court stated that the concepts of liberty and property protected by the amendment included "the right to make contracts for the purchase of labor of others and equal the right to make contracts for the sale of one's own labor." Thus, any legislation that attempted to restrict the individual's liberty and the employer's property interest contravened rights established by the Constitution. The majority explained that "it is not within the functions of government—at least in the absence of contract between the parties—to compel any person in the course of his business and against his will to accept or retain the personal services of another, or to compel any person, against his will, to perform personal services for another." Employers and employees enjoyed equal freedom in establishing employment relationships. Coppage had the right to quit his employment, just as the employer had a right to fire Coppage because he belonged to a labor union.[18] As a second ground for its decision, the majority said that the legislation was not within the constitutional power of the federal government.[19]

The legal doctrine had two important consequences. First, it gave employers an absolute right to threaten and administer disciplinary action against employees, up to and including discharge. This right was necessarily connected with scientific management since, once employers determined the amount of a fair day's work, they could force an employee to do that much work on pain of discharge.[20] Second, the rule provided an ideological basis for invalidating federal legislation because it seemed to rely on such important American values as individual choice, property ownership, and states' rights. The *Adair* case is one illustrative decision in a substantial body of Supreme Court precedent that constrained efforts to curb the power of employers over workers through the legislative process.[21] To emphasize an important point, the constitutional limitations on the power of the federal government meant that political action often proved an exercise in futility; even if unions could obtain meaningful legislation, such as the Erdman Act, courts stood ready to strike down laws that exceeded constitutional bounds.

Courts went even further in their efforts to minimize the effectiveness of workers' collective action. The move to undo federal legislation such as the Erdman Act meant that employers could exercise their rights of discharge without interference, and employees had no protection against the loss of their jobs. Another legal concept provided affirmative benefits to employers by protecting their property rights against interference from workers. To accomplish that task, courts construed the meaning of property very broadly to include the intangible assets of goodwill and reputation. Unions that injured an employer's right to enjoy the full use of his or her property, by, for example, establishing a picket line at the employer's place of business, became subject to judicial sanction. The specific weapon against labor's injury to an employer's property was an order to stop all collective action directed against the employer.

Injunctions and Antitrust

One crucial aspect of judicial control over labor arose from judges' willingness to grant employers' requests for injunctive relief in labor disputes. The value of this judicial tool against labor was illustrated by the prosecution against Debs in the Pullman strike, and the number of injunctions issued in labor disputes continued to grow through the 1920s. One study estimates that 410 injunctions were issued in the 1890s, and that figure rose to 2,130 in the 1920s.[22] The reason for the increase was that the character of strike activity changed from localized disputes to ones involving sympathy strikes by other workers and widespread boycotts against the employer's product. Judges were particularly antagonistic toward secondary activities not confined to the actual work site. Because of the common law sanctions applied against their methods, labor leaders were eventually convinced to abandon their program for broad class-based legislation, such as the eight-hour workday, and instead dedicated themselves to defensive action trying to eliminate judge-made law. Gompers's experience with the antitrust laws illustrates the vicissitudes that labor suffered at the hands of judges.

Congress enacted the Sherman Act in 1890 to prohibit combinations in restraint of trade. Anyone injured by an unlawful combination would be entitled to recover treble damages. Organized labor presumed that labor organizations were not subject to the law and its penalties, but in the *Danbury Hatters* case, the judiciary ruled otherwise. An official of the United Hatters Union, Martin Lawlor, approached the hatmaking firm of Loewe & Company, located in Danbury, Connecticut. The union represented most employees in the hatmaking trade. Lawlor asked Loewe for union recognition and a contract; in exchange, the company would be allowed to use the union label. When Loewe refused, the union began a boycott against Loewe's products and asked hat retailers not to sell those products. It also urged the public not to patronize stores that sold Loewe's hats. As a result, Loewe lost $85,000 in one year.

In 1903, Loewe sued the union under the Sherman Act contending that the boycott was an unlawful combination in restraint of trade. Lower federal courts held that there was no violation, but the U.S. Supreme Court reversed. It stated that Congress had intended to cover labor organizations under the law and that boycotts were combinations that obstructed the free flow of commerce. The Court remanded the case for determination of damages, and seven years later, it affirmed an award of $252,000 against the union. Justice Holmes ruled that the union officers were acting as agents for individual union members, and therefore each member was liable, jointly and severally, for the entire judgment.[23]

Enraged by the decision, Gompers focused his political efforts on reform of the antitrust laws, and in 1914, Congress passed the Clayton Act, which President Wilson signed. The Clayton Act stated that "the labor of a human being is not a commodity or article of commerce," and nothing in the antitrust laws should be construed to forbid the existence and operation of labor organizations or to restrain individuals from carrying out their legitimate objectives. Despite this apparently clear language, the Supreme Court ruled in the *Duplex Printing Press Company* case that a nationwide boycott could be prosecuted under the antitrust laws. Interpreting Section 6 of the Clayton Act, the Court said that only the "normal and legitimate" objects of labor organizations were protected. Because secondary boycotts were unlawful at common law, they were not normal and legitimate activities. Consequently, Congress did not intend to authorize illegal secondary boycotts under the Clayton Act. Gompers's political victory was thus rendered useless by the judiciary.[24]

A similar pattern of judicial hostility to unions emerged in connection with the "yellow dog" labor contracts. The yellow dog contract, which could be made a condition of the worker's employment, stated that the worker agreed not to join a union so long as he was employed at the specific place of business. In the *Hitchman Coal & Coke Co. v. Mitchell* case, an organizer for the United Mine Workers of America (UMWA) attempted to organize miners in West Virginia. Relying on its yellow dog contracts, the employer obtained an injunction prohibiting the UMWA organizer from entering the coal fields or soliciting the miners. The Supreme Court approved enforcement of the contracts by means of injunctive relief.[25] Used primarily by small employers, the device became a popular antiunion device in the 1920s.[26]

Obviously, then, labor law played a central role in the development of employment relations during the late nineteenth and early twentieth centuries. The employment at will rule guaranteed the employer's legal right to exercise discipline and thus fit neatly with the practice and ideology of Taylorism, which relied on absolute control over workers; the constitutional dimension of *Adair* meant that no legislation would succeed in abridging that control. Injunctions prevented labor from using the tactic of secondary boycotts, a powerful means of bringing pressure on recalcitrant employers. The yellow dog contracts provided yet another weapon with which judges could intimidate employees and union organizers. Political gains, as with the Clayton Act, were always subject to interpretation by the courts. Accordingly, Gompers and the AFL, not surprisingly, tended to abandon broad political goals and seek instead a narrow, voluntaristic strategy that aimed at keeping state interference out of labor affairs.[27]

Scientific Management and the Efficiency Movement

The concept of scientific management was among the most important developments in management thought between 1880 and 1920. First conceived by Frederick Winslow Taylor in the 1870s, scientific management revolutionized workplace relations of the time. Taylor's ideas had both a practical and an ideological significance; although relatively few employers completely adopted his prescriptions for workplace design, the basic notions of scientific management profoundly changed the relationship between labor and management. According to a well-known labor historian, "The historical role of the scientific-management movement was to explain, guide, and justify the changes in the hierarchy of human relations in the workplace that accompanied the turn-of-the-century transformation of American industry."[28] Essentially, that transformation involved eliminating workers' control over production.

Taylor spelled out his program in various publications, speeches, and testimony before the Industrial Relations Commission. Taylor's emphasis was on attaining the greatest possible level of productivity or efficiency in the workplace. He insisted that the most important function of management "should be the training and development of each individual in the establishment, so that he can do (at his fastest pace and with the maximum of efficiency) the highest class of work for which his natural abilities fit him." But managers of the time, according to Taylor, allowed workers to *soldier,* or withhold their labor and avoid doing a full day's work. For Taylor, soldiering was pervasive in U.S. industry and constituted the greatest evil facing workers. Both workers and managers contributed to the practice. Workers believed wrongly that if they increased their output, they would have less work. Managers were ignorant of the amount of time actually necessary to the performance of a task. As a result, *systematic soldiering* prevailed in industry, where workers collectively deceived employers concerning the process of production. Taylor advocated the substitution of scientific procedures for the old rule of thumb style of management in which workers had to be given special incentives to put forth their best efforts. The scientific method, Taylor said, produced cooperative, harmonious, and mutually beneficial relationships between employers and employees.[29]

Taylor specified certain requirements for introducing his system. First, managers were to carefully observe the work process, "gathering together all of the traditional knowledge which in the past has been possessed by the workmen" and developing the rules and laws of production. The next step was to scientifically select the workman and train him to execute the tasks *planned by management.* Management thus took responsibility for the conception and planning of all work, and workers were responsible for its execution.[30] Taylor's most famous illustration of his system involved the loading of pig iron at Bethlehem Steel Company. The story of a worker named Schmidt epitomizes how Taylor enabled managers to gain significant control over the labor process by objectifying and quantifying labor, enforcing output through a system of rewards and punishment. The case is presented here as Taylor reported the incident in his writings.

Taylor's Tale of Pig Iron

[Bethlehem Steel had stockpiled a large amount of pig iron, which it subsequently sold. To move the iron, workers carried ninety-two-pound pigs up an inclined plank and threw them into railroad cars. The gang loaded an average of twelve and one-half long tons per day. After studying the process, Taylor concluded that a worker could load between forty seven and forty eight long tons. Taylor's first step was to select a workman whom he called "Schmidt." Schmidt was of Pennsylvania Dutch extraction and had a reputation for thrift and industry. In Taylor's words:]

The task before us, then, narrowed itself down to getting Schmidt to handle 47 tons of pig iron per day and making him glad to do it. This was done as follows. Schmidt was called out from among the gang of pig-iron handlers and talked to somewhat in this way:

"Schmidt, are you a high-priced man?"

"Vell, I don't know vat you mean."

"Oh yes, you do. What I want to know is whether you are a high-priced man or not."

"Vell, I don't know vat you mean."

"Oh, come now, you answer my questions. What I want to find out is whether you are a high-priced man or one of these cheap fellows here. What I want to find out is whether you want to earn $1.85 a day or whether you are satisfied with $1.15, just the same as all those cheap fellows are getting."

"Did I vant $1.85 a day? Vas dot a high-priced man? Vell, yes, I vas a high-priced man."

"Oh, you're aggravating me. Of course you want $1.85 a day—everyone wants it! You know perfectly well that that has very little to do with your being a high-priced man. For goodness' sake answer my questions, and don't waste any more of my time. Now come over here. You see that pile of pig iron?"

"Yes."

"You see that car?"

"Yes."

"Well, if you are a high-priced man, you will load that pig iron on that car to-morrow for $1.85. Now do wake up and answer my question. Tell me whether you are a high-priced man or not. . . ."

"Vell, den, I vas a high-priced man."

(Continued)

(Continued)

"Now, hold on, hold on. You know just as well as I do that a high-priced man has to do exactly as he's told from morning till night. You have seen this man [Taylor's assistant] here before, haven't you?"

"No, I never saw him."

"Well, if you are a high-priced man, you will do exactly as this man tells you to-morrow, from morning till night. When he tells you to pick up a pig and walk, you pick it up and you walk, and when he tells you to sit down and rest, you sit down. You do that right straight through the day. And what's more, no back talk. Now a high-priced man does just what he's told to do, and no back talk. Do you understand that? . . . Now you come on to work here to-morrow morning and I'll know before night whether you are really a high-priced man or not."

[The next day Schmidt loaded forty-seven and one-half long tons of pig iron. Taylor calculated that Schmidt carried 106,400 pounds of iron and walked about sixteen miles. He was under load 42 percent of the day, about .22 minutes per pig.][31]

What's "Scientific" About Management?

1. Considering the work being done, what sort of physical specimen do you think Schmidt was? Taylor said one of the first requirements for a pig-iron handler was "that he shall be so stupid and so phlegmatic that he more nearly resembles in his mental make-up the ox than any other type." Is that why Schmidt was chosen for career advancement? In fact, Schmidt weighed 135 pounds and was 5'7" tall.

2. Why were the other workers only loading twelve and one-half tons per day? Were they even smaller than Schmidt? Would it matter that they came from different ethnic backgrounds than Schmidt or are their backgrounds irrelevant?

3. Note the pay Schmidt received for the amount of pig iron he loaded. Who got the benefit of the transaction?

4. Taylor always insisted that it was management's job to determine a fair day's work. If so, then who should determine a fair day's pay?

5. Sometimes the story of scientific management features improved technology that enabled workers to work harder (e.g., a shovel with a bigger scoop). Do you think the essence of scientific management has any necessary relationship to better tools?

There is considerable debate today about how widely scientific management was used in industry. Some scholars argue that Taylor's program had only modest acceptance and did not greatly affect workers.[32] Others perceive scientific management to be the single most important concept in work organization and a crucial historical development in U.S. capitalism.[33] In any event, it is clear that most unionists initially opposed scientific management. The most famous example is the strike at Watertown Arsenal in 1909, when iron molders at a government armory refused to work under the bonus system set by a "time and motion" expert. Arsenal managers capitulated, and Congress later adopted legislation prohibiting time studies in federal facilities.[34]

Taylor himself insisted that because scientific management involved a code of laws, unionism was irrelevant to the question of wages and work standards. "You would not think of collective bargaining in the matter of whether there was an eclipse of the moon," Taylor told the Industrial Relations Commission. "You would in that case go to an astronomer." He emphasized that cooperation between employers and employees was necessary to his system.[35] The cooperation depended on workers' realizing that increased production led to higher compensation, a proposition that sometimes failed to materialize.

After Taylor's death, his followers took a more flexible approach toward collective bargaining, and the AFL responded by engaging in mutually advantageous exchanges with management theorists. Gompers met with Morris Cooke, a well-known disciple of Taylor's, on various occasions. Others, such as Louis Brandeis, publicized the virtues of scientific management and efficiency. The result was a popular wave of enthusiasm for efficiency and higher productivity in the 1920s. Unions were hardly in a position to oppose such widespread sentiment.[36] Thus, one noteworthy by-product of Taylorism was greater effort at labor–management collaboration. A related development involves managerial strategies to create a more favorable public image and to deal with the increasing scrutiny of politicians over corporate behavior.

Welfare Capitalism and the Emergence of the Modern Personnel System

As noted in the material dealing with Debs and the rail strike of 1894 in Chapter 2, George Pullman adopted an attitude of benevolent paternalism toward his employees that many observers considered to be an exemplary demonstration of compassionate capitalism. Pullman offered an array of employment benefits associated with his company, although his generosity was sometimes more apparent than real, and Pullman's failure to live up to his expressed ideals contributed significantly to the destructive labor dispute. Many other employers before and after Pullman engaged in activities generically described as *welfare capitalism.* The term is imprecise, but one scholar defined it as "any service provided for the comfort or improvement of employees which was neither a necessity of the industry nor required by law," adding that the strategy "constituted one solution offered by American businessmen to the crisis of labor-management relations of the early twentieth century."[37] In one aspect, welfare capitalism led to the development of fringe benefits associated with the workplace rather than with the state; this dimension of voluntary employer largesse contributed to the maintenance of American exceptionalism by linking income security with specific jobs.

A second dimension of welfare capitalism had to do with the less tangible but equally important question of *representation* in the workplace. This feature is prominently associated with Rockefeller's employee representation plan; it gained widespread popularity in the 1910s and early 1920s and then resurfaced with the rise of company unions in the period from 1933 to 1935. The issue of workers' voice remains a central concern in employment relations; it ties in with our basic under-standing of democratic principles—that is, a right to participate in decisions that affect important areas of our lives—and its importance was recognized by labor experts in the 1920s. The material below traces both strands of welfare capitalism and its impact on organized labor.

The labor problem became a phenomenon of public concern during the first decade of the twentieth century. Strike activity increased significantly between 1896 and 1903, rising from 1,026 to 3,495 occurrences. The number of establishments involved in strikes rose from 5,462 to 20,248, and the number of days lost went from 94,341 to 239,885. Most stoppages involved wage demands and related issues, but more than 20 percent of the strikes were for union recognition. During the same period (1897–1903), union membership more than quadrupled.[38] One important response to the developing labor problem was the founding of the National Civic Federation in 1901. This organization included business and labor leaders, and its goal was to further harmonious labor–management relations through collectively bargained trade agreements. Gompers was an active supporter of the NCF; his interest was in maintaining the AFL's control over the labor move-ment threatened by socialist factions, which was an objective of the NCF's business membership also. Thus, cooperation was possible for the NCF members.[39] Similarly, employers devised welfare programs as a supplement to aggressive antiunionism and as a defensive move to counter negative public opinion.

Welfare programs, as the Pullman story indicates, were in existence as early as the 1890s. Generally, they involved such benefits as profit-sharing, pensions, libraries, recreational activities, and employee representation plans. The welfare programs served at least three important objectives. First, as one study suggests, "welfare work was not just an alternative to unionism; it was also an overt anti-union policy."[40] Regardless of employers' motives, welfare policies were influential in determining workers' attitudes toward the firm, and this dimension of welfarism persisted even after the rise of unions in the postwar period.[41]

Second, welfare policies were crucial for large corporations to fend off state interference and justify their tremendous wealth and power against political attack. An analysis of political processes convincingly documents how U.S. capitalism remade its public image between 1900 and 1916. Public distrust of corporations reached a peak in the 1912 elections, when the Democratic Party platform included explicit criticisms of corporations. Significantly, corporate antitrust cases reached a record level only two years later. One consequence was the appearance of a new business ideology that extended through the 1920s. The new ideology was based on such themes as "cooperation, service, social responsibility, trusteeship, efficiency, and power," and its general thrust was to legitimate the corporation in the public's mind.[42] That legitimating strategy evolved in response to the changing political alignments of the time. A recent study concludes, "Employers eager to check and repel the tide of government regulation proffered welfare capitalism as an alternative to welfare statism."[43]

Third, welfare capitalism helped to stabilize labor markets. Larger firms had an incentive to reduce turnover and create stability in their labor force by paying higher wages and benefits. These employers often supported developments that reduced competition in labor markets and helped to maintain a floor under wages. Consequently, such industries as coal mining could and did encourage extension of union contracts throughout the particular sector. Standard terms and conditions of employment not only meliorated discontent but also clarified relations for firms and workers.[44]

Given its usefulness to management, welfare capitalism contributed to the development of the field of personnel management, the forerunner of the contemporary organizational function referred to as human resource management. Scientific management or Taylorism promoted the rationalization of management activity and when it was brought into contact with the welfare plans in companies, produced a standardized personnel function. A business historian puts those pieces together in the following way:

> To find the sources of personnel administration, we need to turn first to the introduction of Scientific Management. This body of thought contained only incidental reference to personnel matters, but clearly related them to the practices of industrial efficiency. Welfare work, an older movement, constitutes the second source. Out of the practices of philanthropy or paternalism or both developed a system of entrusting responsibility for welfare effort to particular company officers, called social or welfare secretaries.[45]

Contemporary observers in the 1920s began to describe the emerging field of personnel management as a necessary part of business activity. Employment managers had responsibility for hiring, training, compensating, and scheduling labor. They also oversaw such matters as employee health and safety, morale, and general well-being.

While employers' motivations for engaging in welfare work arose from economic, political, and even cultural concerns, the programs had adverse consequences for unions. By fulfilling workers' demands for better working conditions through employer initiatives, welfare capitalism tended to weaken unions by offering an alternative to the collective agreement. A pro-union observer characterized the era as the "employer's offensive against the trade unions" and argued that such devices as the company union intentionally undercut workers' efforts at unionization.[46] Although some historians view the effect of welfare capitalism as marginal, others argue that welfare capitalism constituted a program of employer opposition to unions that persisted into the 1960s.[47]

In any event, by 1920 a field of theory and practice had emerged to address interfirm relations between employees and managers. Ordway Tead and Henry Metcalf noted in the first edition of their pioneering study of personnel administration that a set of principles and practices had evolved covering such activities as employee selection, health and safety, training, employee benefits, and cooperative relations. A few years later, Tead and Metcalf said that the "record of accomplishment in various fields of personnel activity since 1920 could easily fill a volume four times the size of the first edition."[48] The scope of the early domain is comparable to modern treatments of human resource management, including the focus on linkages between various human resource activities and the strategic dimension of management.[49]

Welfare capitalism aided employers in minimizing both workers' demand for unions and public pressures for direct political intervention in workplace matters. Despite general corporate antipathy toward legislative solutions to employment issues, one of the crucial developments in the pre-Depression era demonstrates how the interaction between interest groups and environmental forces could combine to produce seemingly anomalous results. One of the pillars of U.S. employment legislation came into existence during the period from 1910 to 1920. The explanation for the phenomenon of workers' compensation insurance illustrates clearly that when employers' interests coincided with the interests of labor, politicians responded with appropriate legislative action. The next section takes up that topic.

Workers' Compensation Insurance—
An Early Exception to Exceptionalism

Protection against work-related injuries makes up a major component of our employment relations system. Workers' compensation schemes are unique in several respects. First, the legislation consists of state, rather than federal, law and the conditions for recovery of benefits and the amounts of compensation are determined strictly by the respective states. Second, employers supported the enactment of compensation laws even though they represented an important deviation from the principle that contractual agreement governed employment relations. Third, the statutes displaced an existing system of common law that in many cases favored employers and precluded workers from any remedy for workplace injuries. Given the seeming contradictions that workers' compensation posed for the contractual regime of employment, why would employers ever consent to the system? This part of the chapter explains the origins of those laws and their general application to employment.

The current method of dealing with workplace injuries is a workers' compensation system that protects the interests of the three interested parties—employee, employer, and the community—in situations where a worker suffers incapacity in connection with employment. Under a workers' compensation scheme, the injured worker receives regular and fixed amounts of money for job-related illnesses and injuries. In exchange, the worker surrenders the right to sue the employer in court for damages arising out of the worker's loss of earning capacity. The arrangement protects the employer against the costs of litigation and jury awards, which eventually would be passed onto the consumer in the form of higher prices for the product. It protects employees from the uncertainty of a judicial proceeding, and it protects the public from the economic burdens associated with incapacitated workers.

Workers' compensation is essentially an employer insurance program. Employers pay a premium to a state fund or to a private insurance company, and the insurers, in turn, decide which worker claims are compensable and which are not. If a claim is denied and the worker appeals that denial, the dispute will be submitted to an administrative agency or a court. The insurance company defends against the claim as it proceeds through the appropriate state administrative body, such as the state Bureau of Workers' Compensation, or the state court, if necessary. The employer is not forced to expend time and resources in court contesting the employee's claim for compensation, and the employer is insured against large and uncertain damage awards to injured workers. Citizens and communities benefit because compensation to injured workers helps the worker to maintain a percentage of his or her previous income, thus enabling the worker to avoid public assistance and to continue to contribute to the general economic health of the community.

Compensation statutes emerged from common law roots. Judicial doctrine explains both the particular attributes of workers' compensation and the reasons for its creation. As some states exercised control over industrial accidents, others followed suit to realize the advantages of the system.

Common Law Background

The growth of the factory system as a model for industrial production was accompanied by sharp increases in the number of industrial accidents, and the common law rules governing employment were inadequate to deal with the problem of injured workers. The result was a surge of state legislative activity in the first two decades of the century; that activity eventually resulted in the system of industrial insurance that now exists.[50] Prior to the 1830s, the issue of an employer's duty to compensate an employee for injuries received little legal attention.[51] As cases arose, U.S. judges looked to English common law precedent to determine standards of liability. Under the English rule, an employee was required to prove as a condition of recovery that the employer's negligence had caused the injury.[52] That body of judicial doctrine featured a number of defenses available to employers against an employee's claim for damages, which effectively limited recovery. In the case of *Priestly v. Fowler* (1837), for example, Lord Abinger formulated the fellow servant rule, which held that the employer could not be liable for the negligence of one of his employees when that negligence caused the injury of another employee.[53]

U.S. courts followed Abinger's lead in decisions such as *Farwell v. Boston and Worchester R.R. Corp.*, decided in Massachusetts in 1842.[54] In that case, a locomotive engineer was injured when his train ran off the track at a switch negligently opened by a switchman. The accident crushed the engineer's right hand. Chief Justice Shaw ruled in favor of the railroad, stating that the relationship between an employee and his employer was governed by express or implied contract. Citing the *Priestly* case, Shaw continued that there was no implied promise of a master "to be responsible to each person employed by him, in the conduct of every branch of business, where two or more persons are employed, to pay for all damage occasioned by the negligence of every other person employed in the same service."[55] Moreover, Shaw added, the theory of an employment contract presumed that workers accepted the risks of employment in return for higher compensation. His opinion precisely captures the assumptions underlying market conceptions of employment:

> The general rule, resulting from considerations of justice as of policy, is, that he who engages in the employment of another for their performance of specified duties and services, for compensation, takes upon himself the natural and ordinary risks and perils incident to the performance of such services, and in legal presumption, the compensation is adjusted accordingly.[56]

Labor markets, that is, are contractually adjusted for hazardous work, and, in theory, the negligence system promoted an efficient method of allocating the costs of industrial injury.[57]

In practice, however, the effects of *Farwell* and other cases following Shaw's reasoning were disadvantageous to workers, and as the industrial age progressed, it became more and more difficult for the worker to gain a remedy for an industrial accident. In addition to the defenses of the fellow servant and assumption of risk, the common law precluded recovery in situations where the employee, as well as the employer, was negligent. The result, according to a leading authority, was that employees rarely succeeded in their claims. Using data from 1906, Arthur Larson concludes that employees were legally precluded from any remedy in 83 percent of the cases. In the remaining 17 percent of the sample, the claimants were still required to prove their claim against the employer in a legal setting that was relatively biased in favor of employers. The end result was a "picture of helplessness which characterized the position of the injured workman of the precompensation era."[58]

One important feature of the *Farwell* decision was its characterization of employment exclusively as a matter of contract. Any lack of liability could be justified on the ground that a worker contracted for the risk of injury. That is, the more dangerous the work, the higher the wage theoretically demanded by the employee, and, as a result, wages were deemed to reflect the full costs of injury to the employee. That reasoning tended to perpetuate the relative inequities inherent in the employment relationship during the period.[59] And in any event, the common law manifested the conviction that broad employer liability for accidents was contrary to public policy and "would not conduce to the general good."[60]

Generally, then, the common law system of compensation for workers' injuries was inadequate in a number of respects. The injured worker had no recourse for injury other than litigating against the employer. Such litigation was both expensive and time-consuming, and the worker and his family required immediate aid. Even assuming the worker prevailed in the suit, the remedies were often not sufficient to defray the costs of litigation and to provide maintenance for the worker and his family, which resulted in a burden to the community. Finally, the common law system became progressively disadvantageous to the employer during the first decade of the twentieth century. Although it was difficult for a worker to obtain a remedy through the system, there were an increasing number of suits where the employer was found to be at fault, and the damages awarded to the injured worker were sometimes quite large.

With regard to expanding employer liability, one researcher concluded that "the rising value of the injured worker's right of action against the employer was at the center of capital's interest in a new system" of compensation for injury.[61] As industrial injuries became more widespread, public attention focused on the problem, and judges and juries grew more sympathetic to claims. Premiums for insurance against such claims rose from $203,132 in 1887 to $35 million in 1911, and insurance companies were unable to develop sound actuarial standards for industrial injuries.[62] There was also an obvious political dimension at stake; workers as a class reacted against the perceived callousness of employers and the hardships inflicted on workers' families. Several other aspects of labor unrest contributed to a crisis of confidence in business during the period; the compensation issue, however, was particularly symbolic, and it "became the focal point for a debate as to whether the American state could be modified to provide even a minimum floor to cushion the physical and financial risks of the employment relationship." Eventually, then, "The compensation crisis of the first decade reached the point where a solution imported from Europe, Workers' Compensation, presented itself as a form of social insurance that could be adapted to conditions in the United States."[63]

The Elements of Workers' Compensation

The basic concept of insurance for workers first arose in Germany in 1884.[64] A report on the German system was published in the United States in 1893, and several states undertook studies of compensation schemes shortly thereafter. Beginning with a statute enacted in New York in 1910, the growth of legislation was rapid, and, by 1920, all but eight states had adopted workers' compensation systems.[65] The remaining states gradually followed, and presently all states have a legislative scheme pertaining to industrial injury.[66] Although workers' compensation programs are under the exclusive control of the respective states, they share certain similarities. The most common features of those programs are briefly described below.

There Must Be an Employment Relationship

Workers' compensation claims are appropriate only where an actual employer–employee relationship exists, and only the employee is covered. Generally, an employee is an individual who routinely and regularly performs remunerative work for another and is subject to the control and direction of the other. An independent contractor, in contrast, is paid an agreed amount for completion of a task and the accomplishment of the task is typically within the discretion of the contractor, who is in a position to make a profit or suffer a loss from the venture. Some other major exemptions usually found in statutory provisions include those for agricultural employment, for casual employment not in the employer's course of business, and for employers with less than a specified number of employees.[67]

Coverage Is Automatic for Compensable Injuries

A compensable injury is defined as any injury "arising out of and in the course of employment." The standard ensures that the injury has some close and substantial connection to the employment relationship. Courts and administrative bodies interpret the phrase very broadly because the legislation is protective in nature. Thus, if a claimant proves that his or her injury resulted from a risk related to employment, as opposed to risks incurred by the general public, compensation will be awarded. Certain issues are particularly problematic, such as the case of employees who are injured away from the workplace or by a natural phenomenon such as a tornado. In the case of a preexisting condition causing the injury, such as a propensity for heart attacks, the burden of proof rests on the employee to prove that the injury suffered was aggravated by his or her working conditions. Every state now provides coverage for occupational diseases connected with the employment, either through a broad definition of the term *injury* or by specific provisions within the statute.

Negligence Is Not a Necessary Element of Recovery

Under workers' compensation, fault is usually irrelevant. In contrast to the common law, the worker need not prove that the employer's negligence caused the injury in order to recover, nor, typically, will the employee's own negligence defeat recovery. One exception to that rule is the situation in which the employee's acts constitute misconduct that has been expressly prohibited by the employer and that is consequently outside the course of the employment. Examples might include an injury incurred while using the employer's tools to make an item for personal use. A second exception to the no-fault principle is based on specific statutory provisions. For example, defenses to a compensation claim may include a showing of the employee's willful misconduct, the violation of safety rules or positive law, self-induced intoxication, and an intentional self-injury or suicide, unless the suicide is the result of mental derangement produced by the work-related injury.[68] In most cases, nevertheless, the focus is on the source and nature of the harm rather than on an evaluation of the parties' conduct.

The Right to Compensation Is an Exclusive Remedy

In return for a prompt and certain remedy, the worker typically surrenders his or her right to sue the employer for any injury arising out of the employment relationship. Accordingly, the workers' compensation remedy is deemed to be exclusive, and the amount recoverable is the only award to which the employee is entitled. The limitation of the exclusivity concept is offset by the relative ease and efficiency of recovery. Moreover, under some statutes, employer misconduct may affect the principle of exclusive remedy and permit recovery of additional damages. Such misconduct includes intentional injury to the employee, a failure to provide safety equipment, or the employer's willful misconduct that harms the employee. Courts may reach a similar conclusion in the absence of specific provisions when the employer personally inflicts an intentional injury on the employee, under the theory that the injury is no longer accidental.[69] In addition, exclusivity may not apply when the injury arises from the negligence of a third party outside the employment relationship, and the worker may proceed against the third party. It should also be observed that employers may be criminally liable for intentional harm to an employee, regardless of the employee's right to workers' compensation or to a civil remedy. Indeed, criminal prosecutions against employers are sometimes viewed as a more effective means of protecting employees than the workers' compensation systems or the occupational safety and health laws.[70]

The Statutory System Is Administered by a Governmental Body

Workers' compensation is the responsibility in the first instance of a designated agency created by the state. The function of the agency is to provide prompt and efficient handling of claims for compensation by avoiding the expense and delays associated with litigation. The agency is not bound by the formalities of a judicial proceeding and can thus avoid legal technicalities about evidence and procedure. Hearing officers have substantial expertise and familiarity with the statutory provisions. Typically, once a compensable claim is filed, the claimant will become eligible for benefits in two to seven days.

The Employer Bears the Cost of Providing the Compensation Insurance

The employer is not permitted to deduct the cost of workers' compensation premiums from the employee's paycheck, but must assume the initial cost of the insurance. The employer will theoretically pass the costs of the insurance along to customers in the form of higher prices for goods and services. Most economists agree that employers also pass some costs on to employees in the form of lower wages,[71] but, unlike Social Security, the worker does not directly participate in underwriting the scheme. Also, the arrangement gives employers an incentive to provide a safe workplace.

Benefits Under Workers' Compensation

Once a compensable injury has occurred and the claimant has initiated a valid claim for compensation, the claimant may be eligible for several types of cash benefits. It should be emphasized that the primary concern of workers' compensation is the loss of earning capacity or disability. This concept has several dimensions that figure in the policy considerations underlying workers' compensation. The broad categories of benefits available to a worker and his or her family are discussed below.

Medical

In every state an injured worker is entitled to recover for medical expenses incurred as a result of the injury. These expenses broadly include the costs of hospitalization, physician's care, and other necessary expenses, such as transportation and supplies. In addition, the employee may be entitled to rehabilitation services that will enable him or her to return to gainful employment. The medical benefits in most states are not limited either in duration or in length of time, and if limited, the period can be extended by administrative decisions.[72]

Disability Resulting in Loss of Earnings

To deal with the matter of lost wages, compensation systems typically utilize a four-part scheme of classification. Benefits may be paid for disabilities within any of the following categories:

Temporary partial—A disability that incapacitates a worker only in part and only for a limited time

Temporary total—A disability that prevents the worker from performing any suitable work for a definite period of time

Permanent partial—A disability that impairs the workers' earning capacity and that will continue to do so in the foreseeable future

Permanent total—A disability that prevents the worker from performing any suitable work and will continue to do so in the foreseeable future

The amounts paid in each case will depend on the workers' earnings, the extent of disability, and the state's formula for awarding benefits. Those points are discussed more fully below. Keep in mind that the law is subject to legislative modification, so benefits can fluctuate from time to time. One survey concludes that reductions in cash benefits, especially for permanent partial disabilities, are one of the most significant developments in worker compensation law.[73]

Scheduled Benefits

A second type of compensable claim, which is distinct from loss due to impaired earning capacity, is loss of or loss of use of a member of the body. In all but seven states, there is a scheduled award of benefits for a specified injury of this kind. The award is usually computed as an award of a fixed number of weeks of payment. Note that the awards have no necessary relationship to a given worker's capacity to perform work or to whether the worker has suffered a wage loss. For example, if a computer operator suffered the loss of a foot in a compensable injury, but returned to work shortly thereafter at the same salary, the operator nevertheless would be entitled to the scheduled award of compensation. As Professor Larson comments, "If a worker is given $20,000 for some internal organ damage that has no conceivable effect, actual or presumptive, on earning capacity, it is no longer possible to pretend that this is still somehow only an extrapolation of the wage-loss principle aided by the conclusive presumption of eventual wage loss."[74] The inconsistency is compounded when the amount of the award is based on past earnings; in this case, a high wage earner and a low wage earner receive different amounts for the identical injury.[75]

Death and Dependency Benefits

In addition to payments to an injured worker, the compensation system pays benefits to the worker's dependents in the event of his or her death from a work-related injury. The amounts may vary from state to state, in terms of both the maximum benefit and the duration, but most states pay benefits to a widow for life or until remarriage and to children until they reach a specified age.[76] In Pennsylvania, for example, the spouse and family who survive the worker are entitled to the same maximum as the deceased worker, and they receive the award throughout widow/widowerhood and until age 18, unless disabled or a student under age 23. Most states presume the dependency of surviving spouses and children. Other persons may be entitled to benefits if they prove dependency, but in some relationships, proof of dependency does not result in entitlement. The death benefit in all states includes some payment for the expenses of funeral and burial, ranging from $400 in South Carolina to $5,000 in Georgia and Rhode Island.[77]

Calculating the Award

Generally, workers' compensation statutes use a worker's average weekly wage (AWW) as a basis for calculating awards of benefits. This figure is derived from the actual earnings of the worker or from a wage that fairly approximates the worker's earning capacity, including such items as tips, bonuses, or other related income. Once the AWW is determined, it may be reduced to a proportion fixed by statute, such as $66\frac{2}{3}$ percent. The award may be further subject to a statutory minimum and maximum based on a statewide average weekly wage (SAWW) or some other figure.[78]

For example, a worker in Colorado who is temporarily totally disabled as a result of compensable injury will be eligible for payments amounting to $66\frac{2}{3}$ percent of the worker's average weekly wage. However, if the worker has high earnings, the award will be limited by the state maximum. That maximum is set at 91% of the SAWW. In 1999, the most an injured worker could receive was $559.23. Thus, a worker who earns an average weekly wage of $900 would not receive $66\frac{2}{3}$ percent of income, or $600, but the smaller statutory maximum. For temporary partial and permanent partial disabilities, benefits will be determined by the extent of the disability, or, if applicable, a scheduled award of benefits.

Funding

Workers' compensation systems are highly politicized, and states have substantial flexibility to alter benefits according to the political climate. From 1993 to 1995, awards of both cash and medical benefits declined relative to the previous five-year period.[79] In determining levels of benefits, the state must consider the interest of the employee in receiving adequate financial assistance, the interest of the employer in not being unduly burdened by insurance premiums, and the state's own interest in attracting and retaining business activities to provide employment for state citizens. These interests are frequently a topic of legislative and public debate, and they are especially significant in a period of intense competition among states and among the industrialized nations of the world.

The system of workers' compensation illustrates the first important legislative breakthrough in U.S. employment relations. It shows how political alignments can shift in response to environmental conditions and produce state action that creates new labor institutions. That idea has particular application to the legislation enacted during the New Deal, which is taken up in the next chapter. During the first two terms of Franklin D. Roosevelt's presidency, the domestic economy changed in profound ways that continue to exert an influence on the lives of all U.S. citizens. Below is a brief summary of the period leading up to the New Deal.

Summing Up the 1920s

In 1929, the Wertheim Fellowship Committee sponsored an informative set of lectures on problems in industrial relations. The speakers included such notable figures as John R. Commons, William Leiserson, and Elton Mayo, and their published essays reflect the main currents of the time in all their complexity and contradiction. One theme, explored by representatives of management and labor, deals with joint efforts at industrial peace, stability, and cooperation. Railroads offered the most complete and successful example of cooperation. The Baltimore and Ohio Railroad undertook a joint program with its union to develop communication between workers and managers that resulted in "effective and humane" employment conditions.[80] Union leaders in other trades likewise saw that voluntary, as opposed to legislative, cooperation could lead to a "sane and practical industrial relationship" sustained by collective agreements.[81]

Surveying developments in the management of labor, William Leiserson cogently described the confluence of labor economics and industrial relations in the field of personnel management.[82] Leiserson argued that the unitary conception of a "labor problem" had fragmented into specialized areas of inquiry focusing on the relations of employers and employees. He traced the evolution of the self-employed craft worker to the workplace characterized by "bossy management" confronted by "bossy trade unionism." As conflict gave way to the more enlightened welfaristic policies, firms created centralized departments dedicated to labor relations, and Leiserson credited John D. Rockefeller Jr. as the architect of such policies. After reviewing the various economic benefits accruing through the new system, Leiserson turned to the most significant contribution of personnel management—the development of "employee representation machinery" as a means of providing workers with a voice in corporate decision making and a "necessary step toward industrial democracy."[83] Even if managers deployed such organizational tactics from suspect motives, the institutions themselves produced desirable effects. As Leiserson assessed the coincidence of union and management goals through employee representation, management surrendered a measure of autocratic control, swinging "to the left in the direction of collective bargaining, trade unionism, and industrial democracy." For their part, the labor movement accepted the principles of scientific management and wage policies and moved "to the right in the direction of the program of the personnel managers. It is easy, therefore, for the two to meet and to unite in cooperative arrangements where the best of both are combined."[84] Under those circumstances, Leiserson concluded, personnel management led to many of the objectives sought by trade unions.

Despite the laudatory accomplishments of welfare capitalism, economist Frank Taussig cautioned that the industrial system depended on the adjustment of antagonistic interests, which resulted in imbalances of power in the employment relationship. Trade unions served the beneficial end of promoting the aims of workers; when an employer established representation plans, he dealt only with "persons over whom he has the whip hand." Schemes of internal representation ignored the fundamental power of employers to discharge employees, and they were bound to fail in matters of wages, hours, and the pace of work. Moreover, Taussig pointed out, "It is patent that such arrangements as employee representation and the company union are set up in not a few cases for the very reason that they do weaken the bargaining power of the employees."[85] As power tilted in favor of capital, the distribution of economic output likewise shifted.

Taussig's warnings proved to be altogether prophetic. The prosperity of the 1920s grew increasingly unequal and wealth became concentrated in the top segments of society. At the end of the decade, the collapse of the stock market and related developments created the greatest domestic crisis since the Civil War. Out of the defining moment of the Great Depression came massive state involvement in economic matters, rapid growth in union membership, and the creation of collective bargaining processes as the basis of labor markets. The first and most important legislative step had to do with federal protections for unions under the National Labor Relations (Wagner) Act (NLRA). Much of the NLRA's content took shape under the War Labor Board's auspices and reappeared in Section 7(a) of the National Industrial Recovery Act and the decisions of the National Labor Board (1933–1935). The next chapter begins with the genesis of government regulation during the war and its resurgence in the early years of the New Deal.

Summary

- Legal rules were crucial in controlling workers' collective activities and shaping labor strategies. Employment at will gave employers substantial legal powers in the workplace. Constitutional doctrine prevented the federal government from enacting protective labor legislation. Injunctions were the device that judges used to outlaw certain labor tactics.
- Important managerial techniques emerged during the 1920s. Scientific management was an influential method of organizing production. Welfare capitalism marks the beginnings of personnel management in U.S. firms; it was also a means of remaining nonunion.
- In the early 1920s, employers mounted an offensive against unions. Union membership declined significantly over the decade. Wealth became more concentrated in the upper segments of the economic spectrum.
- Workers' compensation systems are an exception to the contractual pattern of U.S. employment relations. Such legislative schemes mandate protections for job-related injuries. Employers supported the introduction of workers' compensation laws because they limit an employer's common law liability for industrial accidents.

Further Analysis

1. The change from Blackstone's rule of presumed yearly hiring to Wood's rule of presumed at-will employment illustrates the distinction between status and contract. That is, in one case the status of the parties determines their legal rights, while in the other case the agreement of the parties is controlling. Which principle is more consistent with the U.S. economic system, and why? Can you think of other instances where status matters more than agreement? If a wife entered into a prenuptial agreement to pay her husband a weekly allowance to clean the house, should a court enforce that contract or is a marital relationship one of status?

2. As noted in Chapter 2, some legal theorists argue that any economic exchanges should be permitted unless they involve force or fraud. The problem is that labor is embedded in physical bodies and some expenditures of labor involve moral issues. For example, if there is an ethical distinction between the services of a prostitute and, say, a chiropractor, how would that ethical principle be articulated? The philosopher John Locke started from the premise that persons own their bodies as a form of property. How does the sale of labor differ from the sale of blood or other body parts?

3. What is the justification for a legal rule that permits employers to fire employees? What is the justification for a rule that restricts the employer's power to fire employees? What might be an acceptable middle ground between an employer's absolute authority to terminate employment and an employee's right to challenge any employment decision he or she wanted to protest?

4. The public policy exception to employment at will protects employees in cases where some important governmental interest is at stake. Should a federal statute be enacted that prohibits an employer from discharging an employee because the employee notifies a governmental agency of the employer's violation of a law or regulation? What other public policies are important to our society? Consider the argument that employment is such an important property right that it should not be taken away from someone without due process protections. What are the weaknesses of that assertion?

5. Assume that you were a citizen of Montana when that state enacted its law protecting employees from discharge except for just cause. Would you have supported or opposed modification of the common law rule? If you were an employer, would you agree to arbitration under the Montana statute? Would employers be likely to voluntarily contract away their right to fire workers? What reasons might they have for doing so?

6. What are the positive aspects of scientific management as a technique of labor relations? What are the negative aspects? Do you think it is still used today in the workplace, and if so, what are some examples of it? What might be a better alternative—let workers wander around doing what they want?

7. Compare the idea of employee representation as advanced by Rockefeller with the idea of trade union representation held by Gompers. Which system is most advantageous to workers?

8. Consider the reasoning of Chief Justice Shaw in the *Farwell* decision. Is it more consistent with our economic system than a rule requiring employers to provide compensation insurance for employees? Assume that the purpose of legal rules in employment is to promote economically efficient contracts. Should states allow employers and employees to agree to opt out of compensation systems and fall under the common law rules of negligence?

9. Self-employed persons and independent contractors have no legislative protection against work-related injuries. Should the federal government impose a tax on them to provide insurance coverage? If your answer is no, consider that the government does force self-employed individuals to pay a tax into the Social Security system. Is it logical to require the self-employed to buy a pension from the government but not to require them to buy insurance against injuries on the job? What differences might there be in the two cases?

10. How are the principles of no-fault recovery and exclusivity of remedy related? Would it be advisable to have one without the other? Consider the case of Karen Silkwood, who worked in a factory with radioactive materials and was the subject of a movie about workplace hazards in the nuclear industry. After she died in an automobile accident, her estate brought suit against the Kerr-McGee Corporation alleging that Silkwood's person and her property had been injured by exposure to radioactive plutonium. The Tenth Circuit Court of Appeals held that any injury to her person was covered by the Oklahoma Worker's Compensation law and could not be the basis of a jury award of punitive damages. However, a jury could award punitive damages because of harm to Silkwood's apartment caused by the

plutonium. See 769 F.2d 1451 (1985). In the trial, the jury found that there was $5,000 damage to Silkwood's property, and it awarded $10 million in punitive damages against Kerr-McGee. Do you think Kerr-McGee should have to pay $10 million to Silkwood's father when her death was already covered by workers' compensation?

11. As noted, scheduled benefits are not altogether consistent with the notion that workers' compensation replaces a worker's lost earnings. For example, if a worker is disfigured by an accident, should the disfigurement be the basis for an award of benefits? Should the worker be forced to show that the disfigurement affected his or her employability as a condition of benefits? How much should the award be? Some states require that the disfigurement affect the employee's employment but others allow recovery for any permanent and serious disfigurement to exposed parts of the body. Which approach is more consistent with the policies of workers' compensation?

12. Most states fix a maximum amount that can be awarded under the compensation system and usually the maximum is linked with the SAWW. What policy justifies the limitation of awards? Is the SAWW an equitable method of determining a maximum or should the legislature be required to set a limit each year?

13. Assume during the 2004 presidential campaign one candidate proposed a system of national health care, which would cover industrial injuries, and an expansion of Social Security disability to provide cash benefits for temporarily or permanently disabled workers. Would you support such a system as a replacement for workers' compensation?

Suggested Readings

Ballam, Deborah. "Exploding the Original Myth Regarding Employment-At-Will: The True Origins of the Doctrine," *Berkeley Journal of Employment and Labor Law* 17 (1996): 91–128.

Bernstein, Irving. *The Lean Years: A History of American Workers, 1920–1933.* Boston: Houghton Mifflin, 1960.

Blades, Lawrence. "Employment At Will vs. Individual Freedom: On Limiting the Abusive Exercise of Employer Power," *Columbia Law Review* 67 (1967): 1404–1435.

Chandler, Alfred. *The Visible Hand: The Managerial Revolution in American Business.* Cambridge, MA: Harvard University Press, 1977.

Epstein, Richard. "In Defense of the Contract at Will," *University of Chicago Law Review* 51 (1984): 947–982.

Feinman, Jay. "The Development of the Employment At Will Rule," *American Journal of Legal History* 20 (1976): 118–135.

Fishback, Price, and Shawn Kantor. *Prelude to the Welfare State: The Origins of Workers' Compensation.* Chicago: University of Chicago Press, 2000.

Forbath, William. *Law and the Shaping of the American Labor Movement.* Cambridge, MA: Harvard University Press, 1991.

Hogler, Raymond, and Guillermo Grenier. *Employee Participation and Labor Law in the American Workplace.* New York: Quorum Books, 1992.

Jacoby, Sanford. *Employing Bureaucracy: Managers, Unions, and the Transformation of Work in American Industry, 1900–1945.* New York: Columbia University Press, 1985.

Larson, Arthur. *The Law of Workmen's Compensation.* Vols. 1–4. New York: Matthew Bender, 1952 (updated looseleaf service).

Montgomery, David. *The Fall of the House of Labor: The Workplace, the State, and American Labor Activism, 1865–1925.* Cambridge, UK: Cambridge University Press, 1987.

National Commission on State Workmen's Compensation Laws. *Report of the National Commission on State Workmen's Compensation Laws.* Washington, DC: Government Printing Office, 1972.

Ramirez, Bruno. *When Workers Fight: The Politics of Industrial Relations in the Progressive Era, 1898–1916.* Westport, CT: Greenwood Press, 1978.

Spieler, Emily, and John F. Burton Jr., "Compensation for Disabled Workers: Workers' Compensation," in *New Approaches to Disability in the Workplace,* ed. Terry Thomason, John F. Burton Jr., and Douglass Hyatt. Madison, WI: Industrial Relations Research Association, 1998, pp. 205–244.

Worrall, John, and David Appel, eds. *Workers' Compensation Benefits: Adequacy, Equity, and Efficiency.* Ithaca, NY: ILR Press, 1985.

Endnotes

1. Richard B. Freeman, "Spurts in Union Growth: Defining Moments and Social Processes," in *The Defining Moment: The Great Depression and the American Economy in the Twentieth Century* (Chicago: University of Chicago Press, 1998), 265–295. For somewhat different estimates, see Leo Wolman, *The Growth of American Trade Unions, 1880–1923* (New York: National Bureau of Economic Research, 1924), 33, Table 2.

2. David M. Gordon, Richard Edwards, and Michael Reich, *Segmented Work, Divided Workers: The Historical Transformation of Labor in the United States* (Cambridge, UK: Cambridge University Press, 1982), 128.

3. See generally, David Brian Robertson, *Capital, Labor and State: The Battle for American Labor Markets From the Civil War to the New Deal* (Lanham, MD: Rowman & Littlefield, 2000).

4. Bruno Ramirez, *When Workers Fight: The Politics of Industrial Relations in the Progressive Era, 1898–1916* (Westport, CT: Greenwood Press, 1978), 65–84.

5. Walter Drew, one of the foremost proponents of the open shop, represented employers in the National Erectors' Association. His career illustrates the lengths to which some U.S. capitalists pursued an overt campaign of union eradication until the Wagner Act gave workers legal rights to unionize. See Sidney Fine, *"Without Blare of Trumpets": Walter Drew, the National Erectors' Association, and the Open Shop Movement, 1903–57* (Ann Arbor: University of Michigan Press, 1995).

6. In 1877, a treatise writer named Horace Gray Wood published a book on the master–servant relationship and declared the rule to be the "inflexible" one that "a general or indefinite hiring is prima facie a hiring at will, and if the servant seeks to make it out a yearly hiring, the burden is upon him to establish it by proof." Horace Wood, *Master and Servant* (Albany, NY, 1877), § 134, p. 272. Regarding the contrary English rule, Wood asserts that he is "aware of no instance in which, for many years, the rule has been approved by any American court." Wood's conclusion is challenged in Jay Feinman, "The Development of the Employment At Will Rule," *American Journal of Legal History* 20 (1976): 118–141.

7. William Blackstone, *Commentaries on the Laws of England.* Book I, ed. George Sharswood (Philadelphia, 1870), 425.

8. Feinman notes, for example, that Scottish miners negotiated some contracts requiring only a minute's notice, thus avoiding criminal liability for unlawful strikes. "Development of Employment At Will Rule," p. 121.

9. For a recent contribution to the debate, see Deborah Ballam, "Exploding the Original Myth Regarding Employment-At-Will: The True Origins of the Doctrine," *Berkeley Journal of Employment and Labor Law* 17 (1996): 91.

10. A leading case is *Martin v. New York Life Ins. Co.*, 148 N.Y. 117, 42 N.E. 416 (1895), in which the New York Court of Appeals cited and approved Wood's rule.

11. Feinman, "Development of Employment At Will Rule," note 2, pp. 132–133. In Feinman's view, the greatest perceived threat to the capitalist owner lay with middle-level employees. That group had sufficient economic leverage within an enterprise to assert a meaningful claim of continued interest.

12. Marx's theory of labor supposes that an available pool of unemployed workers is a necessary condition of capitalism, and any rule enhancing the employer's power to separate workers from employment gives managers greater control over the labor process. For an important treatment of Marx's ideas in the modern employment context, see Harry Braverman, *Labor and Monopoly Capital: The Degradation of Work in the Twentieth Century* (New York: Monthly Review Press, 1975), 377–402.

13. James D. Schmidt, *Free to Work: Labor Law, Emancipation, and Reconstruction, 1815–1880* (Athens: University of Georgia Press), 205.

14. *Payne v. Western & Atlantic R.R. Co.*, 81 Tenn. 507 (1884).

15. 81 Tenn. at 519.

16. 81 Tenn. at 544.

17. *Adair v. United States*, 208 U.S. 161 (1908).

18. 208 U.S. 174–175.

19. The majority held that there was no substantial relation between an employee's membership in a labor organization and the federal authority to regulate interstate commerce. In a prescient dissenting opinion, Justice McKenna wrote that "the test of power is not merely the matter regulated, but whether the regulation is directly one of interstate commerce or is embraced within the grant conferred on Congress to use all lawful means necessary and appropriate to the execution of that power to regulate commerce." Thus, even if labor relations were not in interstate commerce, the legislative effort to eliminate a burden on commerce fell within the federal authority. This reasoning is the basis for modern federal employment regulation.

20. For a discussion of the point, see Raymond Hogler, "Employment At Will and Scientific Management: The Ideology of Workplace Control," *Hofstra Labor Law Journal* 3 (1985): 27–58.

21. The case of *Lochner v. New York*, 198 U.S. 45 (1905), is probably the most extreme example of the Court's substantive due process approach to employment regulation. The Court struck down a state law fixing the maximum number of work hours in the bakery industry on the grounds that it exceeded the permissible exercise of the state's police power and interfered with the individual's freedom of contract.

22. William Forbath, *Law and the Shaping of the American Labor Movement* (Cambridge, MA: Harvard University Press, 1991), 193.

23. *Loewe v. Lawlor*, 208 U.S. 274 (1908); *Lawlor v. Loewe*, 235 U.S. 522 (1915). The labor movement took up a collection for the members of the Hatters, donating one day's wages. The judgment was satisfied.

24. For a brief summary, see Raymond Hogler, "Danbury Hatters Case," in *Labor Conflict in the United States: An Encyclopedia*, ed. Ronald L. Filippelli (New York: Garland, 1990), 147–149.

25. *Hitchman Coal & Coke Co. v. Mitchell,* 245 U.S. 229 (1917).

26. Daniel Ernst, "The Yellow-Dog Contract and Liberal Reform, 1917–1932," *Labor History* 30 (1989): 251–274.

27. Forbath, *Shaping of the Labor Movement,* pp. 134–135.

28. David Montgomery, *The Fall of the House of Labor: The Workplace, the State, and American Labor Activism, 1865–1925* (Cambridge, UK: Cambridge University Press, 1987), 229.

29. Frederick Taylor, *The Principles of Scientific Management* (New York: Harper and Brothers, 1911), 9–29.

30. Taylor, *Principles,* pp. 35–39.

31. Taylor, *Principles,* pp. 42–47; 60, n. 1. In fact, much of Taylor's account of the Schmidt episode is sheer fabrication. For a more factual version of what took place, see Charles Wrege and Amedeo Perroni, "Taylor's Pig-Tale: A Historical Analysis of Frederick W. Taylor's Pig-Iron Experiments," *Academy of Management Review* 17 (1974): 6–23.

32. E.g., Daniel Nelson, "Scientific Management and the Workplace, 1920–1935," in *Masters to Managers: Historical and Comparative Perspectives on American Employers,* ed. Sanford Jacoby (New York: Columbia University Press, 1991), 74–89.

33. Montgomery, *Fall of the House of Labor;* Braverman, *Labor and Monopoly Capital;* Dan Clawson, *Bureaucracy and the Labor Process: The Transformation of U.S. Industry, 1860–1920* (New York: Monthly Review Press, 1980).

34. As N. P. Alifas of the Machinist's Union commented about scientific management before a congressional committee, "We would a good deal rather have the world run on the basis that everybody should enjoy some of the things in it, and if the people of the United States do not want to spend all their time working they have a right to say so, even though the scientific engineers claim that they can do five times as much as they are doing now." Testimony of N. P. Alifas, quoted in "Watertown, Connecticut Arsenal Strike of 1909," Filippelli, *Labor Conflict,* p. 564. For a detailed treatment of the incident, see Hugh G. J. Aitken, *Taylorism at Watertown Arsenal: Scientific Management in Action, 1908–1915* (Cambridge, MA: Harvard University Press, 1960).

35. Testimony of Frederick W. Taylor, United States Commission on Industrial Relations 1914, *Final Report and Testimony.* Vol. 1 (Washington, DC: Government Printing Office), 786–787.

36. See Samuel Haber, *Efficiency and Uplift: Scientific Management in the Progressive Era* (Chicago: University of Chicago Press, 1964).

37. Stuart D. Brandes, *American Welfare Capitalism* (Chicago: University of Chicago Press, 1967), 5–6.

38. See generally Gordon, Edwards, and Reich, *Segmented Workers,* pp. 121–127.

39. For a treatment of labor relations during the period, see Bruno Ramirez, *When Workers Fight: The Politics of Industrial Relations in the Progressive Era, 1898–1916* (Westport, CT: Greenwood Press, 1978).

40. Ramirez, *When Workers Fight,* p. 155. An important study of the subject is David Brody, "The Rise and Decline of Welfare Capitalism," in *Workers in Industrial America: Essays on the Twentieth Century Struggle* (New York: Oxford University Press, 1980), chap. 2.

41. The ongoing importance of welfare capitalism is described in an influential recent book: Sanford Jacoby, *Modern Manors: Welfare Capitalism Since the New Deal* (Princeton, NJ: Princeton University Press, 1997).

42. Neil J. Mitchell, *The Generous Corporation: A Political Analysis of Economic Power* (New Haven, CT: Yale University Press, 1989), 122.

43. Andrea Tone, *The Business of Benevolence: Industrial Paternalism in Progressive America* (Ithaca, NY: Cornell University Press, 1997), 7.

44. Ramirez describes the development of collective agreements in both bituminous and anthracite mining and calls the period between 1895 and 1905 the golden age of the trade agreement. *When Workers Fight,* pp. 17–84.

45. Henry Eilbirt, "The Development of Personnel Management in the United States," *Business History Review* 33 (1959): 345–364.

46. Robert W. Dunn, *Company Unions, Employers' "Industrial Democracy"* (New York: Vanguard Press, 1927).

47. One labor historian concludes, for example, that welfare capitalism had little influence on union decline and that it was not a widespread practice. Howard Gitelman, "Welfare Capitalism Reconsidered," *Labor History* 33 (1992): 5–31. For a detailed analysis of employer antiunionism and its relation to welfare capitalism, see Sanford Jacoby, *Employing Bureaucracy: Managers, Unions, and the Transformation of Work in American Industry, 1900–1945* (New York: Columbia University Press, 1985).

48. Ordway Tead and Henry C. Metcalf, *Personnel Administration: Its Principles and Practices,* 2d ed. (New York: McGraw-Hill, 1926), vii.

49. For example, Tead and Metcalf organize their book into sections dealing with the field of personnel administration, its functions in the firm, selection and hiring, worker health and safety, training, record keeping and analysis, compensation, and employee–employer relations. A modern text consists of the following subject matter: the nature of human resource management, staffing, training and development, compensation, and employee relations. Robert L. Mathis and John H. Jackson, *Human Resource Management,* 10th ed. (Mason, OH: Thomson, 2003). The core elements of strategic human resource management are historically analyzed in Bruce E. Kaufman, "The Theory and Practice of Strategic HRM and Participative Management: Antecedents in Early Industrial Relations," *Human Resource Management Review* 11 (2001): 505–533.

50. For an excellent recent history of workers' compensation systems, see Price V. Fishback and Shawn Everett Kantor, *A Prelude to the Welfare State: The Origins of Workers' Compensation* (Chicago: University of Chicago Press, 2000).

51. The law of industrial accidents is analyzed from a labor history perspective in Christopher L. Tomlins, *Law, Labor, and Ideology in the Early American Republic* (Cambridge, UK: Cambridge University Press, 1993), 331–384.

52. See generally Ben Small, "The General Structure of Law Applicable to Employee Injury and Death," *Vanderbilt Law Review* 16 (1963): 1021–1023.

53. 150 Eng. Ref. 1030 (Exch. of Pleas 1837), cited in Small, "General Structure," p. 1023.

54. 4 Metcalf 49 (1842).

55. 4 Metcalf at 56.

56. 4 Metcalf at 57.

57. For a good discussion of the point, see Fishback and Kantor, *A Prelude to the Welfare State,* pp. 30–34.

58. Arthur Larson, *Larson's Workers' Compensation Law.* Vol. 1 (New York: Matthew Bender, 1952 [1997]) § 4.30, pp. 25–28. This treatise is routinely updated and now consists of twelve volumes. It is generally regarded as the definitive treatment of workers' compensation law.

59. Morton Horwitz, an influential scholar of legal history, comments on the *Farwell* case:

> The doctrine of "assumption of risk" in workmen's injury cases expressed the triumph of the contractarian ideology more completely than any other nineteenth century legal creation. It arose in an economy which already had all but eradicated traces of an earlier model of normative relations between master and servants. And without the practice of enforcing preexisting moral duties, judges and jurists could no longer ascribe

any purpose to legal obligations that were superior to the expressed "will" of the parties. As contract ideology thus emasculated all prior conceptions of substantive justice, equal bargaining power inevitably became established as the inarticulate major premise of all legal and economic analysis. The circle was completed: the law had come simply to ratify those forms of inequality that the market system produced.

The Transformation of American Law, 1780-1860 (Cambridge, MA: Harvard University Press, 1977), 210.

60. Larson, vol.1, § 4.30, quoting Justice Shaw in *Farwell* and citing other authorities.

61. Anthony Balle, "American's First Compensation Crisis: Conflict Over the Value and Meaning of Workplace Injuries Under the Employer's Liability System," in *Dying for Work: Workers' Safety and Health in Twentieth-Century America,* ed. David Rosner and Gerald Markowitz (Bloomington: Indiana University Press, 1987), 34.

62. Balle, "America's First Compensation Crisis," p. 41.

63. Balle, "America's First Compensation Crisis," pp. 47, 49; see also Fishback and Kantor, *A Prelude to the Welfare State,* chap. 5.

64. Larson, *Worker's Compensation,* vol. 1, § 5.10.

65. Larson, *Worker's Compensation,* § 5.20.

66. For a summary, see Department of Labor, "State Workers' Compensation Laws" (revised January 2000) at the following Web site: www.dol.gov/esa/regs/statutes/owcp/stwclaw/stwclaw.htm. The site includes information about insurance systems, methods and amounts of payment, and other useful information.

67. See generally, Mark A. Rothstein et al., *Employment Law,* 2d ed. (St. Paul, MN: West Publishing, 1999).

68. Typical statutes and cases are collected in Larson, *Worker's Compensation,* vol. 1A, §§ 32.00–36.63.

69. Larson, *Workers' Compensation,* vol. 2A, §§69.10 and 68.10.

70. See, for example, Garth Magnum, "Murder in the Workplace: Criminal Prosecution v. Regulatory Enforcement," *Labor Law Journal* 39 (1988): 220–231.

71. E.g., Fishback and Kantor, *A Prelude to the Welfare State,* p. 18, note that as a result of the shift to employer liability for injuries, "Workers essentially paid for an improvement in their insurance."

72. See generally Larson, *Worker's Compensation,* vol. 2, § 61.00.

73. Emily A. Spieler and John F. Burton Jr., "Compensation for Disabled Workers: Workers' Compensation," *New Approaches to Disability in the Workplace,* ed. Terry Thomason, John F. Burton Jr., and Douglass Hyatt (Madison, WI: Industrial Relations Research Association, 1998), 205–244.

74. Larson, *Worker's Compensation,* vol. 2, § 57.14(d). Larson describes the origins of scheduled benefits in § 57.14(c).

75. Consider two Minnesota workers, the first earning $400 per week and the second $100 per week. If both lost their voice mechanisms in an accident, A would receive $98,500 and B's award would be $50,000. Larson points out that "if what is being compensated for has nothing to do with loss of earning capacity, of what relevance are prior earnings?" Larson, *Worker's Compensation,* § 57.14(i).

76. Larson, *Worker's Compensation,* vol. 4, App. B, Table 16.

77. Survivors' and death benefits on a state-by-state basis are listed on the Department of Labor Web site at www.dol.gov/esa/regs/statutes/owcp/stwclaw/stwclaw.htm, Tables 12 and 13.

78. See Larson, *Worker's Compensation,* Tables 6–10 for a listing of benefits. Benefits are also compiled in Larson, vol. 4, App. B, Tables 8 (permanent total), 9 (permanent partial), 10 (temporary total), and 11 (certain schedules).

79. Spieler and Burton, "Compensation for Disabled Workers," p. 218.

80. O. S. Beyer Jr., "Experiences With Cooperation Between Labor and Management in the Railway Industry," in *Wertheim Lectures on Industrial Relations 1928,* ed. Otto S. Beyer Jr. (Cambridge, MA: Harvard University Press, 1929), 3–31.

81. John P. Frey, "Industrial Relations," in *Wertheim Lectures,* p. 69.

82. William M. Leiserson, "Contributions of Personnel Management to Improved Labor Relations," in *Wertheim Lectures,* pp. 125–164.

83. Leiserson, "Contributions," p. 154.

84. Leiserson, "Contributions," p. 158.

85. Frank Taussig, "The Opposition of Interest Between Employer and Employee: Difficulties and Remedies," in *Wertheim Lectures,* pp. 197–229; quote, p. 220.

PART II

The Evolution of Collective Bargaining

CHAPTER 4

The Creation of Federal Labor Policy

World War I Through the New Deal

I n the two decades from 1916 to 1935, U.S. society underwent dramatic and wrenching changes. World War I provided the opportunity for extensive federal involvement in key sectors of the economy; as a result, workers gained a greater voice than ever before in workplace matters.[1] The new employment conditions raised workers' expectations about better pay, working conditions, and relations with management. At the end of the war, employers made clear that they would not willingly adopt collective bargaining as the primary means of employment administration, and they took concrete steps to reduce the power and influence of unions. The Great Steel Strike of 1919, described in Chapter 2, which ended in defeat for workers and unions, proved that capital had both the power and the will to defeat labor's organizational attempts. By the end of the 1920s, union membership stood at about one-half its level in 1919, and employers had instituted the employment practices that laid the foundation for future personnel management programs.

The economic crash beginning in 1929 led to the election of Franklin D. Roosevelt in 1932 and the inauguration of the New Deal program. It featured a radical transformation of our economic system and the establishment of the modern U.S. welfare state. The pillars of the new capitalist state were protections for collective bargaining and basic components of social insurance, such as retirement security, unemployment insurance, and minimum wage and overtime laws. Together, these programs are the basis of employee workplace benefits in the United States. By encouraging collective bargaining procedures through the National Labor

Relations (Wagner) Act (NLRA) of 1935, federal law aimed at a system of equitable wealth distribution and enhanced consumer demand to sustain the system of capitalism. The Wagner Act sparked a massive increase in union membership that generated real wage and benefit gains for workers from 1945 to 1975. That trend ended with the inflationary spiral of the 1970s, the decline of union density, and the erosion of economic gains for most workers, developments that are described in more detail in the next chapter.

Wartime Policies and the Effect on Collective Bargaining

The United States entered World War I in April 1917. To ensure that production of vital war materials continued without interruption, President Wilson appointed a War Labor Board (WLB) headed by former president William Howard Taft and labor attorney Frank Walsh. The WLB was given authority "to settle by mediation and conciliation controversies arising between employers and workers in fields of production necessary for the effective conduct of the war." From April 30, 1918, to May 31, 1919, the WLB handled 1,245 cases and issued 426 awards.[2] The WLB's objective was to stabilize labor relations, and through its guiding principles and administrative decisions, it laid the foundations for the New Deal labor legislation. Among other precepts, the WLB held that workers had a right to organize in trade unions and to bargain collectively through their representatives; employers were accordingly prohibited from denying such rights or discriminating against workers for engaging in legitimate trade union activities. Women were entitled to equal pay when performing equal work, and all workers, "including common laborers," had a right to a living wage. In addition, the WLB often established internal shop committees or employee representation plans on the Rockefeller model to give workers a method of adjusting grievances.[3] In an "extraordinary business-labor accommodation," employers tended to support the WLB principles and decisions even though their compliance was voluntary.[4] Altogether, the WLB established the conditions necessary for an effective national program of labor–management relations.[5]

In an attempt to continue the practices initiated by the WLB, President Wilson convened an Industrial Relations Conference in October 1919 to formulate a national labor relations policy. Wilson envisioned a mutual accord between workers and firms that would provide a smooth transition to the postwar economy. For the trade union delegates, it was assumed that the policies of collective bargaining favored by the WLB would provide an appropriate industrial model for the future. Following the WLB's lead, union members at the conference proposed a comprehensive program, beginning with the recognition of the employees' basic right to organize and be represented by a trade union of their choosing. They also advocated the creation of national industrial unions covering all workers in a particular occupation, standards regulating minimum wages and maximum hours, and child labor prohibitions. But the key point of the union program was the right of outside representation. On this issue, however, the employers demonstrated utter intransigence, and the Industrial Conference disintegrated in an atmosphere of hostility.[6]

Employers believed that as a matter of constitutionally protected property rights, they had a duty to resist union expansion. The postwar environment of strikes, union growth, and radicalism threatened basic ideals of the business community, most notably their prerogatives to manage their firms without interference from outsiders. In this climate, employers assumed a responsibility "not to limit their actions to the refusal to deal with unions but to destroy the movement itself."[7] The employers' plan for postwar labor relations emphasized activities at the level of the firm, not on a national level, and employee representation—limited to the workers at a particular location—was the proper mode of collective bargaining. In this way, the shop councils could serve as "the way to kill unionism with kindness while maintaining labor in its proper place and the employer in his rightful position of ultimate control."[8]

The environment of the immediate postwar period favored the employers' agenda of curtailing union power. The failure of the strike at U.S. Steel and a wave of political conservatism fueled the drive for retrenchment. As a consequence, the antiunion movement of the early 1920s was a resounding success. In 1920, total membership of U.S. trade unions was 4,551,000, but by 1923, that figure had dropped 27 percent to a total of 3,281,000. Thereafter, membership continued to decline slightly, and by 1929, unions represented 10.5 percent of the nonagricultural workforce, compared with the 16.6 percent in 1920.[9] Although the decade of the 1920s was generally one of economic growth, a diversified labor force, employer opposition, changing work environments, and judicial antagonism all contributed to union decay. Strikes became less frequent and less effective; to illustrate, the relative proportion of workers involved in strikes from 1926 to 1930 was only one-tenth of the level of 1916 to 1921.[10]

Labor suffered during the 1920s from two other problems, high unemployment and the unequal distribution of income in the country. According to some estimates, unemployment remained between 10 and 13 percent of the labor force for the period 1924 to 1929. Turnover in employment was low, and the implementation of labor-saving technology displaced many workers. In terms of comparative income, 21 percent of families received less than $1,000 annual income, and 71 percent received less than $1,500. At the same time, the combined total income of the top 0.1 percent roughly equaled that of 42 percent of families at the bottom.[11] The Republican dominance of the 1920s resulted in a capitalist heyday, in which wealth was redistributed from lower to upper classes of society, similar to the economic revolution beginning in the 1980s. In both cases, attacks on labor, conservative political environments, and financial restructuring were key elements of the transformation.[12]

The stock market crash in October 1929 signaled the collapse of the U.S. economy. The reasons for the sudden decline of investment had much to do with international relations and the enactment of stringent tariff legislation, which affected global financial mechanisms. In one expert's view, "The desperate state of the commodity producers along with the reparations-induced problems of Germany set off a domino reaction. In this sense, the depression was directly a product of disorderly financial markets."[13] Despite the international dimensions of the economic downturn, however, U.S. policymakers viewed the event as a domestic crisis amenable to domestic remedies. The Great Depression-era legislation rested on policies of consumer demand, redistribution of wealth, and economic stimulus. Those policies explain in large part the objectives and content of such programs as collective bargaining, Social Security, wage and hour standards, and unemployment insurance. They continue to dictate the terms of the debate about state intervention in economic matters.[14]

Whatever the origins of the Great Depression, it resulted in dire circumstances for many Americans. According to one calculation, nearly 30 percent of U.S. workers were unemployed in March 1933, and even that figure underestimated the magnitude of the problem.[15] President Herbert Hoover, although a great humanitarian, offered little active leadership to deal with the abysmal situation, and his popularity fell with the worsening conditions. Franklin Delano Roosevelt, the Democratic presidential candidate, won the 1932 election and immediately began a program of economic and legislative reform that became known as the New Deal. The National Industrial Recovery Act (NIRA) undertook a massive reconstruction of the economic regime, including, for the first time, federal protections for all workers to unionize. The Supreme Court in May 1935 declared the NIRA, Roosevelt's attempt at recovery, an unconstitutional extension of federal power. The failure of that law created the opportunity for Robert Wagner to introduce his own collective bargaining bill in Congress. Wagner's statute had important forerunners that explain the peculiar characteristics of the U.S. system.

Labor Legislation Before the Wagner Act

The Railway Labor Act of 1926

As the historical materials in earlier chapters show, labor disputes on railroads severely affected the national economy, and the increasing number of disturbances eventually brought about federal action. The Knights of Labor mounted a series of strikes against Jay Gould's Southwest railroad system in 1886, and those disturbances first prompted Congress to explore alternative legislative methods for resolving disputes and minimizing the damaging consequences of railway strikes. Two years later, in 1888, Congress enacted the Arbitration Act, which authorized voluntary arbitration of issues and allowed a presidential commission to investigate labor-specific incidents of strife. The law contained no procedures for enforcement, and during its ten-year existence, between 1888 and 1898, the voluntary arbitration process was never used.[16] Congress's first attempt at railroad labor regulation, then, proved to be a failure.

After the Pullman strike in 1894, Congress realized that more stringent legislative measures were called for. The Erdman Act of 1898 provided for both mediation and the voluntary arbitration of disputes. That law also had a section protecting union members from employer discrimination, but, as discussed in Chapter 3, the Supreme Court in the *Adair* case invalidated that particular section of the law. Other features of the Erdman Act continued in force, and a number of disputes were resolved by mediation or arbitration. In the Newlands Act of 1913, Congress created a permanent board of mediation and conciliation for railroad disputes. During the war years of 1917 to 1920, Congress nationalized the railroads and placed them under the jurisdiction of a federal administrative agency. Once the war ended, Congress relinquished control to private ownership, but it also adopted a new law in the Transportation Act of 1920; this statute created a Railroad Labor Board that engaged in mediation and arbitration. The act proved unpopular with both labor and management, and eventually, under the urging of President Coolidge in 1924, a joint labor–management committee eventually developed its own law.[17]

In early 1926, Congress passed the Railway Labor Act (RLA). The RLA forms the basis of railroad and airline labor law, and it is the oldest continuous federal collective bargaining statute. The law describes its general purposes as follows: to maintain transportation services, to allow employees to unionize, and to aid the parties in settling disputes in negotiations and contract administration.[18] As one of the committee members responsible for drafting the law emphasized, "This bill is the product of a negotiation between employers and employees which is unparalleled, I believe, in the history of American industrial relations."[19] The Supreme Court in 1930 upheld the constitutionality of the law, stating that it was a proper exercise of Congress's power over interstate commerce.[20] The Air Line Pilots Association successfully lobbied Congress in 1936 for an extension of the law to cover air carriers.[21]

The RLA established a National Mediation Board (NMB) to administer its provisions, and, under the RLA, the NMB is authorized to hold elections and certify union representatives within designated crafts. As its name implies, the NMB engages in mediation to assist the parties in reaching settlements. When mediation fails to resolve a bargaining impasse, the board offers to establish arbitration. If the parties accept arbitration, the decision of the arbitration tribunal is final. If they do not accept arbitration, a thirty-day cooling-off period follows. The NMB may in the interim notify the president that a strike of an airline or rail carrier would result in the deprivation of essential transportation services, whereupon the president may convene an emergency board to investigate the dispute and offer recommendations. One criticism of the law is that the parties have relied too heavily on the emergency boards, particularly in the postwar years.[22] The recommendations of the emergency boards are not binding on the parties, and if that procedure fails, the parties are free to engage in economic action. To prevent a strike or lockout, however, the president may ask Congress to enact emergency legislation.[23]

The RLA was an early model for collective bargaining activities. However, it was confined to a relatively small, well-defined group of employees who had an obvious connection with the nation's commercial system, and Congress had been actively legislating in the field for years. Furthermore, to attain some degree of industrial peace and stability, employers in the industry supported the statute. Despite its limited coverage, the RLA remains an important part of our labor relations law. An example that occurred during Clinton's second term as president demonstrates how the RLA allows government oversight of the collective bargaining process.

Clipping Their Wings: The Pilots' One-Minute Strike at American Airlines

After several years of unsuccessful negotiations with American Airlines, the Allied Pilots Union in 1997 declared its intention to strike the carrier. The strike deadline approached, and neither party made any concessions. President Bill Clinton took no position in the dispute, other than to insist that the economy remained vulnerable to economic disruptions. On February15, 1997, at 12:00 midnight, pilots at American Airlines began the strike. Captain Jim Sovich, the union president, directed all members to stop work immediately. At 12:01 A.M., President Clinton notified the union that he had invoked the provisions of the RLA and was referring the matter to an emergency board. A few minutes later, Sovich called off the strike and ordered pilots back to work. In a message posted on the union's Web site, he explained his decision:

> Just after midnight tonight, [the union's] Board of Directors authorized a strike of American Airlines in the absence of an agreement with [American's] management. Moments after I instructed Strike Chairman Captain Matthew Field to proceed with shutting down the airline, we received word that President Clinton had intervened by announcing the appointment of a Presidential Emergency Board. That word was verified 24 minutes later, so after a 24-minute strike the status quo was put back in place and status quo will remain.[24]

Clinton's intervention was the first such action in more than three decades, and it alienated some of Clinton's political support from unions. In the end, the parties agreed to a labor contract without any further interruption of service.

Was President Clinton Wrong?

1. From a policy standpoint, what arguments can be made for and against Clinton's action? If voluntary agreement is the ideal in employment relations, what would justify state intervention in a collective bargaining activity?
2. Assume that economic conditions in 1997 were actually much better than they were in 1992 or in 2003. Are strikes more economically palatable in bad times or good times?
3. The mechanism of emergency dispute procedures appears in the 1947 amendments to the National Labor Relations Act, and President George W. Bush relied on that law to intervene in a dock workers strike in 2002. Do you think dock workers or pilots pose a greater threat to the economy? What proof might support a conclusion one way or the other? The case is discussed more fully in Chapter 5.
4. Do you think Clinton's decision could be characterized as pro-union or antiunion? As to the eventual outcome, pilots received substantial pay increases in the new contract. By early 2003, American Airlines contemplated going into bankruptcy, in part to relieve itself of high labor costs.

The Norris-La Guardia Act of 1932

Court injunctions, discussed in Chapter 3, were an effective weapon against organizing activities and strikes. Union hostility toward the common law doctrine culminated in the anti-injunction movement of the late 1920s and early 1930s. The Supreme Court's approval of yellow-dog contracts enforceable through injunctions, and the availability of injunctions to halt most kinds of strikes, provoked strong reaction from the labor movement and, increasingly, from the public. Federal Circuit Judge John Parker, in a notorious 1927 decision, upheld an injunction against the United Mine Workers of America (UMWA) under the Sherman Antitrust Act; three years later, the Senate rejected Parker's nomination to the Supreme Court because of his apparent approval of the yellow-dog contract.[25]

The leader of the anti-injunction movement was Republican Senator George Norris of Nebraska. Motivated by his own background of poverty and deprivation, Norris was determined to assist workers in their struggle against inequitable labor laws. After the Supreme Court upheld the RLA's constitutionality in 1930, organized labor decided to support Norris's efforts to obtain anti-injunction legislation. Norris's bill was introduced into the Senate in March 1932 and approved by a vote of 75 to 5. Representative Fiorello La Guardia of New York sponsored the legislation in the House, where it was enacted by a majority of 362 to 14. Given the statute's overwhelming approval, President Hoover had no choice but to sign it.[26] The major provisions of the law are summarized below.

First, Norris-La Guardia limits the power of federal courts to issue injunctions in labor disputes. It does so by limiting the jurisdiction of courts, a power clearly within Congress's constitutional scope. Section 4 of the act specifies circumstances in which courts have *no* authority to intervene in a labor dispute, including cases in which individuals have ceased or refused to perform work, have become or remain members of a labor organization, are lawfully participating in or aiding a labor dispute, or are entering into agreements to participate in lawful acts. Section 5 aims particularly at the common law conspiracy doctrine and declares that injunctions cannot be issued on the ground that strikers "are engaged in an unlawful combination or conspiracy." Section 7 of the law permits federal courts to issue permanent and temporary injunctions if certain specific conditions are satisfied, including proof in open court that unlawful acts will be committed and will cause irreparable injury to the person's property and that public officials are unable or unwilling to protect the property.

Second, Norris-La Guardia declared that yellow-dog contracts would not be enforceable in federal courts. Such contracts included all undertakings "not to join, become or remain a member of any labor organization" and the promise that a person "will withdraw from an employment relation in the event that he joins, becomes, or remains a member of any labor organization." The contracts were deemed to be contrary to the policy of the United States. From this point in our industrial history, employers have been unable to legally enforce promises from employees that they will forego union involvement.

Third, with respect to federal labor policy, Norris-La Guardia emphasized workers' needs for freedom of association; this emphasis marked a departure from the government's previous stance of nonintervention in labor markets. Although Congress's policy declaration was provided as an aid to interpreting the statute and was not intended as a grant of enforceable rights, it does reflect a different view of labor relations than previously existed. The statute also specifically repudiates much Supreme Court jurisprudence, as the text below indicates.

Excerpt From the Norris-La Guardia Act

Section 2. In the interpretation of this Act and in determining the jurisdiction and authority of the courts of the United States, as such jurisdiction and authority are herein defined and limited, the public policy of the United States is hereby declared as follows:

Whereas under prevailing economic conditions, developed with the aid of governmental authority for owners of property to organize in the corporate and other forms of ownership association, the individual unorganized worker is commonly helpless to exercise actual liberty of contract and to protect his freedom of labor, and thereby to obtain acceptable terms and conditions of employment, wherefore, though he should be free to decline to associate with his fellows, it is necessary that he have full freedom of association, self-organization, and designation of representatives of his own choosing, to negotiate the terms and conditions of his employment, and that he shall be free from the interference, restraint, or coercion of employers of labor, or their agents, in the designation of such representatives or in self-organization or in other concerted activities for the purpose of collective bargaining or other mutual aid or protection. . . .

Discussion Questions

1. How does the act define "liberty of contract"? In what respects does this definition differ from the one offered by the Supreme Court in *Adair*?
2. Of what importance are the "prevailing economic conditions" to the enactment of this legislation?
3. How would you define "concerted activities"? Can you think of any examples of "mutual aid and protection" as applied to workers?
4. The Norris-La Guardia Act mentions certain rights that workers should have, such as the right to choose representatives, to negotiate contracts, and to be free from employer coercion. Could you draft a statute that would guarantee those things to workers? What would its major features be?

The National Industrial Recovery Act

With Franklin D. Roosevelt's inauguration in March 1933, the new administration moved to deal with problems in U.S. industry. The National Industrial Recovery Act was an attempt to reduce destructive competition and stabilize industry. Title I of the NIRA was designed to promote cooperative action among trade groups by allowing industries to establish codes of fair competition exempt from the antitrust laws. Those codes aimed at restoring purchasing power by setting labor standards governing hours of work and wages. Title II of the act established a public works program to stimulate employment. In addition, the law contained a provision, Section 7(a), specifically dealing with collective bargaining. President Roosevelt enthusiastically declared that the NIRA was "the most important and far-reaching legislation ever enacted by the American Congress."[27]

Section 7(a) was included in the NIRA as a result of lobbying by American Federation of Labor (AFL) President William Green. During congressional debate, one important issue involved the legitimacy of company unions, or employee groups organized within the individual firm. Employers proposed amendments that would have allowed such organizations to compete for rights of representation along with the independent trade unions.[28] As enacted, Section 7(a) provided that every code of fair competition should contain three protections for workers. First, employees had the right to organize and bargain collectively through their representatives and to be free from employer coercion. Second, no employee would be forced to join a company union or to refrain from supporting a union of his or her own choosing. Third, the employer agreed to comply with the maximum hours of labor and minimum rates of pay prescribed by the codes for the industry.

Two immediate and related developments followed Roosevelt's signing of the NIRA in June 1933. The first was a sharp increase in union organizing activity, and the second was an upsurge of strikes. John L. Lewis, for example, rebuilt the membership of the UMWA to its 1920 levels and established collective bargaining contracts throughout most of the bituminous coal industry.[29] But the union drives encountered serious employer opposition, which included the creation or revival of the company unions. During July 1933 alone, 1,375,574 worker hours were lost in labor disputes, and the number rose to 2,377,886 in August.[30] One immediate result of the strike wave was President Roosevelt's formation of a National Labor Board (NLB) to administer the labor provisions of the NIRA. The NLB consisted of three labor members, three employer members, and an impartial chair—Senator Robert Wagner.

Under Wagner's leadership, the NLB issued a number of decisions interpreting Section 7(a). Importantly, the NLB advocated the selection of representatives through a process of secret ballot elections and through exclusive representation by the organization selected by a majority of workers.[31] Employers began to resist the NLB's orders, however, and without any enforcement powers, the NLB's authority began to wane. Differences of opinion likewise developed within the Roosevelt administration and eventually led to the demise of the NLB.[32] Senator Wagner, convinced that more comprehensive legislation was necessary, drafted a Labor Disputes bill that he introduced into the senate in March 1934. The legislation proved unsatisfactory to both labor and business; as a compromise measure, Wagner supported Public Resolution No. 44 put forward by President Roosevelt to deal with a threatened steel strike. The resolution created the first or "old" National Labor Relations Board (NLRB), which had authority under the NIRA to investigate labor matters, hold union elections, adjudicate claims of antiunion discrimination, and issue regulations.[33] Wagner persisted in his efforts to bring about a federal labor law statute, and the next year, he was successful.

The National Labor Relations (Wagner) Act of 1935

The NLRA was one of the most innovative and controversial laws ever enacted by the U.S. Congress. It brought labor relations under federal, rather than a state's, control, and it removed the judiciary from a central role in regulating employment through common law doctrine. Perhaps most important, the constitutional theory underlying the NLRA provided the basis for many future laws, including those dealing with civil rights and worker health and safety. Senator Wagner's bill incorporated past attempts at labor legislation, but went far beyond those earlier measures. The policies articulated by Wagner and supporters of the statute are still topics of debate among economists and policymakers, as further examined in Chapter 8. The legislative history of the bill clarifies those policies and helps to explain employers' opposition to the law.

Background

Wagner introduced his bill (S. 1958) into the Senate on February 21, 1935. In his explanatory statement accompanying the draft, Wagner pointed out that employees who attempted "to exercise their liberties under section 7(a) have met with repeated rebuffs." The NLB and the NLRB, Wagner continued, were unable to effectively protect the rights of employees because those bodies lacked enforcement powers. If employers refused voluntarily to accept administrative decisions, the government was virtually powerless to force compliance. One result of the breakdown of Section 7(a) was a wave of costly strikes. But more significantly, Wagner said, workers denied the right to act in concert "cannot participate in our national endeavor to coordinate production and purchasing power." The "widening gap between wages and profits" threatened economic recovery. Wagner emphatically denied that the law favored any particular form of organization or would create a labor dictatorship. While it did prohibit the sham company unions controlled by the employer, that prohibition did not deny freedom of choice. "There can be no freedom in an atmosphere of bondage," Wagner said. "No organization can be free to represent the workers when it is the mere creature of the employer."[34]

The economic dimensions of the NLRA were set forth in a speech by Francis Biddle, Chairman of the NLRB. According to Biddle, the fundamental economic problem facing the country was a decline in domestic consumption. One theory of recovery, he said, advocated "leaving business alone" to adjust to prevailing conditions by cutting labor costs. On that theory, lower wages would eventually lead to higher profits, to greater investment, and therefore to higher employment. Biddle rejected the idea for historical reasons. In 1842, he noted, wage earners received

51 percent of each dollar in manufacturing. The figure dropped to 42 percent in 1919 and to 36 percent in 1933. Labor productivity between 1919 and 1933 almost doubled, but during that period, labor's share of income fell 6 percent. The New Deal, Biddle continued, was grounded on the idea that wealth should be more equitably distributed. He then summarized the self-evident truths supporting the Wagner legislation. He said,

> I believe that prosperity must have a broad basis; that it cannot balance on the apex of the pyramid: that we cannot drift back into good times; that lower real wages tighten the circle of economic destruction; that the profit motive, uncontrolled, will not distribute wealth; that we have been for many generations interfering artificially with the natural law of supply and demand, so that it no longer works, if indeed it ever did work in a society maintained by the haphazard balancing of everyone's individual striving for advantage; that a few must be content with less if indeed they are to get anything at all; that the future, the very present, in fact, demands an economy consciously controlled to the desired end.[35]

Where collective bargaining exists, Biddle concluded, real wages are higher and work is more secure. The NLRA would permit workers to deal with employers from a position of strength and relative equality.

During March and April 1935, committees in the Senate and the House held hearings on the proposed statute. The Senate passed S. 1958 on May 16, and the House approved its bill in the following month. President Roosevelt signed the law on July 5, 1935, declaring, "A better relationship between labor and management is the high purpose of this act. By assuring the employees the right of collective bargaining, it fosters the development of the employment contract on a sound and equitable basis." Furthermore, the orderly bargaining procedures set forth in the law would "remove one of the chief causes of economic strife."[36]

As the legislative history and other evidence makes clear, employers lobbied vigorously against the Wagner Act.[37] Yet, the bill passed by substantial margins in Congress with little debate. Two explanations account for this surprising development. One was the political strength of the labor movement and the reform coalition throughout the country. The second reason had to do with the judiciary. On May 27, at a critical moment, the Supreme Court invalidated the NIRA. In the *Schechter Poultry Company* case, the Court ruled that Congress did not have power to regulate commercial activities that occurred only within a state. Most observers believed that the *Schechter* decision likewise invalidated the NLRA, and rather than expend effort to defeat the statute in Congress, opponents decided simply to wait for the Court to declare it unconstitutional.[38] Wagner and his assistants, however, worked carefully to provide a clear constitutional basis for the NLRA resting on the federal power over interstate commerce. Wagner remained convinced that the law could survive constitutional challenge, and, in the end, he was correct. Before examining judicial interpretations of the Wagner Act, we will first consider the main provisions of the 1935 law.[39]

Findings and Policies

The first section of the act contains its basic economic and legal theories. The statute declares that employers' denial of employees' rights to organize and bargain leads to industrial strife, which affects interstate commerce in certain specific ways. Industrial strife impairs the operations and instrumentalities of commerce, occurs within the current of commerce, affects the flow of raw goods and finished products, and diminishes employment and wages so as to disrupt markets. Because employees lack equality with employers, they do not have actual freedom of association or liberty of contract. Such inequality also burdens the flow of commerce and aggravates business depressions by depressing the wages and purchasing power of workers. Historically, the protection of employees' rights to organize and bargain collectively safeguards commerce from harmful disruption. Therefore, the section concludes, it is the federal policy to remove obstructions to commerce "by encouraging the practice and procedure of collective bargaining and by protecting the exercise by workers of full freedom of association, self-organization, and designation of representatives of their own choosing, for the purpose of negotiating the terms and conditions of their employment or other mutual aid or protection."

Definitions

The definitional section of the Wagner Act excluded important groups of workers from the law's coverage. Section 2(2) defined *employer* to include all persons directly acting in the employer's interest, but *employer* did not include the United States or any state or political subdivision; accordingly, public sector or government workers were not—and are not now—covered by the law. Because the federal government declines coverage of public sector workers, states can enact their own laws regulating collective bargaining. Most states have done so, and public sector bargaining is an important component of the contemporary labor movement.[40]

Section 2(3) defined *employees* to include strikers who had not obtained "any other regular and substantially equivalent employment." The term employee did not include agricultural laborers, domestics, or immediate family members. As with public employees, the exclusion of agricultural labor permits states to regulate collective bargaining in this area. Cesar Chavez, the well-known activist who founded the United Farm Workers, was instrumental in the passage of the California Agricultural Labor Relations Act (1975), which protected migrant workers' rights to engage in union activities in that state.

Section 2(5) defined the meaning of a *labor organization* very broadly to mean "any organization of any kind, or any agency or employee representation committee or plan, in which employees participate and which exists for the purpose, in whole or in part, of dealing with employers concerning grievances, labor disputes, wages, rates of pay, hours of employment, or conditions of work." This definition has considerable significance in today's workplace because it may include participatory systems in the nonunion employment context and make those systems unlawful. Note particularly the discussion of the employer unfair labor practices below and how this definition relates to unlawful employer conduct.

National Labor Relations Board

One of Senator Wagner's important objectives was to create an independent federal body with authority to administer the law. Various parts of the statute deal with the composition of the board and its authority. Sections 3 through 6 established a national board made up of three members appointed by the president and also provided for terms of appointment and compensation. The board's principal office is located in Washington, D.C., but its power extended throughout the United States. The board also had the authority to make, amend, and rescind appropriate rules and regulations. Presently, the board maintains thirty-four regional offices across the country and in Puerto Rico. Its two main activities are to conduct secret ballot elections to determine if employees want union representation and to investigate unfair labor practice charges.[41]

Rights of Employees

Section 7 is the heart of U.S. labor law. By this time, the concepts should be familiar to you. The section reads in its entirety: "Employees shall have the right to self-organization, to form, join, or assist labor organizations, to bargain collectively through representatives of their own choosing, and to engage in concerted activities, for the purpose of collective bargaining or other mutual aid or protection." Consider whether these fundamental principles are adequate in themselves to ensure a system of collective bargaining and industrial democracy. In most European countries, for example, employees have a right to form works councils inside the firm to deal with management. That form of representation might be a useful supplement to formal collective bargaining. The topic is taken up again in Chapter 7.

Employer Unfair Labor Practices

To enforce the rights guaranteed in Section 7, the statute made it unlawful for an employer to engage in certain prohibited acts. Sections 8(1) through (5) of the NLRA set forth the employer unfair labor practices, which were subsequently renumbered in 1947 as 8(a)(1) through (5). Those illegal practices are summarized below.

Section 8(a)(1) provides that it is unlawful for an employer to "interfere with, restrain, or coerce employees in the exercise of the rights guaranteed in section 7." Thus, for example, an employer who only threatens to discharge an employee for joining a union, but who does not actually take any action affecting the employee's job, nevertheless violates the law. Nor could an employer threatened with a union drive give workers a pay raise in hopes of "buying off" their desire to unionize.

Section 8(a)(2) says that an employer cannot "dominate or interfere with the formation or administration of any labor organization or contribute financial or other support to it." This provision was intended to outlaw the company union that was exemplified by Rockefeller's Colorado Plan and that flourished after the enactment of the NIRA. But the problem is that this prohibition may cover the employee involvement programs that are an important organizational tool in the modern industrial enterprise. The board has decided several important cases on this subject, but the law remains uncertain.[42]

Section 8(a)(3) states that it is unlawful for an employer to discriminate "in regard to hire or tenure of employment or any term or condition of employment to encourage or discourage membership in any labor organization." Generally, this section is designed to prevent an employer from discouraging a union drive by firing or demoting the union sympathizers. An important issue here is how the board determines whether the employer had an improper motive or was taking legitimate disciplinary action; generally, the rule is that if the employer shows discipline would have occurred even without the protected conduct, then there is no violation of the act.[43] Because the law also prohibits employers from acting to encourage union activity, a question arises about employer enforcement of contract language requiring an employee to join or support the union. An exception written into the section legalizes union security clauses in a labor agreement that require an employee to pay union dues or be discharged.

Under Section 8(a)(4), employees cannot be discriminated against because they use the resources of the board. For example, if an employee who testifies before the board or files a charge with the board is subsequently disciplined or discharged, the board carefully scrutinizes the employer's asserted reasons for the action.

Section 8(a)(5) states that an employer cannot refuse to bargain collectively with the union representing his employees. The duty to bargain is a complex matter explored in greater detail in Chapter 8. At this point, you should appreciate that this section required an employer to at least meet and discuss wages and working conditions with the union. Note that the law does *not* require an employer to enter into a contract with the union, nor to grant any union demands, but merely to approach negotiations with an open mind. The obligation imposed by Section 8(a)(5), consequently, tries to accommodate the idea of freedom of contract with the policy favoring collective bargaining. At bottom, these two goals might conflict with one another.

Representation

Section 9 of the Wagner Act dealt with representatives and elections. It established a number of important labor relations concepts. First, the representative selected by a majority of employees was to be the *exclusive representative* of all employees in the unit, regardless of union affiliation or sympathies. Second, the board had authority to decide what unit was appropriate for collective bargaining in any case. The unit might be an employer unit, a craft unit, a plant unit, or any subdivision thereof.

Administration

Sections 10 through 12 gave the board various powers to carry out its duties. The board has authority to issue complaints and hold hearings where testimony and evidence are presented. Following the hearing, the board issues its findings and order in the case. Importantly, the board's orders are not self-enforcing, but must be presented to a federal court of appeals for enforcement. The federal appeals courts are to review the board's decision and enforce, modify, or set aside the board's order. The board's findings of fact must be upheld if they are supported by substantial evidence. Further, any person affected by a *final* order of the board may request court review. Congress also authorized the board to issue subpoenas requiring a person to attend a hearing and produce evidence. The board's subpoenas are enforced through the federal court system.

Strikes

In Section 13, Congress clarified the common law regarding strikes and provided broad and specific protection for workers' rights. The provision states: "Nothing in this Act shall be construed so as either to interfere with or impede or diminish in any way the right to strike." As a general rule, a striking employee is not entitled to compensation while on strike, and his or her job can be given to a replacement on either a temporary or a permanent basis. When the strike concludes, the striker will be given an opportunity to return to work as jobs become available and in accordance with the employee's qualifications and seniority. In addition, the Supreme Court and the board have defined a number of strike activities as *unprotected* and beyond the scope of the law. For example, the Court ruled that sit-down strikes illegally burdened an employer's property rights and subjected strikers to discharge rather than replacement. Other unprotected conduct involves picket line violence, sporadic or intermittent stoppages, unauthorized wildcat strikes, and similar activities.[44]

As noted, the board enforces laws protecting employees and also ensures a right of free choice to workers concerning union representations. What follows is a brief summary of the steps necessary to gain formal union recognition and some of the difficulties employees may encounter in undertaking an organizing effort. The board's rules include procedures for initiating an election, for regulating the parties' conduct during the election campaign period, and for devising remedies to deter unlawful conduct. The discussion concludes with a case study of how the largest employer in the United States—Wal-Mart Corporation—remains nonunion.

How to Form a Union: Certification Procedures Under the NLRA

The Election Petition

Once a union decides to attempt an organizing drive at a particular firm, the union organizers begin to solicit authorization cards from employees. The cards typically give the union a right to act as the employee's representative for purposes of collective bargaining and to seek an election at the NLRB. They may also commit the employee to join the union at some future point, such as the signing of a labor agreement. As a practical matter, the cards have little binding effect on employees, but they are crucial as a means of showing union support at the board.

If a union obtains authorization cards from 30 percent of employees in a suitable unit, the union can file an election petition with the board (usually, though, the union attempts to build up a sizeable majority before it requests a vote). The petition is a formal document that starts a lengthy procedure and requires considerable effort by both the union and the employer. To begin with, the union will specify an *appropriate bargaining unit* that separates the employees who will or will not be part of the collective bargaining process. In a manufacturing facility, to illustrate, the union would probably ask for a unit consisting of all production and maintenance employees, including all custodial, shipping, and warehouse workers. The union would exclude office workers, supervisors, and professional employees. These groups are not legally prohibited from bargaining, but they do involve special characteristics that make them different from the blue-collar workers. The crucial concept is whether workers share a sufficient *community of interest* to be placed in a single group; if they do not, the union cannot effectively represent them. Note that the concept will be used to determine whether employees of the same employer at different locations should be incorporated into one unit. For example, if Wal-Mart has ten stores in a large metropolitan area, should all ten stores be combined into a single voting bloc? The board decides that question based on such factors as centralized labor policies, similarity of operations, and geographical proximity.

Once the board decides who will be permitted to vote, it sets the date for the election. Generally, the board tries to conduct an election soon after the petition is filed. The parties can agree on the details of the vote, or they can rely on the board to resolve any disputed issues. Once the election date is set, the employer must provide the union with a list of the names and addresses of employees. This list, known as the Excelsior list from a case involving the Excelsior Underwear Co., allows the union to contact employees.[45] Both parties then embark on a vigorous campaign trying to persuade employees how to vote.

The Campaign Period

Both sides have legal rights and responsibilities in dealing with employees. Neither unions nor employers can coerce or intimidate employees to influence their vote, nor can they bribe them with gifts or better wages and working conditions. Aside from that, they have important techniques available that have proved to be powerful motivators in the contest over unionization. Among the most important devices are the captive audience speech for the employer and the home visit by union supporters.

In Section 8(c) of the Taft-Hartley Act, Congress explicitly gave employers the right to state their views about unions, provided they did not threaten or coerce employees. Because employees are subject to the direction and control of the employer, they can be required to attend mandatory sessions dealing with unions. Employers have become quite sophisticated in conveying their sentiments regarding unionization, and the captive audience speech may effectively persuade undecided voters. Most employers use this device extensively during a campaign.

On the union side, organizers can visit employees at their homes and explain the benefits of unions to the employees in a setting away from the influence of the employer. Managers are prohibited from this tactic because the board believes it to be intimidating and coercive for workers; having the boss inside your home might be unsettling, particularly if the visit is coupled with a request not to support the union. If a worker does not want to speak to the union supporter, he or she can tell the organizer to leave. Research shows that an integrated program of grassroots activity emphasizing personal contact is the best way to communicate the union message.[46]

Both sides can also use other forms of communications such as letters, leaflets, e-mail, and telephone contact. Management often instructs supervisors to conduct one-on-one meetings with employees, which is legal if supervisors do not promise, threaten, or interrogate employees about their union views. Modern unions also attempt sometimes to bring pressure on management through a corporate campaign focusing on an employer's customers or the general public. When janitors in Los Angeles mounted a "Jobs with Justice" publicity campaign, they successfully persuaded the public that the cleaning companies were exploiting their labor and they should be given higher wages and benefits. Altogether, then, unions and managers have an array of tactics suitable for campaigning. Many labor experts conclude, however, that the law tends to favor employers because it does not provide adequate deterrents to unlawful activities. Employers have the power to discharge or threaten to discharge workers as a consequence of union organizing, and such power gives them considerable influence over voting behavior. Take, for example, recent attempts to unionize Wal-Mart stores.

Collective bargaining formed the core of the New Deal employment legislation. Wagner aimed to create a system of industrial self-governance based on mutual agreements and sustained by relatively equal participants in the economic process. To that extent, the NLRA promotes U.S. ideals of voluntary adjustment of conflicting interests. But the policy framework of unionism failed to address immediate issues of unemployment and poverty. The New Deal legislators therefore laid the basic foundations for a scheme of social insurance.

Rolling the Dice: Workers Try to Unionize a Las Vegas Wal-Mart

According to reports in the national media, the United Food and Commercial Workers (UFCW) union initiated a campaign to organize workers at the largest employer in the United States, the Wal-Mart Corporation.[47] The struggle between the company and the union played out most recently at a Sam's Club store in Las Vegas, Nevada. The UFCW obtained a sufficient number of authorization cards to petition for an election at Club 6382. At that, Wal-Mart "mounted a blistering counteroffensive." Among other tactics, the company "parachuted in a dozen labor-relations troops from its Bentonville (Ark.) headquarters, instructing local managers in a fierce anti-union campaign, including surveillance of employees and the firing of several union sympathizers, the union claims." The campaign ground to a halt when the union dropped its request for an election and filed a number of unfair labor practice charges against the employer.

The event underscores the reasons for union decline in this country. Wal-Mart effectively penetrated retail sales and moved into the grocery industry, where it competes with unionized chains such as Safeway and Kroger with its trademark low-wage strategy. UFCW represents about 800,000 members in the retail industry, many in groceries. Under their collective bargaining agreements, unionized employers pay nearly 20 percent more in labor costs. Pressures from Wal-Mart force the unionized chains to demand concessions from the UFCW, and the union is responding by trying to "take wages out of competition" by organizing Wal-Mart. "'We have no choice but to [unionize Wal-Mart] if we want to survive,' says William A. Meyer, the UFCW staffer who's heading up the Las Vegas effort."

Given the fact that unionized retail workers earn $30,000 a year plus benefits, how could Wal-Mart successfully convince their employees that a union is not in their best interests? According to one study, the main reason is employer opposition. When faced with threatened organization, 92 percent of employers hold mandatory captive audience meetings, 78 percent require supervisors to hold one-on-one meetings with employees, 75 percent hire an antiunion consultant, 70 percent send antiunion mailings to employees' homes, and 25 percent fire union activists.[48] Those tactics, including illegal discrimination, are evident in the Wal-Mart case. They illustrate the failure of our labor law to protect workers' rights in the contemporary environment. It is unlikely that legal reform will occur in the foreseeable future. It is also unlikely that the UFCW will make substantial inroads in its efforts to unionize Wal-Mart.

What If the Union Won?

1. Assume the union is certified as the bargaining representative. Does Wal-Mart legally have to enter into a collective bargaining agreement with the union?

2. If the union does not have a right to compel agreement by law (which it does not), what rights does it have? In fact, the union can only present demands to the employer that the employer must consider in good faith.
3. What can the union do to force Wal-Mart to make concessions? Recall that employers have a right to operate their business during a strike and to hire replacement workers. Do you think Wal-Mart would have any problem finding people to work in their stores during a strike? What factors might determine whether Wal-Mart could successfully hire replacements?
4. If Wal-Mart successfully continued to operate their stores, what options would the union have? If the union doesn't get an agreement, what incentive would it have to keep representing employees?
5. Assume that the union in fact did succeed in negotiating a labor agreement at one Wal-Mart store. What would be the effect on the corporation's personnel practices?
6. Do you think the labor laws should force an employer to sign a standardized labor contract if workers voted to have a union? If it did not increase labor costs, why would an employer object to a contractual relationship?

Social Legislation: Retirement, Unemployment, and Labor Standards

During the New Deal, Congress fashioned the major components of our economic safety net. Each program aimed at the macroeconomic objective of stabilizing the economy by providing security against loss of income for working Americans. Incidentally, the programs served a welfare objective of ensuring that significant portions of the population did not suffer financial destitution. The Social Security Act (SSA) created a retirement scheme for the elderly. It also contained provisions dealing with families and individuals in need, but those welfare programs were not funded by the trust fund system. Title III of the SSA established an unemployment insurance system that, again, has no connection with the retirement concept. Last, the Fair Labor Standards Act (FLSA) legislated a "floor on wages and a ceiling on hours" by adopting a minimum wage and a standard workweek of forty hours. Each of those programs is summarized below; the important contemporary policy debates about them are discussed more fully in Chapter 8.

The Social Security Act

Since its inception, Social Security has been a target of political criticism and manipulation. Once voters overwhelmingly endorsed the concept in 1936, Congress began adding to and modifying the basic Social Security provisions. That process resulted in important changes in the structure of Social Security, which in turn affected its economic foundations. In the 1970s and 1980s, Congress undertook significant reforms to strengthen Social Security. Again in the 2000 political campaigns, Social Security was a topic of national contention and will undoubtedly continue to occupy a central place in domestic policy. Without a historical context, however, any public discussion of Social Security tends to be unproductive. The Social Security program is a labyrinthine scheme that embodies two conflicting goals. On the one hand, it attempts to provide a measure of individual equity by basing benefits on a worker's lifetime contributions to the system. But simultaneously, Social Security aims for social adequacy by establishing a minimum level of benefits for all recipients.

After his inauguration in March 1933, Roosevelt commenced swift legislative action to deal with the economic crisis. In June 1934, he created a committee to study economic insecurity, including the problems of the aged. It had gradually become accepted by most of the nation's leaders that a comprehensive federal program of social insurance or public assistance was necessary. This change in philosophy came as a direct result of the evidence of widespread poverty and hardship throughout the country. Ordinary savings and future planning were no longer adequate to protect an individual and provide for his or her economic security.[49]

Roosevelt's Committee on Economic Security prepared a comprehensive analysis of social insurance. It recommended a retirement plan based on three basic principles. First, the plan was to be national in scope and overseen by the federal government. Second, it was to be contributory, with both employers and workers paying into the fund. Third, benefits were to be a matter of right, based on previous earnings. From January through July 1935, the committee's proposals were debated and amended by Congress.[50] On August 14, President Roosevelt signed the bill into law after Congress had overwhelmingly passed it, and almost all the recommendations of the committee were included. The SSA was adopted, to take effect on January 1, 1937.

During the 1936 election campaign, the Republican Party nominated Alfred Landon, governor of Kansas, as its candidate and targeted Social Security as an issue. Republicans described Social Security as communistic and un-American. One employer, to illustrate, placed signs in his factory reading, "You're sentenced to a weekly tax reduction for all of your working life. You'll have to serve the sentence unless you help reverse it November 3."[51] Roosevelt reacted to such tactics by condemning big business and "organized money." Several polls and political commentators predicted that Landon would win the election, but Roosevelt was reelected by an electoral vote of 523 to 8, the largest margin in U.S. history. The public accepted Social Security.

Almost every U.S. worker now participates in the Social Security system; the only exceptions are some public sector employees covered by state pension plans. The SSA was initially conceived as a means to protect the aged workers in our society, but as Social Security evolved, it has become much broader and more inclusive. Currently, Social Security pays benefits not only to retired workers, but also to a deceased retiree's survivors, to disabled workers, to dependent members of the worker's family, and to divorced spouses of qualified recipients, among others. In addition, the Medicare portion of Social Security helps to provide health and hospital insurance for Social Security recipients. Originally presented as a retirement program, Social Security now forms the foundation of the United States' social insurance system.

The first part of Social Security was enacted in 1935 and was designated as old age insurance (OA). Congress amended the act in 1939 to provide coverage for the survivors (S) of deceased workers qualified under the program. The next major modification was the addition in 1956 of coverage for disabled workers (D). Then, in 1965, Congress added the Medicare or health insurance (HI) portion to the act, and the final product is now known as OASDHI. In addition to those specific programs, the act also dealt with other welfare programs such as Aid to Families With Dependent Children (AFDC), Supplemental Security Insurance (SSI), and medical assistance to the needy (Medicaid). The welfare components of Social Security are funded out of general revenues as a joint endeavor with state and local governments and not from the Social Security trust funds. Nevertheless, the administration of the means-tested welfare system is intimately connected with the Social Security bureaucracy.

Entitlements Under Social Security

In order to qualify for Social Security benefits, a worker must earn credits based on work history. Credits are based on quarters of coverage; in 2003, an individual is credited for one quarter of coverage if he or she earned $890 in covered wages during the quarter. (The earning amounts necessary for coverage are increased regularly.) An individual who has earned forty quarters of coverage is deemed to be fully insured for any program under Social Security. Some programs, such as disability, require fewer quarters to qualify. Once a worker is fully insured and meets the other requirements for benefits, such as age 62 for retirement or a disabling condition for disability, Social Security will begin paying cash amounts. In addition to cash payments, Social Security recipients also qualify for certain health insurance programs. The basic Social Security medical program is Medicare (*Medicaid* is a much different program based only on need and not on participation in Social Security); it offers basic health and hospitalization insurance. Medicare Part A is a hospital insurance program and Part B is the medical insurance aspect. Part A is furnished to Social Security recipients as part of the basic package. Part B is an optional feature of Medicare, and in 2002, it cost $54 per month for covered individuals. Medicare does not cover such things as routine checkups, eyeglasses, and prescription drugs.[52]

Financing Mechanisms

Social security was initially conceived as a "pay as you go system" that relied on revenues collected from active workers to pay the benefits for Social Security recipients.

(This feature has important implications for the future of the Social Security program, as explained in Chapter 8.) Congress made substantial changes to the law in 1983, and one change was to begin accumulating reserves to deal with demographic trends in the population. Those reserves, held in a trust fund, are invested in U.S. government securities and will be used to provide Social Security benefits for the large cohort of workers born in the baby boom generation after World War II. Discussions about the solvency of Social Security focus on the point at which trust funds are depleted and cash outlays exceed income.

The Social Security program is funded by means of a payroll tax on workers and employers, each of whom pays equally into the system. The total 2003 tax was 7.65 percent on a taxable wage base of $87,000; altogether, the joint employer–employee contribution is 15.3 percent of the earnings amount. Medicare contributions make up 1.45 percent of the 7.65 percent, but Medicare taxes cover all earnings without any limit. Self-employed persons are liable for the entire amount of the tax. The taxes and the wage base have varied over the years, and both taxes and benefits can be adjusted by congressional action without constitutional or contractual limitation. Benefits are calculated by a formula that takes into account amounts of earnings and years of coverage. The maximum monthly individual retirement payment in 2003 was $1,741.[53]

The Trustees of SSA issue annual reports analyzing the fiscal state of the program, but a great deal of skepticism and cynicism surrounds Social Security. On the one hand, some presently retired individuals are enjoying benefits far in excess of the amounts they paid into the system. For example, a retired chemical engineer in his mid-seventies, who described himself as an "old geezer," calculated that he had received $104,761 in benefits to date; that sum amounted to 193 percent of the total amount he and his employer contributed to Social Security. The old geezer also expected to live at least another decade based on actuarial figures. As he pointed out, everything above his total contribution and reasonable interest was a gift from the generations succeeding him.[54]

After the 1983 payroll tax increases, however, future retirees did not reap the same windfall. One expert testified before the Senate Finance Committee in March 1993 that based on moderate interest rates, "high earning single men who retire today at age 65 cannot expect to get the present value of their taxes back." The rates of return for future retirees, he continued, will be even worse. "For men retiring 35 years from now, the expected return ratio will be less than 50 percent; that is they can expect to get less than half their money back in present value terms."[55] Rather than a mandatory government pension plan to which workers contribute, Social Security thus appears more like a program of taxation that transfers wealth from some citizens into the hands of others.

Quite clearly, the Social Security system poses troubling policy questions about our employment system. The goals of Social Security are sometimes characterized as those of *equity* and *adequacy*. Neither by itself explains the system, and, at bottom, they are irreconcilable with each other. The notion of equity suggests that workers are entitled to the amounts they contribute to Social Security, plus interest. But the idea of adequacy holds that all individuals can expect certain minimal protections from the system; consequently, for example, the nonworking spouse of a retired insured worker qualifies for 50 percent of the working spouse's benefit. One scholar describes Social Security as an "intergenerational compact" that expresses our sense of community and our belief in the future.[56] To the extent that the Social Security compact breaks down, it pits generations of workers against one another. Those issues will be exacerbated in the first several decades of the twenty-first century as the large cohort of post–World War II babies enters retirement.

Unemployment Insurance

During the 1930s, levels of unemployment rose above 25 percent of the work force. After World War II, unemployment stabilized at relatively low levels, fluctuating between approximately 4 and 7 percent in the 1950s and 1960s. Unemployment gradually increased in the 1970s, ranging between 4.9 and 8.5 percent. In the 1980s, it reached its highest postwar levels, climbing above 10 percent nationally in the early part of the decade.[57] Unemployment declined to a low of 5.1 percent during the first Bush administration, but it rose to 7.8 percent before the 1992 elections. When Bill Clinton assumed office, the rate was 7.2 percent; in April 1994, it was 6.4 percent, and economists speculated that continued declines might lead to inflationary wage pressures because of some presumed "natural" level of noninflationary unemployment.[58] That view proved utterly incorrect, however, and through Clinton's presidency, the economy continued to thrive. In late 2000, unemployment stood at approximately 4 percent and inflation was negligible. The rate began to rise in 2001 and continued to climb to 6.4 percent in June 2003. Both the Bush administration and Democratic presidential hopefuls continue to debate policies for job growth.

The Federal–State Relationship

The unemployment insurance system in this country is a joint federal–state undertaking. It was established as part of the Social Security Act of 1935 (Title III), and the cooperative relationship between federal and state administration was the direct result of President Roosevelt's desire that social insurance should be financed through contributions and the states should have responsibility for managing the system. The Committee on Economic Security, which drafted the law, decided that "the federal bill should contain only a few necessary standards, leaving to the states complete freedom as to benefit rates, employee and governmental contributions, and practically everything else that is customarily included in an unemployment compensation law."[59] Consistent with that objective, the federal government adopted certain labor standards in the original law and has enacted others over the years. An example of a standard is the one passed in 1976 to protect pregnant workers, who cannot be denied unemployment benefits solely on the grounds they are pregnant.[60]

At this point, you might consider why a state would voluntarily adopt a system of unemployment insurance. Logically, if the state taxed employers to fund a system of benefits, employers would move to a state that did not have the unemployment insurance tax. How, then, did the federal government persuade states to enact unemployment insurance laws? The answer is that through the Federal Unemployment Tax Act (FUTA), federal government imposes a payroll tax on designated employers. If the employer pays unemployment insurance taxes to the state under an approved program, however, the federal government would waive 90 percent of the employer's tax liability.[61] Moreover, an employer may reduce his or her tax liability to the state by minimizing employee turnover. In short, a state without an unemployment insurance program exposes employers to the full federal tax on the wage base. Employers would therefore move to a state that did have the program.

Characteristics of Unemployment Insurance Programs

Even though states are free to establish their own legislation, unemployment insurance systems have basic common features. Some of the more important characteristics are discussed below.

Coverage. The coverage under FUTA is broad. All employees in industry and commerce are covered if the employer had at least one employee during specified periods. Congress in 1976 required states to provide unemployment insurance benefits for state and local government employees. Altogether, about 97 percent of workers in this country now have some financial protection against temporary layoffs. Persons not covered include independent contractors and the self-employed.

Eligibility. Because unemployment insurance is intended to replace income lost because of separation from work, only those individuals with work experience will be eligible for benefits. Typically, an unemployment insurance claimant must show a specific amount of earnings within a designated period, usually the *base year*. The base year consists of the first four of the last five completed calendar quarters preceding the quarter in which unemployment occurred. The amount of necessary earnings varies from state to state; some states have a relatively high standard of qualification, while others have less.

Disqualifications. Even if a worker satisfies the eligibility requirements, the worker may be disqualified from the receipt of benefits or have the amount of benefits reduced. There are four main grounds for reducing or denying an award. First, the worker must be able to work and available for work. If not, no unemployment insurance benefits are authorized. Second, the worker must not have voluntarily quit work without justification because unemployment insurance is designed for people who are involuntarily out of work. Third, workers discharged for job-related misconduct are not entitled to full benefits. Misconduct may include such offenses as theft, absenteeism, poor performance, insubordination, and the like. Fourth, an unemployment insurance recipient must accept suitable employment when offered, or future benefits will be terminated.

Financing. The unemployment insurance system is financed by means of a payroll tax on employers. The present federal rate is 6.2 percent of a taxable wage base of

$7,000. States are permitted to increase the wage base as appropriate, and some states have relatively high bases. If a state has a qualified unemployment insurance system—as all fifty states do—then employers may claim a credit of 5.4 percent against their federal tax liability. This tax offset mechanism is important because an employer may reduce the amount of tax payable to the state but still claim the full 5.4 percent offset. The federal government uses its 0.8 percent share of the unemployment insurance tax to pay administrative costs of supervision and to provide additional funds for benefits, as in times of high unemployment.[62] In most states, employers pay the entire unemployment insurance tax although states may require employee contributions if they wish; only Alaska, New Jersey, and Pennsylvania currently do so. Taxable wage bases and rates can vary considerably from state to state.[63]

Experience Rating. All states offer incentives to employers to provide stable employment. By means of the experience rating concept, the state reduces the unemployment insurance contribution of an employer depending on the number of unemployment insurance claims against the employer. As a result, some employers have no state tax liability and pay only the residual federal contribution. Note that the experience rating mechanism encourages employers to challenge claims for benefits rather than simply allowing a discharged worker to collect unemployment insurance. Managing unemployment is an important aspect of the human resource function.

Benefits. An individual worker's benefits are calculated according to past earnings. The formula may be a fraction of the worker's total wages, such as one-twenty-fifth of the highest quarter's earnings, or it may be a percentage of the worker's average weekly wage. Regardless of how it is figured, the weekly benefit amount is capped at some maximum amount. In most states, the maximum is set at a part of the state's average weekly wage in selected industries.

The recessionary periods beginning in the early 1980s placed severe strains on the unemployment insurance system. Many workers exhausted their benefits before finding other jobs. The result was that fewer workers actually received benefits. Before 1984, for example, over 40 percent of the unemployed work force received unemployment insurance benefits in an average month. From 1984 to 1989, the proportion was 33 percent. Although that percentage increased in 1990 and again in 1991, it remained low by historical standards.[64] Congress enacted legislation in early 1993 appropriating $4 billion to extend benefits for up to fifty-two weeks, depending on the region of the country. When unemployment rates dropped during the late 1990s, the supplemental benefits ceased to be a political issue. It surfaced once again in early 2003, when Congress voted, at the urging of President George W. Bush, to extend benefits using federal funds for those individuals who had exhausted their state entitlement.[65]

Fair Labor Standards

The Fair Labor Standards Act (FLSA) of 1938 was the last major labor legislation of the New Deal. The law established a floor under wages and a ceiling over hours by fixing a minimum wage for designated workers and requiring the payment of overtime after a specified number of hours of work. The regulation of wages and hours had particular importance for women and children, who suffered severe exploitation in factories during the industrial revolution. The concept of labor standards also incorporated the theme of a *living wage,* which was advocated by social reformers of the time. A prominent Catholic clergyman, for example, proposed in 1906 a minimum wage law, a prohibition on child labor, and an eight-hour workday.[66]

Near the end of the nineteenth century, government commissions and social reform groups investigated the predicament of children and women in work environments.[67] The reformers' initial efforts were aimed at prohibiting child labor, and by 1909, many states had enacted laws regulating the age of employment in factories and limiting the working day for youths under the age of sixteen. Labor activists also achieved success in legislating protections for female workers. The U.S. Supreme Court, in its 1908 decision in *Muller v. Oregon,* upheld state legislation limiting the hours of work for women;[68] that case led other states to adopt similar laws.

Shortly after Roosevelt took office in 1933, Congress adopted minimum wage and maximum hour standards as part of the NIRA. The NIRA required employers and unions to establish codes of fair competition that were to include maximum hours, minimum rates of pay, and the abolition of child labor under age sixteen. According to a leading historian of the period, "By February 1935, there were in effect 517 basic codes and 178 supplements, a total of 695, covering much of American industry and over 22 million workers."[69] The NIRA codes ended with the 1935 Supreme Court decision in *Schechter Poultry Corp.* mentioned earlier. Anticipating the expanded view of the Commerce Clause announced in *Jones & Laughlin Steel,* the Court held in *West Coast Hotel v. Parrish* that the state of Washington could establish minimum wages for women without infringing upon the employer's constitutional freedom of contract. The Court's change of position is reflected in the following quotation: "The Constitution does not speak of freedom of contract. It speaks of liberty and prohibits the deprivation of liberty without due process of law. In prohibiting that deprivation the Constitution does not recognize an absolute and uncontrollable liberty."[70]

Two dominant public policy considerations support the underlying principles of the FLSA. The first is that every person who is ready, willing, and able to work is entitled to at least a minimally adequate standard of living. Second, economic policy suggests that a sound national economy requires reasonable levels of purchasing power among employees and a reasonably stable and healthy workforce. The act is intended to further these objectives, and the basic issues under the FLSA are still pertinent. The minimum wage of $5.15 per hour was set in Clinton's second term and has not been raised since that time. Workers who earn the minimum wage fall below the official poverty guidelines for a family standard of living.

Generally, the FLSA can be described in terms of its coverage, basic standards, exemptions, record keeping, and enforcement. In 1974, Congress extended the minimum wage and overtime provisions to state and local government employees, but the Supreme Court invalidated the new law through an unusual interpretation of the Tenth Amendment. After the Court reversed itself in 1985, Congress again covered that group of public workers.[71] Rather than requiring cash compensation for overtime, however, Congress permitted governmental employers to offer compensatory time off in lieu of wages. Despite the FLSA's broad scope, it specifically exempts many classes of employees and occupations from its provisions.

Coverage

Coverage under the FLSA is quite comprehensive. Congress intended that the law should extend to the furthest reach of its constitutional power under the interstate commerce clause, and the law contains several tests for determining whether a specific employer is covered by the law. The FLSA uses two approaches to determine whether an employee is covered by the act, and either of them can be applied to a given situation. The approaches are individual employee coverage and enterprise coverage. An employee is covered if he or she is engaged either in interstate commerce or in producing goods for transportation in interstate commerce. An example of the former would be a worker employed on a railroad. The latter would include a worker who prepares goods for shipping across state lines. Enterprise coverage, which brings all employees in the enterprise under FLSA coverage, depends on the type of business and on a "dollar volume" test. Some enterprises, such as laundries and nursing homes, are covered because they satisfy a commerce requirement, such as having employees engaged in commerce. Other enterprises must satisfy a dollar test; retail services, to illustrate, must have a yearly gross volume of $500,000.[72] In addition, coverage extends to employees of the states and political subdivisions, but public agencies may provide compensatory time off in lieu of cash payments for overtime.[73]

Exemptions

Because of the political compromises underlying the act, numerous categories of employees are wholly or partially exempt from its provisions. The most significant exclusions pertain to executive, administrative, and professional employees, who are exempt from the minimum wage and maximum hour provisions of the act. Generally, those employees are defined as persons exercising discretion as a manager or on management's behalf or who have advanced, specialized training; the common element in the three categories is a consistent measure of discretion in the performance of job duties. Illustrative employees who are exempt from the overtime pay provisions include employees of motor carriers and air carriers subject to federal regulation, agricultural employees, and salespeople employed by automobile, truck, or farm implement dealers. Hospital employees may be paid overtime on the basis of a two-week period rather than a single workweek. The partial minimum wage exemptions include, among others, learners, apprentices, handicapped persons, and students working in specified employment. In 1996, Congress added an exemption designed to accommodate employers in high technology workplaces; the law exempts computer systems analysts, programmers, and software engineers from overtime standards if they earn at least a specified hourly rate ($27.63).[74]

Minimum Wage Standards

The FLSA establishes a minimum wage that must be paid to all covered, non-exempt workers. The precise amount must be adjusted by congressional action, and it is subject to political exigencies. The figure increased from $0.25 per hour in 1938 to $0.75 in 1955, $1.25 in 1965, and $2.10 in 1975. It was raised to $5.15 effective September 1, 1997, and remains at that level as of 2003. Because the minimum wage is politically volatile, Congress periodically debates whether and when it should be increased. Both the House and the Senate had bills pending in September 2000; they differed on the minimum wage by the amount and timing of the increases.[75] The argument against the minimum wage is that it prices some workers out of the labor market, thereby increasing unemployment. But as a popular book written by journalist Barbara Ehrenreich demonstrated, it is difficult even for one person to survive on minimum wages. (Ehrenreich actually worked at various low-wage jobs and described her experience in a best-selling account.[76]) Many communities and states have taken a proactive approach on this issue and established minimum wages above the federal statute.[77]

Overtime Standards

The FLSA provides that covered, nonexempt employees must be paid one and one-half times their regular hourly rate for hours worked in excess of forty per week, but it does not prohibit employers from assigning overtime work and requiring it as a condition of employment. One issue that arises in this connection involves the definition of a regular rate of pay. The regular rate is generally an employee's weekly earnings divided by the number of hours worked; it does not include discretionary bonuses, holiday pay for time not worked, premium pay for holiday or overtime work, and other similar remuneration. In contrast, remuneration that is guaranteed and is a fixed part of compensation, such as a production bonus or piecework earnings, may be counted as part of the regular rate.

A second important concern under the FLSA has to do with classifying employees as exempt for purposes of the law. In April 2003, the Bush administration proposed a major overhaul of this aspect of the FLSA. The new regulations would change the methods for determining whether an employee falls within certain exempt occupations and outside the requirement of overtime. The justification for the change includes an expanded base of covered employees and a modernization of law more consistent with contemporary organizational realities. According to the Department of Labor news release,

> For the first time since 1975, the Department's proposed regulations would raise the salary threshold—below which workers would automatically qualify for overtime—from $155 a week to $425 a week. This increase of $270 a week would be the largest since Congress passed the FLSA in 1938. The impact of this revision will be to increase the wages of 1.3 million lower-income workers and reduce the number of low-wage salaried workers currently being denied overtime pay.

In addition, the proposal would clarify the job duties that make up exempt types of work and allow employers to more easily "determine overtime entitlement for millions of workers whose status is currently unclear."[78] Organized labor opposes the regulation as a tactic to reclassify employees for purposes of longer working hours without additional compensation.[79]

Working Time

The FLSA also determines which activities constitute time worked and which the employer must therefore compensate. That determination includes activities performed both during working hours and outside the normal working day. For example, compensable time includes meal periods if workers cannot leave their posts or if less than one-half hour in duration, travel time to worksites or out of town, rest periods of less than 20 minutes, on-call time if the employee's liberty is significantly restricted, and changing clothes if required by the work. In contrast, meal times of more than one-half hour and involving no duties, traveling from the work site to home, waiting to check in or out, and changing clothes for personal convenience are all noncompensable. If the employer "suffers or permits" the employee to work, such time will be compensable. As the examples suggest, there are a number of specific situations in which the employee may be entitled to compensation, even though it is not direct productive labor.[80] Recently, the country's largest employer made news when it lost a case involving overtime work. The details are given below.

Working for Nothing? Wal-Mart Employees Win FLSA Suit Against Company

In an important case about working time, a jury in federal district court found that Wal-Mart had forced employees to work overtime without pay over a five-year period.[81] Two former employees in Portland, Oregon, claimed that managers forced them to work a regular shift and then punch out and continue working. Those who failed to do so suffered demotion or termination. One attorney for the plaintiffs observed, "Wal-Mart's smiley-faced logo simply doesn't apply for the company's employees." Wal-Mart representatives, however, insisted that the company had clear policies prohibiting the practice of unpaid overtime and blamed local managers for violating the policy. One executive said, "It's hard to imagine how we could put more emphasis on this issue."

The verdict is important because there are about forty similar suits pending against Wal-Mart in other states. The named plaintiff in the litigation, Carolyn Thiebes, believes the jury's conclusion will set a precedent for other employees and force Wal-Mart to settle those claims. Damages under the Fair

(Continued)

(Continued)

Labor Standards Act are limited to double the amount of back wages due, and no punitive damages can be awarded. In earlier lawsuits, Wal-Mart reportedly paid $50 million to settle a Colorado overtime claim for 69,000 employees in that state. Obviously, FLSA claims can be very costly to an employer.

Why Do It?

1. Given Wal-Mart's focus on low prices (and low labor costs), are there any incentives for managers to violate the rules about overtime? Do you think the penalties under the FLSA are sufficient to deter such managerial behavior?
2. Envision a situation where an employee clocks out and is getting ready to leave when a manager asks the employee to "help out just a minute" with a particular task. What realistic options do you think an employee would have under the circumstances?
3. Wal-Mart executives claimed they could not "put more emphasis" on the problem of forced and uncompensated overtime. Assume the company's CEO directed every store to implement a grievance procedure to deal with the issue. It would guarantee any employee a right to file a grievance over unpaid work, provide for outside arbitration of the claim, and protect against retaliation. Would that work? Wal-Mart and every other company of any significance already has such a process in place to deal with sexual harassment. Why not offer the same thing for wage claims?

Child Labor

The FLSA protects children from "oppressive child labor." The definition of oppressive labor depends upon the nature of the work and the child's age. There are several exemptions from the standard; the most common example is the exemption for children who deliver newspapers to consumers. Other specific occupations have restrictions for children of a certain age. Some hazardous occupations, such as coal mining, cannot employ children under the age of eighteen. There are also occupations with restrictions for children under sixteen and under fourteen. For agricultural work, the law permits some activities as described in Section 13(c) of the act. Congress also provided specific exemptions for apprentices, learners, students, and handicapped workers in Section 14, with respect to both working hours and minimum wages. Congress directed the secretary of labor to promulgate regulations dealing with the matter of child labor.[82]

Record Keeping

The FLSA imposes an obligation on employers to keep adequate records. It is the employer's duty to compile and preserve records showing an employee's hours of work and earnings, in addition to certain other information concerning the individual worker. Records need not be in any specific form, but they must be sufficiently clear to permit inspection. The records must be maintained for a period of three years. Employers are also required to display a poster informing workers of their rights under the FLSA, including the methods of presenting claims and obtaining relief for violations of the law.[83]

Enforcement

There are several methods of enforcing the act. The Wage and Hour Division of the Department of Labor has broad authority to investigate alleged violations of the statute, including the power to issue subpoenas and to conduct hearings. The secretary is empowered to seek injunctive relief in federal courts to restrain future violations of the act and to collect back pay due employees; the employer has no right to a jury trial in such suits. The terms of the injunction are enforced through contempt proceedings. For claims of minimum and overtime wages, both the government and employees individually or collectively may sue the employer. The employer will be entitled to a jury trial if the suit is in federal court. Employees may recover attorney fees and unpaid wages, and on a showing that the employer did not act in good faith, additional damages may be awarded. Civil penalties may also be sought where a defendant has violated child labor laws or engages in repeated or willful violations of the act.[84]

According to a 2002 press release from the Employment Standards Administration, which administers the FLSA, "The U.S. Department of Labor announced [on December 18, 2002] that $175 million in back wages collected for 263,593 workers in FY 2002 is the largest amount collected by the department in 10 years. The Employment Standards Administration's Wage and Hour Division achieved a 33 percent increase over FY 2001 in back wages as well as increases in the number of concluded cases and enforcement hours."[85] As such figures indicate, the FLSA remains an important source of protections for workers. The statute continues to be relevant to today's work environment in several respects, including the safeguards against long work hours and child labor. The principle of wage equity embodied in the minimum wage will remain an issue of policy debate.

The Federal Mandates and the Collective Bargaining Process

With the major components of the modern employment system in place by the end of Roosevelt's second term, the United States entered another period of historical transition—the onset of global conflict triggered by events in Europe and the attack on Pearl Harbor in late 1941. Labor relations during World War II fell under government control through the National War Labor Board (NWLB), as with the War Labor Board in 1917 and 1918. The NWLB, however, had much greater authority than its predecessor, and its influence over industrial policy was both more extensive and more permanent. After the war, unions bargained for increasing real wage gains and an elaborate system of fringe benefits that further contributed to the persistence of private rather than public provision for pensions, health care, leisure time, and other social goods. Almost one-third of U.S. workers belonged to unions at the merger of the AFL and Congress of Industrial Organizations (CIO), and collective bargaining dictated the policies and procedures even in nonunion firms. Large employers like Delta Airlines, Coca-Cola, and many others tracked the wage and benefits packages of union employers, and smaller firms tried to emulate them as well. The next chapter takes up those subjects in greater detail.

Summary

- Collective bargaining legislation in the United States has been closely associated with political developments since the New Deal era. Unions have become extensively involved in politics.
- The Wagner Act marked a radical shift in political direction; that shift is explained in large measure by the unique conditions of the 1930s.
- After the Supreme Court upheld the NLRA in 1937, the new constitutional doctrine permitted a vast expansion of federal power under the Interstate Commerce Clause. The reach of that power continues to attract the Court's attention.
- The Social Security Act began as a program of retirement benefits. It has evolved into the basic platform of our social insurance system.
- Unemployment insurance is a joint federal–state program and offers the only legislative source of income for workers who suffer involuntary unemployment.
- The Fair Labor Standards Act of 1938 sets a floor on wages and a ceiling on hours. The Department of Labor in March 2003 proposed a major revision of the law's coverage.

Further Analysis

1. How did labor's alliance with the Democratic Party come about? Do you think labor's political values are compatible with those of the Republican Party? Then why did many workers vote for Republican Ronald Reagan in 1984 and 1988, despite the AFL-CIO's endorsement of the Democratic candidate?
2. All things considered, do you think that the AFL-CIO should remain neutral in political affairs, as Samuel Gompers advised? What advantages and disadvantages might there be to such a strategy?

3. Why did the Supreme Court change its constitutional views in 1937? What differences in the Railway Labor Act and the National Industrial Recovery Act might explain the Court's treatment of those two statutes?

4. Is the economic justification for the Wagner Act convincing to you? To what extent, if any, is the NLRA incompatible with the idea of a free labor market?

5. Sit-down strikes are now illegal, and workers engaging in them can be immediately discharged and removed from the employer's premises by legal compulsion. Could you make an argument that workers have a property interest in the physical assets of an enterprise equal to that of the employer, and, consequently, sit-downs should be a legitimate weapon of unions?

6. Assume Medicare goes broke in 2020 when outlays exceed income. What strategies should Congress pursue to deal with that problem?

7. Organized labor opposes the Bush proposal to modify the FLSA. Why not simply let employers make employees work any hours the employer deems necessary, with or without overtime pay? Presumably, the labor market would force payment of overtime if workers wanted it. Is there any difference between this argument and the argument that a minimum wage is irrelevant? Does it matter that U.S. workers now spend more hours on the job than any other workers in the industrialized world, including the Japanese?

Suggested Readings

Bernstein, Irving. *A Caring Society: The New Deal, The Worker, and the Great Depression.* Boston: Houghton Mifflin, 1985.

Bernstein, Irving. *The Lean Years: A History of the American Worker, 1920–1933.* Boston: Houghton Mifflin, 1960.

Bernstein, Irving. *The New Deal Collective Bargaining Policy.* Berkeley: University of California Press, 1950.

Bernstein, Irving. *The Turbulent Years: A History of the American Worker, 1933–1941.* Boston: Houghton Mifflin, 1970.

Brody, David. *Workers in Industrial America.* New York: Oxford University Press, 1980.

Lorwin, Lewis, and Arthur Wubnig. *Labor Relations Boards: The Regulation of Collective Bargaining Under the National Industrial Recovery Act.* Washington, DC: Brookings Institution, 1935.

Rehmus, Charles, et al. *The Railway Labor Act at Fifty: Collective Bargaining in the Railroad and Airline Industries.* Washington, DC: National Mediation Board, 1976.

Tomlins, Christopher. *The State and the Unions: Labor Relations, Law, and the Organized Labor Movement in America, 1880–1960.* Cambridge, UK: Cambridge University Press, 1985.

Endnotes

1.   One highly regarded study of the period identifies workplace industrial democracy as the dominant political theme of the era. Joseph McCartin, *Labor's Great War: The Struggle for Industrial Democracy and the Origins of Modern American Labor Relations, 1912–1921* (Chapel Hill: University of North Carolina, 1997).

2. U.S. Department of Labor, *Report of the Secretary of the National War Labor Board to the Secretary of Labor for the Twelve Months Ending May 31, 1919* (Washington, DC: Government Printing Office, 1920). W. Jett Lauck, a labor economist, served as the board secretary and prepared the report.

3. U.S. Department of Labor, Bureau of Labor Statistics, Bulletin No. 287, *National War Labor Board: A History of Its Formation and Activities, Together With Its Awards and the Documents of Importance in the Record of Its Development* (Washington, DC: Government Printing Office, 1922), 32–33. One of the most important WLB awards created a shop committee at war-related industries in Bridgeport, Connecticut. The plan set forth in elaborate detail provisions for the election of representatives, committee procedures, and dispute resolution. The Bridgeport plan served as the model for the board's later representation systems. The plan is described at pp. 37–41.

4. H. M. Gitelman, "Being of Two Minds: American Employers Confront the Labor Problem, 1915–1919," *Labor History* 26 (1984): 206.

5. Valerie Jean Conner, *The National War Labor Board: Stability, Social Justice, and the Voluntary State in World War I* (Chapel Hill: University of North Carolina, 1983).

6. "With an eye focused on the steel strike, the employer group held out for a written guarantee that 'no employer should be required to deal with men or groups of men who are not his employees or chosen by and from among them.'" Connor, *The National War Labor Board*, p. 179.

7. Haggai Hurvitz, "Ideology and Industrial Conflict: President Wilson's First Industrial Conference of October 1919," *Labor History* 18 (1977): 521.

8. Hurvitz, "Ideology and Industrial Conflict," p. 521.

9. Richard B. Freeman, "Spurts in Union Growth: Defining Moments and Social Processes," in *The Defining Moment: The Great Depression and the American Economy in the Twentieth Century*, ed. Michael D. Bordo, Claudia Goldin, and Eugene N. White (Chicago: University of Chicago Press, 1998), Table 8A.2, pp. 291–292; and see also Leo Wolman, *The Growth of American Trade Unions, 1880–1923* (New York: National Bureau of Economic Research, 1924), 33–34.

10. See generally Irving Bernstein, *The Lean Years: A History of the American Worker, 1920–1933* (Boston: Houghton Mifflin, 1960), 83–90.

11. Bernstein, *Lean Years*, pp. 59–63.

12. Kevin Phillips, *The Politics of Rich and Poor: Wealth and the American Electorate in the Reagan Aftermath* (New York: Random House, 1990), 56–57. For a more comprehensive treatment of politics and inequality in the United States, see Kevin Phillips, *Wealth and Democracy: A Political History of the American Rich* (New York: Broadway Books, 2002).

13. Harold James, *The End of Globalization: Lessons From the Great Depression* (Cambridge, MA: Harvard University Press, 2001), 29.

14. The seminal attack on New Deal liberalism is Milton Friedman, *Capitalism and Freedom* (Chicago: University of Chicago, 1961), published during a period of liberal political dominance. Friedman begins his argument by pointing out that New Deal lawmakers wrongly interpreted the causes of the Great Depression. Friedman contends that monetary policy was the most important factor, and, as a result, social legislation is essentially misguided.

15. Irving Bernstein, *A Caring Society: The New Deal, the Worker, and the Great Depression* (Boston: Houghton Mifflin, 1985), 18.

16. See Charles Rehmus, "Evolution of Legislation Affecting Collective Bargaining in the Railroad and Airline Industries," in *The Railway Labor Act at Fifty: Collective Bargaining in the Railroad and Airline Industries* (Washington, DC: National Mediation Board, 1976), 1–22; and also, National Mediation Board, *Administration of the Railway Labor Act by the National Mediation Board, 1934–1970* (Washington, DC: National Mediation Board, 1970), 20–21.

17.   Rehmus, "Evolution of Legislation," pp. 4–7.

18.   The RLA is codified at 45 U.S.C. §§ 151–88 (1988). For an overview of the law, see Frank N. Wilner, "The Railway Labor Act: Why, What, and for How Much Longer?, Part I," *Transportation Practitioners Journal* 55 (1988): 242–287.

19.   Quoted in Rehmus, "Evolution of Legislation," p. 8.

20.   *Texas & New Orleans R. Co. v. Brotherhood of Railway and Steamship Clerks,* 281 U.S. 548 (1930).

21.   For a treatment of the RLA as applied specifically to airlines, see William Thoms and Frank Dooley, *Airline Labor Law: The Railway Labor Act and Aviation After Deregulation* (New York: Quorum Books, 1990), 57–62.

22.   Donald E. Cullen, "Emergency Boards Under the Railway Labor Act," in Rehmus, ed., *Railway Labor Act,* pp. 151–186.

23.   Congress intervened to halt national rail strikes a dozen times between 1968 and 1992. Mike Mills, "Congress Ends Rail Shutdown by Forcing Mediation," *Congressional Quarterly,* June 27, 1992, p. 1870.

24.   Allied Pilots Association Hotline, February 15, 1997. Sovich's speech is archived online at www.alliedpilots.org/Public/Publicrelations/hotline/archive/19970215.html

25.   Bernstein, *Lean Years,* p. 409.

26.   Bernstein, *Lean Years,* p. 413.

27.   Quoted in Arthur Schlesinger, Jr., *The Age of Roosevelt: The Coming of the New Deal* (Boston: Houghton Mifflin, 1958), 102.

28.   For a good contemporary analysis, see Lewis Lorwin and Arthur Wubnig, *Labor Relations Boards: The Regulation of Collective Bargaining Under the National Industrial Recovery Act* (Washington, DC: Brookings Institution, 1935), 26–45.

29.   Irving Bernstein, *The Turbulent Years: A History of the American Worker, 1933–1941* (Boston: Houghton Mifflin, 1970), 40–46.

30.   Lorwin and Wubnig, *Labor Relations Boards,* pp. 89–90.

31.   For a discussion of the point, see Christopher Tomlins, *The State and the Unions: Labor Relations, Law, and the Organized Labor Movement in America, 1880–1960* (Cambridge, UK: Cambridge University Press, 1985), 103–119.

32.   Irving Bernstein, *The New Deal Collective Bargaining Policy* (Berkeley: University of California Press, 1950), 57–60.

33.   Bernstein, *New Deal Collective Bargaining,* pp. 76–83.

34.   National Labor Relations Board, *Legislative History of the National Labor Relations Act, 1935,* vol. 1 (Washington, DC: Government Printing Office, 1985), 1311–1313.

35.   *Legislative History, NLRA,* vol. 1, p. 1315.

36.   Reprinted in *Legislative History, NLRA,* vol. 2, p. 3269.

37.   The testimony presented to the Senate Committee on Education and Labor is reprinted in *Legislative History, NLRA,* vol. 1, pp. 1373–1616, and vol. 2, pp. 1617–2276. See also Kenneth Casebeer, "Clashing Views of the Wagner Act: Leon Keyserling's Files," *Labor's Heritage* 2 (1990): 44–55. Keyserling was a member of Wagner's staff and one of the principle drafters of the NLRA.

38.   Bernstein, *New Deal Collective Bargaining,* pp. 116–121; and see Peter Irons, *The New Deal Lawyers* (Princeton, NJ: Princeton University Press, 1982), 231.

39.   For the original version of the law, see 49 Stat. 449 (1935).

40.   In 2002, overall union density stood at 13.2 percent of the nonagricultural work-force. Public sector union density was 37.5 percent, while the private sector was only 8.5 percent. Bureau of Labor Statistics, http://stats.bls.gov/news.release/union2.nr0.htm. For a good treatment of government employment, see Dale Belman, Morely Gunderson, and Douglas Hyatt, eds., *Public Sector Employment in a Time of Transition* (Madison, WI: Industrial Relations Research Association, 1996).

41. For information about the board, visit www.nlrb.gov/index.html.

42. An informative study on this point is Michael LeRoy, "Do Employee Participation Groups Violate Section 8(a)(2) of the National Labor Relations Act? An Empirical Analysis," in *Nonunion Employee Representation: History, Contemporary Practice, and Policy,* ed. Bruce E. Kaufman and Daphne Gottlieb Taras (Armonk, NY: M. E. Sharpe, 1997), 287–306.

43. See *NLRB v. Transportation Management Corp.,* 426 U.S. 393 (1983).

44. On the rights of strikers, see Patrick Hardin, ed., *The Developing Labor Law: The Board, the Courts, and the National Labor Relations Act,* 3d ed., vol. 2 (Washington, DC: Bureau of National Affairs, 1992), 1087–1127.

45. *Excelsior Underwear, Inc.,* 156 N.L.R.B. 1236 (1966). The rule was upheld in *NLRB v. Wyman-Gordon,* 394 U.S. 759 (1969).

46. Kate Bronfenbrenner and Tom Juravich, "It Takes More Than House Calls: Organizing to Win With a Comprehensive Union-Building Strategy," in *Organizing to Win: New Research on Union Strategies,* ed. Kate Bronfenbrenner, Sheldon Friedman, Richard W. Hurd, Rudolph A. Oswald, and Ronald Seeber (Ithaca, NY: ILR Press, 1998), 19–36.

47. "How Wal-Mart Keeps Unions at Bay," *BusinessWeek,* October 28, 2002, pp. 94–96. Quotations in the case study are from this source.

48. Bronfenbrenner and Juravich, "It Takes More Than House Calls."

49. The background of economic assistance for the elderly is traced in Carolyn Weaver, *The Crisis in Social Security: Economic and Political Origins* (Durham, NC: Duke University Press, 1982), 28–56. Weaver points out that there was little public interest in the subject of retirement security prior to the Great Depression.

50. The legislative background of the act is described by Edmund Witte, who was executive director of the Committee on Economic Security, in his book titled *Development of the Social Security Act* (Madison: University of Wisconsin, 1962).

51. William Manchester, *The Glory and the Dream: A Narrative History of America, 1932–1972* (Boston: Little, Brown, 1974), 143.

52. The federal program is described at www.medicare.gov.

53. For information about the program, including a calculation of individual benefits, begin with the page at www.ssa.gov/understanding.htm.

54. Alvin T. Ehrensing, "Embarrassed by My Greedy Fellow Geezers," *Wall Street Journal,* February 14, 1991, p. A16, col. 4.

55. John B. Shoven, "An Economic Evaluation of Social Security Retirement Benefits," testimony before the United States Senate, Committee on Finance, March 11, 1993 (reprinted in Center for Economic Policy Research Policy Discussion Series, Stanford University).

56. Andrew Achenbaum, *Social Security: Visions and Revisions* (New York: Cambridge University Press, 1986).

57. A book analyzing the historical causes of unemployment in the United States is Richard Vedder and Lowell Gallaway, *Out of Work: Unemployment and Government in Twentieth-Century America* (New York: Homes & Meier, 1993). Their estimates of unemployment by decades for 1900–1990 are listed in Table 1.1, p. 4.

58. David Wessel, "Jobs vs. Inflation: Never an Easy Call," *Wall Street Journal,* May 23, 1994, p. A1, col. 5.

59. Witte, *The Development of the Social Security Act,* p. 125.

60. For a good analysis of the federal–state relationship, see Murray Rubin, *Federal–State Relations in Unemployment Insurance* (Kalamazoo, MI: W. E. Upjohn Institute, 1983).

61. The federal legislation is codified at 26 U.S.C. §§ 3301–3311.

62. The Department of Labor provides basic information on unemployment insurance under FUTA at http://workforcesecurity.doleta.gov/unemploy/taxinfo.asp.

63.   For data on state unemployment insurance taxes, see http://ows.doleta.gov/unemploy/pdf/2001comptax.pdf.

64.   Isaac Shapiro and Marion Nichols, *Far From Fixed: An Analysis of the Unemployment Insurance System* (Washington, DC: Center on Budget and Policy Priorities, 1992), 2–3.

65.   David Rogers, "Senate Passes Jobless-Aid Package," *Wall Street Journal,* January 8, 2003, p. A6, col. 1.

66.   Rudolph Oswald, "Fair Labor Standards," *Federal Policies and Worker Status Since the Thirties,* ed. Joseph Goldberg et al. (Madison, WI: Industrial Relations Research Association, 1976), 108.

67.   For an overview of the historical context, see Willis Nordlund, *The Quest for a Living Wage: The History of the Federal Minimum Wage Program* (Westport, CT: Greenwood Press, 1997); Jonathan Grossman, "Fair Labor Standards Act of 1938: Maximum Struggle for a Minimum Wage," *Monthly Labor Review* (1978) (available online at www.dol.gov/dol/esa/public/minwage/history.htm).

68.   *Muller v. Oregon,* 208 U.S. 412 (1908).

69.   Bernstein, *New Deal Collective Bargaining,* p. 118. Grossman, "Fair Labor Standards," provides further statistics about the NIRA provisions and its incentives for business. He says, "Employers signed more than 2.3 million agreements, covering 16.3 million employees. Signers agreed to a workweek between 35 and 40 hours and a minimum wage of $12 to $15 a week and undertook, with some exceptions, not to employ youths under 16 years of age. Employers who signed the agreement displayed a 'badge of honor,' a blue eagle over the motto 'We do our part.' Patriotic Americans were expected to buy only from 'Blue Eagle' business concerns."

70.   *West Coast Hotel v. Parrish,* 300 U.S. 379 (1937).

71.   The Court's opinions are *National League of Cities v. Usery,* 426 U.S 833 (1976) and *Garcia v. San Antonio Metropolitan Transit Authority,* 469 U.S 528 (1985).

72.   29 U.S.C. § 203(s)(2) (1996).

73.   29 U.S.C § 207(o) (1996).

74.   Exemptions are set forth in Section 13 of the FLSA. Some exemptions apply to both minimum wage and overtime requirements, while others pertain only to the latter. Complete definitions of each category are set forth in 29 Code of Federal Regulations (CFR) §§ 541.1–541.3 (1997).

75.   S. 2284 proposed an increase to $6.15 per hour on April 1, 2001. In the House, a Republican bill proposed increases to $5.81 in April 2001 and $6.15 in 2002 (H.R. 3081).

76.   Barbara Erenreich, *Nickled and Dimed: On Not Getting By in America* (New York: Metropolitan Books, 2001).

77.   The city of Santa Fe, New Mexico, passed a law raising the minimum wage in the city to $8.50 per hour in 2004 and to $10.50 by 2008. Tom McGhee, "Minimum Wage Jumps in Santa Fe," *Denver Post,* March 17, 2003, p. 1C.

78.   "U.S. Department of Labor Proposal Will Secure Overtime for 1.3 Million More Low-Wage Workers," www.dol.gov/opa/media/press/esa/ESA2003146.htm.

79.   Visit the site at www.aflcio.org/issuespolitics/ns03282003a.cfm.

80.   For detailed information about computing overtime pay, see generally 29 CFR Part 5, §§ 548.1–548.502.

81.   "Portland, Ore., Jury Finds Wal-Mart Broke Laws on Overtime," *Oregonian,* December 20, 2002. Quotations in the case study are from this article.

82.   See generally 29 CFR Part 570.

83.   To view the poster, go to www.dol.gov/esa/regs/compliance/posters/flsa.htm.

84.   The penalties are set forth in Section 16 of the act.

85.   For the press release, see www.dol.gov/opa/media/press/esa/ESA2002694.htm.

CHAPTER 5

Rise and Decline of the Labor Movement, 1935–2000

As the previous chapter shows, the National Labor Relations (Wagner) Act (NLRA) represented a profound historical shift in the relations between labor and capital in the United States. That change in dimensions of power provided the impetus for workers to join unions at an unprecedented rate, and even though many employers continued to oppose collective bargaining, labor made key breakthroughs that formed the groundwork for the contemporary labor system. This chapter examines the major events in the rise and decline of organized labor from 1935 to the end of the twentieth century. Over the course of nearly seven decades, unions created and sustained important patterns in labor markets that still persist.[1] The weakening of the collective bargaining system raises serious questions about future directions in our industrial system.

Major gains in union organizing took place under the auspices of the Committee for Industrial Organization, later named the Congress of Industrial Organizations (CIO). In April 1937, the Supreme Court upheld the constitutionality of the Wagner Act, thus ensuring that trade unions enjoyed a legitimate status in our political system. During World War II, the government assumed broad control over the economy and preserved, and in some cases enhanced, the relative strength of unionism. The business community, however, never accepted the prolabor Wagner Act, and after the war, it successfully lobbied Congress for changes in the law. The result was the Taft-Hartley Act of 1947, which dramatically altered the legal environment. After Taft-Hartley, labor continued to thrive for a time, but its

Table 5.1   Overview of Union Growth and Decline

Historical Event	Descriptive Summary	Significance
Formation of the Congress of Industrial Organizations, 1936	Rival of the American Federation of Labor, 1936–1955	Responsible for organizing victories in the steel, auto, and rubber industries
Supreme Court decision in *Jones & Laughlin Steel Corp.*	Court upholds the constitutionality of the National Labor Relations Act	Legal foundation for modern employment legislation
General Motors strike of 1946–1947	United Auto Workers demand right to bargain over strategic managerial decisions	Union concedes its demand in exchange for economic benefits; turning point in modern labor relations
Passage of the Taft-Hartley Act, 1947	Legislation amending the Wagner Act and adding new legal provisions regulating unions	Marks the start of labor's continuing decline; provisions are antiunion in nature
The "Labor Accord," 1950s–1970s	Maturation of union–management relations and collective bargaining; consistent gains in real wages for workers	Creates particular employment patterns in the United States (health insurance, pensions, vacations, other fringe benefits)
Labor Reform Act of 1978	Organized labor's attempt during the Carter administration to modify the National Labor Relations Act, with the objective of facilitating organizing activity	Proposed legislation defeated by Senate filibuster; signals a turning point in labor's contemporary political power and influence

weaknesses had become apparent by the late 1970s. With a Democratic administration and Congress, unions attempted to modify the NLRA in 1977. Labor's failure to achieve a legislative victory marked an acceleration of union membership declines. Table 5.1 summarizes major developments.

Founding of the CIO

John L. Lewis rose to prominence as president of the United Mine Workers of America (UMWA) union. As a member of the American Federation of Labor's (AFL's) executive council, Lewis agitated for the principle of industrial unionism to organize workers in the mass-production industries. The issue of industrial versus craft unionism was debated at the AFL convention in October 1935, and Lewis's proposals to expand organizing activity were defeated. After a heated exchange with William Hutcheson, president of the Carpenters Union, Lewis stormed out of the convention hall. Two days later, Lewis met with eight other labor leaders to form the CIO.[2]

The CIO's major organizing successes occurred in the steel, auto, and rubber industries. In January 1936, workers at the Firestone plant in Akron, Ohio, stopped the production line and began a sit-down strike. Further strikes followed at

Goodrich and Goodyear, and employers in the industry granted important concessions to the Rubberworkers Union.[3] But the most effective of the sit-downs, and the turning point in CIO organizing, was the sit-down strike at the General Motors (GM) plant in Flint, Michigan.

In late 1936, workers at GM's Fisher Body No. 2 seized control of the plant and demanded union recognition. The strike was clearly an unlawful appropriation of the company's property, but state officials decided against removing the strikers by force. For several weeks, workers occupied the premises supported by pickets outside. The strike gradually spread to other GM facilities. Management remained opposed to recognition and bargaining until February 1937, when the union took control of Chevrolet No. 4, a large plant essential to the GM operation. Realizing that sufficient force to remove the strikers would lead to bloodshed and destruction of its property, GM signed a labor contract with Lewis and the CIO in March 1937. Workers did not attain the degree of control over production they demanded, but the CIO leadership was not altogether sympathetic toward the sit-downs. Because rank-and-file members often defied both management and their own union leaders, John L. Lewis repeatedly assured employers that a labor contract was their best protection against shop floor militancy.[4]

Another important victory came in the steel industry. Lewis created the Steel Workers Organizing Committee (SWOC) in June 1936 and named UMWA vice-president Philip Murray as head of the new organization. Through SWOC's infiltration of the company's employee representation plans, Murray persuaded rank-and-file leaders at U.S. Steel to switch their allegiance to the CIO.[5] Murray was so successful that management at U.S. Steel conceded union recognition without a strike. Myron Taylor, chairman of the U.S. Steel board, met with Lewis in January 1937. Two months later, Benjamin Fairless, head of the Carnegie-Illinois subsidiary, signed a labor agreement that one historian calls "the most important single document in the history of the American labor movement."[6] Selected provisions from that document are set forth below.[7]

The Steel Industry's First Contract With the CIO

[The contract between SWOC and Carnegie-Illinois, dated March 17, 1937, was effective for one year. It consisted of thirteen sections and five typed pages. Some of the more important sections are the following:]

SECTION 2—RECOGNITION. The Corporation recognizes the Union as the collective bargaining agency for those employees of the Corporation who are members of the Union. The Corporation recognizes and will not interfere with the right of its employees to become members of the Union. There shall be no discrimination, interference, restraint or coercion by the Corporation or any of its agents against any members because of membership in the Union. The Union agrees not to intimidate or coerce employees into membership and also not to solicit membership on Corporation time or plant property.

(Continued)

(Continued)

SECTION 5—VACATIONS. Each employee, who is a member of the Union, and who, prior to July 1, 1937, was continuously in the service of the Corporation five (5) years or more . . . shall receive one week's vacation with pay, such vacation to be taken in a single period. . . . The total hours of vacation pay will be the average hours worked per week during [the two prior pay periods] but not less than 40 hours nor more than 48 hours.

SECTION 6—SENIORITY. It is understood and agreed, however, that in all cases of promotion or increase, or decrease of forces, the following factors shall be considered, and where factors (b), (c), (d), and (e) are relatively equal, length of continuous service shall govern.

   a. Length of continuous service.
   b. Knowledge, training, ability, skill and efficiency.
   c. Physical fitness.
   d. Family status; number of dependents, etc.
   e. Place of residence.

SECTION 8—MANAGEMENT. The management of the works and the direction of the working forces, including the right to hire, suspend or discharge for proper cause, or transfer, and the right to relieve employees from duty because of lack of work, or for other legitimate reasons, is vested exclusively in the Corporation; Provided that this will not be used for purposes of discrimination against any member of the Union.

More About the Contract

1. The recognition clause only covers union members. Is this consistent with the provisions of Section 9 of the Wagner Act? The clause also prohibits employer discrimination against union members. Is such language necessary in an agreement if the law already protects rights of association? In understanding this clause, it might be helpful to know that the *Jones & Laughlin* decision was issued on April 12, 1937. Does that fact explain the union's strategy here?

2. If you work in a situation where the employer grants vacations, how much vacation do you get? Generally, how much vacation do you think employees should receive? Are vacations now mandated by federal law? Then why do nonunion employees get vacations?

3. In the seniority clause, why did the negotiators agree that seniority would prevail if other factors were "relatively equal"? Do you think the union or the employer insisted on the "relatively equal" language?

4. Regarding the management's rights clause, does it sufficiently protect managerial authority? Why would the union concede all those rights? If management failed to spell out its rights in the contract, would they no longer have them? Then who would run the operation?

Part of Lewis's success in dealing with employers can be attributed to his political support for the Democratic Party and for the Roosevelt administration in particular. Roosevelt's New Deal policies had failed to produce sustained economic recovery by mid-1936, an election year. The Republicans nominated Alf Landon as their presidential candidate, and a Gallup poll taken in July showed that Landon had a majority of electoral college votes. Nevertheless, Roosevelt, with labor's help, defeated Landon by one of the largest margins in our political history, 523 electoral votes to 8. Roosevelt thereafter claimed a mandate for continuing his programs.[8]

Lewis was a powerful and influential ally of the Democratic Party, and he used his political connections to assist the CIO's organizing efforts. According to one analysis, "The role of the state was the determining factor in the General Motors sit-down strike of 1937." If either Frank Murphy, Michigan's governor, or President Roosevelt had used armed force to remove the strikers, GM probably would have prevailed in the struggle. But public officials urged GM executives to recognize the United Auto Workers (UAW), and the GM-UAW agreement in turn led to the U.S. Steel–SWOC contract.[9]

The CIO's momentum slowed after its victory at U.S. Steel. Other smaller steel companies, known as Little Steel, steadfastly refused to deal with Lewis. At the Republic Steel plant in Chicago, SWOC organizers held a rally on Memorial Day (May 30) in 1937. Pickets marched to the plant gates and confronted a squadron of Chicago police. The police fired into the crowd, killing ten men and injuring thirty others. Union appeals to President Roosevelt produced no results; Roosevelt distanced himself from the conflict by declaring, "a plague on both your houses." Temporarily defeated by the Little Steel group, SWOC pursued unfair labor practices through the National Labor Relations Board (NLRB), and several years later, SWOC won contracts with Bethlehem, Republic, and two other Little Steel members. But Lewis's close relationship with the federal government had suffered lasting damage.[10]

The Supreme Court
and the Wagner Act

Between April 1937 and December 1941, the Supreme Court rendered a number of significant decisions interpreting the new labor law. From the *Jones & Laughlin* case establishing the constitutionality of the act up until the creation of the National War Labor Board (NWLB) in 1941, the Court decided many important issues of labor relations. Scholars associated with the critical legal studies movement have examined those cases in terms of power, ideology, and the interests of employers. In an often-cited 1978 article, Karl Klare argued that the Court actually weakened or "deradicalized" the Wagner Act by protecting the legal prerogatives of employers and discouraging worker activism.[11] After the war, according to other commentators, the Taft-Hartley amendments decisively tilted labor law in favor of employers, and the law's proemployer bias continues up to the present time.[12]

The landmark labor decision, and one of the Court's most important opinions in this century, was that of *NLRB v. Jones & Laughlin Steel Co.*[13] In response to a SWOC drive, Jones & Laughlin threatened and discharged in-plant organizers. The union filed charges with the NLRB, and, following a hearing, the agency found the employer guilty of violations of Sections 8(1) and 8(3). On the advice of its attorneys, the company did not contest the unfair labor practice charges themselves; the company's defense before the board was that the Wagner Act itself was unconstitutional. When the board ordered reinstatement of the discharged employees and sought enforcement of the order, Jones & Laughlin successfully argued in the court of appeals that the act was invalid. The Supreme Court reversed.

Upholding the NLRA, the Court said that Congress had constitutional authority to regulate interstate commerce and to pass all laws "necessary and proper" to its control over commerce. Because labor strife disrupts commerce, laws regulating labor relations have a significant connection with commerce. The Jones & Laughlin plant, the Court noted, received shipments of raw materials from various states and Canada, and shipped its finished steel products throughout the country. Consequently, strikes at the Aliquippa plant could burden or affect production at other locations. For that reason, the act had a constitutionally sound basis under the interstate commerce clause. As the Court observed, "It is a familiar principle that acts which directly burden or obstruct interstate or foreign commerce, or its free flow are within reach of the congressional power."

With respect to Jones & Laughlin's rights of liberty and property, the Court held that the NLRA did not arbitrarily deny constitutional protections. The company was free to hire and fire employees as it wished; the law did not "interfere with the normal exercise of the right of the employer to select its employees or to discharge them." But at the same time, employers were not permitted to intimidate or coerce employees in the legitimate exercise of their rights. This distinction effectively overruled previous doctrine holding that any constraint on hiring and firing violated due process principles, and it constituted the first major breakthrough in the employment at will rule.

Importantly, the Court also made clear that the company was under no obligation to enter into a contract with the union. Its only obligation was to *bargain* with the union, not concede to union demands. Thus, the Court preserved the idea of freedom of contract, assuring the employer that relations between it and its employees was a private one in which the government would not interfere. The NLRB would not oversee the bargaining process to guarantee fair contracts for workers. Whatever terms and conditions were agreed upon by the parties would constitute the labor bargain. Thus, even while recognizing workers' rights to bargain with an employer, the Court rejected any suggestion that the state could redress imbalances of power between union and employer.

Following *Jones & Laughlin,* the Court issued other opinions establishing principles that still form core concepts in labor law doctrine. One of them was the *Mackay Radio Company* case of 1938, which allowed employers to temporarily or permanently replace employees engaged in a strike for economic demands with other employees who were willing to work on the employer's terms.[14] The *Mackay Radio Co.* doctrine was debated in Congress in 1992, and Congress rejected a proposed legislative modification of the rule.[15] Other important rulings prohibited sit-down strikes[16] and strikes while a contract was in effect, even if the contract did not include a no-strike clause.[17] On the whole, the cases helped to reinforce the idea that a union's primary functions are to negotiate for wages and govern the activities of workers. Unions thus provide industrial stability by regulating the use of the strike weapon and controlling worker militancy. Unfortunately, the law's tendency to entrench union bureaucracies and suppress employee discontent may actually discourage workers from seeking union representation.

Labor Relations During World War II

The United States entered the war immediately after the Japanese attack on Pearl Harbor on December 7, 1941, and Germany in turn promptly declared war on the United States. President Roosevelt convened a joint labor–management conference on December 17, 1941, and the participants agreed upon three general principles concerning wartime labor relations. First, there were to be no strikes and no lockouts for the duration of the war; second, all disputes would be settled by peaceful means; and third, the president would establish a National War Labor Board. Roosevelt issued an executive order on January 12, 1942, providing for a tripartite board representing labor, management, and the public, which had jurisdiction over all nongovernmental industries and employees. The board's structure consisted of twelve regional offices headed by regional directors and a number of commissions dealing with specific industries such as steel, shipbuilding, trucking, and textiles.[18] Among the NWLB's responsibilities were the adjustment of grievances, wage stabilization, and supervision of collective bargaining relationships.

During its relatively brief existence, the NWLB greatly influenced the course of the U.S. labor movement. With the economic downturn of 1937–1938, the CIO's organizing onslaught ground to a halt. Management regained the offensive in many cases, defeating union drives and taking the upper hand in negotiations. For that reason, CIO leaders in the late 1930s were more concerned with matters of union security than with efforts to expand their membership. But when the government initiated its rearmament program in 1940, demand for labor grew rapidly and Philip Murray, president of the CIO, launched another organizing attack. A wave of strikes during early 1941 led to government intervention in labor relations to maintain production of military equipment. Because of the CIO's ties to the administration, union leadership supported Roosevelt's strategies for mediating labor conflict and discouraging strikes.[19]

Featuring the no-strike policy as its centerpiece, the NWLB forged new doctrines of labor relations. It granted maintenance of membership clauses to the unions that honored the no-strike pledge, thus ensuring union stability and growth. The maintenance of membership clause is a form of union security requiring that any individual who is a union member at a specified point in time agrees to remain a member for the duration of the contract. By granting unions a guaranteed source of membership dues, the NWLB expected in return that union leadership would control rank-and-file discontent, particularly wildcat strikes. Thus, CIO leadership became more aligned with governmental policies, often at the expense of its authority over the rank and file.[20]

At the end of the war, President Truman convened a labor–management conference to ease the transition to a peacetime economy. He informed the conference members that the U.S. public expected labor and management to settle their differences without resort to conflict.[21] Unfortunately, management was determined to recapture prerogatives that it believed had been inappropriately seized by unions under the NWLB's protection. One of the conference subcommittees insisted that "management has functions that cannot be compromised in the public interest." To protect those rights, the subcommittee proposed that "labor must agree that certain specific functions and responsibilities are not subject to collective bargaining."[22] Labor leaders refused to accede to that demand, believing that the partnership between labor, government, and management created during the war should continue. Once President Truman removed wage and price controls in late 1945, a series of strikes began that eventually surpassed even the strike wave of 1919. Among the more important strikes was the UAW-GM dispute, in which Walter Reuther attempted to force the employer to grant a wage increase without increasing prices. Reuther also demanded that the corporation open its books to public scrutiny. After a 113-day strike, Reuther settled for a wage increase only.[23]

The postwar labor turbulence added to growing congressional concern over union power. In the 1946 elections, the Republicans gained control of both houses and cemented the conservative political ideology of the cold war era. The intense, relentless criticism of the Wagner Act culminated in the passage of the Taft-Hartley amendments. In general, Taft-Hartley constituted a direct effort to curtail union rights and to enhance rights of individual union members. Because Republicans dominated Congress, President Truman's opposition to the bill proved futile. Organized labor, for its part, refused to compromise on any significant legislative changes and had to accept the more onerous law.[24]

The Labor Management Relations (Taft-Hartley) Act, 1947

Between 1937 and 1947, opponents of the Wagner Act kept up a sustained political attack against the law. More than two hundred pieces of legislation dealing with labor law were introduced into Congress, and many states adopted laws attempting to regulate and control unions. The antiunion acts were often comprehensive, such as Colorado's 1943 Labor Peace Act, and served as a model for the later federal legislation.[25] Three major arguments were repeatedly made against the Wagner Act and accounted in part for the popular appeal of the legislation. Those arguments can be summarized as follows:[26]

Organized labor had become too powerful. The increases in union membership and the 1945–1946 wave of strikes were a matter of great public concern. Wartime shortages created a tremendous demand for consumer goods; strikes in major industries exacerbated consumers' frustration. Moreover, unions abused their economic weapons, particularly the secondary boycott against neutral employers, to enhance their bargaining leverage. Labor disputes spilled across entire sectors of the economy. With union growth came greater political influence, which was viewed with apprehension by other groups in society.

Unions lacked social responsibility. Given their substantial power, unions failed to protect the rights of individual employees and the interests of the public. Critics argued that bureaucratic unions stifled the voice of their individual members and forced compliance with union objectives. Unions called unnecessary strikes and created labor disruption harmful to other social interests. In all, then, union power appeared threatening to individuals and communities.

The labor law was not equitable. Because the Wagner Act outlawed only employer unfair labor practices, critics claimed that it was biased and unequal. Management likewise attacked the NLRB as prejudiced in favor of unions. Accordingly, proponents of legal change characterized the amendments as balanced and impartial. From this perspective, Taft-Hartley did not disadvantage unions, but merely leveled the playing field of labor relations. The notion of fairness appealed to many moderate voters.

On the day Congress convened in 1947, more than seventeen bills dealing with labor reform were introduced in the House. In April, the Committee on Education and Labor reported favorably on H.R. 3020, the Hartley bill. In its report, the committee stated that industrial strife had at times "brought our country to the brink of general economic paralysis." Comprehensive legislation was needed to define the legitimate rights of labor and management and to protect the public interest. The committee also criticized the negative aspects of the Wagner Act, as illustrated in the text below. Note especially the tone of the committee report.

Legislative History of the Taft-Hartley Act, House
Report No. 245: What's Wrong With Unions

[The following is taken from the official House document that accompanied H.R. 3020.[27] It was prepared by the Committee on Education and Labor.]

For the last 14 years, as a result of labor laws ill-conceived and disastrously executed, the American workingman has been deprived of his dignity as an individual. He has been cajoled, coerced, intimidated, and on many occasions beaten up, in the name of the splendid aims set forth in section 1 of the National Labor Relations Act. His whole economic life has been subject to the complete domination and control of unregulated monopolists. He has on many occasions had to pay them tribute to get a job. He has been forced into labor organizations against his will. At other times when he has desired to join a particular labor organization he has been prevented from doing so and

(Continued)

(Continued)

forced to join another one. He has been compelled to contribute to causes and candidates for public office to which he was opposed. He has been prohibited from expressing his own mind on public issues. He has been denied any voice in arranging the terms of his own employment. He has frequently against his will been called out on strikes which have resulted in wage losses representing years of his savings. In many cases his economic life has been ruled by Communists and other subversive influences. In short, his mind, his soul, and his very life have been subject to a tyranny more despotic than one could think possible in a free country.

The employer's plight has likewise not been happy. He has witnessed the productive efficiency in his plants sink to alarmingly low levels. He has been required to employ or reinstate individuals who have destroyed his property and assaulted other employees. When he has tried to discharge Communists he has been prevented from doing so by a board which called this valid reason for the discharge a mere pretext. He has seen the loyalty of his supervisors undermined by the compulsory unionism imposed upon them by the National Labor Relations Board. He has been required by law to bargain over matters to which it was economically impossible for him to accede, and when he refused to accede has been accused of failing to bargain in good faith. He has been compelled to bargain with the same union that bargains with his competitors and thus to reveal to his competitors the secrets of his business. He has had to stand helplessly by while employees desiring to enter his plant to work have been obstructed by violence, mass picketing, and general rowdyism. He has had to stand mute while irresponsible detractors slandered, abused, and vilified him.

His business on occasions has been virtually brought to a standstill by disputes to which he himself was not a party and in which he himself had no interest. And finally, he has been compelled by the laws of the greatest democratic country in the world—or at least by their administrators—to treat his employees as if they belonged to a different class or caste of society.

This sordid story was unfolded before the committee in its hearings. Those hearings demonstrate the need for action by Congress—and action now.

Evaluating the Attacks

1. With which of the foregoing criticisms of unions would you agree? Why?
2. What is the committee's attitude toward the NLRB? What statements explain that attitude?

3. In what ways, according to the report, have the rights of individuals been sacrificed by the law? Assume you were a member of a work team entitled to bonuses based on productivity. If one of your team members shirked his or her performance, how would you deal with that member? Does that justify coercion against union members who try to cross picket lines? How are the cases different?

4. Consider the case of a union steward who was a member of the Communist Party. Is party membership alone a "valid reason" for discharge, as the report suggests? What might the board have meant by the word "pretext"?

5. Should supervisors have the right to form and join unions, or do they owe a paramount duty of loyalty to the employer?

Taft-Hartley's Major Provisions

Definitions

To protect the employers' right to their supervisors' loyalty, Congress defined *employee* to exclude any individual employed as a supervisor. Supervisors, in turn, were individuals having authority to hire, discipline, and direct employees, to adjust grievances, or to effectively recommend such action in the exercise of their independent judgment. Congress also excluded independent contractors from the definition of employee and defined *professional employees* as persons having specialized learning or skills who are involved in intellectual work that normally requires the use of discretion. Those employees can choose in a representation election to be part of the larger unit or to have separate representation.

Modification of the Board

Congress expanded the board from three to five members to expedite procedures, and it also created the office of General Counsel to deal with unfair labor practices. The General Counsel was appointed by the president and remained independent from the board's authority. By this device, Congress removed the function of prosecuting unfair labor practices from the board's direct control.

Rights of Employees

In an important symbolic change from the Wagner Act, Congress added language to Section 7 clarifying that employees had the right to refrain from all of the activities protected in the provision. Therefore, unless a union security agreement required union membership, employees were guaranteed the right *not* to engage in collective bargaining, concerted activity, or assisting labor organizations. A related and significant change regarding union security was made in Section 8(a)(3). Under the Wagner Act, unions and employers could enter into an agreement requiring union membership as a condition of employment. This device was referred to as the *closed shop*. New language in Section 8(a)(3) specified that union security requirements were effective no sooner than thirty days after the employee commenced employment. Closed shops no longer legally exist in the U.S. workplace, although the term is still sometimes erroneously used to refer to any form of union security.

Union Unfair Labor Practices

As mentioned, one of the major objectives of Taft-Hartley was to equalize the law. Congress therefore added seven prohibitions against union activities considered unlawful. The union unfair labor practices, designated as Sections 8(b)(1) through (6) in the 1947 amendments, are summarized below. Section 8(b)(7), which deals with picketing, was added in 1959, but it is discussed here for the sake of convenience.

Section 8(b)(1) provides that unions cannot restrain or coerce employees in the exercise of Section 7 rights, nor can unions coerce employers in the selection of their representatives for collective bargaining. Unions can, however, prescribe rules for membership in their organization.

Under Section 8(b)(2), unions cannot cause an employer to discriminate against an employee based on union activities, unless that employee fails to comply with a union security arrangement and tender dues to the union. The counterpart to this unfair labor practice is Section 8(a)(3), which forbids employer discrimination to encourage or discourage union activity.

Section 8(b)(3) corresponds to an employer's duty to bargain. Thus, unions have an obligation to bargain collectively with an employer if they represent the employer's employees. Congress also added provisions clarifying the extent of the duty, as discussed below.

Section 8(b)(4) makes it unlawful for unions to engage in secondary activities for certain specified objectives, such as forcing an individual to stop dealing with any other person or forcing an employer to assign work to a particular group of employees. This section also contains provisos to the effect that nothing in the sections makes primary strikes or picketing unlawful, that employees may honor picket lines at another place of business, and that unions can truthfully advise the public that a secondary employer distributes the products produced by the primary employer. The prohibitions against secondary activities were modified by subsequent legislation in 1959.

According to Section 8(b)(5), if a union security clause is in effect, a union may not charge an excessive membership fee. In determining whether a fee is excessive, the board will consider "the practices and customs of labor organizations in the particular industry, and the wages currently paid to the employees affected."

Section 8(b)(6) forbids unions from exacting money from an employer "for services which are not performed or not to be performed." This section was aimed at union featherbedding tactics, but as interpreted by the courts, it does not prohibit unions from negotiating over work preservation clauses. For example, it is permissible for unions to negotiate an agreement whereby workers perform specified jobs, even if the employer may regard the work as unnecessary. In early 2003, musicians struck New York theatres demanding that musical productions hire a specific number of union musicians for each performance; because actors supported the strike, management agreed to grant the demand.[28]

An additional unfair labor practice, Section 8(b)(7), was added to the law in 1959. It prohibits union picketing to force an employer to recognize the union under specified conditions. Those conditions include situations in which the employer has lawfully recognized another union, where a valid election has been held within the past twelve months, and where the picketing union has failed to file an election petition. Similar to Section 8(b)(4), however, unions may picket to advise the public that the employer does not employ members of, or have a contract with, the labor organization.

Employer's Free Speech

In one of the most important changes made by Taft-Hartley, Congress assured employers that they could voice an opinion about unions. Board doctrine on this point was unclear, and Congress eliminated any ambiguity by enacting Section 8(c), which reads as follows: "The expressing of any views, argument, or opinion, or the dissemination thereof, whether in written, printed, graphic or visual form, shall not constitute or be evidence of an unfair labor practice under any of the provisions of this Act, if such expression contains no threat of reprisal or force or promise of benefit."

Duty to Bargain

To facilitate an orderly process of negotiations, Congress added Section 8(d) to the act. It imposes a mutual obligation on employers and unions "to meet at reasonable times and confer in good faith with respect to wages, hours, and other terms and conditions of employment." The obligation, however, "does not compel either party to agree to a proposal or require the making of a concession." Further, the party wishing to terminate a contract must so notify the other party in writing sixty days prior to the contract's expiration date, or sixty days prior to termination, and offer to meet with the other party to negotiate a new contract. The contract must be continued in force for sixty days after the notice or until the contract expires, whichever is later. Further, if a dispute arises, the union must notify the Federal Mediation and Conciliation Service (FMCS) and any applicable state agencies within thirty days. Failure to comply with notice periods may result in the employee's loss of protections under the act. In 1974, Congress added language to Section 8(d) and a new Section 8(g) regulating bargaining in health care institutions. Those amendments generally provide for extended notice periods and require the union to notify the institution at least ten days prior to engaging in a strike.

Representatives and Elections

Congress made substantial changes in the law regarding election procedures. It allowed professional employees to vote on whether they wished to be included in a bargaining unit including nonprofessionals and excluded guards from bargaining units of other employees; guards were permitted to bargain in their own exclusive units. In 9(c)(1), Congress authorized the filing of election petitions by labor organizations seeking certification, by groups of employees seeking union decertification, and by employers presented with a claim by a labor organization to represent the employer's employees. If a valid election was held in a particular unit, no further elections were to be held within twelve months. Striking employees would be permitted to vote in elections for a period of twelve months from the date of the strike. Section 9(f) of Taft-Hartley is a revealing example of the effects of the cold war on labor. That provision, since repealed, stated that no labor organization would be entitled to rights under the act unless officers of the labor organization and the international affiliate had signed an affidavit that the officer was not a member of the Communist Party and did not support any organization advocating the illegal overthrow of the U.S. government.

Preventing Unfair Labor Practices

The statute of limitation period for unfair labor practice charges was fixed by Taft-Hartley at six months from the date of the incident, and the board cannot issue a complaint on a charge filed outside the limits. To address the problem of workers guilty of misconduct being reinstated by the board, Congress specified that "No order of the Board shall require the reinstatement of any individual as an employee who has been suspended or discharged, or the payment to him of any back pay, if such individual was suspended or discharged for cause." Section 10(j) authorized the board to seek an injunction in federal district court to prevent the occurrence of unfair labor practices, and Section 10(1) further details the granting of injunctions in the case of unlawful secondary activity by unions.

Supervisors and "Right to Work"

Two important but unrelated provisions are contained in Sections 14(a) and (b) of the act. Section 14(a) states that nothing shall prohibit a supervisor from joining a union, but employers are not required to "deem individuals defined . . . as supervisors as employees." In short, although supervisors are not legally forbidden from joining a union, the employer can take action—such as discharge—against any supervisor who does so. Section 14(b) is perhaps the most repugnant provision of Taft-Hartley to unionists. It permits states to pass laws forbidding union security arrangements in a contract. To date, twenty-two states are "right to work" states where employees cannot be forced to join the union.

Other Provisions of Taft-Hartley

In addition to the amendments to the National Labor Relations Act, the Taft-Hartley Act contained two other major components; those are Titles II and III, which deal with a range of labor relations matters. The more significant of the provisions are briefly summarized.

In Section 202, Congress established the Federal Mediation and Conciliation Service. Its duties are to mediate labor disputes and to prevent or minimize interruptions in commerce. Generally, the FMCS intervenes in disputes at the mutual request of the employer and the union, but it has no authority to impose settlements in any case. The parties remain free to engage in a strike or lockout if mediation is unsuccessful. In health care institutions, however, mediation is mandatory rather than voluntary; employers and unions "shall participate fully and promptly in such meetings as may be undertaken by the Service for the purpose of aiding in a settlement of the dispute."

To control strikes that might threaten the U.S. economy, Congress adopted legislation in Sections 206 through 210 dealing with national emergencies. This provision authorizes the president to intervene in a labor dispute "affecting an entire industry or a substantial part thereof" if the continued dispute will "imperil the national health or safety." Among other powers, the president may appoint a board of inquiry to report on the dispute, and that board may direct the attorney general to seek an injunction against the strike. Recall that similar procedures exist under the Railway Labor Act (RLA); to avoid duplication, Congress exempted matters arising under the RLA from the Labor Management Relations Act's (LMRA's) coverage.[29] The national emergency provision was not used for many years, but President George W. Bush resurrected it in October 2002 to halt a strike of dock workers on the Pacific coast.[30] His action had the desired effect when the parties reached an agreement a short time later.

Title III of the LMRA deals with federal court jurisdiction in labor matters. Section 301 allows suits for enforcement of collective bargaining agreements to be brought in federal district courts. This provision provided the basis of "duty of fair representation" suits, in which an individual worker jointly sues the employer and the union. In order to prevail under such a theory, the individual must prove two elements: that the employer in fact breached the contract and that the union failed to adequately represent the employee by acting arbitrarily, perfunctorily, discriminatorily, or in bad faith regarding the employee's interests. Although most cases involve grievance and arbitration proceedings, the doctrine is sometimes applied to contract negotiations.[31] Section 303 of Title III permits suits to recover damages resulting from an unlawful secondary boycott. The statute states that any injury arising out of activity unlawful under Section 8(b)(4) entitles the injured person to sue in any district court.

The consequences of the Taft-Hartley amendments were not immediately apparent to organized labor, which continued to gain members and economic power. Unions negotiated key agreements in such basic industries as automobiles, steel, rubber, and other manufacturing concerns. Much of the impetus for particular bargaining strategies came from the oversight of the National War Labor Board, which favored increases in benefits as less inflationary than wage increases. A shift in social attitudes toward greater security after the Great Depression helped to orient both labor and management toward improved benefits. Accordingly, one labor expert noted, "Union attitude shifted from limited interest to strong endorsement."[32]

As a result of union strength and aggressiveness, workers made real gains in wages and economic conditions of employment. The key to their success lay in formalized agreements that incorporated historical industrial relations practices; those agreements could be enforced through a system of private dispute resolution—that is, arbitration—or through the jurisdictional authority conferred on federal courts by Section 310 of the LMRA. To understand the significance of collective negotiation, the process is discussed below in some detail, including the bargaining obligation, the practical aspects of the process, and the usual contents of a collective agreement.

Consolidation of Collective Bargaining and Employment Policies

According to one survey, the overall growth in wages and benefits between 1948 and 1973 increased at an annual rate of 3 percent; but from 1973 to 2000, growth ranged from 0.8 percent to 2 percent, and in some years, benefits actually declined. Benefits as a share of compensation in 1948 made up 5.1 percent of compensation and had risen to 14.1 percent in 1973. They reached a peak level of 18.5 percent of compensation in 1989, but declined to 15.4 percent in 2000.[33] The Bureau of Labor Statistics reported in March 2003 that "in December 2002, employer costs for employee compensation for civilian workers in private industry and State and local government in the United States averaged $23.66 per hour worked. . . . Wages and salaries, which averaged $17.06, accounted for 72.1 percent of these costs, while benefits, which averaged $6.60, accounted for the remaining 27.9 percent."[34] Costs for union employees typically exceed those for nonunion workers by a significant margin.[35] The union wage differential can be explained as an effect of the power that organized workers have when they bargain from a monopoly position by controlling the employer's access to labor. That differential also explains why employers seek to avoid unionization and engage in antiunion strategies.[36] The next section summarizes collective bargaining procedures, the nature of labor contracts, and the typical elements of a negotiated agreement.

A Summary of the Bargaining Obligation

Taft-Hartley more fully addressed the nature and obligations of the collective bargaining process. As noted, Section 8(d) states that the union and the employer have an obligation to meet and to "confer in good faith with respect to wages, hours, and other terms and conditions of employment." The latter term is ambiguous and could be construed to cover almost every dimension of work. That is, any matter affecting the enterprise could be characterized as a condition of employment because it has implications for workers. The Supreme Court, however, has interpreted the language of Section 8(d) to mean that only *mandatory* items are subject to the obligation to negotiate. As a result, the Court's narrow interpretation of the subjects of bargaining means that unions are precluded from exercising an effective voice in many important managerial decisions because unions cannot demand a resolution of those matters.

If a subject is a mandatory one, the employer cannot legally change existing practices without negotiating with the union, and either party can insist on an impasse on its bargaining position. Conversely, if the subject is nonmandatory, or permissive, the party may offer the matter for discussion, but it cannot demand that it be a part of the agreement. The Supreme Court's earliest effort to define the meaning of "wages, hours, and other terms and conditions of employment" was its 1958 decision in the *Borg-Warner* case, in which it set forth the conceptual framework for the mandatory–permissive distinction.[37]

The Court refined the concept of bargaining subjects in a series of cases following *Borg-Warner*. In *Fibreboard Paper Products v. NLRB* (1964),[38] the Court held that the employer's subcontracting out of work was under the circumstances a mandatory subject. In a concurring opinion, Justice Stewart noted that while certain managerial decisions, such as capital investment choices, might "affect" employees, those decisions were nevertheless beyond the scope of labor–management negotiations. Stewart observed, "Nothing the Court holds today should be understood as imposing a duty to bargain collectively regarding such managerial decisions, which lie at the core of entrepreneurial control." That insight is central to the Court's current conception of entrepreneurial rights and collective bargaining duties.

In an important case dealing with plant closures, the Court ruled in *First National Maintenance Corp.* (1981) that the employer had no duty to bargain with the union prior to terminating a part of its operation.[39] The Court distinguished three types of managerial decisions relative to the employment relation, the first two of which were discussed previously. The third type of decision has to do with entrepreneurial interests concerning the scope and direction of the enterprise, such as whether to close down a part of the operation. While those decisions directly affect the employee, the employer's need for "unencumbered decision-making" must be balanced against the requirements of the collective bargaining process. When collective bargaining would further managerial economic decision making, unions can demand bargaining.

In 1991, the board announced a set of principles in *Dubuque Packing Co.* to govern bargaining over relocations and closings.[40] If the employer relocates bargaining unit work in the absence of a change in the basic nature of the operation, then the board presumes the decision was a mandatory subject of bargaining. The employer can rebut the presumption by showing the work at the new location is significantly different than the work at the old plant, that no work from the old plant will be performed at the new one, or that the decision involved a change in the "scope and direction of the enterprise." As an alternative, the employer can prove an affirmative defense based on labor costs. The defense is that labor costs were not a factor in the decision, or even if they were, the union could not have offered cost concessions that would have changed the employer's decision.

Overview of a Bargaining Session

As to actual negotiations, the first bargaining session usually begins with an initial statement by both sides where the parties offer general statements about their respective positions and objectives. Typically, for management, the opening statement is a public relations effort aimed at the rank-and-file members on the union negotiating committee. The union begins by offering a list of proposals for management's consideration. The common understanding is that language, and not economic, items are dealt with first because language items are often easier to resolve. If discussed at the beginning of bargaining, wages could lead to an impasse before anything else is resolved. Moreover, economic items are typically settled in a package offer that the union must accept or reject as a totality—such as a wage increase, an additional holiday, and an improvement in health insurance.

Once the contract proposal is on the table, the parties take up discussion of the respective items. If an item is acceptable, it can be marked "tentatively agreed." The tentative agreement means that if the entire package is finally agreed to and ratified by the union membership, the tentative agreements will become effective. Until agreement is reached on the document itself, none of the tentative agreements are implemented. If a party cannot accept a particular item, it may offer a counterproposal. Parties are not obligated to make a counterproposal on any item; they can merely refuse to agree. Any item on which agreement is not reached is at impasse. The impassed item is set aside and the parties go on to a new item. Eventually, if other outstanding items are agreed to, the impassed issue will be reexamined and possibly resolved. Should the negotiations as a whole reach a point of impasse, the parties are free to exercise economic weapons—a strike or a lockout—against one another.

Language Items in a Labor Agreement

Contract issues not directly involving money have implications for the daily operations of the firm. Managers try to retain as much flexibility and discretion as possible in order to respond to a changing business environment. Unions negotiate for language that will ensure a strong organization with high membership levels and adequate financial resources. Workers value job security and clear rules governing their employment. All parties to the collective bargaining process can benefit from an orderly procedure for resolving disputes about the meaning and enforcement of the contract's terms.

Management Rights

The core of a union–management relationship consists of rights bargained for by the union and agreed to by management. A fundamental rule of the contractual relationship is that any prerogatives not surrendered by the employer in the contract are retained by it.[41] The theory of reserved rights is critical in interpreting the contract's meaning, because any doubts concerning management's authority are resolved in favor of management. It may also place unions at some disadvantage, because they must begin bargaining from a relative imbalance of power. The following statement from an arbitration award concisely summarizes the general rule: "The underlying premise of collective bargaining agreements is that management retains all rights of a common law employer which are not bargained away or limited by the collective bargaining agreement. . . . That is, it is free to set the conditions of employment in any manner it desires without any limitation, except those imposed by law."[42] Among the more basic managerial rights are the power to discipline and discharge workers, set work standards, assign work, determine the size of the workforce, and control methods of operation.

Dispute Resolution Mechanisms

As noted, the general concept of labor agreements is that management exercises any authority not inconsistent with law or contract, unless a union forces explicit concessions from the employer. Those concessions are extracted through a strike or threat of strike. When the employer agrees to provide the specified wages, hours, and conditions of employment, the union promises in return not to engage in a strike or slowdown during the life of the contract. If the union surrenders its only means of coercing the employer, how can it enforce the employer's commitments? The answer is by means of grievance and arbitration, which the U.S. Supreme Court described as the quid pro quo (the "this for that") in exchange for the union's surrendering the strike weapon. Arbitration thus forms the foundation of industrial peace.

Grievances are disputes about the interpretation and application of the contract. If an individual employee believes that the employer has violated the agreement, such as wrongfully disciplining the employee, the employee files a grievance by contacting his or her steward and filling out a grievance form. This document contains a simple statement of the facts and refers to the section of the contract that is at issue. The steward presents the grievance to the supervisor, who grants or denies the grievance. If it is denied, the union proceeds to the next level of supervision. Eventually, the union's international representative and a company official hear the matter. If they disagree, the case is scheduled for arbitration. The arbitration clause sets forth the method of selecting an arbitrator and the arbitrator's authority to hear the case and render a decision. The arbitrator's decision is deemed to be final and binding on the parties.[43]

Arbitration has become increasingly popular as a form of nonjudicial dispute resolution and is used in many fields, such as construction and insurance.

Nonunion employers find it an efficient means of adjusting workplace conflict and avoiding litigation. Because arbitration plays a central role in union–management administration, it offers the prospect of union expansion into workplaces not currently covered under a collective bargaining agreement. The subject is explored in greater detail in Chapter 8.

Union Security

One of the union's most important concerns is maintaining a strong organiza-tion. To do so, it needs dedicated members and adequate financial resources. One method of achieving those goals is to negotiate a contract clause requiring that all employees in the bargaining unit will become members of the union after thirty days of employment, or, if they do not, they will be discharged from employment. The union's right to negotiate for a union shop clause is regulated both by the National Labor Relations Act and by state law. A number of states, known as right to work jurisdictions, outlaw compulsory union membership or fee payments. First, we will consider various union security arrangements and their restrictions and then take up arguments about right to work legislation.

A typical union security clause states that, as a condition of employment, employees hired into the bargaining unit will be required to become union members on their thirty-first day of employment. The reason for the delay between hiring and required union membership is that the Taft-Hartley amendments to the Wagner act prohibited the closed shop, which required union membership as a prerequisite to hiring. Section 8(3) of the Wagner act was modified in Section 8(a)(3) of Taft-Hartley to permit union membership "on or after the thirtieth day" of employment.

Despite references to union membership, the employee's union shop obligation actually amounts only to a payment of money. Section 8(a)(3) contains a proviso prohibiting discrimination against an employee for nonunion membership where the employee was subjected to different terms of membership or if membership "was denied or terminated for reasons other than the failure of the employee to ten-der the periodic dues and the initiation fees uniformly required as a condition of acquiring or retaining membership." The result of the Section 8(a)(3) proviso is that the membership requirement is reduced to a financial core. Unions, in other words, cannot demand that employees comply with such membership rules as an oath of membership or attendance at meetings. More important, unions cannot subject nonmembers to internal disciplinary procedures for violating union rules, particu-larly the rule prohibiting members from crossing picket lines during an authorized strike. Furthermore, the U.S. Supreme Court ruled in *Communications Workers v. Beck* that unions cannot use compulsory dues money to finance political or frater-nal activities as distinct from activities related to bargaining and representation, and employees subject to a union security provision can seek proportional reimburse-ment for any sums expended by the union for the former purposes. [44]

A second type of union security device is known as the *agency shop*. The contract in this case does not refer to union membership, but instead provides that covered employees agree to pay the union a service fee equivalent in amount to the dues obligation. The agency shop concept arose in part as a theoretical alternative to the union shop and in part as labor's practical attempt to circumvent the right to work laws.[45] The law has developed in such a way that the agency shop and the union shop are for practical purposes indistinguishable. Employees' obligations under either form of union security are the same—to pay money, but not to accept all the incidents of union membership. States, moreover, can prohibit the agency shop as well as the union shop.

The final form of union security is the maintenance of membership clause. Such provisions require that if a unit employee is or becomes a union member at a specified point in time or thereafter—which point is usually the effective date of the contract—he or she agrees to remain a member for the duration of the contract. Employees who are not union members at the designated time have no obligation to tender dues to the union. Like the union and agency shops, the maintenance of membership clause actually requires only the payment of dues. When the collective bargaining agreement expires, employees are free to leave the union.[46]

Union security in the construction industry is covered by a specific provision of the NLRA. Section 8(f) stipulates that employers engaged primarily in construction and construction industry unions can enter into *prehire* contracts that include union shop provisions enforceable after a seven-day period of employment. Those contracts are lawful even though the union's majority status has not been established at the time of agreement. The contract may also provide that employees will be hired through referral from the union hiring hall. In order to screen referrals, the union must rely on objective criteria such as training and experience, seniority with an employer in the industry, and area residency. Referrals cannot be based on membership or nonmembership in a union, nor can they be made arbitrarily or capriciously.[47] Table 5.2 summarizes the various forms of union security and their basic features.

Right to Work Laws

State laws prohibiting union security devices originate with Section 14(b) of the Taft-Hartley amendments. Recall that Section 14(b) provides that nothing in the federal labor law shall authorize agreements "requiring membership in a labor organization as a condition of employment" when state law forbids such arrangements. Section 14(b) specifically mentions membership in a labor organization, but for the reasons just explained, union security clauses do not force workers to actually join unions. At present, twenty-two states have enacted right to work laws. One state, Colorado, has a modified right to work law that requires union security be approved in a special referendum election conducted by state officials. Such a clause must be passed by a majority of those in the unit who are eligible to vote, or three-quarters of those actually voting, whichever number is greater. Thus, even if the employer and union agree to a security provision, it will be unlawful without the second election.[48]

Table 5.2 Union Security Provisions

Type of Clause	Language	Comments
Closed shop	Requires employer to hire only union members	Unlawful since 1947 Taft-Hartley amendments
Union shop	Requires membership in union after thirty days of employment as condition of continued employment	Interpreted as obligation to tender dues and fees; membership is financial core; no obligation to contribute to union's political activities; exemption for religious objectors
Agency shop	Requires payment of fee to union as condition of continued employment	Functional equivalent of financial core obligation; can be prohibited under Section 14(b) of the NLRA
Maintenance of membership	Must remain union member for specified period as condition of continued employment Obligation is to tender dues; resignation permitted at end of period; no duty imposed on nonmembers to join or pay dues	Gained widespread use under the National War Labor Board; unions agreed not to strike in exchange for security
Construction industry prehire agreement	Join construction industry union after seven days as condition of continued employment	Permitted under Section 8(f) of the NLRA; allows union and employer to negotiate a prehire agreement before union has majority status

The reasons given in support of right to work laws include reduced labor costs, economic competitiveness, and individual choice. Economic arguments for right to work legislation have proved inconclusive with respect to job creation. Opponents of such laws also point out that in states with low union density, per capita income also tends to be lower, and there is a correlation between high levels of union opposition and low levels of social capital, or effective communal institutions. Proponents of right to work argue that fundamental values of free choice and association are undermined by compulsory unionism, which forces workers to support an organization to gain employment. In any event, the debate is a long-standing one in U.S. labor relations.[49]

Seniority Systems

Seniority is the linchpin of a unionized employee's job rights. Unions insist on seniority as a fair, objective criterion by which to measure an employee's worth to the company and his or her entitlement to various benefits. Seniority may be granted at different organizational levels, such as the department, the plant, or the firm. The most common uses of seniority are in the areas of compensation, promotion, layoffs, and job assignments. Because employees tend to perceive seniority as a matter involving equity, it may serve beneficial managerial ends. At the same time, seniority cuts against unilateral management discretion. Note how those concerns are balanced in specific applications of seniority.

Many contracts provide for wage increases and promotions based on seniority. The underlying idea is that an experienced worker is more valuable than one who has less time on the job. Thus, unions generally prefer that employees advance to better jobs strictly as a matter of seniority. Managers, on the other hand, insist that superior employees be promoted to ensure a qualified, efficient workforce. As a compromise, contracts often specify that promotions will be made on the basis of ability, and where ability is relatively equal, seniority will govern. If a junior employee is selected, the union files a grievance claiming that the seniority provision was violated. Management defends its selection by attempting to show that the junior selectee was the clearly superior candidate—that is, he or she was head and shoulders above the senior candidate. Arbitrators will ordinarily place the burden in such cases on management to prove the junior's superior qualifications.[50]

Another essential feature of seniority is protection against layoffs. A layoff is a cessation from work either on a temporary or on an indefinite basis, and it contemplates that the employee might return at some point to the company's employment. Seniority protects workers by establishing a method to determine both who will be laid off and the order in which workers are to be recalled after layoff. For employers, the primary concern in layoffs is to retain a productive, competent workforce. Contract language may reflect that concern by stipulating that senior employees must have the ability to perform necessary jobs. If a layoff is implemented, junior employees in classifications not scheduled for reduction may be bumped by senior workers in other classifications. Arbitrators hold that when bumping is not explicitly prohibited, "it is almost universally recognized that senior employees, under a plant-wide seniority system, have the right to bump junior employees from their jobs in order to avoid their own layoff, provided they can perform the work of the juniors."[51] Seniority can also benefit employees in cases of work assignment. If a job bid becomes available on a different shift, but does not involve a promotion, the bid is typically awarded according to seniority. Lateral transfers, likewise, may be determined by seniority. Vexing problems of overtime and weekend work may be partly resolved by the seniority principle by offering overtime by order of greater seniority and requiring it by order of less seniority. The procedure is carried through the unit on rotation until every employee has either voluntarily or mandatorily received extra work. Thus, for many daily decisions regarding assignments, seniority is a handy method of distributing work.

It bears emphasizing that even nonunion employers rely on seniority for some purposes. Vacations, pensions, and other valuable benefits are tied to an employee's longevity, and few employers would try to dispense with seniority altogether. Simplistic notions of pay for performance that reject the concept of seniority tend to discount fundamental notions of fairness and loyalty, and managers who condemn seniority as having no value in the modern workplace may overlook the virtues of a neutral, wholly objective standard of distributing awards and the advantages of accumulated training and experience. Indeed, it could be argued that if a manager's subordinates do not improve their performance with length of service, the manager should be terminated. Used properly, seniority offers a means of avoiding arbitrary action and the appearance of favoritism.

Job Security

Global competition in labor markets has brought issues of job security to the forefront in the U.S. workplace, and lack of security is one of the hallmarks of the new employment relations described by contemporary analysts.[52] The economic deterioration of 2002–2003 affected not only blue-collar manufacturing workers, but those employed in services and management as well. Between January and March 2003, the economy lost 525,000 jobs, and over two million since March 2001.[53] Other than unemployment insurance, workers have little protection against job loss. The only significant federal legislation dealing with job security is the Worker Adjustment and Retraining Notification Act (WARN) of 1988, which requires notice to designated parties in the event of a plant closing or mass layoff.[54] WARN does not prevent employers from getting rid of employees, and traditional methods of providing job security such as internal labor markets and psychological contracts are disappearing.

One way to analyze the issue is by comparing different models of job security. The first model is the industrial union model, which applied to blue-collar workers. It consisted of elaborate job descriptions, wages tied to a particular job, and seniority as the key to a worker's rights in getting or keeping the job. While employees had no entitlement to job security in times of economic distress, they expected that personnel decisions would be made according to length of service rather than some other criterion. The salaried model, in contrast, applied largely to white-collar employees. There was greater flexibility in terms of compensation and duties; employees having the same job title, in fact, might receive different pay, and seniority was of less consequence than merit or ability. In return for the employee's loyalty to the firm, the employer tacitly agreed to protect him or her against business fluctuations. In either case, employees had expectations regarding the company's treatment of them during economic downturns. But in the contemporary environment, neither blue- nor white-collar workers can rely on a firm's previous practices.[55] Through labor contracts, employees have several avenues of attaining some degree of job security. Those avenues include restricting the employer's right to assign work to outsiders or to shift it to nonunion workplaces, preventing the sale of the operation unless the collective bargaining agreement is accepted by the new owner, and dealing with relocations and closings. If language is included in the contract, the employer's discretion to shift bargaining unit work is limited by the terms of the agreement. Likewise, contracts may contain a *successors and assigns* clause, which means that a purchaser of the company also agrees to abide by the terms of the existing contract. Without such express limitations, however, workers have little entitlement to protections against loss of work. A purchase of assets during corporate restructuring does not end a previous collective bargaining relationship, but it will force the union to negotiate a new contract.[56]

Bankruptcy is another area that threatens the job security of employees. This technique was put to use most effectively by Frank Lorenzo when he took over Continental Airlines in a leveraged buyout in the early 1980s. After Lorenzo acquired the carrier, he took action to reduce labor costs in order to remain competitive. He declared bankruptcy, unilaterally rejected the collective bargaining agreements negotiated with Continental employees, and asked a bankruptcy court to approve a new organizational plan without the former labor agreement. The bankruptcy judge approved Lorenzo's actions. Organized labor promptly moved to amend the bankruptcy laws, and Congress passed an act in 1984 requiring the debtor or trustee in possession to bargain with the union representative before terminating or altering the labor contract.[57]

Health and Safety

The Occupational Safety and Health (OSH) Act requires employers to furnish a safe and healthy workplace and has elaborate procedures for enforcement that are covered in Chapter 7. Contractual safety and health provisions have several important advantages over the OSH Act both in terms of substantive protections and in effectiveness of enforcement. For example, the contract may establish joint labor–management safety committees with broad authority to deal with safety matters. They meet on a regular basis and have basic responsibility for handling employee complaints, implementing necessary safety measures, and conducting routine evaluations of safety practices. They may also have delegated authority to suspend unsafe operations that pose an immediate hazard to workers.

Contract language can give employees more rights than those available under the OSH Act, and contractual remedies are usually superior to the ones provided by law. An illustration is the employee's right to refuse unsafe work. Under the OSH Act, the employee must make a personal decision whether the job assignment in fact constitutes a condition that is imminently dangerous and will result in serious physical injury or death. If the employee decides that it does, then he or she may risk a refusal to perform the work. If the employer disagrees and fires the employee, he or she files a charge with the Occupational Safety and Health Administration (OSHA) and proceeds through an elaborate system of administrative and judicial determinations that may continue for years. If the employee wins, he or she will be reinstated with back pay less any interim earnings. A system of safety committees and arbitration can supersede any rights available under the OSH Act.

Unpaid Leaves

Employees may want to take a leave without compensation but with the right to return to their job after the specified period. The Family and Medical Leave Act (FMLA) discussed in Chapter 7 superceded rights negotiated by union agreements and established a legal entitlement to certain kinds of leaves. The statutory provisions can be supplemented and expanded by collective bargaining agreements. For example, the contract may allow workers to use allocations of sick leave or vacation as part of an otherwise unpaid leave. In addition, unions typically bargain for

Table 5.3   Elements of Compensation

Goal	Means	Outcome
Alignment	Define content of jobs	Employee equity
Competitiveness	Respond to market conditions	Employer efficiency
Incentives	Evaluation of employees	Employee equity; employer efficiency
Administration	Clear procedures	Employee compliance; employer efficiency

several kinds of unpaid leave not covered by the FMLA. Those leaves might include time off for designated employees for union business, such as attendance at training sessions or union conventions. Unpaid leaves can also be useful if employees wish to pursue further schooling or other training opportunities.

Compensation in a Labor Agreement

Employees may receive remuneration in many forms, including wages, vacations, health insurance, holiday pay, and other kinds of financial benefits. Direct compensation includes a base wage or salary and any additional payments such as bonuses, cost of living adjustments (COLAs), or profit-sharing arrangements. Compensation plans deal with four main areas of employer concern. First, pay practices must have some degree of internal consistency or alignment, so that employee morale is not undermined by arbitrary rewards. Second, because the employer must recruit qualified workers, the pay plan must be competitive with external labor market conditions. Third, pay should be based on the employee's actual or presumed contribution to the firm. Fourth, a pay plan must be administered according to some scheme or system. The overall employer objectives achieved by a pay system are efficiency, equity, and compliance. Table 5.3, drawn from a widely used textbook, summarizes some of those strategic concerns.[58]

Employers and unions have common interests in attaining the objectives of compensation plans, but they may have much different approaches in implementing pay strategies. As a rule, unions presume that seniority is a reliable guide to ability and contribution and that the best pay plan has the least employer discretion. The union's basic strategy—in addition to getting the maximum amount of pay available—is to fashion objective, formalized, and fairly rigid methods of direct compensation. Such an approach leads to conflict with newer compensation strategies that link pay with performance. Indeed, a study advocating the new pay strategies identifies unionism as one of the primary impediments to performance-based compensation. Schuster and Zingheim observe, "As the result of many factors that occurred from 1900 to 1970, the union movement primary among them, U.S. pay programs tend to be based on factors unrelated to the performance of organizations or employees." Among those factors are "how long the employee has been with the organization, what the cost-of-living increase is over the last year, what other employees in the organization are paid, what other organizations are doing under similar circumstances, or what the value of the job is in terms of how many people the job supervises or how 'clean' or 'dirty' the job is to perform."[59] The quotation accurately describes the union view of wages. How unions negotiate for agreements based on those criteria is discussed next.

Job Classifications

Many union contracts contain an appendix that sets forth the jobs available in the bargaining unit and the wages attached to the jobs. The framework emphasizes job content rather than the person holding the job, and unions try to increase the amounts tied to the classification. Generally, unions request wage increases either as a percentage of compensation (e.g., 5 percent) or as an across-the-board increment to the hourly rate (e.g., $0.55 per hour). The latter method tends to flatten pay differentials among classifications. In important contrast to the flexibility of the new pay conceptions, labor agreements assume that individuals qualified for a job will perform the job adequately. Thus, pay goes with the position, not with the individual. The classification may also be linked to seniority, as when, for example, a worker moves to a higher classification after a specified term of service.

Cost-of-Living Adjustment Clauses

In addition to lump sum job classification payments, the contract may also provide for pay increments based on increases in the Consumer Price Index (CPI). The CPI is a measure of price increases in the economy compiled by the Department of Labor. By comparing the cost of certain items in a shopping basket of goods over time, the CPI accurately reflects inflationary pressures in the economy. The CPI is further broken down into an index for wage earners, the CPI-W, and an index for urban areas, the CPI-U. Typical formulas might call for a one-cent increase in hourly rates for every 0.3- or 0.4-point increase in the CPI. Rates may be adjusted quarterly or annually. As a further limitation, the clause may specify that no benefits are payable until the CPI increases by a set amount. According to a Bureau of National Affairs pattern contract survey, the frequency of COLA clauses declined from 48 percent of contracts in 1983 to 34 percent in 1992. The moderate inflation rate from the late 1980s into the 2000s reduced the attractiveness of COLA clauses for unions as a bargaining item; the corresponding increases in health care insurance pose a much more difficult problem for employers and employees alike.

Bonuses

An employer may wish to provide some productivity incentives for workers or inducements to sign a labor agreement. The incentives could be calculated as a profit- or gain-sharing arrangement, a payment-based percentage of the base wage, payment linked to seniority, or a flat lump sum amount. Unions may be reluctant to accept wages contingent upon factors not entirely under workers' control, but bonuses may be more acceptable. Consider the following alternative proposals made as part of a wage package in a manufacturing facility: (1) Upon ratification of the contract, the employer offers to pay current employees a bonus equal to one

Table 5.4   Benefits as Percentage of Overall Compensation, 2002

Item	Percentage
Benefits mandated by law (Social Security, workers' compensation insurance, etc.)	7.9
Insurance benefits (life, health)	7.1
Paid leaves (vacations, holidays, sick leave, etc.)	6.8
Retirement and savings programs	3.5
Supplemental pay (premium, shift differentials)	2.4

percent of their previous year's gross earnings. (2) The employer agrees to pay a $400 bonus to all bargaining unit employees on the first pay date after contract ratification. Think about the equities of these two approaches and which one would most likely be preferred by a majority of unit employees, by the union leadership, and by the employer. Note also the advantage to the employer of paying a one-time bonus as against an increase in the classification rate.

Two-Tier Wage Systems

Nonunion employers may vary pay according to their inclinations and objectives. Because union wage classifications pay jobs, not individuals, they offer less flexibility to address needs for labor cost savings. A solution to that dilemma is to pay workers hired after a certain date at a lower wage than the wage paid to current employees for the same job. The employer gains several advantages by this technique. First, the two-tier system lowers direct wage costs beginning with any new hires. In addition, it decreases overall labor costs associated with fringe benefits calculated by the wage base, such as vacations, holidays, premium pay, and other benefits. One disadvantage of the two-tier system is the conflict it creates between new workers and more senior employees who enjoy the higher rate. During the concessionary era of the 1980s, some unions acquiesced in the two-tier system rather than accepting wage cuts across the workforce. But a dual-wage structure conflicts with basic union principles of equality and may be accepted only as a strategy of last resort.[60]

Fringe Benefits

The attachment of various fringe benefits to the employment relationship is extremely important in this country. Health insurance, for example, has traditionally been linked with employment. But other benefits, such as pensions, life insurance, and many other items are also associated with work. According to the Bureau of Labor Statistics, total compensation costs for the civilian workforce in 2002 amounted to $23.66 per hour. Benefits made up 27.9 percent of the total, or $6.60. Table 5.4 lists the benefits and percentages of distribution in the total package.[61] As we proceed, note which benefits seem most attractive to employees and what reasons might account for those preferences. Chapter 8 pursues some of the policy implications of health care and retirement.

Health Insurance

On November 19, 1945, President Harry Truman proposed to nationalize the medical system in the United States. He stated in his address to Congress, "We should all resolve now that the health of this nation is a national concern; that financial barriers in the way of attaining health shall be removed; that the health of all of its citizens deserves the help of all the Nation."[62] Truman's call for legislation failed. In the 1992 election, President Bill Clinton campaigned on a program of health care reform. The Clinton model was based on a payroll tax, a network of regional health alliances, and extensive reliance on Health Maintenance Organizations (HMOs) as providers.[63] President Clinton presented his proposed legislation to Congress in November 1993. That legislation, titled the "Health Security Act of 1993," consisted of eleven separate titles and 1,368 pages of text.[64] Only a year later, Americans had decisively rejected Clinton's plan.

In early 2003, the national media warned that the health care system faced a crisis of affordability and accessibility.[65] Contributing factors included pressures generated on the system by the federal government in the form of Medicare and Medicaid. A second was the rising of health care costs. Third, increasingly expensive technology permitted the medical system to prolong the lives of critically ill patients and imposed new costs on the providers. The result was an escalation of health insurance premiums that reached an average rate of 18 percent in 1989 compared with a general inflation rate of around 7 percent. Costs began to moderate and fell to less than 1 percent in 1996. Thereafter, they began to rise and stood at 12.7 percent in 2002, compared with an overall inflation rate of less than 2 percent.[66]

Clearly, health care poses a difficult problem for unions and employers. In one bargaining situation, for example, transit workers in Denver threatened to strike over the issue of health care costs. The employer proposed to pass all increased costs of care on to the employees, but the union insisted that the employer maintain the previous levels of insurance. The parties compromised on a labor agreement that froze wages for the three-year term of the contract and capped the employer's contribution to health insurance at $436 per month. Workers obviously valued continued health coverage more highly than an actual increase in wages.[67]

Pensions

As noted, employers are not required to provide retirement programs for employees. Should they choose to do so, employees may receive tax-deferred compensation, or income that is not taxed until the pension plan begins to pay out benefits. Employers also receive favorable tax treatment for their contributions. A popular kind of retirement plan known as the 401(k) takes its name from the section of the Internal Revenue Code that specifies the tax consequences of the plan. Pensions offer an incentive for savings programs associated with employment, and because they involve matters of taxation, the federal government may monitor their administration.

The two major types of pensions are the *defined benefit* and *defined contribution* plans. In the former type, the amount of benefits is calculated as the fixed amount of income based on the employee's earnings and years of service. The defined contribution plan places the risk of investment on the employee; if the investment fund performs poorly, the employee will have less money available at retirement. The defined contribution plan became more popular during the 1980s. One reason is that it is more portable than the defined benefits plan. Therefore, it is attractive to a relatively young and mobile workforce. The disadvantage is that poor investment performance will severely influence retirement income. The major statutory treatment of retirement plans, the Employee Retirement Income Security Act (ERISA), came into existence in 1973. It is discussed in Chapter 7.

Holidays and Vacations

Many employers offer paid holiday and vacation benefits even though they are not required to do so by law. According to the Bureau of Labor Statistics, "Paid time off continued to be the most prevalent benefit available to workers in private establishments in 2000. Paid vacations were available to 80 percent of employees and paid holidays to 77 percent of employees in private industry."[68] Common holidays are Christmas, New Years, Memorial Day, July 4th, Thanksgiving, and Labor Day. Additional days may include certain religious days, Martin Luther King Jr. Day, the employee's birthday, or floating holidays taken at the employee's option. To control absenteeism, contracts often specify that the employee must work the day before and after a scheduled holiday in order to receive holiday pay or present a valid reason for absence.

Most employers offer vacations as a reward for length of service. Generally, employees are given one week of paid vacation time after one year of employment. At some point, usually between three and eight years, the employee earns additional vacation benefits. A fourth week is typically granted after ten or twelve years of employment. Some employers continue to increase the benefit by adding fifth and sixth weeks. If an employee fails to take his or her vacation, the employer may offer various options, such as allowing vacation to accumulate or paying the employee a lump sum in compensation for accrued time. Another alternative is to require employees to use vacation time or to forfeit their entitlement. Those options will be specified in a union agreement; in the nonunion setting, the employer's policy handbook sets out the rules for vacations.

Sick Leave

Sick leave benefits supplement workers' compensation insurance by protecting the employee against temporary illness or injury that did not occur as a result of employment. If an employee suffers an attack of appendicitis, for example, and is hospitalized for several days, the company's sick leave program compensates for lost wages during that time. Sick leave programs, however, present unique problems. Some plans allow accumulation of sick leave and apply it to family leave situations under the Family and Medical Leave Act. Workers who take time off for domestic reasons may cause resentment among healthy, unmarried employees who do not use their allotment. Indeed, the healthy employee may be encouraged to use his or her sick leave in place of vacation. This problem can be alleviated by cash compensation for unused benefits or by allowing accumulation of both sick leave and vacation time. Regardless of the policies, administration of sick leave benefits is not as simple as vacation benefits.

Other Paid Time Off

A number of labor contracts and nonunion employment policies provide compensation for such eventualities as funeral leave or jury duty. Funeral (or bereavement) leave is pay for time lost due to a death in the immediate family, as defined in the policy. A similar benefit is parental leave, used on the occasion of birth or adoption. All policies are limited in duration. Under the 1992 FMLA legislation, employers of more than a specified number of employees are required to grant a period of time off to new parents, but they are not required to pay compensation for the leave. In other industrialized countries, parental leave with pay is common.

Uniforms, Tools, and Other Expenses

Employer policies or federal regulations may require certain clothing and equipment to be worn in the workplace. For example, police departments specify the type of uniforms worn by officers and OSHA mandates the use of safety shoes in construction projects. Who pays for such expenditures? Although OSHA requires certain protective clothing, it does not oblige the employer to pay for it. The same issue arises in the context of special tools or equipment. For a carpenter, machinist, or mechanic, some tools might be furnished by the worker and some by the employer. Custom in the industry may answer part of the problem, but the contract also may contain specific provisions about who is responsible for the purchase and maintenance of equipment. Express contract language protects workers from making an investment in expensive equipment that more appropriately should be furnished by the employer.[69]

To summarize, unions imposed substantial costs on employers through negotiated packages of wages and fringe benefits. Their success in doing so had two important consequences. First, the threat of unionization convinced many large nonunion employers to offer comparable compensation in order to deflect unionization. Second, as labor costs escalated in the late 1970s, employers reacted with various containment strategies. If collective bargaining was a cause of higher wages, then union avoidance or eradication was the cure. The economic conditions of the 1980s proved conducive to a program of labor cost retrenchment, the first prong of which focused on collective bargaining relationships.

Union Decline: 1970s to the Millennium

For nearly three decades after Taft-Hartley, labor relations achieved a level of maturity and stability sometimes characterized as the labor accord. Its main components included a relative balance of power, mutual acceptance of conflicting interests, and compensation gains offset by rising productivity and profits. So long as the system remained in balance, unions and employers could negotiate agreements that provided mutual satisfaction. The accord, as one study summarizes, represented "a program for orderly industrial government and for avoiding class confrontations." Negotiated labor agreements were supported by both political parties, and "many of the most important corporate leaders supported reliance on collective bargaining, 'responsible' unionism, and the integration of the union movement into the legitimized institutional structure of American society as means for achieving industrial and class peace."[70] Beginning in the early 1970s, economic conditions led to a much less favorable environment for bargaining.

A number of adverse developments combined to erode the status quo of unionism. An important factor was the decline of productivity during the period, particularly between the union and nonunion sectors. High rates of inflation forced employers to seek labor cost savings, which were much more easily realized in the nonunion setting. As unemployment rose during the 1980s, unions lost substantial bargaining power. Employment tended to shift out of manufacturing, a union stronghold, and into services, where unions had less organizing success. The business transformations during the time—consolidation, takeover, bankruptcy, and relocation—all tended to undermine the pattern of negotiated increases in compensation.[71]

Employer Strategies and Union Density

One of the most obvious features of the new environment was the rapid growth of employer antiunion strategies. A number of studies argue that the single most important factor in union decline in the 1980s was employer hostility to unions.[72] Organized labor was aware of those problems by the late 1970s and attempted a legislative solution to alleviate the perceived shortcomings of the National Labor Relations Act. Politically, the moment appeared propitious for reform, as Congress was heavily Democratic and President Jimmy Carter indicated his support for a bill. Accordingly, labor supporters introduced legislation in 1977 called the Labor Reform Act.

Backers of the law defined it as a procedural change in the law designed to level the playing field so that employers had less opportunity to defeat organizing drives. Its main elements are summarized below, with an explanation of the purpose of the change. The bill proposed to do the following:

- Expand the board from five to seven members. This change was intended to facilitate decision making and expedite rulings on important points of law.

- Fix a mandatory campaign period not to exceed thirty days. Union organizers believed—and research supports their belief—that a delay between the filing of a petition and the election worked to the advantage of employers.
- Penalize employers who discriminated against union supporters during an organizing drive by requiring double back pay. This provision would have discouraged retaliation against union supporters. Research shows that workers generally respond to such actions by withdrawing their support for the union.
- Authorize the board to draft and implement a collective bargaining contract if the employer violated its duty to bargain in negotiations for a first agreement. Because employers often undermined the union by bad faith bargaining, and thus avoided a contract, the bill permitted the board to impose an agreement based on specified factors such as industry wage increases and similar objective criteria.
- Permit union organizers to give a rebuttal (on the employer's property) to the employer's captive audience speech. Under Section 8(c) of Taft-Hartley, employers had a right to state their views about unions if they did so without threats or promises. The reform legislation allowed unions access to employees to counteract the speech.
- Require the board to seek injunctive relief for specified unfair labor practice charges. If employers could engage in unlawful discharges, for example, and the remedy was reinstatement at some time in the future, workers might be discouraged from exercising their rights. To correct that problem, the bill utilized injunctions against that activity.

The Labor Reform Act passed the House of Representatives by a sizeable margin. When it arrived in the Senate, however, senators sympathetic to business interests mounted a filibuster against the legislation. After a number of cloture votes, the AFL-CIO conceded defeat for the legislation. That moment marked a pivotal event in the modern labor movement's political effectiveness. Labor tried for reform in 1992 under the Clinton administration when Democrats once again controlled Congress, but with smaller margins than in 1978. Labor introduced the Caesar Chavez Workplace Fairness Act to restrict an employer's right to hire permanent replacements in the event of a strike. The legislation was based on similar laws in Canada, which require employers to justify by economic necessity the hiring of permanent rather than temporary replacements. Even this relatively minor adjustment to the labor law proved unacceptable to business interests, however, and Senate Republicans again mounted a filibuster. The result was the same as for the Labor Reform Act, and the striker replacement bill was killed without a floor vote.[73]

Altogether, the antiunion offensive of the 1980s was as successful as that of the 1920s. Figure 5.1 shows levels of union membership at five-year intervals since 1955. By 2002, membership was 13.2 percent of the nonagricultural workforce and showed few signs of resurgence.[74]

As is obvious, the decline of union membership has been steep and inexorable. What, if anything, should be done legislatively to improve labor's prospects is discussed in Chapter 8.

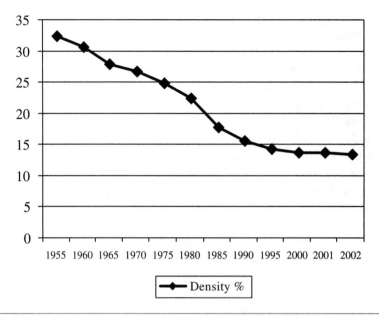

Figure 5.1   Union Membership Density, 1955–2002

Conclusion

This chapter traces the rise and decline of unionism in the United States. Collective bargaining is inextricably linked with the patterns of compensation and employment practices that persist in today's environment. Unlike in other countries, many aspects of social welfare in the United States—retirement, health insurance, and other protections against risk—attach to employment relationships. The explanation for that phenomenon lies in the ascendancy of collective bargaining after World War II and the impact on labor markets. As those benefits begin to disappear from employment, it is unlikely—and considering the history of American exceptionalism, politically impractical—to substitute government legislation for the failures of private dealing. One deviation from that pattern emerges when conditions make it so onerous for employers to continue a particular practice that they cooperate with labor and politicians to create legislation addressing the problem. That point proved true with workers' compensation programs in the 1920s, and future events could create a favorable environment for other changes. Chapter 8 takes up the matter in greater detail.

Summary

- Collective bargaining legislation in the United States has been closely associated with political developments since the New Deal era. Unions have become extensively involved in politics.
- The Wagner Act marked a radical shift in political direction; that shift is explained in large measure by the unique conditions of the 1930s.

- After the Supreme Court upheld the NLRA in 1937, management marshaled its political strength to change the law in the 1947 Taft-Hartley amendments. Those changes were to the advantage of employers.
- When organized labor tried in 1977–1978 to amend the labor law to make organizing easier, business mobilized to defeat the proposed legislation. That defeat was a significant blow to the labor movement.
- Labor's decline continues unabated. The causes of decline are a subject of scholarly interest because of the labor movement's role in economic policy.

Further Analysis

1. How did labor's alliance with the Democratic Party come about? Do you think labor's political values are more compatible with those of the Republican Party? Why did many workers vote for Republican Ronald Reagan in 1984, despite the AFL-CIO's endorsement of the Democratic candidate, Walter Mondale? More recently, the Carpenters Union expressed its support for the economic policies of George W. Bush at a rally on Labor Day, 2002. Are carpenters historically among the skilled craft workers who tended to be politically conservative?

2. All things considered, do you think that the AFL-CIO should remain neutral in political affairs? What advantages and disadvantages might there be to such a strategy?

3. Why did the Supreme Court change its constitutional views in 1937? What differences in the Railway Labor Act and the National Industrial Recovery Act might explain the Court's treatment of those two statutes?

4. Is the economic justification for the Wagner Act convincing to you? To what extent, if any, is the NLRA incompatible with the idea of a free labor market? If Congress were considering a national law prohibiting compulsory union membership, what arguments might be made against the proposal?

5. Review the provisions of Taft-Hartley. Which do you think are most detrimental to unions? When President George W. Bush exercised his legal right to intervene in the dockworkers' strike of 2002, did that decision benefit labor or management or both equally?

6. In January 2003, a national right to work bill prohibiting compulsory union membership or dues payment was introduced into the House. If states can already enact such legislation, why should the federal government become involved? Should the federal government repeal Section 14(b) of the NLRA and abolish the idea of right to work?

7. Was the government's method of dealing with labor during the war an effective one? Would it be a good idea to establish an Industrial Labor Board like the National War Labor Board to oversee workplace relations? If the notion of such excessive governmental regulation is repugnant to you, consider the legislation now in effect giving workers various rights and protections in employment. Why not channel all matters arising out of employment into one single agency?

8. The Labor Reform Act was defeated by a Senate filibuster. Is the device of a filibuster consistent with fundamental notions of democracy? If Congress is so concerned about the manipulation of elections by union bosses, why does it have rules allowing a minority to control the political will of this country? If the filibuster against the Labor Reform Act was a courageous act based on commitment to important principles, can the same thing be said about the Democratic filibusters against the Bush administration's judicial nominees in 2003?

9. What arguments can be made for and against legislation dealing with the replacement of strikers? If employers were not permitted to hire more workers, how would they operate their business? What might be the result if workers had the power to close down an operation? If unions in fact had such power, do you think union members would be more, or less, likely to vote for a strike?

Suggested Readings

Atleson, James. *Labor and the Wartime State: Labor Relations and Law During World War II.* Urbana: University of Illinois Press, 1998.

Bennett, James, and Bruce E. Kaufman, eds. *The Future of Private Sector Unionism in the United States.* Armonk, NY: M. E. Sharpe, 2002.

Bernstein, Irving. *The Lean Years: A History of the American Worker, 1920–1933.* Boston: Houghton Mifflin, 1960.

Bernstein, Irving. *The New Deal Collective Bargaining Policy.* Berkeley: University of California Press, 1950.

Bernstein, Irving. *The Turbulent Years: A History of the American Worker, 1933–1941.* Boston: Houghton Mifflin, 1970.

Brody, David. *Workers in Industrial America.* New York: Oxford University Press, 1980.

Clark, Paul F., John T. Delaney, and Ann C. Frost, eds. *Collective Bargaining in the Private Sector.* Champaign, IL: Industrial Relations Research Association, 2002.

Dubofsky, Melvyn. *The State and Labor in Modern America.* Chapel Hill: University of North Carolina, 1994.

Dubofsky, Melvyn, and Warren Van Tine, eds. *Labor Leaders in America.* Urbana: University of Illinois, 1987.

Goldfield, Michael. *The Decline of Organized Labor in the United States.* Chicago: University of Chicago Press, 1987.

Kaufman, Bruce E., and Roy B. Helfgott, eds. *Industrial Relations to Human Resources and Beyond: The Evolving Process of Employee Relations Management.* Armonk, NY: M. E. Sharpe, 2003.

Kochan, Thomas A., Harry C. Katz, and Robert B. McKersie, *The Transformation of American Industrial Relations.* New York: Basic Books, 1986.

Lichtenstein, Nelson. *Labor's War at Home: The CIO in World War II.* Cambridge, UK: Cambridge University Press, 1982.

Tomlins, Christopher. *The State and the Unions: Labor Relations, Law, and the Organized Labor Movement in America, 1880–1960.* Cambridge, UK: Cambridge University Press, 1985.

Wheeler, Hoyt. *The Future of the American Labor Movement.* Cambridge, UK: Cambridge University Press, 2002.

Endnotes

1. In a fine study of labor's role in social policy, one scholar describes the private sector union–management system of fringe benefits as the "shadow welfare state." Marie Gottschalk, *The Shadow Welfare State: Labor, Business, and the Politics of Health Care in the United States* (Ithaca, NY: ILR Press, 2000).

2. See Irving Bernstein, *The Turbulent Years: A History of the American Worker, 1933-1941* (Boston: Houghton Mifflin, 1970), 352–399.

3. Jeremy Brecher, *Strike* (Boston: South End Press, 1977), 185.

4. Brecher, *Strike,* pp. 201–206.

5. Raymond Hogler, "Worker Participation, Employer Anti-unionism, and Labor Law: The Case of the Steel Industry, 1918–1937," *Hofstra Labor Law Journal* 7 (1989): 1–69; and see also Raymond Hogler and Guillermo Grenier, *Employee Participation and Labor Law in the American Workplace* (New York: Quorum Books, 1992).

6. Robert R. R. Brooks, *As Steel Goes . . . : Unionism in a Basic Industry* (New Haven: Yale University Press, 1940), 108.

7. A copy of the SWOC-Carnegie Illinois agreement is attached as Appendix A in Frederick Harbison, "Collective Bargaining in the Steel Industry: A Factual Summary of Recent Developments" (Typescript, Industrial Relations Section, Department of Economics, Princeton University, 1938).

8. For a revisionist treatment of the New Deal, see Gary Dean Best, *Pride, Prejudice, and Politics: Roosevelt Versus Recovery, 1933–1938* (Westport, CT: Praeger, 1991). Best argues that Roosevelt's policies were misguided and ineffectual, and the 1936 landslide is accounted for by the massive amount of federal relief spending just before the election (pp. 131–137).

9. Melvyn Dubofsky and Warren Van Tine, "John L. Lewis and the Triumph of Mass-Production Unionism," in Melvyn Dubofsky and Warren Van Tine, eds., *Labor Leaders in America* (Urbana: University of Illinois, 1987), 197–198.

10. Peter Gottlieb, "Steel Strike of 1937," in *Labor Conflict in the United States: An Encyclopedia,* ed. Ronald Filippelli (New York: Garland, 1990), 502–509.

11. Karl Klare, "Judicial Deradicalization of the Wagner Act and the Origins of Modern Legal Consciousness," *Minnesota Law Review* 62 (1978): 265–339.

12. The critical labor law movement led to important reinterpretations of legal doctrines. For examples, see James Atleson, *Values and Assumptions in Labor Law* (Amherst: University of Massachusetts Press, 1983); Karl Klare, "Critical Theory and Labor Relations Law," in *The Politics of Law: A Progressive Critique,* ed. David Kairys (New York: Pantheon Books, 1982), 65–88; Raymond Hogler, "Critical Labor Law, Working-Class History, and the New Industrial Relations," *Industrial Relations Law Journal* 10 (1988): 116–143.

13. *NLRB v. Jones & Laughlin Steel Co.,* 301 U.S. 1 (1937).

14. *NLRB v. Mackay Radio & Telegraph Co.,* 304 U.S. 333 (1938).

15. Albert Karr, "Backers of Bill on Replacing Strikers Fail to Head Off Expected Filibuster," *Wall Street Journal,* June 12, 1992, p. A4, col. 4.

16. *NLRB v. Fansteel Metallurgical Corp.,* 306 U.S. 240 (1939).

17. *NLRB v. Sands Manufacturing Co.,* 306 U.S. 332 (1939).

18. The most complete description of the NWLB and its activities is U.S. Department of Labor, *The Termination Report of the National War Labor Board: Industrial Disputes and Wage Stabilization in Wartime, January 12, 1942–December 31, 1945,* 3 vols. (Washington, DC: Government Printing Office, 1946). An excellent study of the period is James B. Atleson, *Labor and the Wartime State: Labor Relations and Law During World War II* (Urbana: University of Illinois Press, 1998).

19. See generally Nelson Lichtenstein, *Labor's War at Home: The CIO in World War II* (Cambridge, UK: Cambridge University Press, 1982), 44–53.

20. For a detailed analysis of strike rates and issues, see Atleson, *Labor and the Wartime State,* pp. 130–157.

21. In Truman's words, "Under the patriotic pressure of a desperate war crisis, management and labor have performed a miracle of production for four years—working together voluntarily but under a measure of Government control. Those controls must soon disappear. Many have already gone. And yet as soon as the first ones were taken off, industrial strife appeared." Harry S. Truman, "Address at the Opening Session of the Labor–Management Conference," November 5, 1945. Online at www.trumanlibrary.org/trumanpapers/pppus/1945/184.htm.

22. For documents relating to the conference, see *The President's National Labor–Management Conference, November 5–30, 1945: Summary and Committee Reports,* U.S. Department of Labor, Division of Labor Standards, Bulletin No. 77 (Washington, DC: Government Printing Office, 1946).

23. Barton Bernstein, "Walter Reuther and the General Motors Strike of 1945–46," *Michigan History* 49 (1965): 261–262.

24. Christopher Tomlins, *The State and the Unions: Labor Relations, Law, and the Organized Labor Movement in America, 1880–1960* (Cambridge, UK: Cambridge University Press, 1985), 252–281.

25. See, for example, Raymond Hogler and Steven Shulman, "The Law, Economics, and Politics of Right to Work: Colorado's Labor Peace Act and Its Implications for Public Policy," *University of Colorado Law Review* 70 (1999): 871–952.

26. See Harry A. Millis and Emily Clark Brown, *From the Wagner Act to Taft-Hartley: A Study of National Labor Policy and Labor Relations* (Chicago: University of Chicago Press, 1950), 272.

27. For the complete text of the report, see U.S. Senate, 93rd Congress, 2nd Session, *Legislative History of the Labor Management Relations Act, 1947* (Washington, DC: Government Printing Office, 1974), 292–354.

28. "A Broadway Showstopper: Musicians' Strike," *Christian Science Monitor,* March 10, 2003. Online at www.csmonitor.com/2003/0310/p03s01-ussc.html.

29. For a treatment of the topic, see Donald Cullen, *National Emergency Strikes* (Ithaca, NY: ILR Press, 1968).

30. Neil King Jr., Jeanne Cummings, and Carlos Tejada, "Open Door Policy," *Wall Street Journal,* October 8, 2002, p. A1, col. 6.

31. See generally, Patrick Hardin, ed., *The Developing Labor Law: The Board, the Courts, and the National Labor Relations Act,* 3d ed., vol. 2 (Washington, DC: Bureau of National Affairs, 1992), 1464–1471.

32. Sumner H. Slichter, James J. Healy, and E. Robert Livernash, *The Impact of Collective Bargaining on Management* (Washington, DC: Brookings Institution, 1960).

33. Lawrence Mishel, Jared Bernstein, and Heather Boushey, *The State of Working America, 2002/2003* (Ithaca, NY: ILR Press, 2003), 120.

34. Bureau of Labor Statistics, "Employer Costs for Employee Compensation—December 2002," March 18, 2003. Online at http://stats.bls.gov/news.release/ecec.nr0.htm.

35. According to one analysis, the union effect on total compensation in 2001 amounted to 27.8 percent. Mishel, Bernstein, and Boushey, *State of Working America,* p. 191.

36. For an application of the concept, see Edward P. Lazear, *Personnel Economics for Managers* (New York: John Wiley & Sons, 1998), 521–523.

37. *NLRB v. Wooster Division of Borg-Warner Corp.,* 357 U.S. 342 (1958).

38. *Fibreboard Paper Products Corp. v. NLRB,* 379 U.S. 203 (1964).

39. *First National Maintenance Corp. v. NLRB,* 452 U.S. 666 (1981).

40. *Dubuque Packing Co.,* 303 NLRB No. 66 (1991).

41. Frank Elkouri and Edna Elkouri, *How Arbitration Works,* 5th ed. (Washington, DC: BNA Books, 1997), 655–801.

42. Quoted in Elkouri and Elkouri, *How Arbitration Works,* p. 659.

43. On grievance procedures, see Elkouri and Elkouri, *How Arbitration Works,* pp. 214–295.

44. *Communications Workers v. Beck,* 487 U.S. 735 (1988).

45. Hardin, *The Developing Labor Law,* pp. 1523–1526.

46. Hardin, *The Developing Labor Law,* pp. 1526–1528.

47. The application of the Section 8(f) proviso is discussed in Hardin, *The Developing Labor Law,* pp. 1517–1523, and the rules about hiring halls at pp. 1533–1543.

48. Hogler and Shulman, "The Law, Economics, and Politics of Right to Work."

49. Raymond L. Hogler and Robert LaJeunesse, "Oklahoma's Right to Work Initiative: Labor Policy and Political Ideology," *Labor Law Journal* 53 (2002): 109–121. For a rebuttal to this article, see Stan Greer and Charles W. Baird, "Reply to Hogler and LaJeunesse's 'Oklahoma's Right to Work Initiative: Labor Policy and Political Ideology,'" *Labor Law Journal* 54 (2003): 89–100.

50. Elkouri and Elkouri, *How Arbitration Works,* pp. 857–883.

51. Elkouri and Elkouri, *How Arbitration Works,* p. 772.

52. According to one commentator, "The old employment system of secure, lifetime jobs with predictable advancement and stable pay is dead." Peter Cappelli, *The New Deal at Work: Managing the Market-Driven Workplace* (Boston: Harvard Business School Press, 1999), 17.

53. David Leonhardt, "Jobless Rate Rose to 6 Percent in April," *New York Times,* May 3, 2003.

54. Worker Adjustment and Retraining Notification Act, 28 U.S.C. §§ 2101–2190 (1988).

55. For useful treatments of the topic, see Stephen A. Herzenberg, John A. Alic, and Howard Wial, *New Rules for a New Economy: Employment and Opportunity in Postindustrial America* (Ithaca, NY: ILR Press, 1998); Paul Osterman, ed., *Broken Ladders: Managerial Careers in the New Economy* (New York: Oxford University Press, 1996); David T. Ellwood et al., eds., *A Working Nation: Workers, Work and Government in the New Economy* (New York: Russell Sage Foundation, 2000).

56. For a discussion of the effects of a change in employers, see Hardin, *The Developing Labor Law,* vol. 1, pp. 761–838.

57. U.S. Bankruptcy Code, 11 U.S.C. § 1113; for a comment, see also, Steven Kropp, "Collective Bargaining in Bankruptcy: Toward an Analytical Framework for Section 1113," *Temple Law Review* 66 (1993): 697–749.

58. See generally George Milkovich and Jerry Newman, *Compensation,* 7th ed. (Boston: McGraw-Hill/Irwin, 2002), 7–12.

59. Jay Schuster and Patricia Zingheim, *The New Pay: Linking Employee and Organizational Performance* (New York: Lexington Books, 1992), 21.

60. Milkovich and Newman, *Compensation,* p. 520. For an early overview of two-tier systems and their problems, see Marvin Levine, "The Evolution of Two-Tier Wage Agreements: Bane or Panacea in Labor-Intensive Industries," *Labor Law Journal* 40 (1989): 12–21.

61. Bureau of Labor Statistics, Employee Costs for Employee Compensation, 2002. Online at http://stats.bls.gov/news.release/ecec.t01.htm.

62. For a copy of the document, see Harry S. Truman, Special Message to the Congress Recommending a Comprehensive Health Program, Public Papers of the Presidents, www.trumanlibrary.org/trumanpapers/ppus/1945/192.htm.

63. Hilary Stout and Rick Wartzman, "With Health-Care Package Nearing Completion, Clinton Now Must Make Some Tough Decisions," *Wall Street Journal,* May 18, 1993, p. A22, col. 1.

64. U.S. Congress, House Doc. 103–174, *Proposed Legislation: "The Health Security Act of 1993,"* (Washington, DC: Government Printing Office, 1993).

65. E.g., Sarah Lueck, "Health-Care Spending Rises 8.7%, Fastest Expansion in 10 Years," *Wall Street Journal,* January 8, 2003, p. D2, col. 5.

66. Kaiser Family Foundation, "2002 Employer Health Benefits Survey (Summary of Findings)," online at www.kff.org/content/2002/20020905a/.

67. George Merritt, "Dispute Didn't Derail RTD Pact," *Denver Post,* April 3, 2003, p. B1.

68. Bureau of Labor Statistics, Employee Benefits in Private Industry, 2000. Follow links available online at www.bls.gov/ncs/ebs/.

69. For example, a construction contract states, "No Carpenter will be allowed to furnish, rent, lease or supply any workbench, mitre box, jackscrews, power tools, electric and acetylene welding and cutting equipment, sawhorses, or heavy steel bars exceeding thirty (30) inches in length, drill bits, taps and dies, or files or tools other than those found in the Carpenter's regular tool chest, and Carpenters shall not furnish cars or trucks for hauling or transporting tools and materials of the Employer." Statewide Building Construction Agreement Between Colorado Centennial District Council of Carpenters and Independent Contractors, May 1, 1990–April 30, 1995, p. 21.

70. Richard Edwards and Michael Podgursky, "The Unraveling Accord: American Unions in Crisis," *Unions in Crisis and Beyond,* ed. Richard Edwards, Paolo Garonna, and Franz Todtling (Dover, MA: Auburn House, 1986), 14–60.

71. One of the most influential studies of declining unionism is Thomas Kochan, Harry C. Katz, and Robert B. McKersie, *The Transformation of American Industrial Relations* (Ithaca, NY: ILR Press, 1994).

72. For an excellent collection of essays on union decline, including discussions of employer antiunion tactics, see James Bennett and Bruce E. Kaufman, *The Future of Private Sector Unionism in the United States* (Armonk, NY: M. E. Sharpe, 2002).

73. Helen Dewar and Frank Swoboda, "Republican-Led Filibuster Kills Striker Replacement Bill in Senate," *Washington Post,* July 14, 1994, p. 47, cols. 1–6.

74. Bureau of Labor Statistics, Union Membership Summary, February 25, 2003. Online at http://stats.bls.gov/news.release/union2.nr0.htm.

PART III

Individual Employment Rights, 1960s–2000s

CHAPTER 6

Protecting Individuals From Discrimination

Beginning in the mid-1960s, Congress undertook a radical expansion of civil rights for individuals previously affected by social and economic discrimination. Such legislation had its historical roots in the period of reconstruction just after the Civil War; unfortunately, the older laws failed to end racial discrimination and a system of de facto segregation endured for another century. The evolving legal environment reflected changes in the social and political composition of the country. With the election of Democrat John Kennedy as president in 1960, and the administrations of his successor Lyndon Johnson from 1963 to 1968, government commenced initiatives to reduce poverty, discrimination, and workplace inequality.[1] The centerpiece of the legislative revolution was the Civil Rights Act of 1964, a landmark statute outlawing race discrimination in most aspects of public life. Title VII of the bill applied specifically to employment. It prohibited covered employers from discriminating against any individual "because of such individual's race, color, religion, sex, or national origin."[2] Other laws followed, including the Age Discrimination in Employment Act (ADEA) in 1967 and the Americans With Disabilities Act (ADA) of 1990. The major statutory developments are supplemented by numerous related laws at both the federal and the state levels.

The defining element of antidiscrimination laws is the concept of protected classes. The laws identify characteristics unique to the class of persons and grant protections to individuals based on those characteristics, such as gender, race, age, or disability. The public policy justifying this extensive scheme of workplace regulation is the elimination of arbitrary bias in the employment relationship. For example, the characteristic of age may have little relevance to job performance, and employers now are generally prohibited from using age as a factor in employment decisions.[3] From a labor market perspective, however, it could be argued that age indeed predicts certain factors of physical performance such as strength, endurance, and other desirable attributes, and employers should not be precluded from making assessments of potential employees using that kind of information. Despite such arguments, Congress decided that employers must show that the characteristic has some relevance to the job in question when it affects employment decisions.

The structure of individual discrimination claims follows certain well-defined stages. First, the person claiming the legal protection must prove that he or she falls under the terms of the statute—that is, he or she is a member of the protected class. Next, the claimant must show that an adverse job action occurred affecting his or her wages, hours, or conditions of employment. Once those elements are established, the claimant must then produce some evidence that the employer acted with an unlawful intent toward him or her. Those factors make out a prima facie case of employment discrimination, which, if not defended by the employer, will generally entitle the claimant to relief. If the employer articulates a legitimate reason for the employment decision, the employee may try to show that the employer's justification lacked plausibility. To prevail in the case, the employee must ultimately prove the employer's improper motivation.[4] One important exception to this formula involves discrimination that affects a protected class even when the employer did not necessarily intend discriminatory consequences. Requiring a high school diploma for a job of manual labor, for example, may have an adverse or disparate impact on racial groups that do not obtain diplomas at the same rate as whites. This legal theory entails different procedural elements, which are explained later in the chapter.

When Congress enacted Title VII and related laws, it created administrative tribunals to handle complaints against employers. Like the National Labor Relations Board described in Chapter 4, these administrative bodies perform an important function of screening complaints, assessing the merit of charges, and advocating the interests of workers. Different agencies may exercise authority over enforcement of employment laws, and the scope of their powers depends on the particular statute involved. The Equal Employment Opportunity Commission (EEOC), which has the most extensive jurisdiction, deals with Title VII, the ADEA, the Equal Pay Act (EPA), the ADA, and the Civil Rights Act of 1991. The EEOC procedures are summarized at the end of this chapter.

The coverage of the statutes varies considerably. Title VII and the ADA cover employers in the private sector, state and local governmental employers, and educational institutions that employ fifteen employees or more. The ADEA covers private employers and state and local governments, including school districts, with twenty employees or more. These laws also cover private and public employment agencies, labor organizations, and joint labor management committees controlling apprenticeship and training. Title VII, the ADEA, and the EPA apply to employees in the federal government, but disabilities are protected under the federal Rehabilitation Act of 1973. Note that states may supplement the terms of the federal laws by adding

Table 6.1   Overview of Individual Rights Legislation

Statute	Basic Provision	Coverage	Comments
Equal Pay Act, 1963	Requires equal pay for women performing equal work with men	Coverage based on the Fair Labor Standards Act (FLSA); adopted as an amendment to FLSA	Does not apply to comparable work; must be interpreted in relation to Title VII
Title VII, Civil Rights Act of 1964	Prohibits employment discrimination because of race, color, religion, sex, or national origin	Covers employers having fifteen or more employees, including government; part of a comprhensive civil rights law	Supreme Court issued key interpretive opinions about scope and meaning of law
Age Discrimination in Employment Act, 1967	Prohibits employment discrimination against workers because of their age (over forty)	Covers employers having twenty or more employees, including state and local governments	Contains exemptions for certain occupations and employment benefit plans
Civil Rights Act of 1991	Expands protections for victims of discrimination under Title VII	Extends civil rights coverage to designated federal agencies	Congressional response to Supreme Court decisions that weakened Title VII
Americans With Disaiblities Act, 1990	Prohibits employment discrimination against workers with disabilities	Covers employers having fifteen or more employees, but excludes the federal government	Requires employers to make a reasonable accommodation for employees with disability who are otherwise qualified for employment

other categories (e.g., sexual orientation) or by covering smaller employers. States may share enforcement responsiblities with the EEOC under the scheme of *deferral* set out in the statute. That is, if the state elects to create its own administrative body, the federal government will defer any charge until the state has a specified period of time to investigate the matter (see Table 6.1).[5]

Before proceeding to the specific laws, some comment on the managerial implications of civil rights law is warranted. Chapter 3 emphasized that many employers in the 1920s voluntarily adopted personnel programs very similar to contemporary practices. Welfare capitalism included systems of employee participation and complaint procedures as well as economic benefits for workers. If employers act rationally when they pursue strategies to hire, motivate, and retain loyal and satisfied employees, why are laws against discrimination needed? Put another way, competitive labor markets will theoretically compel employers to make personnel decisions based on relevant worker characteristics and to treat employees fairly in matters of compensation and job tenure.[6] According to this line of reasoning, the existence of laws protecting some groups of workers contradicts the basic ideas of liberty and property on which capitalism rests. The author of a sustained attack on civil rights legislation contends, "An antidiscrimination law is the antithesis of freedom of contract, a principle that allows all persons to do business with whomever they please for good reason, bad reason, or no reason at all." Because this concept forms the bedrock of employment relations, he continues, antidiscrimination laws interfere with the moral and economic premises of our society.[7] Consider such criticisms in the context of the respective statutes below.

Equal Pay Act

In 1963, Congress enacted the EPA as an amendment to the Fair Labor Standards Act (FLSA), which is the Great Depression-era law regulating minimum wages and overtime described in Chapter 4. Both the World War I and World War II labor boards recognized the problem of gender-based pay systems and took steps to alleviate their effects. The EPA continued the objective of eliminating gender-based wage differentials, and it specifically prohibits discrimination on the basis of sex in the payment of wages. As an amendment to the FLSA, the EPA reinforces the policy goals of the FLSA to reduce poverty and expand employment opportunities. Congress noted that wage differentials based on sex depressed wages and living standards for employees necessary for their health and efficiency, prevented the maximum utilization of available labor resources, burdened the free flow of goods in commerce, and constituted an unfair method of competition.[8] Aside from simple notions of equity, the EPA promotes the macroeconomic agenda developed during the New Deal.

Coverage under the EPA is coextensive with coverage under the minimum wage provisions, with one important exception. In 1972, Congress provided for coverage of executive, administrative, and professional employees under the EPA. The EPA generally states that males and females must be paid the same wages for equal work, where the job duties involve equal skill, effort, and responsibility and work is performed under similar working conditions. *Equal* does not necessarily mean identical, but only *substantially* equal. For example, the assignment of different job titles is not sufficient evidence to justify wage differentials, if the classification is an artificial one not materially different from the genuine one; rather, the specific job duties in the particular case must be analyzed. Determinations of equal skill, effort, and responsibility similarly necessitate detailed examination of the jobs in question.

The EPA also sets forth specific circumstances in which an employer will not be liable for wage differentials. Congress stated that equal pay was not required where compensation was made "pursuant to (i) a seniority system; (ii) a merit system; (iii) a system that measures earnings by quantity or quality of production; or (iv) a differential based on any other factor other than sex."[9] Consequently, employers may defend equal pay claims by demonstrating that a difference in pay is based on one of the three grounds specified or, in any event, is not based on the sex of the employee. For example, market conditions may justify higher salaries for a male college professor in the field of engineering compared with a female professor teaching English even though both jobs involve educating students.

One point that has generated considerable sensible interest is the relationship between the EPA and Title VII. When Congress enacted the latter statute in 1964, it devoted little attention to the problem of sex discrimination and equal pay. Title VII provides that an employer may not discriminate with regard to terms and conditions of employment because of sex. If discrimination includes pay practices, then, in one view, Title VII makes superfluous the narrow equal pay for equal work standard of the EPA. That is, a woman might claim that she received less pay because she was a woman, even though she did not perform work equal to that of a male employee. The Ninth Circuit addressed the issue in the leading case of *AFCSME v. Washington.* In an opinion by Judge Anthony Kennedy, now a member of the Supreme Court, the appellate court rejected the plaintiffs' argument that employers violated the law if they did not pay job classifications held mostly by women equivalent pay for jobs held mostly by men, if those jobs were of comparable value to the employer (e.g., the job of a nurse and a maintenance worker).[10]

Although courts generally do not recognize claims based on the idea of comparable pay for comparable work, inequality in compensation occasionally surfaces as an issue in the contemporary workplace. Presidential candidate Al Gore campaigned on that subject in August 2000. Gore urged the enactment of federal legislation strengthening laws to protect women from wage discrimination. Two proposed bills in the Senate addressed the matter. Both took the approach that where women workers dominate jobs, employers should eliminate pay disparities not justified by the value of the job to the organization. While Gore did not support all aspects of the comparable worth theory, he believed that equal pay was an issue of concern to U.S. women and would advance his political prospects. According to media reports, "With women overall earning on average about 76 cents to every dollar earned by a man, the Gore camp hopes equal pay is a sleeper issue that will help to trump [Bush's] 'compassionate conservativism' by attracting working women to the Democratic ticket."[11] By mid 2003, however, neither political party had identified wage equality as an important issue.

Civil Rights Acts

Statutes protecting individuals from certain kinds of discrimination arose in the aftermath of the Civil War. In 1866, Congress enacted legislation guaranteeing the right of all persons in this country to make contracts on the same basis as white people.[12] The statute directly abolished racially motivated discrimination in all commercial transactions, including employment. It was reenacted in 1870 after passage of the Fourteenth Amendment, which constitutionally mandated equal protection of the laws for all persons. For many years, Section 1981 was interpreted to apply only to state action consistent with the interpretation of other constitutional provisions. In 1975, the U.S. Supreme Court ruled that it also prevented race discrimination in private employment because the Fourteenth Amendment specifically authorizes Congress to enact remedial legislation pursuant to the equal protection concept. Presently, the provision is a common basis for race-related employment claims, and Congress reaffirmed that principle in the Civil Rights Act of 1991 discussed later.

Another Reconstruction law, 42 U.S.C. Section 1983, authorizes suits for damages against any person who, acting under governmental authority, denies any other person rights and privileges secured by the U.S. Constitution. Among those rights is freedom from racial discrimination. Because it is expressly limited to "state action," Section 1983 applies generally to the public sector, but it provides broad guarantees for such rights as free speech and due process in governmental employment.[13] Sections 1981 and 1983 continue to be important laws affecting rights in the workplace. An important point is that, in addition to any statutory rights, public workers also enjoy constitutional protections. For example, a police officer who is arbitrarily discharged without notice or an opportunity to present relevant information in his or her defense could bring a claim that he or she was denied liberty or property rights.

The Reconstruction-era civil rights legislation failed to end racial discrimination in this country, largely because of U.S. Supreme Court decisions that undermined the congressional purposes. That sad chapter of judicial history was eloquently recounted by Justice Thurgood Marshall, an African American who served on the Supreme Court from 1967 to 1991. In a case involving a white plaintiff who claimed he was unlawfully discriminated against because of his race, Justice Marshall wrote a concurring opinion explaining why affirmative protections for racial minorities were necessary in this country. Portions of that opinion are reprinted below. Note particularly Marshall's description of how judicial interpretation frustrated the obvious intent of legislative action.[14]

Concurring Opinion of Justice Thurgood Marshall,
Bakke v. University of California, 438 U.S. 265 (1978)

Three hundred and fifty years ago, the Negro was dragged to this country in chains to be sold into slavery. Uprooted from his homeland and thrust into bondage for forced labor, the slave was deprived of all legal rights. It was unlawful to teach him to read; he could be sold away from his family and friends at the whim of his master; and killing or maiming him was not a crime. The system of slavery brutalized and dehumanized both master and slave.

The denial of human rights was etched into the American Colonies' first attempts at establishing self-government. When the colonists determined to seek their independence from England, they drafted a unique document cataloguing their grievances against the King and proclaiming as "self-evident" that "all men are created equal" and are endowed "with certain unalienable Rights," including those to "Life, Liberty and the pursuit of Happiness." The self-evident truths and the unalienable rights were intended, however, to apply only to white men. An earlier draft of the Declaration of Independence, submitted by Thomas Jefferson to the Continental Congress, had included among the charges against the King that "[he] has waged cruel war against human nature itself, violating its most sacred rights of life and liberty in the persons of a distant people who never offended him, captivating and carrying them into slavery in another hemisphere, or to incur miserable death in their transportation thither."

The Southern delegation insisted that the charge be deleted; the colonists themselves were implicated in the slave trade, and inclusion of this claim might have made it more difficult to justify the continuation of slavery once the ties to England were severed. Thus, even as the colonists embarked on a course to secure their own freedom and equality, they ensured perpetuation of the system that deprived a whole race of those rights.

The implicit protection of slavery embodied in the Declaration of Independence was made explicit in the Constitution, which treated a slave as being equivalent to three-fifths of a person for purposes of apportioning representatives and taxes among the States. Art. I, § 2. The Constitution also contained a clause ensuring that the "Migration or Importation" of slaves into the existing States would be legal until at least 1808, Art. I, § 9, and a fugitive slave clause requiring that when a slave escaped to another State, he must be returned on the claim of the master, Art. IV, § 2. In their declaration of the principles that were to provide the cornerstone of the new Nation, therefore, the Framers made it plain that "we the people," for whose protection the Constitution was designed, did not include those whose skins were the wrong color. As Professor John Hope Franklin has observed, Americans "proudly accepted the challenge and responsibility of their new political freedom by establishing the machinery and safeguards that insured the continued enslavement of blacks."

The individual States likewise established the machinery to protect the system of slavery through the promulgation of the Slave Codes, which were designed primarily to defend the property interest of the owner in his slave. The position of the Negro slave as mere property was confirmed by this Court in *Dred Scott* v. *Sandford*, 19 How. 393 (1857), holding that the Missouri Compromise—which prohibited slavery in the portion of the Louisiana Purchase Territory north of Missouri—was unconstitutional because it deprived slave owners of their property without due process. The Court declared that under the Constitution a slave was property, and "[the] right to traffic in it, like an ordinary article of merchandise and property, was guarantied to the citizens of the United States. . . ." The Court further concluded that Negroes were not intended to be included as citizens under the Constitution but were "regarded as beings of an inferior order . . . altogether unfit to associate with the white race, either in social or political relations; and so far inferior, that they had no rights which the white man was bound to respect. . . ."

(Continued)

(Continued)

The status of the Negro as property was officially erased by his emancipation at the end of the Civil War. But the long-awaited emancipation, while freeing the Negro from slavery, did not bring him citizenship or equality in any meaningful way. Slavery was replaced by a system of "laws which imposed upon the colored race onerous disabilities and burdens, and curtailed their rights in the pursuit of life, liberty, and property to such an extent that their freedom was of little value." *Slaughter-House Cases,* 16 Wall. 36, 70 (1873). Despite the passage of the Thirteenth, Fourteenth, and Fifteenth Amendments, the Negro was systematically denied the rights those Amendments were supposed to secure. The combined actions and inactions of the State and Federal Governments maintained Negroes in a position of legal inferiority for another century after the Civil War.

The Southern States took the first steps to re-enslave the Negroes. Immediately following the end of the Civil War, many of the provisional legislatures passed Black Codes, similar to the Slave Codes, which, among other things, limited the rights of Negroes to own or rent property and permitted imprisonment for breach of employment contracts. Over the next several decades, the South managed to disenfranchise the Negroes in spite of the Fifteenth Amendment by various techniques, including poll taxes, deliberately complicated balloting processes, property and literacy qualifications, and finally the white primary.

Congress responded to the legal disabilities being imposed in the Southern States by passing the Reconstruction Acts and the Civil Rights Acts. Congress also responded to the needs of the Negroes at the end of the Civil War by establishing the Bureau of Refugees, Freedmen, and Abandoned Lands, better known as the Freedmen's Bureau, to supply food, hospitals, land, and education to the newly freed slaves. Thus, for a time it seemed as if the Negro might be protected from the continued denial of his civil rights and might be relieved of the disabilities that prevented him from taking his place as a free and equal citizen.

That time, however, was short-lived. Reconstruction came to a close, and, with the assistance of this Court, the Negro was rapidly stripped of his new civil rights. In the words of C. Vann Woodward: "By narrow and ingenious interpretation [the Supreme Court's] decisions over a period of years had whittled away a great part of the authority presumably given the government for protection of civil rights."

The Court began by interpreting the Civil War Amendments in a manner that sharply curtailed their substantive protections. See, *e. g., Slaughter-House Cases, supra; United States* v. *Reese,* 92 U.S. 214 (1876); *United States* v. *Cruikshank,* 92 U.S. 542 (1876). Then in the notorious *Civil Rights Cases,* 109 U.S. 3 (1883), the Court strangled Congress' efforts to use its power to promote racial equality. In those cases the Court invalidated sections of the Civil Rights Act of 1875 that made it a crime to deny equal access to "inns, public conveyances, theatres and other places of public amusement." According to the Court, the Fourteenth Amendment gave Congress the power to proscribe only discriminatory action by the State. The Court ruled that the Negroes who were excluded from public places suffered only an invasion of their social rights at the hands of private individuals, and Congress had no power to remedy that. "When a man has emerged from slavery, and by the aid of beneficent legislation has shaken off the inseparable concomitants of that state," the Court concluded, "there must be some stage in the progress of his elevation when he takes the rank of a mere citizen, and ceases to be the special favorite of the laws. . . ." As Mr. Justice Harlan noted in dissent, however, the Civil War Amendments and Civil Rights Acts did not make the Negroes the "special favorite" of the laws but instead "sought to accomplish in reference to that race . . . what had already been done in every State of the Union for the white race—to secure and protect rights belonging to them as freemen and citizens; nothing more."

The Court's ultimate blow to the Civil War Amendments and to the equality of Negroes came in *Plessy v. Ferguson,* 163 U.S. 537 (1896). In upholding a Louisiana law that required railway companies to provide "equal but separate" accommodations for whites and Negroes, the Court held that the Fourteenth Amendment was not intended "to abolish distinctions based upon color, or to enforce social, as distinguished from political equality, or a commingling of the two races upon terms unsatisfactory to either." Ignoring totally the realities of the positions of the two races, the Court remarked: "We consider the underlying fallacy of the plaintiff's argument to consist in the assumption that the enforced separation of the two races stamps the colored race with a badge of inferiority. If this be so, it is not by reason of anything found in the act, but solely because the colored race chooses to put that construction upon it."

Mr. Justice Harlan's dissenting opinion recognized the bankruptcy of the Court's reasoning. He noted that the "real meaning" of the legislation was "that colored citizens are so inferior and degraded that they cannot be allowed to sit in public coaches occupied by white citizens." He expressed his fear that if like laws were enacted in other States, "the effect would be in the highest degree mischievous." Although slavery would have disappeared, the States would retain the power "to interfere with the full enjoyment of the blessings of freedom; to regulate civil rights, common to all citizens, upon the basis of race; and to place in a condition of legal inferiority a large body of American citizens. . . ."

The fears of Mr. Justice Harlan were soon to be realized. In the wake of *Plessy,* many States expanded their Jim Crow laws, which had up until that time been limited primarily to passenger trains and schools. The segregation of the races was extended to residential areas, parks, hospitals, theaters, waiting rooms, and bathrooms. There were even statutes and ordinances which

(Continued)

(Continued)

authorized separate phone booths for Negroes and whites, which required that textbooks used by children of one race be kept separate from those used by the other, and which required that Negro and white prostitutes be kept in separate districts. In 1898, after *Plessy*, the *Charlestown News and Courier* printed a parody of Jim Crow laws: "If there must be Jim Crow cars on the railroads, there should be Jim Crow cars on the street railways. Also on all passenger boats. . . . If there are to be Jim Crow cars, moreover, there should be Jim Crow waiting saloons at all stations, and Jim Crow eating houses. . . . There should be Jim Crow sections of the jury box, and a separate Jim Crow dock and witness stand in every court—and a Jim Crow Bible for colored witnesses to kiss." The irony is that before many years had passed, with the exception of the Jim Crow witness stand, "all the improbable applications of the principle suggested by the editor in derision had been put into practice—down to and including the Jim Crow Bible."

Nor were the laws restricting the rights of Negroes limited solely to the Southern States. In many of the Northern States, the Negro was denied the right to vote, prevented from serving on juries, and excluded from theaters, restaurants, hotels, and inns. Under President Wilson, the Federal Government began to require segregation in Government buildings; desks of Negro employees were curtained off; separate bathrooms and separate tables in the cafeterias were provided; and even the galleries of the Congress were segregated. When his segregationist policies were attacked, President Wilson responded that segregation was "not humiliating but a benefit" and that he was "rendering [the Negroes] more safe in their possession of office and less likely to be discriminated against."

The enforced segregation of the races continued into the middle of the 20th century. In both World Wars, Negroes were for the most part confined to separate military units; it was not until 1948 that an end to segregation in the military was ordered by President Truman. And the history of the exclusion of Negro children from white public schools is too well known and recent to require repeating here. That Negroes were deliberately excluded from public graduate and professional schools—and thereby denied the opportunity to become doctors, lawyers, engineers, and the like—is also well established. It is of course true that some of the Jim Crow laws (which the decisions of this Court had helped to foster) were struck down by this Court in a series of decisions leading up to *Brown* v. *Board of Education,* 347 U.S. 483 (1954). See, *e. g., Morgan* v. *Virginia,* 328 U.S. 373 (1946); *Sweatt* v. *Painter,* 339 U.S. 629 (1950); *McLaurin* v. *Oklahoma State Regents,* 339 U.S. 637 (1950). Those decisions, however, did not automatically end segregation, nor did they move Negroes from a position of legal inferiority to one of equality. The legacy of years of slavery and of years of second-class citizenship in the wake of emancipation could not be so easily eliminated.

The modern civil rights employment law dates from 1964, when Congress outlawed discrimination in employment based on race, color, religion, sex, and national origin under Title VII of a comprehensive bill dealing with other areas such as housing and transportation. After a series of Supreme Court decisions in 1989 that overturned much established precedent, Congress supplemented Title VII with the Civil Rights Act of 1991. This legislation corrected the Court's aberrational interpretations of the basic statutory framework. Two other employment laws are included in the discussion in this section; they are the Age Discrimination in Employment Act and the more recent Americans With Disabilities Act. Taken together, the Civil Rights Acts, the ADEA, and the ADA make up a complex and challenging scheme of regulation for employers. Rights under those laws cannot be waived by collective bargaining agreement, nor can grievance and arbitration procedures completely displace the statutory remedies. As a result, employers may face several overlapping claims generated from a single fact situation.

Title VII and the 1991 Civil Rights Act

As noted earlier, the Supreme Court has shaped the application of civil rights law to employment in some surprising ways. The plain language of Title VII says no discrimination "because of" race, which seems to imply that employers are only forbidden from making employment decisions that deliberately harm an individual or racial group. The disparate treatment theory of unlawful discrimination in fact follows that general idea by requiring proof of intent. At the same time, the Court developed a much different approach to Title VII that is based on impact rather than intent. That theory of discrimination, known as disparate impact, profoundly affected the way U.S. employers hired workers.

Disparate or Adverse Impact as Discrimination

The relevant language of Title VII appears to be straightforward enough. For all covered organizations, it is an unlawful employment practice to treat protected employees less favorably than others, when the discrimination is because of the individual's race, color, religion, sex, or national origin. Despite the seeming simplicity of the law, the Supreme Court has rendered interpretations of Title VII that altered the apparent meaning of the words and added to this country's continuing social turmoil over questions of race. We begin with the Court's 1971 decision in *Griggs v. Duke Power Co.*[15]

In *Griggs,* the employer selected employees for certain entry-level jobs by requiring applicants to have either a high school diploma or a passing score on specified general intelligence tests. The selection procedures excluded relatively more black applicants than white. It was undisputed, however, that the company did not intend to discriminate on the basis of race; in fact, the company provided assistance to its minority employees so they could meet the qualifications for more desirable jobs. Because there was no showing of intent to discriminate, the district court and the court of appeals found for the employer.

The U.S. Supreme Court reversed. According to the Court, the company failed to demonstrate that its selection procedures were related to the specific jobs in question. In one of the most well-known passages in civil rights jurisprudence, the Court stated: "The Act [Title VII] proscribes not only overt discrimination but also practices that are fair in form, but discriminatory in operation. The touchstone is business necessity. If an employment practice which operates to exclude Negroes cannot be shown to be related to job performance, the practice is prohibited." This language contains some dubious propositions, and the Court cites no source of authority to support its conclusion. For example, why would an employer ever engage in an employment practice that had no job relevance unless it was the result of an intent to discriminate?

Nonetheless, as a result of this pronouncement, employers throughout the country were forced to reexamine their hiring practices. Even an employment requirement that was neutral on its face might become suspect in its application. Of more consequence, when the minority applicants showed that the employer's practice disqualified proportionately more of them than it did nonminorities, the employer had to justify the practice in terms of its job-relatedness. If the employer could not, the practice was prohibited.

To defend against the *disparate impact* types of claims, as they are now called, employers hired psychologists to design selection procedures that could be related to the jobs, and an elaborate set of principles emerged in the aftermath of *Griggs*.[16] Psychologists used techniques based on content, criterion, and construct validation to prove job-relatedness. Thus, for example, a firefighter might be required to carry a heavy length of hose up a ladder and remove obstacles from his or her path; because this is part of the actual job, it is a means of *content* validation. An applicant for a welder's job might be asked to examine a set of drawings and answer questions about their meaning; the ability to conceptualize three-dimensional spatial relationships is a *criterion* related to successful job performance as a welder. As the EEOC describes this method of validation, "Evidence of the validity of a test or other selection procedure by a criterion-related validity study should consist of empirical data demonstrating that the selection procedure is predictive of or significantly correlated with important elements of job performance."[17] The construct approach is based on such abstract notions as leadership ability and is so difficult to prove that it is hardly used.[18] In any event, *Griggs* introduced a new approach to the law of discrimination and one with significant implications.

A skillful legal analysis of the *Griggs* case by Michael Gold in 1985 made clear that in the first place Congress never contemplated forcing an employer to prove that its selections techniques were related to a given job.[19] Indeed, all the pertinent legislative history of Title VII points in the other direction—that the use of tests would be permitted unless it was shown that the employer deliberately and intentionally used tests as a means of discriminating against minorities. For that reason, the impact or outcome of a test was irrelevant according to Congress's original understanding of the bill. It might be argued, of course, that forcing employers to use job-related hiring criteria is both fair and consistent with the capitalist idea that competition for productive workers will lead to nondiscriminatory practices.

This argument is a variation on the idea that markets will eventually eliminate discrimination without government intervention.

Conversely, *Griggs* had a tendency to encourage hiring by quotas rather than widespread adoption of job-related hiring criteria. As Gold explains, the basic assumption of *Griggs* was incorrect and so its effect has been to burden rather than facilitate selection practices. In his words,

> Employers have not adopted valid criteria because such criteria do not presently exist, and the cost of developing them may often exceed the gain of using them. Consequently, employers have been motivated to find a way around the law. They have looked for the loophole in the rule, and they have found it. They hire by quotas. If a selection criterion does not have an adverse impact, the rule does not require the employer to validate the criterion. So employers merely ensure that proportionate numbers of blacks are hired.[20]

Gold's article was written nearly two decades ago. Has the problem he so cogently identified been corrected? Hardly—in fact, the Supreme Court, Congress, and the administration of the first President Bush made the situation even more complicated.

In its series of 1989 decisions undermining existing civil rights law, the Supreme Court decided the case of *Wards Cove v. Antonio* involving cannery workers in Alaska.[21] The plaintiffs in *Wards Cove* claimed that the employer's hiring practices resulted in disparate impact because most minorities worked in less desirable cannery jobs and most whites held better-paying and more prestigious noncannery jobs. The Ninth Circuit Court of Appeals found sufficient evidence of disparate impact to shift the burden of proof to the employer to defend its hiring practices.

In an opinion by Justice White, the Supreme Court reversed. The Court said that disparate impact was not proved because the plaintiffs had used the wrong labor market data in their statistical comparisons and did not consider whether ethnic applicants were qualified for jobs where they were underrepresented. That conclusion could have disposed of the case. Nevertheless, the Court then went on to overrule the core principles of *Griggs* by changing the burden and standard of proof in disparate impact cases. According to White, employers were not obliged to prove selection criteria were job related, but merely to produce evidence showing that the practice significantly serves the employer's legitimate employment goals. The Court did not expressly overturn *Griggs,* but its failure to do so was merely duplicitous. Most legal commentators, as well as the federal Congress, immediately realized that *Wards Cove* had repudiated *Griggs.*

The *Wards Cove* case led to a prolonged conflict between Congress and former president Bush, and finally to the Civil Rights Act (CRA) of 1991. Declaring a 1990 version of the law to be a quota bill, Bush vetoed it and demanded changes in the language to minimize its consequences for employers. Following extensive debate and revision in Congress, the 1991 act successfully passed. Although the 1991 act purported to adopt the business necessity standard of *Griggs,* there was some question about whether employers must prove that a practice having disparate impact was related to a particular job or only to some legitimate business objective. In any event, the law is clear that if a plaintiff proves disparate impact, the burden of proof in the lawsuit then shifts to the employer.[22] Consequently, employers may still be tempted to hire by quotas in an effort to avoid civil rights liability, and that trend can exacerbate workplace conflict. Managers strive for diversity among employees even though the economic and interpersonal benefits of a diverse workplace are the subject of ongoing academic debate.[23] As shown later, private sector employers can legally undertake diversity programs, and many do so.

Disparate Treatment and Discrimination

The second kind of discrimination under Title VII involves intentional discrimination against a particular individual or individuals. In these cases, the complaining party must show that he or she suffered an adverse employment decision and produce some evidence that the decision was based on the employee's protected status. Next, the employer must present evidence, but need not prove, that the decision was made for legitimate, nondiscriminatory reasons. The employee can in turn prove that the employer's asserted justification is only pretextual. For example, assume a woman is discharged and files a charge claiming that her male supervisor often criticized women workers for "being lazy, talking too much, and not caring about the job." In response, the employer produces the woman's attendance record showing a large number of absences, which is a legitimate reason for discipline. But other women at the firm testify that the male supervisor routinely granted excused absences to men and routinely refused to accept a female's explanation for absence. Therefore, absenteeism is actually a pretext for discriminating against women.

The U.S. Supreme Court continues to adhere to this formula for presenting evidence under Title VII. As it succinctly stated the rule in a leading case,

> First, the plaintiff has the burden of proving by the preponderance of the evidence a prima facie case of discrimination. Second, if the plaintiff succeeds in proving the prima facie case, the burden shifts to the defendant to articulate some legitimate, nondiscriminatory reason for the employee's rejection. Third, should the defendant carry this burden, the plaintiff must then have an opportunity to prove by a preponderance of the evidence that the legitimate reasons offered by the defendant were not its true reasons, but were a pretext for discrimination.[24]

With regard to the element of pretext, the Court has held that plaintiffs have the burden of proving unlawful intent, and proof that the employer's reason is false is not by itself sufficient to prevail in the litigation.[25] In its recent decision in *Reeves v. Sanderson Plumbing Products,* however, the Court clarified its earlier precedent and held that a trier of fact could conclude that the employer's untruthful explanation of its motives, along with the evidence of a prima facie case, supported a finding in favor of the employee.[26]

A more difficult case, and one affected by the CRA, involves mixed motive cases in which the employer has a legitimate reason for the job decision but there is also some evidence of a discriminatory motive. In the highly publicized case of *Price Waterhouse v. Hopkins,* the employer refused to promote a female accountant in part because she was not sufficiently feminine.[27] The employer also said that she did not work well with subordinates. The Supreme Court, in another of its 1989 civil rights interpretations, held that an employer acting with both good and bad motives would not be liable under Title VII if the employer could show that the same employment decision would have been made in the absence of a discriminatory motive. Thus, if Price Waterhouse could demonstrate that good interpersonal skills were required of all applicants for partnership, the company could legally refuse to promote the woman candidate regardless of the fact that part of the decision was based on a gender stereotype. The rule allows an employer to act with a discriminatory motive if the employee also acts improperly. Congress did not accept the result.

The 1991 CRA provides that "an unlawful employment practice is established when the complaining party demonstrates that race, color, religion, sex, or national origin was a motivating factor for any employment practice, even though other factors also motivated the practice." In the example above, it would be unlawful for Price Waterhouse to deny a woman a promotion even if sound business reasons are mixed with the discriminatory motives. But to confuse the situation and clog the courts with more litigation, the remedial section of the CRA limits the remedies available to employees in mixed motive cases; the CRA states if the employer shows it would have taken the same action in the absence of the impermissible motivating factor, a court can award declaratory relief and damages only in the amount of attorney's fees and costs directly attributable to the claim. The plaintiff cannot be reinstated or granted back pay. That provision provokes more litigation, because claimants can always try to gain attorney fees even when it is clear that the employer had a legitimate reason, as well as a possibly illegitimate one, to support its employment decision. [28]

The Bona Fide Occupational Qualification

Both the disparate impact and the disparate treatment types of analysis involve defenses that the employer can use to defeat a claim. In the disparate impact situation, the employer proves that the qualification was based on business necessity. If the claim involves disparate treatment, the employer shows that the action was a legitimate business decision and thereby rebuts the allegation of discriminatory intent. Another, and much different, kind of defense available to employers is the *bona fide occupational qualification* (BFOQ). In this type of case, the employer openly discriminates against a protected group. An example is a rule that states that women capable of bearing children will not be permitted to work in a production area where lead is present. If women claim sex discrimination, the employer can try to demonstrate that the rule is justified as an essential part of the business operation. In *Johnson Controls v. UAW,* the employer based such a BFOQ on safety considerations—protecting women employees from injury to their reproductive capacity and potential offspring. The U.S. Supreme Court held that the employer did not prove the existence of a BFOQ because safety of unborn children was not a legitimate concern of an employer. That is, since the lead was not unsafe for adult employees or customers, the BFOQ defense failed.[29]

The BFOQ defense has limited application because the characteristics defining the protected classes under Title VII rarely determine an individual's ability to perform a job. The EEOC states flatly that the BFOQ defense is not available in cases of race discrimination; consequently, an employer could not advertise for white applicants to work in a department store in a predominantly white suburban neighborhood. A notorious attempt to use the BFOQ defense in a gender case involved the lawsuit brought against Hooters by male applicants for a server's job. The company argued unsuccessfully before the EEOC that it could legally refuse to hire men in the job because Hooter's business was entertainment, not the sale of food and beverage.[30] As summarized in a news report, "The restaurant said its hiring practice conformed with the Civil Rights Act because the chain is 'in the business of providing vicarious sexual recreation and female sexuality is a bona fide occupational qualification.'" But that explanation failed to convince the plaintiffs, and Hooters eventually paid a total of $3.75 million to settle the men's lawsuit.[31] More recently, the EEOC brought another suit against a chain of restaurants on behalf of male employees who claimed they were denied access to jobs that offered tips to servers. The employer cited the Hooters settlement and asserted that it had not violated any civil rights laws.[32]

Unlawful Discrimination and Sexual Harassment

Title VII prohibits discrimination based on sex. Because the category of "sex" was added to the statute near the end of the legislative process, the legislative history underlying that part of Title VII is sparse and ambiguous.[33] Presumably, Congress meant to protect women against unfair treatment in terms of hiring, wages, and other benefits of employment—that is, against economic disparity. As the law developed, however, it was applied to discrimination connected with sexual favors. A male supervisor might demand sexual intercourse as a condition of a woman's promotion or hiring. This type of discrimination was described as quid pro quo sexual harassment and was recognized as an unlawful employment practice in the 1970s.[34] It is relatively uncontroversial as a legal principle because the objective of the law is to provide fair treatment in the workplace based on qualifications, not on submission to sexual demands.

Courts also found a violation of Title VII when a supervisor made unwelcome sexual advances to female employees but did not discriminate in terms of job benefits. Such harassment is known as the hostile working environment theory of discrimination, and the U.S. Supreme Court adopted this interpretation of Title VII in the 1986 case of *Meritor Savings Bank v. Vinson*.[35] More recent lower court decisions expand the definition of sexual harassment to include sexually suggestive pictures in the workplace, graffiti of an offensive nature, or practical jokes such as spying on female workers in toilets. Some courts dealing with harassment suggested that whether or not conduct is offensive must be determined from the perspective of a reasonable person of the victim's gender because what is acceptable to most males may not be acceptable to most females.[36] In late 1993, the U.S. Supreme Court clarified the issue by holding that harassment need not cause serious psychological injury in order to be unlawful; it must only be offensive to a reasonable person.[37]

The Court continued to expand the scope and content of sexual harassment doctrine in important cases decided in 1998. One of the most debatable rulings applied Title VII to situations involving persons of the same sex. In *Oncale v. Sundowner Offshore Services*, heterosexual men engaged in harassing behavior against another heterosexual male employee, and the Court held that workplace harassment having a sexual content was unlawful discrimination "because of" sex.[38] Even though the harassers had no intention of engaging in sex with the victim, the fact that their behavior contained explicit references to sex brought the conduct under legal prohibition. *Oncale* effectively obliterates the notion that Title VII was designed to protect women on the basis of their gender because gender is now irrelevant to the creation of a hostile work environment if the offensive element is sexual.[39]

Employers are not liable for all situations involving a hostile working environment but only for the misconduct of supervisors, coemployees, and other persons allowed into the workplace when the employer was or should have been aware of the misconduct.[40] That rule is based on common law doctrines of agency relationships in organizations. Further, if the employer has a policy against sexual harassment and provides effective methods of dealing with its occurrence, the policy may shield the employer from liability. The point becomes important in the context of both litigation and human resource management policies because it provides an incentive for employers to enact grievance procedures so that employees can voice complaints about unacceptable sexual behaviors.[41] Those procedures can have financial consequences.

When it enacted the 1991 CRA, Congress expressed concern that the remedies for women victimized by a hostile working environment were inadequate to compensate them for the emotional trauma associated with harassment. The testimony of Lois Robinson, a shipyard welder, before the House Committee on Education and Labor contained graphic descriptions of harassment and abuse on the job. Despite her suffering, a trial judge awarded only $1 in damages. Robinson said, "That seemed like a slap in the face to me."[42] Congress agreed, and it added a special provision to the CRA that was extremely controversial in the business community. Under the law, damages in the case of intentional discrimination may include both compensatory and punitive damages. The compensatory damages exclude back pay and any other monetary relief available under Title VII, but they do cover emotional pain, suffering, inconvenience, loss of enjoyment of life, and other nonpecuniary losses. Cleverly drafted, the provisions apply only to cases of a hostile work environment, although the law does not expressly so state.[43] At the insistence of former president Bush, damages are limited by the size of the establishment involved. An employer with more than 14 and fewer than 101 employees is subject to a maximum of $50,000 in damages; the amount increases in three additional increments to employers of more than 500 employees, who are liable for up to

$300,000 in damages. The caps on damages were inserted as a compromise to gain White House support for the bill.

Affirmative Action

Clearly, most citizens support the idea that no one should be denied access to employment because of some immutable characteristic that has little to do with a job—such as race or gender. Title VII aimed to level the playing field by outlawing the use of specified criteria in employment decisions. But employers may sometimes use those criteria to benefit, rather than penalize, certain individuals. This form of discrimination appears in many aspects of public life as well as in the employment setting. Despite its ubiquity, the phenomenon of affirmative action or reverse discrimination is quite controversial as a matter of legal policy. In the employment setting, standards vary considerably depending on whether the employment is in the private or public sector. Title VII, covering both the public and the private sector, allows great latitude to employers. The Fifth and Fourteenth Amendments, which apply only to governmental employers, are interpreted much more narrowly.

In the landmark case of *Steelworkers v. Weber*,[44] the Kaiser Aluminum Company and the Steelworkers union negotiated a collective bargaining contract that gave black workers a substantial advantage in access to an apprenticeship program. The contract provided that regardless of seniority, for every white admitted to the program, one black apprentice would also be accepted. Brian Weber, a qualified white man, applied for an apprenticeship but was rejected. A black applied and was accepted because he was black, even though he had less seniority than Weber. Weber sued claiming that he was denied his seniority rights because of race. The Supreme Court ruled there was no violation of Title VII. A surprising result? Consider the Court's reasoning.

One way of analyzing the problem would be to say that Congress intended *race* to mean only racial minorities and not whites. That interpretation squares with the basic purpose of Title VII because whites historically gained from race discrimination that eliminated minority workers from desirable jobs. However, the Court had already decided in an earlier case that Title VII protects whites as a race as well as blacks. If, as Weber argued, whites are a race protected by law, and if the only reason Weber was not apprenticed was because he was white, how could he lose his case? The language seems so obvious that the only conclusion would be to prohibit race-conscious policies under the law. Nonetheless, the Court reached a conclusion that afforded employers protection against reverse discrimination claims.

To start with, the Court said that even though a literal construction of Title VII would have required a finding in Weber's favor, the law was not to be read literally. It is a "familiar rule," the opinion says, "that a thing may be within the letter of the statute and yet not within the statute, because not within its spirit, nor within the intention of the makers." According to the Court, Congress intended in Title VII to advance the economic status of blacks, and voluntary affirmative action programs consistent with that objective are permissible if they meet three other criteria. First, the plans must mirror the purposes of the statute in breaking down patterns of race discrimination. Second, the plan must not "unnecessarily trammel" the rights of the white employees. Third, the plan must be temporary and flexible, rather than imposing a strict, permanent racial quota. Because the plan in *Weber* satisfied those criteria, it was lawful.

Even though the Court has decided a number of cases dealing with reverse discrimination, *Weber* still remains intact as the definitive statement on private sector affirmative action plans. Employers can utilize policies to achieve diversity without fear of successful litigation so long as they adhere to the fairly loose requirements of *Weber.* In the public sector, where the U.S. Constitution rather than Title VII is the dominant law, the Court has failed to articulate a consistent rule or a coherent rationale for its decisions. It concedes that its precedents on the point cannot be reconciled with one another, and the constitutional rule with respect to employment seems to depend on the particular membership of the Court at a given point in time. That being the situation, tracing the contradictory path of doctrinal development is of little use in understanding the Court's recent pronouncements.[45] Instead, we examine the prevailing state of affairs in further detail.

In *Adarand Constructors, Inc. v. Pena,* the plaintiff Adarand submitted the low bid as a subcontractor to furnish guard rails on a transportation project. The primary contractor rejected the Adarand bid and offered the work to a minority business enterprise. The reason for that decision was purely economic; even though Adarand's bid was low, the contractor received a bonus for hiring a minority business to work on the project. As a result, the contractor made more money on the deal by selecting somewhat more expensive guard rails provided by a subsidized firm. The nonminority owner of Adarand, a man named Randy Pech, sued claiming a violation of his constitutional rights.

When the case reached the Supreme Court, a bloc consisting of O'Connor, Rehnquist, Thomas, Kennedy, and Scalia agreed that the lower courts had incorrectly approved the scheme of preferential treatment. The coalition endorsed at least one basic principle applicable to the facts: any racial classifications used by federal, state, or local governmental employers are subject to "strict judicial scrutiny" and will be constitutional only if they are "narrowly tailored" remedial efforts which further a "compelling governmental interest." Scalia and Thomas wrote concurring opinions to emphasize that, in their view, the state never had a compelling interest in conferring benefits based on race. The case was reversed and remanded for further consideration.

After reconsideration of the facts and the Court's opinion, the Tenth Circuit Court of Appeals found that the government's minority preference program had been modified and the case was no longer suitable for trial under the new standards. More appeals followed, including another trip to the Supreme Court, which finally held in November 2001 that the case was indeed moot and should finally be disposed of. However, the federal government agreed to pay over $300,000 in legal fees on behalf of Adarand.[46] At present, the following rule articulated in *Adarand* governs public sector employment: Affirmative racial preferences are permissible only if they are narrowly tailored programs that are based on a compelling governmental interest.

In June 2003, the Court upheld an affirmative action admissions policy at the University of Michigan.[47] Justice O'Connor's opinion stated the issue to be "Whether diversity is a compelling interest that can justify the narrowly tailored use of race in selecting applicants for admission to public universities." The Court's conclusion that diversity may rise to a compelling state interest has important implications for public sector employment and will undoubtedly encourage private sector employers to continue their diversity programs. Justice Ginsburg noted in a concurring opinion that the Michigan policy satisfied the standards announced in *Adarand*, and, as a result, the precedent in the educational setting may translate directly to the workplace.

The CRA addresses affirmative action in several important but ambiguous provisions. Section 107, which deals with intentional discrimination, states that employment decisions may be unlawful if based even *in part* on race or sex. Members of Congress disagreed during debate on the bill whether affirmative action plans—which are by definition based on race—are affected by the section. Another section of the CRA (Section 116) states that the new law does not affect affirmative action plans that are "in accordance with the law." The sections together suggest that judicial interpretations of the controlling law apply to the issue of whether discrimination occurs, and the standards developed under *Weber* and *Adarand* now constitute the law of affirmative action.

Another provision of the CRA affecting affirmative action is Section 106's prohibition of race norming of scores on employment-related tests. Under the race-norming procedure, the scores on employment screening tests are adjusted to different racial categories, or *normed*. Whites, for example, would be ranked with other white applicants, and African Americans and Hispanics would be compared with test takers in their groups. Through the adjustment, any differential racial impact of the test is eliminated. In a case involving Chicago firefighters, the race norming of promotion exams resulted in a $2.2 million verdict against the city. The district court characterized the city's practice as outright race discrimination against the white plaintiffs and upheld the jury's verdict.[48] However, the CRA and existing case law does not prohibit the practice of *banding*, which involves selecting a candidate who scores within an acceptable range on a selection test. A minority who met the minimum score might be chosen over a nonminority with a higher test score without violating the proscription against norming. Judge Richard Posner, writing for the Seventh Circuit Court of Appeals, said, "We have no doubt that if banding were adopted in order to make lower black scores seem higher, it would indeed be a form of race norming, and therefore forbidden. But it is not race norming per se. In fact it's a universal and normally an unquestioned method of simplifying scoring by eliminating meaningless gradations. Any school that switches from number grades to letter grades is engaged in banding."[49]

The civil rights laws and their interpretation have not eliminated debate about the general policies underlying affirmative action; in fact, the issue may now be more contentious than it was several decades ago.[50] The arguments for and against minority preferences turn on basic notions of equality in this country. Supporters of affirmative action programs point to engrained patterns of social and economic discrimination and conclude that only an effort to systematically undo institution-alized forms of race and gender bias will meliorate the built-in disadvantages suf-fered by some groups in this country.[51] Opponents of such programs take an ahistorical perspective based on assumptions about individual merit, opportunity, and the values embodied in the ideal of American equality. That view has been strongly endorsed by Justice Clarence Thomas, who wrote a separate opinion in the *Adarand* case to express his own views on race. Thomas observed,

> As far as the Constitution is concerned, it is irrelevant whether a government's racial classifications are drawn by those who wish to oppress a race or by those who have a sincere desire to help those thought to be disadvantaged. There can be no doubt that the paternalism that appears to lie at the heart of this pro-gram is at war with the principle of inherent equality that underlies and infuses our Constitution. . . . These programs not only raise grave constitu-tional questions, they also undermine the moral basis of the equal protection principle. Purchased at the price of immeasurable human suffering, the equal protection principle reflects our Nation's understanding that such classifica-tions ultimately have a destructive impact on the individual and our society.[52]

For Justice Thomas, nothing justifies governmental preferences conferred on the basis of an individual's race. Because the conflicting positions about affirmative action rest on fundamental beliefs and values, they are not easily reconciled. In this regard, compare Justice Thomas's position with that of Justice Marshall in the *Bakke* case. The significant point about the Court's jurisprudence in this area is that because it turns on subjective views, new appointments to the Court could very well lead to changes in its doctrine.

Age Discrimination in Employment Act

Congress enacted the ADEA in 1967 and has added various amendments since that time. Like Title VII, the ADEA's coverage is based on the number of employees employed by an entity affecting commerce; however, the ADEA extends to employ-ers with twenty employees rather than fifteen as under Title VII. State and local government employees are protected by the ADEA, but some occupations, such as firefighters, warrant special exemptions. The federal government is not an employer within the ADEA definition, but the statute contains separate provisions covering federal employment. As a result, most employment is subject to the ADEA provisions.

The ADEA prohibits employment decisions that discriminate against workers aged forty years or older. Before 1986, the ADEA protected workers aged forty to seventy, but Congress removed the upper limit. Accordingly, an employer cannot force an employee to retire at *any* age above forty, nor treat any employee over forty differently from younger workers, regardless of the employee's age. Since 1978, the EEOC has exercised authority over ADEA enforcement. The agency can bring a suit on its own initiative, but it must engage in conciliation before doing so. Individuals are entitled to sue in a private action provided they have filed a charge with the EEOC or the appropriate state agency and the EEOC or agency chooses not to proceed on the employee's behalf. Plaintiffs are entitled to a jury trial under the ADEA.[53] The methods of proving age discrimination are similar to those used in Title VII litigation. Most cases under the ADEA involve the issue of intent and are resolved by means of structure of proof discussed in connection with Title VII disparate treatment analysis. A recent example involving a television news reporter will illustrate the points above.

To boost its ratings, KMGH Channel 7 news in Denver, Colorado, hired a new management team. The team developed a strategy to appeal to younger viewers, which included hiring attractive female news anchors and adopting a more contemporary approach. A fifty-three-year-old reporter named Dave Minshall was fired shortly after the station decided on its new look. Minshall, who had worked in the Denver area for twenty-four years and had won eight Emmys, allegedly failed to proofread his work and reported incorrect facts. Minshall sued for age discrimination. Rejecting the company's reasons for discharge as pretextual, a federal jury found that KMGH had willfully violated Minshall's civil rights. The jury awarded him $212,326 in back pay, which was doubled because of the deliberate nature of the employer's action. Minshall also received $137,000 in lost future earnings and approximately $150,000 in attorney's fees. Minshall's lawyer summarized the moral of the case in the following statement to the press: "All the media need to understand that age does not mean ineffectiveness. Age can mean experience and wisdom. Walter Cronkite was the god of all television newscasters. Why was Channel 7 thinking it needed to get rid of a guy just because he's been around a long time?"[54] The publicity surrounding this case did not improve Channel 7's ratings.

A particularly problematic area of the ADEA has to do with corporate restructuring and cost reduction. Assume a company wants to trim its payroll costs, and it decides to lay off workers within a specific range of salaries. That range contains a disproportionate number of older employees, who by virtue of seniority and advancement have relatively high earnings. If the company proceeds with its plan, will it be liable under a disparate impact theory that statistically demonstrates an adverse effect on workers protected under the ADEA, or must workers prove intent to discriminate? The answer to this question generates some conflict among appellate courts. Some earlier cases assumed that the theory of disparate impact would apply in this situation, but that view is now questionable in light of some Supreme Court opinions. In any event, the defense of business necessity may succeed even if there is a disparate impact on older workers through a program of labor cost reduction. Whether those decisions are consistent with the underlying policies of the ADEA are debatable.[55]

The ADEA has a number of exclusions and defenses. Certain jobs, such as law enforcement officers and firefighters, may be subject to different standards than other occupations. Under Federal Aviation Authority regulations, airline pilots can be forced to retire from their positions at age sixty, although they may continue to work as flight engineers. More generally, employers may also differentiate among employees if age is an occupational qualification or in cases of reasonable factors other than age, including seniority systems, employee benefit plans, or discharge or discipline for good cause.[56] Also, benefits to older workers can be reduced to the extent they are based on differences in costs, such as life insurance policies. Congress amended the ADEA in the Older Workers' Benefit Protection Act of 1990 to clarify the statutory language regarding benefit plans. Under this provision, reductions are legal "where, for each benefit or benefit package, the actual amount of payment made or cost incurred on behalf of an older worker is no less than that made or incurred on behalf of a younger worker."[57]

Proving the bona fide occupational qualification defense based on age requires a specific approach. In a case involving Western Airlines, the U.S. Supreme Court held that an employer's rule discriminating against flight engineers over sixty did not constitute a lawful BFOQ. To prove the BFOQ, the Court held, Western could prove either that all or nearly all employees above the specified age lack qualifications for the job or, alternatively, that the age limit was one at which it was highly impractical to ensure by testing that an individual had the necessary job qualifications. Western argued that it was unsafe to have flight engineers over age sixty in the cockpit of an aircraft, but the jury rejected Western's defense and the Supreme Court affirmed.[58] The EEOC has adopted a similar formulation of an age-related BFOQ. Given the articulation of the BFOQ standard, is there some trait associated with age that affects an individual's ability to perform a particular job that it is impractical to determine except by knowing the individual's age? What might that trait be?

As a matter of policy, the ADEA eliminated a common type of employment discrimination that affected all workers. Attitudes about age and abilities have changed as social perceptions of the aging process have changed. Simple economics will continue to shape workforce demographics; given the impending retirement of baby boomers, the strains of funding pension plans may induce many to remain in the workforce, and Social Security funding, including Medicare, is a political issue of some visibility. The ADEA provides options for workers who prefer not to retire, which may be a substantial public benefit in the coming decades.

Americans With Disabilities Act of 1990

In 1973, Congress enacted the federal Rehabilitation Act designed to protect individuals in the federal sector from discrimination because of a disability. The Rehabilitation Act provided a model for various state statutes and for the comprehensive federal Americans With Disabilities Act in 1990. The ADA became effective in July 1992; two years later it was extended to cover employers of more than fifteen employees employed during a specified period. State and local governments are also subject to the ADA as employers. Federal government workers continue to be protected under the Rehabilitation Act as modified.

The ADA prohibits discrimination against a "qualified individual with a disability because of the disability of such individual." The definition of a disability has several elements; disabilities are defined as a physical or mental impairment that substantially limits a major life activity. Numerous medical conditions are encompassed within this broad language. A physical condition may include, for example, diabetes, cancer, heart defects, and the HIV virus that causes AIDS. Mental disabilities include retardation, dyslexia, emotional illness, and schizophrenia. Alcoholism and drug addiction may be disabilities, but employers can prohibit drug and alcohol use that interferes with job performance. Congress specifically excluded certain medically recognized conditions from coverage under the act; those include homosexuality, transsexualism, pedophilia, bisexuality, kleptomania, and transvestism. Individuals having a record of impairment or who are regarded as being impaired also fall within the definition of persons protected under the law.[59]

An individual may have one of the listed disabilities, but unless it limits a major life activity, it does not fall within the protection of the ADA. The Supreme Court made clear in a recent opinion that the definition of a major life activity has a broad scope. An employee of the Toyota Corporation sued under the ADA claiming a disability due to carpal tunnel syndrome. The Court, in a unanimous decision, held that her condition did not affect any major life activities. Conceding that the plaintiff could not perform her regular work duties of repetitive lifting, it offered the following test to determine the impact of a disability: "'Major' in the phrase 'major life activities' means important. 'Major life activities' thus refers to those activities that are of central importance to daily life. In order for performing manual tasks to fit into this category—a category that includes such basic abilities as walking, seeing, and hearing—the manual tasks in question must be central to daily life." The impairment's impact must also be permanent or long term.[60] Her major life activities, consequently, were not limited by the disability.

The key element of the ADA in relation to employment is the meaning of the word *qualified*. A person may have a disability but nonetheless be qualified for employment. Take the case of an individual confined to a wheelchair. That condition limits major life activities such as walking and performing some manual tasks. The meaning of a qualified individual under the ADA is a person who *with or without reasonable accommodation* can perform the *essential* functions of a job. This requirement imposes a duty not only to consider whether a person can perform a job, but whether the job can be modified to accommodate the disability. Thus, a nonwalking person could probably perform the job of a computer programmer with some minor modifications of the work process, such as providing access to areas where work is done. The ADA specifically mentions modifying facilities as a possible accommodation, as well as restructuring jobs, acquiring new equipment, or providing minor assistance to the disabled person. If the accommodation would result in undue hardship for the employer, it need not be undertaken. But the employer must prove that the suggested accommodation is an undue hardship taking into consideration the expense, the resources available, the number of persons employed, and the impact on the operation.[61]

The request for an accommodation may sometimes conflict with the employer's obligations toward other employees, such as a seniority system in a collective bargaining contract. On this point, the Supreme Court ruled in a 2002 decision that an employee of US Airways could not rely on the ADA to deprive another employee of his seniority rights. The disabled employee sought a job in the employer's mail room. Rather than agreeing to deprive a senior employee of the job, the employer refused to make the change. The Court found no violation of the ADA under those circumstances.[62] It rejected the employee's argument with the following response:

> The statute seeks to diminish or to eliminate the stereotypical thought processes, the thoughtless actions, and the hostile reactions that far too often bar those with disabilities from participating fully in the Nation's life, including the workplace. These objectives demand unprejudiced thought and reasonable responsive reaction on the part of employers and fellow workers alike. They will sometimes require affirmative conduct to promote entry of disabled people into the workforce. They do not, however, demand action beyond the realm of the reasonable.

Accordingly, the rights of nondisabled employees must be taken into consideration as part of the accommodation process.

Questions of employer motivation in making employment decisions are resolved using an analysis similar to that under the CRA and the ADEA. To illustrate, a male applicant confined to a wheelchair may possess educational qualifications and experience similar to a nondisabled applicant for a job in a retail clothing store. If the employer rejects the disabled applicant and hires another applicant with no disability, the disabled person can make out an inference of unlawful discrimination. The employer must then present evidence of a legitimate, nondiscriminatory reason for the decision—such as the explanation that the job requires transporting boxes of garments from a loading dock some distance from the sales floor, which could not be done in a wheelchair. The disabled person then has an opportunity to refute the proffered explanation. For example, the disabled individual might show that the employer never required female sales clerks to move goods into the store but always assigned males to work at times of deliveries.

The ADA also incorporates the disparate impact model of analysis into its statutory language. Specifically, the ADA provides that discrimination includes the use of selection criteria that "tend to screen out" disabled individuals or classes of individuals unless the selection device "is shown to be job-related for the position in question and is consistent with business necessity."[63] For example, a test of reading comprehension and written communication skills given to an applicant with the disability of mental retardation might be discriminatory if the job involved is sweeping a warehouse, picking up litter, and emptying trash containers. But a test requiring the interpretation of a schematic diagram might be lawful for the job of an electrical technician, even if it disqualified persons who lacked the mental capacity to comprehend such documents.

Another important part of the ADA deals with medical examinations. Generally, employers may not inquire into a person's physical or mental condition or past medical history. Applicants may be questioned about their ability to perform essential job tasks, such as operating the mechanical controls on a piece of equipment. Once an offer of employment is made, the employer may require a physical examination if all other employees in the classification are given the same examination and if the results of the examination are confidential. Should the examination reveal a disability that prevents the individual from being qualified for the job—even with reasonable accommodation—then the employer may rescind the offer of employment. To illustrate, an oil drilling company legally denied a job to an individual with a severe liver malfunction where the individual would be exposed to dangerous chemicals.[64] Safety considerations protect the individual claiming a disability as well as other employees.

Conclusion

As the foregoing discussion makes clear, the law of individual employment protection began with a narrow focus on groups that suffered historical and unambiguous discriminatory treatment in the workplace. Employers, along with social institutions in general, treated racial minorities and women differently than they treated white males. The political movements in the 1960s aimed to reduce barriers to economic progress. By the end of the twentieth century, the concept of a "protected class" had lost much of its definition. Included within the civil rights protections were workers having no discernible association with historical patterns of discrimination, such as males protected against sexual harassment by other heterosexual males. The evolving interpretation of compensatory damages for sexual harassment likewise moved civil rights law beyond the area of economic justice that provided the intellectual and moral impetus for the early legislation. Employers can now be financially liable even though the aggrieved employee suffered no loss of compensation or benefits.

Given the risk of litigation, some employers have reacted with attempts to contract out of the statutory minefield of employee rights. That strategy involves a binding agreement to arbitrate any disputes arising out of employment. The Supreme Court in *Circuit City Stores, Inc., v. Saint Clair Adams* (2001) encouraged the use of private arbitration clauses by holding that an employee could be compelled to arbitrate before seeking judicial remedies for age discrimination.[65] This trend will undoubtedly continue, and its policy implications are explored in detail in Chapter 8.

Summary

- The elimination of racial discrimination has been an ongoing project in this country since the Civil War. The Supreme Court stymied early federal legislative efforts by its interpretations of relevant constitutional and civil rights law.
- The modern era of civil rights employment legislation begins with Title VII of the Civil Rights Act of 1964. Congress expanded and supplemented the law with the Civil Rights Act of 1991.

- The Supreme Court developed two distinct theories of unlawful discrimination based on protected classes. The disparate treatment theory involves intentional discrimination against an individual or group of individuals because of their race. The disparate impact theory has to do with the outcomes of an employer's policies on a protected class, even though the policy is fair and neutral on its face.

- Because civil rights laws protect some workers but not others, they can have controversial applications in the workplace. An example is affirmative action preferences for minorities that can disadvantage whites. There is an important difference between the law of affirmative action in private and public sector employment; to date, the Supreme Court has been notably unsuccessful in creating stable and coherent legal doctrine to deal with the issue.

- In addition to Title VII, Congress also enacted laws that prohibit discrimination because of age or disability. Those areas now make up an important part of the EEOC caseload.

Further Analysis

1. The argument has been made that competitive labor markets will eliminate irrelevant and invidious discrimination because it forces employers to select and retain employees based strictly on their productivity. If that is true, will civil rights laws eventually become irrelevant? What are the major weaknesses in that argument?

2. Historically, discrimination persisted in this country for many years after the Civil War, despite constitutional amendments granting equal rights to all citizens. Does the historical evidence suggest that courts accommodate their opinions to social values? The Supreme Court decided *Brown v. Board of Education*—which outlawed segregated schools—in 1955. Were most Americans in 1955 ready to accept integrated schools? In this regard, consult Justice Marshall's opinion and consider why so little changed after the Civil War.

3. Does the prohibition against sex discrimination make the Equal Pay Act superfluous? Note the elements necessary to an EPA claim—how are they different than proof of discrimination under Title VII? Should the law attempt to evaluate the comparable worth of jobs in occupations segmented along lines of gender? More males are now entering the field of nursing, largely because of good wages and benefits. Does this support Justice Kennedy's contention that "neither law nor logic deems the free market system a suspect enterprise"?

4. How does the concept of disparate impact discrimination fit in with the purpose of economic opportunity? It is fairly clear that the Supreme Court had no basis for its decision in either the law or the legislative history of Title VII, but the rule might be justified as an effort to force employers to hire minorities by eliminating unfounded bias in selection. How does that rationale coincide with Justice Kennedy's notion of a free market system?

5. Disparate treatment claims require proof that an individual in a protected class was treated differently than a member of a nonprotected class. How does the burden and allocation of proof affect an employer's human resource policies? Assume, for example, that a claimant presents testimony that she had fewer absences than a male worker but she was fired for poor performance. What could the employer do to rebut this evidence?

6. Assume a transgendered individual applies for a job in a Las Vegas chorus line. The musical director states that no person who has, or did have, male sex organs will be hired as a topless dancer. Is this a bona fide occupational qualification? If it is, why did Hooters settle the claims against it instead of litigating?

7. What core values distinguish the positions of Justice Marshall and Justice Thomas regarding affirmative action? Which position do you think is most consistent with core American values? What are those values?

8. Prohibitions against age discrimination are conceptually different than other nondiscrimination laws (we aren't all minorities, but if we live long enough, we all get old). If the policy behind the ADEA is to promote the hiring of older workers, wouldn't a tax offset to employers be a more efficient approach? For example, if an employer hired a person over forty, the employer would get additional tax credit as a business expense. Would that same idea work for women and minorities?

9. The Americans With Disabilities Act has an important feature in that it requires an employer to accommodate a disability. Consider the free labor market attack on regulation in this context. If an employer could hire a loyal and competent employee by making some minor adjustment in work organization, is not the employer in the best position to decide what accommodation is reasonable? Are people with disabilities subject to the same kinds of discrimination as ethnic minorities? If Congress wanted to protect people who were historically discriminated against, why did they exclude homosexuality from the list of disabilities?

10. Title VII prohibits discrimination because of religion, and court decisions require employers to make some reasonable adjustments in work schedules to accommodate religious beliefs. In July 2001, a federal jury awarded an air traffic controller $2.25 million for a claim of religious discrimination.[66] The employee refused to work from sundown Friday to sundown on Saturday, and a supervisor fired him for missing several days of scheduled work. The employee belonged to no formal religious group. His celebration of the Sabbath was based on his reading of the book of Genesis, which prescribes rest on the seventh day. Since the 1991 Civil Rights Act puts a cap on damages, the $1.5 million in punitive damages was reduced to $300,000. But the employer also paid $248,356 in back pay, $508,088 in future lost pay, and about $100,000 in attorneys' fees to the American Civil Liberties Union. Since air traffic controllers are federal government employees, the money will be provided by taxpayers. Does this case illustrate the continuing need for civil rights laws or the unwarranted extremes to which such laws have been taken?

11. All things considered, would it not be simpler to do away with all existing civil rights laws and establish an employment tribunal that would hear the grievances of anyone not selected for, or separated from, employment and provide a standard remedy of six months' wages if the employer acted arbitrarily or discriminatorily?

Suggested Readings

Equal Employment Opportunity Commission. "The Story of the United States Equal Employment Opportunity Commission: Ensuring the Promise of Opportunity for 35 Years, 1965–2000." Online at www.eeoc.gov/35th/history/index.html.

Gold, Michael Evan. *An Introduction to the Law of Employment Discrimination*, 2d ed. Ithaca, NY: IRL Press/Cornell University Press, 2001.

Gregory, Raymond F. *Age Discrimination in the American Workplace: Old at a Young Age.* New Brunswick, NJ: Rutgers University Press, 2001.

Gutman, Arthur. *EEO Law and Personnel Practices,* 2d ed. Thousand Oaks, CA: Sage Publications, 2000.

Hawkins, Michael W., ed. *The HR Survival Guide to Labor & Employment Law.* Cincinnati, OH: National Underwriter, 2001.

Moran, John Jude. *Employment Law: New Challenges in the Business Environment,* 2d ed. Upper Saddle River, NJ: Prentice Hall, 2002.

Rothstein, Mark, et al. *Employment Law,* 2d ed. Minneapolis, MN: West, 2001.

Stefan, Susan. *Hollow Promises: Employment Discrimination Against People With Mental Disabilities.* Washington, DC: American Psychological Association, 2002.

Endnotes

1. Following civil rights demonstrations in Alabama in June 1963, President Kennedy addressed the country on national television. In his speech, he said,

We are confronted primarily with a moral issue. It is as old as the scriptures and it is as clear as the American Constitution. The heart of the question is whether all Americans are afforded equal rights and equal opportunities, whether we are going to treat our fellow Americans as we want to be treated. . . . One hundred years of delay have passed since President Lincoln freed the slaves, yet their heirs, their grandsons, are not fully free. They are not yet free from the bonds of injustice. And this nation, for all its hopes and all its boasts, will not be fully free until all of its citizens are free.

For additional background on Title VII, visit the Web site at www.eeoc.gov.

2. 42 U.S.C. § 200e-2(a)(1).

3. Indeed, U.S. employers traditionally took age into consideration when hiring workers, and even into the 1960s, job advertisements might specify that applicants over the age of forty were not acceptable. During the 1920s, social activists attempted to influence companies through a publicity campaign, but their efforts had little effect until changes in the law. For a historical study of the topic, see Kerry Seagrave, *Age Discrimination by Employers* (Jefferson, NC: McFarland, 2001).

4. *St. Mary's Honor Center v. Hicks,* 509 U.S. 502 (1993).

5. According to the EEOC, state agencies in 2001 "resolved 54,851 charges under contract with the EEOC. These charges are in addition to the 80,840 received by the EEOC in FY 2000." For more information, see the materials on enforcement online at http://eeoc.gov/enforce.html [vistited May 27, 2003].

6. The field of human resource management focuses on the development of comprehensive workplace policies covering all phases of employment; those policies include procedures for hiring and evaluating employees on a fair and nondiscriminatory basis. See, for example, Gary Dessler, *Human Resource Management,* 9th ed. (Upper Saddle River, NJ: Prentice Hall, 2003).

7. Richard A. Epstein, *Forbidden Grounds: The Case Against Employment Discrimination Laws* (Cambridge, MA: Harvard University Press, 1992), 3.

8. Public Law 88-38 (1963).

9. 29 U.S.C. § 203(d).

10. *American Federation of State, County and Municipal Employees v. State of Washington,* 770 F.2d 1401 (9th Cir. 1985). Kennedy pointed out that compensation systems are based on supply and demand operating in labor markets, and therefore, "Neither law nor logic deems the free market system a suspect enterprise."

11. Jeanne Cummings, "Gore's Equal-Pay Refrain Is Played for Working Women," *Wall Street Journal,* August 28, 2000, p. A20.

12. The statute is codified at 42 U.S.C. § 1981.

13. For representative cases, see *Rankin v. McPherson,* 487 U.S. 378 (1987) (upholding free speech rights of a public employee) and *Cleveland Bd. of Education v. Loudermill,* 470 U.S. 532 (1985) (public employees have right of procedural due process when deprived of property interest in employment).

14. Justice Marshall relies on three principal sources in his opinion. Those sources are John Hope Franklin, *From Slavery to Freedom: A History of African Americans,* 4th ed. (New York: Alfred A. Knopf, 1974 [8th ed., 2000]); Richard Kluger, *Simple Justice: The History of Brown v. Board of Education and Black America's Struggle for Equality* (New York: Alfred A. Knopf, 1975); C. Vann Woodward, *The Strange Career of Jim Crow,* 3d ed. (New York: Oxford University Press, 1974). Specific citations have been deleted from the quoted material.

15. *Griggs v. Duke Power Co.,* 401 U.S. 424 (1971).

16. For a discussion of the relationship between law, psychology, and the *Griggs* rule, see Raymond Hogler and Jeanette Cleveland, "*Wards Cove* and the Theory of Disparate Impact: From Bad Law to Worse Policy," *Labor Law Journal* 41 (1990): 138–150.

17. Uniform Guidelines on Employee Selection Procedures, 29 *Code of Federal Regulations* § 1607.5 (B) (2000).

18. For a good discussion of testing in the employment context, see Frank Landy, *Psychology of Work Behavior,* 4th ed. (Pacific Grove, CA: Brooks/Cole, 1989), 54–86.

19. Michael Gold, "*Griggs'* Folly: An Essay on the Theory, Problems, and Origin of the Adverse Impact Definition of Employment Discrimination and a Recommendation for Reform," *Industrial Relations Law Journal* 7 (1985): 429–598.

20. Gold, "*Griggs'* Folly," p. 587.

21. *Wards Cove Packing Co. v. Antonio,* 490 U.S. 642 (1989).

22. On this point, see David Cathcart and Mark Snyderman, "The Civil Rights Act of 1991," *Labor Lawyer* 8 (1992): 869–873.

23. For a collection of essays on conflict, diversity, and human resource practices, see *Journal of Business and Management* 8, no. 3 (Summer 2002) [special issue on conflict management].

24. *Texas Dept. of Community Affairs v. Burdine,* 450 U.S. 248 (1981).

25. See *St. Mary's Honor Center,* 509 U.S. 502 (1993). In this case, a black worker was demoted, and the employer presented various reasons for the action. The worker proved that those reasons were false, and the appeals court ruled in his favor. Justice Scalia said that the lower court incorrectly presumed that an employer's false statement was necessarily proof of race discrimination. Scalia explained:

> We have no authority to impose liability upon an employer for alleged discriminatory employment practices unless an appropriate factfinder determines, according to proper procedures, *that the employer has unlawfully discriminated.* We may, according to traditional practice, establish certain modes and orders of proof, including an initial rebuttable presumption. . . . But nothing in law would permit us to substitute for the required finding that the employer's action was the product of unlawful discrimination, the much different (and much lesser) that the employer's explanation of its action was not believable.

100 U.S. 515, emphasis in original.

26. Compare *Reeves v. Sanderson Plumbing Products,* 503 U.S. 133 (2000). This case appears conceptually incompatible with *St. Mary's Honor Center.* Justice Scalia declined to raise the question of whether the latter opinion is now defunct, although Justice Ginsburg wrote a short concurring opinion which casts doubt on the continuing viability of the Scalia approach.

27. *Price Waterhouse v. Hopkins,* 490 U.S. 228 (1989).

28. Civil Rights Act of 1991, Pub. Law 102–166 (1991). For a case applying the rule, see *Garcia v. City of Houston,* 201 F.3d 672 (5th Cir. 2000).

29. *United Auto Workers v. Johnson Controls, Inc.,* 499 U.S. 187 (1991).

30. At one point in this dispute, Hooters mounted an advertising campaign that featured a muscular, unshaven male wearing a (bad) blonde wig and a scanty costume and a text message chastising the EEOC for its lack of humor. The EEOC was not amused.

31. [New Orleans] *Times-Picayune,* October 1, 1997.

32. Dina Berta, "EEOC Sues Jillian's Chain for Alleged Denial of Tipped Jobs to Men," *Nation's Restaurant News,* December 4, 2000.

33. As the 1964 legislation moved through Congress, some opponents of the bill attempted to delay its passage by amending the statute in the House of Representatives to prohibit discrimination because of "sex." That tactic failed when both the House and the Senate approved the amendment without significant debate. As a result, the intent of the provision was never fully addressed. See, e.g., *Congressional Record,* 1964: 2577–2584.

34. See, e.g., *Barnes v. Costle,* 561 F.2d 983 (D.C. Cir. 1977); *Tompkins v. Public Service Co.,* 568 F.2d 1044 (3d Cir. 1977).

35. *Meritor Savings Bank v. Vinson,* 477 U.S. 57 (1985).

36. See generally Mack Player, *Federal Law of Employment Discrimination,* 3d ed. (St. Paul, MN: West, 1992), § 24.02, pp. 208–212.

37. *Harris v. Forklift Systems,* 510 U.S. 17 (1993).

38. *Oncale v. Sundowner Offshore Services, Inc.,* 523 U.S. 75 (1998).

39. For example, it was illegal in *Oncale* for men to ridicule the plaintiff for his effeminate appearance and to make lewd statements about his sexuality. But, presumably, it would not be unlawful to harass another person because he or she was ugly, stupid, incompetent, lazy, or some other undesirable attribute having no gender or sexual connotations.

40. If a manager exercises authority over wages, hours, and working conditions to extract sexual favors from subordinates, the company is liable because it granted the power to the supervisor. A hostile working environment, in distinction, can be created by nonsupervisory personnel. See EEOC, "Enforcement Guidance: Vicarious Employer Responsibility for

Unlawful Harassment by Supervisors." Online at www.eeoc.gov/policy/guidance.html [visited May 5, 2003].

41.   *Faragher v. City of Boca Raton,* 524 U.S. 775 (1998). For a discussion and empirical study of the effects of employer policies, see Raymond L. Hogler, Jennifer H. Frame, and George Thornton, "Workplace Sexual Harassment Law: An Empirical Analysis of Organizational Justice and Legal Policy," *Journal of Managerial Issues* 14 (2002): 234–250.

42. Statement of Lois Robinson, Committee on Education and Labor, *Hearings on H.R. 1, The Civil Rights Act of 1991* (Washington, DC: Government Printing Office, 1991), 78–82.

43. CRA, § 102(a)(1).

44. *United Steelworkers of America v. Weber,* 443 U.S. 193 (1979).

45. The opinion in *Johnson v. Transportation Agency,* 480 U.S. 616 (1987), represents the most liberal view of affirmative action taken by the Court. In the case, a woman applied for a skilled job on a highway crew, and the employer gave the woman preferential consideration because of her gender. Six Justices voted to uphold the employer's action as within the legal scope of Title VII and the Fourteenth Amendment. For the Court, Justice Brennan wrote,

> We therefore hold that the Agency appropriately took into account as one factor the sex of Diane Joyce in determining that she should be promoted to the road dispatcher position. The decision to do so was made pursuant to an affirmative action plan that represents a moderate, flexible, case-by-case approach to effecting a gradual improvement in the representation of minorities and women in the Agency's work force. Such a plan is fully consistent with Title VII, for it embodies the contribution that voluntary employer action can make in eliminating the vestiges of discrimination in the workplace.

Justices Rehnquist, White, and Scalia dissented in this case. In their view, discrimination in favor of minorities should not be permitted under either the Constitution or Title VII. Former president Bush appointed Clarence Thomas, an African American, to the Court in 1991, and Thomas has expressed similar views.

46. The *Adarand* case was litigated by the Mountain States Legal Foundation. The foundation specializes in attacking government regulatory activity that interferes with the liberty and property interests of employers, landowners, and nonunion workers. For a description of its activities, visit www.mountainstateslegal.org/index.cfm.

47. *Grutter v. Bollinger,* 123 Sup. Ct. 2325 (June 2003). The Court struck down the University of Michigan's undergraduate affirmative action policy because it awarded a fixed number of points to all minority applicants. Therefore, the policy was not narrowly tailored to achieve its objective. *Gratz v. Bollinger,* 123 Sup. Ct. 2411 (June 2003).

48. *Biondo v. City of Chicago,* 2002 U.S. Dist. LEXIS 3463 (February 2002). According to the opinion, "[The] evidence established that the defendant City of Chicago was liable to the class of white plaintiff-intervenors whose promotions to the rank of Lieutenant in the CFD were delayed or denied as a result of the City's unconstitutional, intentional use of race in the making of the City's decisions regarding promotions to the rank of Lieutenant."

49. *Chicago Firefighters Local 2 v. City of Chicago,* 249 F.3d 649 (7th Cir. 2001).

50. See, for example, Samuel Issacharoff, "Law and Misdirection in the Debate Over Affirmative Action," *University of Chicago Legal Forum* (2002): 11–44.

51. For an overview of the arguments about affirmative action and a detailed survey of legal developments, see Giradeau A. Spann, *The Law of Affirmative Action: Twenty-five Years of Supreme Court Decisions on Race and Remedies* (New York: New York University, 2000).

52. *Adarand Constructors v. Pena,* 515 U.S. at 240.

53. The availability of a jury trial has resulted in some sizeable awards under the ADEA. In June 2001, an employee won an award of $10.3 million from Level 3 Communications.

The amount included $5 million in punitive damages, $5 million in compensatory damages, and $300,000 in lost stock options. Those damages, however, were subject to the limits specified in the Civil Rights Act of 1991 and the trial judge reduced the amount to a total of $900,000. John Accola, "Judge Cuts Award in Level 3 Age-Discrimination Case," *Rocky Mountain News,* June 15, 2001, p. 4B. The act provides, "The sum of the amount of compensatory damages awarded under this section for future pecuniary losses, emotional pain, suffering, inconvenience, mental anguish, loss of enjoyment of life, and other non-pecuniary losses, and the amount of punitive damages awarded under this section, shall not exceed, for each complaining party," an amount determined by the size of the firm, not to exceed $300,000. Section 102(b)(3). For a case discussing the limits, see *Lansdale v. Hi-Health Supermarket Corp.,* 314 F.3d 355 (9th Cir. 2002).

54. Mike McPhee, "Ex-reporter Wins Age-Bias Lawsuit," *Denver Post,* September 6, 2001, p. 1B.

55. For a thoughtful discussion of the point, see Judith D. Fischer, "Public Policy and the Tyranny of the Bottom Line in the Termination of Older Workers," *South Carolina Law Review* 53 (2002): 211.

56. 29 U.S.C. § 623(f)(1).

57. 29 U.S.C. § 623(f)(2)(B)(i).

58. *Western Airlines v. Criswell,* 472 U.S. 400 (1985).

59. See generally James Frierson, *Employer's Guide to the Americans With Disabilities Act* (Washington, DC: Bureau of National Affairs, 1992), 48–52.

60. *Toyota Motor Co. v. Williams,* 534 U.S. 184 (2002).

61. An informative reference on these and other points is Equal Employment Opportunity Commission, *A Technical Assistance Manual on the Employment Provision (Title I) of the Americans With Disabilities Act* (Washington, DC: Equal Employment Opportunity Commission, 1992).

62. *U.S. Airways v. Barnett,* 535 U.S. 391 (2002).

63. Americans With Disabilities Act, 42 U.S.C. § 12112(b)(6)–(7).

64. *Chevron U.S.A., Inc. v. Echazabal,* 536 U.S. 73 (2002).

65. *Circuit City Stores, Inc. v. Saint Clair Adams,* 532 U.S. 105 (2001).

66. Mike McPhee, "Sabbath Observer Wins Suit on Firing," *Denver Post,* July 18, 2001.

CHAPTER 7

Workplace Rights and Benefits

This chapter surveys post–New Deal legislation that protects employees by conferring specific rights and benefits on them by virtue of their employment rather than their inclusion in a designated classification, such as ethnicity. Recall that the main components of the employment benefit system were in place by the end of the 1930s and are covered earlier in the book. To reiterate briefly, the first important development was in the area of workers' compensation legislation that displaced common law doctrine. With the legislative revolution of Franklin D. Roosevelt's New Deal, workers gained economic rights through Social Security, fair labor standards, and unemployment insurance. Congress continued to expand the New Deal programs and supplemented employment legislation with civil rights laws. As distinct from antidiscrimination laws, the focus here is on legislation that benefits workers as a class.

The chapter begins with the right to a safe and healthy workplace under the Occupational Safety and Health Act (OSHA). We then examine the Employee Retirement Income Security Act (ERISA), which gives employees rights to information and participation in an employer's retirement plan. Most recently, the Family and Medical Leave Act (FMLA) entitles workers to take unpaid leaves for medical reasons. Congress has also adopted measures addressing the provision of health insurance in the workplace; these measures fall far short of mandating universal coverage, but they do offer some protections against loss of insurance. In addition, one state—Montana—enacted a statute protecting employees against a wrongful discharge. Table 7.1 summarizes the main content of the chapter.

Table 7.1   Overview of Protective Workplace Legislation

Law	Coverage	Main Focus	Approach	Comment
Occupational Safety and Health Act, 1970 (OSHA)	Private and public sectors	Safety and health regulation	Enforced through system of inspections and penalties	Ergonomics is an example of the ongoing debate over workplace health
Employee Retirement Income Security Act, 1976 (ERISA)	Workers covered under employer pension plans	Stability and coverage of retirement income	Requires disclosure of information; insurance system for plans	Most relevant to defined benefit plans, which are declining in coverage
Coverage for continued health insurance benefits (COBRA, HIPAA, PPRA)	Continuation of health insurance benefits	Amendments to ERISA	Allows extension of benefits in case of termination or change of employment	Does not mandate health insurance; requires employee to pay premiums
Family and Medical Leave Act, 1993 (FMLA)	Employers having more than fifty employees, including public sector	Provides unpaid leaves for family health purposes	Guarantees rights to return to job and maintain specified benefits	May impose financial burden on employee and operational burdens on employer
Montana Wrongful Discharge Act, 1987	Private sector employees in the state of Montana	Requires just cause for discharge	Preempts common law claims for unlawful discharges	Only state legislation that abrogates the employment at will rule

Workplace Health and Safety: OSHA

The Occupational Safety and Health Act became law on December 29, 1970.[1] It addressed the problem of industrial injuries to workers, which Congress perceived to be a matter of increasing concern to the nation. Prior to OSHA, there was no comprehensive federal statute that protected all U.S. workers against safety and health hazards in the workplace, and regulation was left primarily to the states.[2] The result of federal neglect was that occupational risks had reached crisis proportions. According to a House Report on industrial safety,

> The on-the-job health and safety crisis is the worst problem confronting American workers, because each year as a result of their jobs over 14,500 workers die. In only four years time, as many people have died because of their employment as have been killed in almost a decade of American involvement in Vietnam. Over two million workers are disabled annually through job-related accidents.

The economic impact of occupational accidents and diseases is over-whelming. Over $1.5 billion is wasted in lost wages, and the annual loss to the Gross National Product is over $8 billion. Ten times as many man-days are lost from job-related disabilities as from strikes, and days lost productivity through accidents and illnesses are ten times greater than the loss from strikes.[3]

Other statistics presented to Congress indicated that 2.5 million workers suffered an on-the-job injury every year and that more Americans died as a result of industrial accidents and disease between 1945 and 1970 than died fighting World War II. One congressman observed ironically, "It is a fact that in the States today there are 1,600 game wardens. Elk and deer are better protected than working men and women."[4] Indeed, according to a 1967 study, there were more than twice as many fish and game wardens employed by the federal government as there were safety inspectors employed by the state and federal governments combined.[5]

To alleviate those conditions, Congressman James O'Hara introduced safety and health legislation in January 1969. That measure was followed by bills sponsored by Senator Harrison Williams and by the Nixon administration. Several versions of the legislation were debated and substantially modified by the House and the Senate prior to passage of the final draft.[6] Because of the different drafts considered by Congress and the lobbying of various groups for their respective positions, the final legislation reflected significant adjustments. One commentator describes the con-sequences as follows:

> As the legislative history clearly indicates, OSHA was the result of numerous compromises, a fact evidenced in two important ways. First, the Act is not well drafted: various sections of the Act are vague, redundant and even para-doxical. Second, in construing the Act, the legislative history is seldom con-clusive because the members of Congress never considered the Act in its present form until after the Conference Report. Thus, Commission and judi-cial resort to the legislative history as an aid interpreting the Act has often proved fruitless.[7]

From its inception, OSHA embodied disparate perspectives and agendas.

Occupational safety and health remains a contentious subject after three decades. One of the most controversial standards taken up by the OSHA adminis-tration has to do with the ergonomics of work. After many years of study and dis-cussion, the administration implemented a standard in late 2000 dealing with work-related musculoskeletal disorders (MSDs). It required proactive efforts on the part of covered employers to mitigate repetitive motion injuries, including detailed record keeping, employee participation, and training. The regulation provoked a reaction among employers. One of the first actions in the George W. Bush admin-istration was congressional repeal of the standard. Subsequently, in mid-2001, the secretary of labor conducted a series of national hearings and drafted a four-prong approach to deal with ergonomic issues. The approach focuses on education, information, and cooperation rather than enforcement.[8] The content of the repealed standard is discussed more fully in the section below dealing with standards.

Purpose and Method

The stated objective of OSHA is "to assure so far as possible every working man and woman in the Nation safe and healthful working conditions and to preserve our human resources." Congress provided in Section 2(b) that the statutory purpose was to be effectuated through the following means: (1) by promoting employer and employee efforts to diminish the occurrence of work-related safety and health hazards, (2) by promoting employer and employee efforts to initiate educational programs concerning safety and health, (3) by establishing mutual employer and employee obligations and rights to create a safe and healthy workplace, (4) by imposing upon the secretary of labor the duty of setting standards through research and providing for the efficient enforcement of those standards, (5) by establishing the Occupational Safety and Health Review Commission to judicially oversee the act, (6) by training individuals in the field of occupational safety and health to ensure capable personnel in the area, and (7) by setting record keeping and reporting requirements with respect to job-related safety and health. In all, Section 2(b) contains thirteen separate subsections particularizing the methods by which the legislative intent is to be implemented.

Coverage and General Duties

Consistent with its protective purpose, OSHA is very broad in its scope. In Section 3(5), Congress defined *employer* to mean "a person engaged in a business affecting commerce who has employees, but does not include the United States or any State or political subdivision of a State." Thus, OSHA was designed to extend to the limits of federal power under the Commerce Clause of the Constitution and applied to approximately five million workplaces and sixty-five million workers. Public employees excluded from OSHA coverage can be protected under state or federal laws in their specific workplaces. The federal government, for example, issued an executive order in 1980 expanding the safety and health protections available to federal employees. Three states, New York, New Jersey, and Connecticut, have implemented plans protecting their public sector workers.[9]

In Section 5, the act sets forth the duties imposed on both employers and employees. According to Section 5(a)(1), otherwise known as the General Duty Clause, the employer has an obligation to provide his employees with a safe and healthy workplace "free from recognized hazards that are causing or are likely to cause death or serious physical harm to his employees." Additionally, Section 5(a)(2) requires that the employer adhere to the standards promulgated pursuant to the act. With respect to employees, Section 5(b) requires that each employee shall comply with the job safety and health rules established at the workplace in compliance with OSHA.

Standards

Section 6 of the act provides for the establishment of occupational safety and health standards in the workplace, which determine an employer's duties. The secretary of labor has authority to promulgate standards using three separate procedures. First, under Section 6(a), the secretary was authorized to adopt existing federal standards and national consensus standards, provided the secretary did so within two years of the effective date of the act. The federal standards were those standards that had been promulgated as federal statutes or regulations. National consensus standards were those that had been established by a "nationally recognized standards producing agency," such as the National Institute for Occupational Safety and Health (NIOSH), under conditions in which affected parties had been afforded the opportunity to introduce their positions and have them examined. Consequently, OSHA incorporated a large body of accepted safety practices.

Section 6(b) provides for the promulgation of standards through a process of rule making. Generally, the secretary may develop a standard based on information provided by any interested person or designated group. The proposed rule must first be published in the Federal Register. Sections 6(b)(2) and (3) then afford any interested person an opportunity to submit information and position papers and to request and participate in hearings regarding a proposed standard before the standard goes into effect. Further, any party affected by a standard may file a petition challenging the standard at any time before the sixtieth day of its being made public.

A third type of standard is contemplated under Section 6(c)(1). The secretary has authority to implement an *emergency temporary standard* (ETS), which is effective immediately upon its publication in the Federal Register. There are two requisites that must be satisfied prior to issuance of an ETS. First, the secretary must determine that employees "are exposed to grave danger from exposure to substances or agents determined to be toxic or physically harmful or from new hazards." Second, the secretary must find that the ETS "is necessary to protect employees from such danger." Within six months of the date of the ETS, the secretary must comply with the rule-making procedures of Section 6(b) in order to adopt the ETS as a permanent standard. The ETS as published serves as the proposed rule referred to in Section 6(b). With respect to any promulgated standard, employers are given the right to apply for a variance from the standard or a part of it and they may petition for an interim order until a decision is made on the variance application. Employers must inform affected employees of variance applications and describe alternative methods of protecting workers.

As noted earlier, the OSH administration's recent proposed ergonomics standard illustrates the process and politics of the law. It initially developed a tentative rule dealing with repetitive motion disorders, which can cause a variety of injuries to workers. That rule encountered substantial opposition from business groups, and administrators provided more opportunity for debate and discussion. At a meeting in March 2000, Marthe Kent, head of OSHA's regulatory program, articulated the agency's position on the standard. Among other points, Kent emphasized that "publishing a final rule addressing ergonomic hazards in the workplace will do more to help American workers and fulfill OSHA's Congressional mandate than any other single action this Agency could take." She stated that "conservatively estimated, American employers report that nearly 2 million of their employees suffer work-related musculoskeletal disorders (MSDs) every year. Put differently, this means that 2% of the entire U.S. workforce suffers a work-related MSD every year." Although the regulation would impose costs on employers to correct workplace conditions leading to such disorders, the agency contended that those costs were negligible compared with the benefits of the corrections. According to Kent, "One-third of all the workers' compensation dollars paid out in this country— somewhere between $15 and $18 billion dollars a year—go to pay the medical costs and replace the lost wages of the workers hurt by these disorders."[10] To reiterate, the Clinton administration adopted the standard and Congress in March 2001 rescinded it by resolution.[11]

Record Keeping

In Section 8, OSHA establishes several record keeping, reporting, and posting requirements for the employer. For example, the employer has an obligation to post notices supplied by OSHA that outline the responsibilities and rights afforded by the act. The notices inform employees that more detailed information, including copies of the act and its specific standards, may be obtained through the employer or the Department of Labor. If an employer possesses copies of the act or its standards, he or she is to provide those to employees as promptly as possible upon request. The notices are to be posted in prominent places, such as employee bulletin boards. The employer must, to the extent possible, prevent alteration, defacement, or concealment of the notices.

With respect to record keeping, small employers having less than ten employees are exempted from most of the OSHA record requirements. Generally, covered employers have the responsibility of maintaining and making available certain information relevant to work-related safety and health. The employer must keep a log and summary of all job-related injuries and illnesses, other than minor injuries, at each work location, with log entries being made no later than six working days after the employer becomes aware of an occurrence. The employer must also post an annual summary of work-related injuries and illnesses at each physical location of the employer's operations. The summaries are to be posted no later than February of the year following the year to which the summaries apply and are to remain posted until March 1. The logs and summaries are to be retained by the employer at each physical location for a five-year period, calculated from the end of the year to which the statistics refer. Upon request, such records are to be made available to any employees currently or formerly employed by the employer or their employee representatives, as well as to any representatives of the secretary of labor. In addition, the employer is obligated to report within forty-eight hours any work-related occurrences resulting in the death of one or more employees or the hospitalization of five or more employees to the OSHA area director, either orally or in writing.

Under Section 8(c)(3) and OSHA regulations, employers may be required periodically to monitor employee exposure levels to specified substances and physical agents. Employees and employee representatives are entitled to observe the measurements and monitoring of any potentially dangerous substances or agents that require monitoring under Section 6. Further, employers must keep precise records of employees' exposure levels to these substances. Exposure records include environmental monitoring, biological monitoring that measures the body's intake of substances, material safety data sheets, and any other records that would disclose the presence of toxic substances. Upon request, these records are to be made available to affected employees or former employees or employee representatives, as well as to representatives of the secretary in their attempts to carry out the provisions of the act. The employer is responsible for promptly informing affected employees of levels of exposure to toxic substances or harmful physical agents in excess of those standards established by the act. Toxic substances and harmful physical agents include any chemical or biological substances or physical factors, such as noise, heat, or cold, that are regulated by federal law as a health hazard or that are contained in the latest edition of the NIOSH Registry of Toxic Effects of Chemical Substances.

In the 1980s, several states enacted right-to-know laws requiring designated firms to identify harmful chemical agents and inform affected persons, including community members, of the health effects of the materials. In response to the state activism, OSHA issued its own revised hazard communication standard in August 1987,[12] and the federal legislation generally superceded the state laws. According to a 1996 study group, "There is a need for hazard communication, and employees have a right-to-know about the hazardous chemicals in their workplace." The report continues that OSHA's Hazard Communication Standard "is a good one" and effectively protects against exposure to harmful chemicals.[13]

Inspections

An essential feature of the OSHA enforcement scheme is the inspection system, described in Section 8. If an employee or employee representative suspects that a safety or health violation that threatens physical harm is present at the workplace, or that an imminent danger exists, he or she may make a written request to the area director for inspection. The request is to state "with reasonable particularity" the reasons for the application for inspection and is to be signed by the employee or employee representative. The employer is furnished with a copy of the application for inspection; however, the name of the individual or individuals filing the notice may be omitted from the employer's copy upon request of the individual (Section 8(f)(1)).

Upon receipt of that notice, the area director must make a determination as to whether reasonable evidence of a violation exists. If the area director deems that there is insufficient evidence of a violation, the complainant is notified of the decision. If the area director determines that grounds exist for conducting an inspection, the director orders one held as soon as practicable.[14] Inspections are generally held during working hours at a time determined by the area director or a compliance officer. The inspection begins with the compliance officer first presenting his or her credentials to the individual in charge. The officer then reveals the nature and purpose of the inspection, including its extent and any records he or she may wish to see. Typically, an employee complaint will provide the probable cause necessary to support a search warrant.[15] Inspections are not limited to items cited in the complaint. In fact, any employee or employee representative at the workplace may provide the compliance officer with written notice of a suspected standard violation at any time before or during the inspection.

During inspections, both the employee and the employer representatives are permitted to accompany the compliance officer on the workplace inspection, although the employer is not obliged to compensate employees for their time. If an employee representative is not present in the workplace, the compliance officer will meet with "a reasonable number of employees" to discuss work-related safety and health (Section 8(e)). Further, the compliance officer is entitled to interview the owner, manager, employer representative, or employees confidentially during the course of the inspection concerning matters related to job safety and health. The compliance officer generally investigates conditions, structures, materials, and equipment. In doing so, the officer is authorized to take photographs, environmental samples, and individual employee exposure readings through the use of personal sampling devices, such as badges. Following the inspection, the compliance officer meets with the employer and informs him or her of any evident violations. At this time, the employer may supply the compliance officer with any additional information relevant to workplace conditions.

Employers are not given advance notice of inspections, except in very unusual circumstances. Among the exceptional cases are those in which a probable imminent danger situation exists. In this instance, advance notice may be given to ensure the prompt abatement of the dangerous situation. Advance notice of an inspection may also be given when the inspection can be carried out more efficiently after work hours or where special arrangements must be made prior to the inspection. Similarly, advance notice may be given in order to ensure the availability of employee or employer representatives or trained personnel necessary to the completion of a thorough inspection. Advance notice may also be given in those instances in which the area director believes that it would ensure an efficient and complete inspection. Typically, notice is to be given no sooner than twenty-four hours prior to an inspection. In cases where advance notice of an inspection is given, an employer is obligated to inform the employee representative of the inspection or alternatively may supply the compliance officer with the employee representative's identity in order for the officer to notify the representative of the inspection.

If during an inspection or investigation a compliance officer becomes aware of conditions or practices that could lead to serious injury or death, the officer is to immediately notify the affected employees and employer of the circumstances and of his or her intent to advise that civil action be taken to control the conditions or practices. The employer is then responsible for taking immediate steps to remove the danger. Under Section 13(a), United States district courts are authorized, upon petition by the secretary, to restrain any conditions or practices that may lead to death or serious injury before the circumstances can be remedied. Subsequent court orders may prohibit the employees from being present where immediate danger exists unless their presence is necessary to remedy the dangerous situation. Any injunctions or temporary restraining orders issued without notice pending investigation of the situation are not effective for a period longer than five days (Section 13(b)).

Citations

Citations are the basic mechanism through which OSHA enforces compliance with its standards. Section 9 of the act describes the citation process. Following an investigation or inspection, the area director examines the staff officer's report. If it is determined that a violation exists according to the standards established by the act, a citation will promptly be issued to the employer. The citation must be in writing, and it will include the specific nature of the violation and the provision of the act that was violated. The citation also establishes a period of abatement for the violation. A citation will be issued even if the employer has immediately remedied the violative situation or is taking steps to do so, but citations cannot be issued after six months from the occurrence of a violation. A copy of the citation is sent to the employee or employee representative responsible for filing the complaint against the employer. Upon receiving the citation, the employer must immediately post it or a copy of it at or near the site of the alleged violative occurrence.

Within a reasonable time period after a citation is issued, the employer is to be notified of any penalty imposed. The employer then has fifteen working days from the date of receipt of the proposed penalty during which he or she can notify the area director of intent to contest either the citation or the proposed penalty or both. By filing a proper notice of contest, the employer stops the running of the period of abatement and the secretary will be obligated to prove subsequently that the period was a reasonable one. Similarly, under Section 10(c), the employee or the employee representative is given the opportunity to file a petition challenging the period allotted for abatement. If the employer does not contest the citation or proposed penalty within fifteen days and the employee or employee representative files no notice, both the citation and the penalty become final orders and are not subject to review. The period of abatement begins to run after the issuance of this final order (Section 17(d)).

In the event that the employer intends to contest a citation or proposed penalty, the area director is to be informed in writing within fifteen working days of receiving the notice of proposed penalty and should state whether the citation, proposed penalty, or both are being contested. Likewise, the employee or employee representative wishing to file objections with the area director challenging the abatement period may do so within fifteen working days of the employer's receipt of the notice of proposed penalty. The area director will forward both employer and employee objections to the Occupational Safety and Health Review Commission for examination.

The commission is a three-member board appointed by the president with Senate approval (Section 12(a)). A two-member majority must approve any official action of the commission. An administrative law judge (ALJ) is appointed by the review commission to preside over and rule on proceedings initiated before the commission. Following the hearing, the ALJ submits a report on his or her decision to the review commission and the order will become final after thirty days, barring any decision by the review commission to review the hearing examiner's findings. The period of abatement begins to run after the issuance of a final order. Importantly, the commission is an adjudicatory body and its function is distinct from the enforcement activities of the secretary of labor, whose office has responsibility for the setting of penalties. The secretary of labor or his or her representative is authorized to grant adjustments to abatement periods.

Penalties

Penalties follow through on the inspection and citation process. If a citation results from an inspection, the notification form issued to the employer will include both the citation and the secretary's proposed penalty. Section 17 of the act specifies certain types of employer misconduct and prescribes a series of penalties; generally, the penalties are civil sanctions involving monetary fines. Funds collected under the OSHA scheme must be paid into the U.S. Treasury for the benefit of the federal government.

The penalties range from nonserious to willful, with increasing sanctions at each stage. Employers may receive a notice under Section 9(a) of a de minimus violation, which does not have a direct or immediate relation to safety and health but which must be corrected. A nonserious violation has a connection with safety and health but would not result in death or serious physical harm. For those violations, Congress provided in Section 17(c) that a civil penalty of up to $7,000 "may be assessed." A serious violation is described in Section 17(b) as one involving "a substantial probability that death or serious physical harm could result" from the violation. The statute provides that a penalty of up to $7,000 for a serious violation "shall be assessed" for each violation.

The act also addresses in Section 17(a) employers who "willfully or repeatedly" violate standards, rules, or orders promulgated pursuant to the statute. In order to establish a repeated violation, the secretary must establish the following five elements: "(1) the same employer (2) was cited at least once before (3) and found in violation (4) of the same standard in a similar manner, and (5) the original violation was abated."[16] For willful violations, courts and the commission have required proof that the employer knew of the requirement and that a subsequent violation was "committed voluntarily or with intentional disregard of the standard or demonstrated plain indifference to the Act."[17] Section 17(a) provides that for willful or repeated violations, a civil penalty of not more than $70,000, but not less than

$5,000 for each violation "may be assessed." In Section 17(j), Congress authorized the commission to fix penalties, taking into consideration "the size of the business of the employer being charged, the gravity of the violation, the good faith of the employer, and the history of previous violations."

If an employer's willful violation of an OSHA standard causes an employee's death, Section 17(e) imposes both fines and possible jail terms. According to that provision, conviction for the offense can result in a fine of $10,000 and a term in jail of six months, or both. If the conviction is a repeat offense, the punishment is doubled. Other penalties can be imposed for falsifying OSHA records or giving unauthorized advance notice of an inspection.

Under Section 11 of the act, any individual or employer unfavorably affected by a ruling of the review commission is afforded the opportunity to file an appeal in a federal court of appeals. Petitions for appeal must be filed within sixty days of the issuance of a final order. The court of appeals has the power to uphold, modify, or set aside any order, and its decision is subject to appeal to the U.S. Supreme Court. The secretary of labor may also petition the federal court of appeals in the appropriate circuit for review or for enforcement of an order (Section 11(b)). If no party files a petition for review or enforcement within sixty days, the review commission's order will become final.

Protection Against Discrimination

Section 11(c) of the act protects employees against discrimination because of the exercise of rights under the provisions of the act. The employee is specifically protected from discharge or discrimination resulting from the filing of a complaint or from testifying or offering to testify under the act's provisions. If an employee suspects that he or she has been discriminated against because of activities under the act, he or she may file a complaint within thirty days of the alleged occurrence. An investigation will ensue. If a violation is found to have occurred, the secretary will file a petition in the U.S. District Court for remedial action to be taken. For example, in the event of a discharge, reinstatement with full back pay may be ordered. The secretary is responsible for informing the filing party of the determination in the case within ninety days of the filing of the complaint.

Assessing OSHA's Effectiveness

Many business groups and conservative political leaders bitterly opposed the OSHA scheme and its intrusive presence in the private sector workplace. Following his election in 1980, President Ronald Reagan stated that an objective of his administration would be to "get the government off the backs of employers and workers in America." One method of doing so was to halt or reduce the levels of government regulatory activity in the employment relationship. Deregulation was undertaken in several major industries, such as the airline industry, during the first Reagan administration. The history of the Occupational Safety and Health (OSH) Administration between 1980 and 1986 indicates that such a program was in progress in the area of safety and health.[18] The policy debates about OSHA tend to center on the relative costs and benefits of regulation.

One method of evaluating safety and health legislation relies on economic analysis. For example, in his study of the act during the early Reagan administration, David McCaffrey used a cost–benefit approach to evaluate developments in the OSH Administration.[19] McCaffrey pointed out that one justification for safety and health legislation is that it provides an incentive for employers to invest in safety and health. Because firms do not bear all the costs of occupational injury and illness, they waste a valuable resource—the worker. The premise underlying the act, then, is that "through fines that vary with the severity, frequency, willfulness, or repeated nature of the violations, OSHA can theoretically assure that the firms' expected penalties for violating regulations (penalty for violation multiplied by the probability of inspection and detection) exceeds the expected benefits of violating the regulations (avoidance of regulatory compliance costs)."[20] Consequently, employers will make economically rational choices in matters of safety and health.

Using this theoretical framework, some commentators, McCaffrey said, developed a particular thesis concerning safety and health regulation. They asserted that OSHA should focus on encouraging employee–employer cooperation in dealing with these issues because it would constitute a more efficient allocation of resources if employers were to implement safety programs voluntarily than if the government required them to do so. Therefore, it was argued, OSHA should devote more resources to providing information and training for workers, thus ensuring that management would afford higher priority to safety and health and expend fewer resources on direct regulation in the form of inspections and enforcement. A related assumption was that both management and labor would place greater emphasis on cooperative health and safety activities, which in turn would lead to decentralization. In fact, according to McCaffrey, the relative number of OSHA inspections and the average amount of proposed penalties declined dramatically after a Reagan appointee assumed office as head of OSHA.[21]

Based on a review of data up to 1984, McCaffrey concluded that efforts to decentralize safety and health activity tended to weaken rather than strengthen the foundation of safety and health protection on the job. First, evidence from collective bargaining agreements suggested that "workers' ability to influence health and safety decisions will actually decline in the 1980's." Second, with the exception of the chemical industry, the percentage of capital expenditures for employee safety and health had fairly consistently declined from 1980 levels. There was some indication that the decline in expenditures could be correlated with a decline in OSHA's regulatory activities.[22]

The cost–benefit approach was also used by the White House to limit the financial impact of regulation on business. In an article discussing the future of OSHA in Reagan's second term, another commentator claimed that although many of the OSHA standards required improvement, it was unlikely that any improvement would be forthcoming.[23] As he explained, "The current regime of the Office of

Management and Budget (OMB) does not believe that OSHA safety standards serve any purpose in protecting workers and is openly hostile to any rulemaking activity by OSHA that places any burdens on employers." Because the OMB could effectively veto new OSHA regulations, upgrading of the standards would occur "only if from outside the Executive branch there is pressure to improve these regulations similar to the pressure exerted on the administration in the health area." The author concluded that employers will support safety standards when unsafe conditions are economically counterproductive; but when safety measures are expensive, and the employer's liability is limited to workers' compensation remedies, these measures will be opposed on the ground that the benefit to society is outweighed by the costs of the proposed standard.[24]

The economic aspects of OSHA regulation continued to be a subject of academic debate into the late 1980s. According to an influential scholar, the effectiveness of OSHA enforcement declined by 1986 to such an extent that there was little financial incentive for employers to invest in safety and health.[25] The OSHA scheme, he said, depends on three phases of enforcement—inspections, violations, and penalties—and each phase was relatively weaker in the first half of the 1980s than in the 1970s. The expert noted that the employer's chance of an inspection in any given year was less than one in two hundred. Further, "if inspected, the average employer will be found guilty of less than two violations of the standards, and for each violation the average penalty will be under sixty dollars. Overall, the violation cost per worker is only fifty-seven cents."[26] He concluded that OSHA penalties are insignificant compared with the costs of compliance, and as a result, "OSHA enforcement efforts comprise an inconsequential addition to policies intended to promote workplace safety."[27]

However, another study found that the OSHA inspection system generated important responses by employers.[28] Relying on different data than those used in previous research, Bartel and Thomas determined that "OSHA inspections have had a positive, sizable, and significant effect on investments in employee safety and health." But, they continued, the cost of employer investment in safety and health cannot be justified in terms of the benefits realized in the reduction of lost workdays. Their calculations for the year 1977 showed that U.S. manufacturers spent $1,281 million on safety and health and that OSHA inspections were responsible for 36 percent of that figure, or $461 million. The total dollar amount of lost working days in that year was $850 million. OSHA enforcement reduced lost workdays to generate a savings of $6.4 million. Comparing those figures, Bartel and Thomas concluded that "the costs of OSHA-induced investments overwhelmingly outweighed the benefits."[29]

Safety issues once again captured national attention in September 1991 when a fire at a North Carolina poultry plant killed twenty-five workers. According to *Time* magazine, the tragedy reflected deteriorating safety conditions throughout U.S. workplaces. The article stated, "By almost every measure, America's regulatory safeguards have grown threadbare." It cited declining numbers of inspectors, less union representation, and more stressful labor conditions. Particularly, repetitive motion traumas injured about 20 percent of the workforce in the poultry industry. *Time* noted that Congress planned hearings on OSHA reforms aimed at creating worker–management committees with authority to enforce OSHA rules.[30] However, nothing resulted from those hearings or from other congressional initiatives during the 1990s.

In early 1998, for example, a House subcommittee on workforce protections conducted hearings on various bills. Scott McGinnis, a Republican, summarized the tenor of the proposed legislation. He said, "Throughout my tenure in the House of Representatives, my biggest priority has been to reduce government regulation. One of the most burdensome agencies within the federal government is the Occupational Safety and Health Administration." McGinnis added that although he supported the idea of a safer workplace, OSHA had failed in its mission. In his view, "The safety that OSHA seeks to create is outweighed by unyielding inspectors and onerous regulation."[31] Among other reforms, H.R. 2873 would have required OSHA to ensure that any promulgated standard "is based upon an assessment of the risks to workers in such industry from the hazard which is the subject of the standard, the range of estimates and the best estimate of the quantifiable and nonquantifiable benefits of the standard in each such industry, and an analysis of the costs likely to occur in each such industry as a result of compliance with the standard."[32]

The debate about OSHA's effectiveness continues. According to an agency news release, OSHA increased its budget in fiscal year 2000 to $388.1 million, up from $353 million in 1999. The number of federal inspections rose from 34,100 to 35,500, and state inspections went from 26,000 to 27,500. OSHA staff positions likewise increased from 2,224 to 2,326. However, more inspections and more standards may not be fully justified in terms of safety and health benefits. A comprehensive 1997 review of workplace health and safety reached the following conclusion: "The evidence indicates that the OSH Act has been largely ineffective in reducing workplace fatalities and injuries. Moreover, the evidence suggests that the OSHA standards are of varying stringency and often unjustified in terms of costs and benefits, and thus supports the anti-standards approach to safety suggested by law and economics theory."[33] Consequently, market incentives, such as those associated with workers' compensation programs, may have more impact on health and safety than exclusive reliance on government mandates.

Conceivably, the act's mandate—"to assure so far as possible every working man and woman in the Nation safe and healthful working conditions"—cannot be attained without a fundamental shift in our approach to the matter of health and safety. In a competitive global economy characterized by scarcity of resources, workers' claims to a safe working environment may clash with the financial needs of employers. Business can, and in the early 1980s effectively did, argue that "society's interest in economic growth and capital [is] equal to, if not prior to, its interest in protection."[34] From that perspective, regulation must be balanced in relation to its anticipated social benefit. Moreover, the imposition of federal standards is basically inconsistent with the theory of a free market economy. That is, if workers prefer a safe workplace, employers will be forced to pay a risk premium to attract labor, and, accordingly, the market will reflect efficient levels of health and safety.[35]

Given the conflicting interests at stake and the political constraints on OSHA, the agency's power to implement basic changes in the workplace is tenuous. Its efforts are often stymied by employer opposition and public apathy. As one scholar points out, Americans generally adopt a dichotomous view of economic affairs. That is, we alternate "between bouts of enthusiasm for state intervention and moods of deep distrust of all forms of public life—leaning first to 'big government' and then to the 'free market.'"[36] His solution is to reform safety and health law by radically strengthening the right of workers to participate in decisions at the enterprise level, coupled with increased public control over investment decisions in the economy. That suggestion is obviously incompatible with prevailing notions of managerial prerogative and ownership of property. The contentious debate over OSHA's repetitive motion standard, which was not implemented after years of debate, amply attests to the philosophical tensions underlying the act.

Employee Retirement and Income Security Act

Private pension plans have a long history in the United States. The American Express Company implemented a retirement plan for its employees in 1875, and many other employers followed that example before the end of the nineteenth century.[37] Typically, the early plans provided a set amount of benefits based on an employee's years of service and earnings. Thus, employees had an incentive to continue their employment with the company in order to qualify for the retirement benefit. Retirement programs of this nature are known as *defined benefit plans,* because the amount of retirement can be calculated according to a fixed formula. An alternative type of plan, referred to as a *defined contribution plan,* establishes only the amount of money that will be paid into the retirement fund, not the amount of a worker's benefit upon retiring. The differences are significant, for reasons discussed below.

In 1935, Congress considered the question of whether workers covered under a private pension plan should be excluded from Social Security provisions. It ultimately decided on compulsory coverage for all private sector workers, but company-sponsored plans nevertheless continued to proliferate after adoption of the act. Pension programs expanded rapidly after World War II, due in part to changes in the Internal Revenue Code, the growing interest of labor unions, and favorable economic conditions. By 1950, about 10.3 million workers, or one-quarter of all persons employed in commerce, had pension coverage. Organized labor viewed private pensions as a supplement to the benefits available under Social Security, which labor believed to be inadequate for a decent retirement. Although labor leaders generally favored a public system of pensions, they vigorously pursued retirement security through collective bargaining.[38] The National Labor Relations Board in 1948 held that pensions were a mandatory subject of bargaining, which gave unions the right to negotiate to impasse on the issue.[39]

The private pension scheme, in practice, had certain advantages. For employers, retirement benefits were an important means of attracting and retaining valuable employees, and they were also afforded beneficial tax treatment under the Internal Revenue Code. For employees, a retirement plan provided additional security beyond the federal levels. But a major shortcoming of the private pension schemes was that workers were easily deprived of their benefits through such events as a factory closure, a discharge or layoff, or a sale of the company. Most plans stipulated that eligibility for pension benefits depended on employment status, so employees separated from employment before meeting the criteria for retirement forfeited their entire benefit. Congress addressed the subject of private sector pensions in 1974 and enacted a comprehensive statute, the Employee Retirement Income Security Act.[40]

The congressional objectives underlying ERISA were to ensure that employees' rights in the plan would be adequately protected and that the plans would be financially sound. Congress determined that private plans affected interstate commerce and were thus subject to federal regulation. After reciting the various weaknesses and inequities of existing plans, the statute sets out the policies that support the legislation in the following statement:

> It is hereby declared to be the policy of this chapter to protect interstate commerce and the interests of participants in employee benefit plans and their beneficiaries, by requiring the disclosure and reporting to participants and beneficiaries of financial and other information with respect thereto, by establishing standards of conduct, responsibility, and obligation for fiduciaries of employee benefit plans, and by providing for appropriate remedies, sanctions, and ready access to the Federal Courts.
>
> It is hereby further declared to be the policy of this chapter to protect interstate commerce, the Federal taxing power, and the interests of participants in private pension plans and their beneficiaries by improving the equitable character and the soundness of such plans by requiring them to vest the accrued benefits of employees with significant periods of service, to meet minimum standards of funding, and by requiring plant termination insurance.[41]

The remaining provisions of the act address each of those concerns in greater detail.

With respect to reporting and disclosure, ERISA requires that administrators of plans furnish each plan participant with a summary description containing specified information. The summary description "shall be written in a manner calculated to be understood by the average plan participant."[42] In addition, various other reports must be filed with the secretary of labor; those filings include the summary plan description, any substantial modifications made in the plan, an annual report, and a terminal report. Each mandatory filing must contain specified information, such as a statement of audit prepared by a qualified accountant, an actuarial opinion, and a detailed financial statement.[43]

To ensure broad access to the plan, Congress provided for certain minimal lengths of service as a condition of participation. ERISA defines a *year of service* to consist of at least one thousand hours in a twelve-month period, with exceptions for seasonal and maritime industries. Section 1053 sets forth minimum vesting standards, which guarantee that benefits will not be forfeited after a designated period. To begin with, the employee's contribution must be nonforfeitable. Thereafter, with respect to the employer's contribution, benefits may vest according to three alternatives. Under the first alternative, an employee is fully vested in the plan after five years of service. The second alternative provides for vesting in steps following three years of service; the employee is 20 percent vested at three years and becomes vested at a prescribed rate per year until 100 percent vesting after seven years. The third method involves full vesting after ten years in multiemployer plans pursuant to a collective bargaining agreement.[44]

Another area of concern addressed in ERISA is the financial stability of private plans. Congress established minimum funding standards with which plans must comply[45] and standards of fiduciary responsibility to ensure prudent fund management.[46] In addition, Congress created the Pension Benefit Guaranty Corporation (PBGC) as an independent entity within the Department of Labor.[47] The PBGC has broad power to oversee the activities of private pension funds and to ensure their fiscal integrity. Most important, the PBGC acts as an insurer to guarantee the payment of all valid claims against a pension plan under its jurisdiction. If it makes payments on behalf of an employer, it has the authority to seek reimbursement from the employer. The PBGC is funded through the collection of premiums, which are set at a rate "necessary to provide sufficient revenue to the fund for the corporation to carry out its functions under this [statute]."[48] Conditions of economic distress may severely reduce the PBGC reserves. By early 2003, PBGC funds had fallen from a $7.7 billion surplus in 2001 to a $3.6 billion deficit, and policymakers discussed methods of averting a fiscal catastrophe in the pension system.[49]

Despite the breadth and complexity of ERISA, it has not corrected all of the deficiencies of private pension plans. The Department of Labor does not have a staff large enough for effective enforcement of the law, and there may be substantial conflict of interest in the use of pension funds. Plans may still be inequitable in operation and may discriminate in favor of more highly paid employees. Further, ERISA does not regulate government pension plans. The consequence is that states are free to set levels of funding and vesting in their plans at their discretion, and these plans may provide very inadequate benefits and protections.[50]

As a final point about ERISA coverage, you should be aware that its basic protections are most relevant to the defined benefit type of pension. Defined contribution plans do not fall under the PBGC insurance scheme because there is nothing to insure. For defined contribution plans, employees, and usually employers, pay into a retirement fund that is intended to earn income over the years. But if the fund instead loses money, as when the stock market falls, that risk is borne by the plan participant; Enron and other financially compromised companies serve as contemporary examples. The end result is a potential disaster in our retirement system.[51] Defined contribution plans do have some attractive features such as portability, flexibility, and administrative ease. Younger workers with good career opportunities may prefer to change jobs frequently. Employers may want the defined contribution plan for reasons of simplicity and lower cost. Whatever the reasons, defined benefit plans have become less popular than in the past. In 1990–1991, 48 percent of full-time employees participated in defined benefit plans, but that number had dropped to 42 percent in 1994–1995.[52] Participants in defined contribution plans grew from under 10 percent in 1979 to nearly 25 percent in 1999.[53] Those trends are projected to continue, and the issue of adequate pension coverage presents an ongoing social and political problem.[54]

Health Insurance and Employment

In the Consolidated Omnibus Budget Reconciliation Act of 1985 (COBRA),[55] Congress enacted significant new legislation pertaining to health insurance for unemployed workers and their dependents. Basically, COBRA permits workers and their families to continue their medical benefits by paying their insurance premiums to the employer with whom they previously had health coverage. If the employer refuses to provide continuation, the employer cannot deduct the cost of his or her group health plan under the Internal Revenue Code. COBRA provisions are triggered by a qualifying event and may be terminated under certain specified circumstances.

COBRA's coverage extends to all employers who have more than twenty employees and offer a health plan to employees, and it also extends to all states and political subdivisions that receive funds under the Public Health Services Act. Consequently, the major exclusions from COBRA are the federal government, small employers, and employers who do not provide a group health plan. It should be emphasized that COBRA does not require any employer to offer a health plan for employees, but only to continue coverage for designated persons under an existing plan.

The qualifying events under COBRA include the following occurrences: (1) the death of the covered employee; (2) the termination of the employee's employment, unless the termination is for gross misconduct, or a reduction of hours below stipulated plan levels; (3) the divorce or legal separation of the covered employee from his or her spouse; (4) the covered employee's becoming entitled to Medicare; and (5) a dependent child's ceasing to be a dependent under the plan.[56] Under any of those circumstances, the former employee or ex-spouse or previous dependent, as appropriate, may elect to pay the applicable insurance premium and continue the coverage. The premium may not amount to more than 102 percent of the premium of similarly situated employees covered by the plan. It is the obligation of the plan administrator to provide written notice of continuation rights to employees, and the Department of Labor issued a model statement that described the basic features of COBRA in a concise and understandable manner.[57] The employee or family member must inform the plan administrator of a divorce or a change in dependent status.

The COBRA coverage does not continue indefinitely. If the qualifying event is the termination of the employee, or a reduction in hours, the health care continuation is provided for eighteen months from the date of the event. For all other qualifying events, the period consists of thirty-six months. In addition, coverage may cease under any of the other following conditions: (1) the employer no longer offers a plan to employees, (2) the qualified beneficiary fails to pay the premium, (3) the qualified beneficiary becomes a covered employee under another health plan or becomes eligible for Medicare, or (4) the beneficiary ex-spouse is remarried and becomes covered under the new spouse's plan.[58] At the end of the continuation period, the beneficiary must be offered a conversion option to an individual plan, if that option is normally available under the group plan.

Congress added additional protections for insured workers under the Health Insurance Portability and Accountability Act of 1996 (HIPAA).[59] Generally, the purpose of the law is to protect employees who change jobs and both employers offer health insurance. The HIPAA prohibits insurers from excluding new employees from coverage in a group plan because of preexisting medical conditions. As defined in the statute, exclusions from coverage cannot be "based on the fact that the condition was present before the date of enrollment for such coverage, whether or not any medical advice, diagnosis, care, or treatment was recommended or received before such date." The HIPAA coordinates with insurance coverage provided under COBRA, which allows employees who are unemployed to have access to group insurance from a new employer. The law does not require employers to offer an insurance plan, nor does it prevent employers from terminating a plan. Unlike many other industrialized countries, the United States has no national health care system. In 2003, the House of Representatives took up a proposal for universal health insurance; it promises to become a political issue in forthcoming campaigns.[60]

The Family and Medical Leave Act of 1993

Congress passed legislation in 1993 that affects an employee's rights to job security in the event of certain medical occurrences.[61] The Family and Medical Leave Act provides for unpaid leaves of absences for covered employees under specific circumstances. In enacting the legislation, Congress found that more adults are working, that proper child development requires parental involvement, and that many workers are forced to choose between the demands of a job and their roles as parents. Particularly, Congress noted, women assume most of the responsibility for child care and suffer job discrimination for that reason. The purpose of the FMLA is to balance workplace and family demands by giving eligible employees a right to a period of leave to care for newborns or family members with a serious medical condition.[62] The Supreme Court in May 2003 specifically affirmed Congress's objective of eliminating the inequitable treatment of working women.[63]

The FMLA does not cover employers with less than fifty employees or individuals employed by the federal government. The period of leave is a total of twelve workweeks, and qualified employees are entitled to leave to care for a newborn or newly adopted child or a spouse, son, daughter, or parent of the employee if the family member has a serious health condition, or if the employee has a health condition that renders him or her unable to perform his or her job duties. The employer can require certification of the condition from a health care provider before granting the leave. Most important under the FMLA, the employee has a right to reclaim his or her job or a substantially similar one after the leave (the law exempts certain highly compensated employees from this requirement). The employee is not entitled to any seniority, benefits, or promotions other than those he or she would have gotten if he or she had not taken leave. Employees are not paid their salary during the leave, but they must be covered under any medical plan in effect. They will also be entitled to use any accrued leave available to other employees, such as vacation time or sick pay. Employers are forbidden from interfering with employees' rights under the act or discriminating against individuals because they exercised their rights. Individuals can bring civil suits to enforce the law and recover damages for lost compensation or for expenses arising out of the employer's wrongful denial, including reasonable attorneys' fees. The secretary of labor can also bring a civil action against the employer.[64]

An important policy issue under the FMLA has to do with compensation during leaves. Despite Congress's reference to families and parental involvement, it did nothing to provide income support for women workers. Other countries tend to have much more generous laws in that regard. Norway, for example, allows for fifty-two-week pregnancy leaves supported by an allowance of 80 percent of the woman's previous earnings (or 100 percent for forty-two weeks). The benefit is funded through the National Insurance Act. Most other industrialized countries have similar legislation.[65]

In June 2000, the secretary of labor authorized states to "provide partial wage replacement, on a voluntary, experimental basis, to parents who take approved leave or who otherwise leave employment following the birth or placement for adoption of a child."[66] The rule took effect on August 14, 2000, shortly before the election of President Bush. As unemployment rose in 2002, opposition to the use of unemployment insurance grew. Senator Judd Gregg, for example, urged the Department of Labor to rescind the birth and adoption regulations as an inappropriate use of funds aimed at alleviating problems of unemployment rather than encouraging pregnancy. In his words, "By inviting states to spend down unemployment insurance reserves for the entirely unrelated purpose of compensating leave takers, BAA-UC [birth and adoption unemployment compensation] puts at risk the safety net for unemployed workers. The UI [unemployment insurance] system is a return-to-work program for workers who lose their jobs, not a catch-all form of income support."[67] Whether government should subsidize family leaves through unemployment insurance is one more dimension of employment policy that is open to debate.

Exceptions to the Employment At-Will Rule

As discussed in Chapter 3, the common law of employment contracts states that unless the employment is for a specific duration, employees are free to leave the employment at any time, and the employer has the right to discharge the employee at any time. After enactment of the National Labor Relations Act, and a declaration of its constitutionality in May 1937, the at-will rule did not apply to discharges that contravened legislative protection for the employee—that is, union activity. More legislative exceptions appeared over the years that limited an employer's prerogatives at both the state and the federal level, particularly the civil rights laws. In 1987, Montana adopted a statute that repealed the common law and substituted a standard of just cause. This section analyzes some important exceptions to at-will employment developed under common law and the Montana legislation.

Judicial Modification of the At-Will Rule

One of the significant features of the employment at will rule is its historical durability. Until the mid-1980s, courts rarely interfered with managerial prerogatives in discharging employees. One of the landmark opinions, decided in 1959, remained virtually unnoticed for years until it gained renewed attention in the mid-1980s. The case *Petermann v. Teamsters Local 396*[68] relied on a public policy theory to limit an employer's power to terminate an employee. The *Petermann* case involved a Teamsters business agent who was subpoenaed to testify before a committee of the California state legislature. His employer, the secretary-treasurer of the local union, directed him to make certain false statements that would protect the union official. At the hearing, the plaintiff testified truthfully, and the following day he was discharged.

Deciding that the plaintiff had stated a cause of action under California common law, the Court of Appeals observed that public policy was a legal principle designed to protect against conduct that was "injurious to the public or against the public good." With respect to employment, the court concluded: "To hold that one's continued employment could be made contingent upon his commission of a felonious act at the instance of his employer would be to encourage criminal conduct upon the part of both the employee and employer and would serve to contaminate the honest administration of public affairs."[69] Thus, the plaintiff would be entitled to a civil remedy as a consequence of his wrongful discharge. The *Wagenseller* case, discussed at the end of this chapter, is another example of the public policy exception to the at-will rule. When you read the opinion, ask yourself what public policy forbids compelled displays of a person's buttocks. (If you think it's indecent exposure, pay close attention to the Arizona statute quoted in the opinion.)

California law also offers a good example of the contract theory of employment protection. In *Cleary v. American Airlines, Inc.*,[70] the plaintiff was hired under an oral agreement for an indefinite term. He continued in his employment for eighteen years, with satisfactory performance. When he was discharged for no apparent reason, he brought suit against the airline. The California Court of Appeals said that the plaintiff had stated a viable claim for recovery and the matter should have proceeded to trial. The court's opinion concludes, "we hold that the longevity of the employee's service, together with the expressed policy of the employer (i.e., the adoption of specific procedures for adjudicating employee disputes) operate as a form of estoppels, precluding any discharge of such an employee by the employer without good cause."[71] *Cleary* contains language about an implied contractual commitment of good faith and fair dealing. Later California cases limited the scope of the theory, but *Cleary* nonetheless demonstrates that an employer's oral representations and policies may create a binding promise of job security for long-term employees.

By the end of the 1990s, exceptions to the rule of employment at will had shredded the rule itself, and the employer's previously impregnable and unchallenged power to discharge employees had been limited by many significant qualifications. A basic problem with wrongful discharge litigation is that the judicial process imposes substantial burdens on employees and substantial risks for employers because lawsuits are expensive, time-consuming, and frustrating. To illustrate, a jury in February 2003 awarded a plaintiff in an employment case over $11 million to compensate him for an unlawful termination. The employee, a gay male, claimed that his employer, Leona Helmsley, created "a hostile and abusive work environment" and subsequently fired him because of his sexual orientation. The award included $10 million in punitive damages.[72] But even if a defendant prevails, attorneys' fees and related costs consume valuable resources and add little by way of social or economic benefits. A growing body of academic literature proposes alternative methods of dealing with job security for U.S. workers.[73] The approach adopted in the state of Montana is taken up next.

Legislative Modification— Montana's Wrongful Discharge Act

Given the ambiguous legal environment and the risk of sizable damage awards, a legislative solution might seem reasonable. In 1987, Montana enacted the Wrongful Discharge From Employment Act (WDEA), designed to afford rights to employees and protections to employers.[74] No other states have followed Montana's lead to date, but the WDEA's provisions are a guide to a rational policy of adjudicating employment disputes. Since its enactment, the legislation has successfully reduced lawsuits against employers while guaranteeing employee rights.

The law defines a wrongful discharge to include a discharge in retaliation "for the employee's refusal to violate public policy for reporting a violation" of policy, incorporating one of the major common law exceptions to the at-will rule. The second exception, based on a contractual obligation, is addressed in a section providing that discharge is wrongful if "the employer violated the express provisions of its own written personnel policy." During the employee's probationary period, which is six months unless otherwise stated, the employment will be terminable by either party. The third element of wrongful discharge extends just cause to all nonprobationary employees and prohibits discharge unless cause exists. The statute defines good cause as "reasonable job-related grounds for dismissal based on a failure to satisfactorily perform job duties, disruption of the employer's operation, or other legitimate business reason." As with union agreements, this principle overturns the employer's traditional prerogative of termination at will.[75]

The benefit to employers consists of a limitation of damages. The statute allows recovery for lost wages and fringe benefits for a four-year period. Interim earnings must be deducted from the award, and the employee has a duty to seek employment. If the employer acted with fraud or malice, the employee may recover punitive damages. But, the statute provides, "there is no right under any legal theory to damages for wrongful discharge under this part for pain and suffering, emotional distress," and similar damages except as specifically permitted. This limitation shields employers from large jury verdicts.[76]

One limitation of the law arises in connection with federal employment policies such as civil rights and collective bargaining. Because a state cannot preempt federal regulation, Title VII, the Americans With Disabilities Act, and similar laws remain in force. An employee cannot successfully litigate under a common law theory, but he or she can pursue a remedy under the federal statute. The WDEA exempts any claim that "is subject to any other state or federal statute that provides a procedure or remedy for contesting the dispute. The statutes include those that prohibit discharge for filing complaints, charges, or claims with administrative bodies or that prohibit unlawful discrimination based on race, national origin, sex, age, disability, creed, religion, political belief, color, marital status, and other similar grounds." Because unionized employees have recourse to just cause protections, the WDEA also excludes claims "of an employee covered by a written collective bargaining agreement or a written contract of employment for a specific term."[77]

To facilitate resolution of claims, the WDEA provides for final and binding arbitration of disputes and allocates the costs of the procedure. Section 914 provides that a "discharged employee who makes a valid offer to arbitrate that is accepted by the employer and who prevails in such arbitration is entitled to have the arbitrator's fee and all costs of arbitration paid by the employer." The finality of the award is similar to that of a collective bargaining agreement. If the parties agree to arbitrate, it will provide "the exclusive remedy for the wrongful discharge dispute and there is no right to bring or continue a lawsuit under this part. The arbitrator's award is final and binding, subject to review of the arbitrator's decision under the provisions of the Uniform Arbitration Act." Accordingly, alternative dispute procedures play an important role under the statute.

The WDEA has implications for the future direction of national employment policy. Many commentators have criticized the fragmented, arbitrary nature of employment law, and many cases support that conclusion. In any event, a comprehensive and uniform body of rules would reduce the costs of litigation and the drag on employer administration of human resource policies. Such improvements would enhance workers' ability to resolve disputes with their employers and would standardize conditions across labor markets. The WDEA suggests one unified approach, and its components are scrutinized more fully in Chapter 8. As a final example of why legislation is superior to piecemeal judicial tinkering with employment doctrine, consider the *Wagenseller* opinion summarized at the end of the chapter. This well-known appellate court decision exemplifies judicial overreach in a case where bad facts made bad law.

Conclusion

This chapter surveyed employment laws enacted in the post–New Deal era that protect employees by virtue of their employment status. Employees have a right to a safe and healthy workplace, protection of their pension entitlements, continued health care coverage, family and medical leaves, and, in some circumstances, protection against unjust discharge. Those rights have important restrictions and do not necessarily guarantee any specific benefit, such as a health insurance or a pension plan. Because the statutes are limited in scope, the existence of a right can only be determined under the specific facts of a given situation. This characteristic leads to more complexity and confusion about the legal environment.

Case Study on Employment At Will

Just the Butt of a Bad Joke?

Wagenseller v. Scottsdale Memorial Hospital[78]

Catherine Wagenseller was a registered nurse at the Scottsdale Memorial Hospital. She sued the hospital in 1985 claiming that she had been wrongfully discharged by her employer. Relying on the employment at-will rule, the trial court dismissed her lawsuit. The Arizona Supreme Court, however, decided that employment at will could be limited by an employer's promises or by important public policies. The public policy at stake in this case involved certain immoral activities that the court said could not be used as a basis to terminate employment.

Wagenseller worked in the emergency room at the hospital, where her immediate supervisor was another nurse named Kay Smith. After several years of a congenial working relationship, Smith and Wagenseller, along with a group of other employees at the hospital, took a raft trip down the Colorado River. Wagenseller claimed that, during the trip, Smith and the others engaged in activities that made Wagenseller very uncomfortable. Those activities included public urination and defecation, coed bathing, heavy drinking, and grouping up with different members of the party. Wagenseller did not participate in any of these activities. She also refused to join in the group's staging of a parody of the song *Moon River*. The skit involved a finale that required the participants to bare their buttocks to, or moon, the audience.

After they returned to work, Smith and her fellow rafters performed the *Moon River* presentation on two different occasions at the hospital. Wagenseller refused both times to engage in the behavior, which she found offensive. Wagenseller said that her reluctance to display her nude buttocks caused her relationship with Smith to deteriorate and eventually led to her discharge. Smith allegedly began to harass her, use abusive language toward her, and embarrassed her in the company of the hospital staff. Other emergency department employees reported a similar marked change in Smith's behavior toward Wagenseller after the trip, although Smith denied it. Wagenseller asserted that she had always received favorable performance reviews before the trip, but afterward, Smith began to criticize her work and used that as a pretext to fire her.

Wagenseller presented various theories of litigation in her lawsuit against the hospital. She argued that she had a contract with the hospital that protected her against arbitrary discharge, and even if she did not have such a contract, the law should incorporate a standard of "good faith and fair dealing" into employment relationships. Of more pertinence here, she asserted that her discharge was contrary to public policy and entitled her to a judicial remedy. The Arizona Supreme Court agreed with the public policy argument. Its decision begins with a review of the employment at will doctrine and the emergence of judicially created exceptions and their rationale.

With regard to the public policy doctrine, the court cited another appellate decision for a definition of the term. It began by conceding that there could be no precise definition of public policy and then continued:

> In general, it can be said that public policy concerns what is right and just and what affects the citizens of the State collectively. It is to be found in the State's constitution and statutes and, when they are silent, in its judicial decisions. Although there is no precise line of demarcation dividing matters that are the subject of public policies from matters purely personal, a survey of cases in other States involving retaliatory discharges shows that a matter must strike at the heart of a citizen's social rights, duties, and responsibilities before the tort will be allowed.

Broadly interpreting the notion of "social rights, duties, and responsibilities," the *Wagenseller* opinion declared that it should not adhere to a rule that permitted an employer to fire someone for "cause morally wrong."

The court ventured into the realm of economic theory to reconcile the apparent conflict between employers' established historical rights and the newly discovered judicial solicitude for workers. Noting that the "rise of large corporations" has limited the opportunity and mobility of employees, the court observed that employers and employees do not deal on a basis of equality; moreover, concentrations of corporate power may threaten important public policies. For that reason, the court emphasized, "It is now recognized that a proper balance must be maintained among the employer's interest in operating a business efficiently and profitably, the employee's interest inearning a livelihood, and society's interest in seeing its public policies carried

(Continued)

(Continued)

out." Having decided that an employer's prerogatives must be limited, the court formulated a rule balancing the interests of employers, employees, and society. The new legal principle was that "an employer may fire for good cause or for no cause. He may not fire for bad cause—that which violates public policy."

The court's next task involved the problem of defining and discovering public policy. The opinion started with the general proposition that public policy was embodied in the state's constitution and statutes because those documents reflected the "public conscience of the people of this state." For that reason "an employer may not with impunity violate the dictates of public policy found in the provisions of our statutory and constitutional law." But statutes and constitutional law did not exhaust the sources of public policy, the court added. Common law, with its tradition of social responsiveness, also created public policy. In short, "we will look to the pronouncements of our founders, our legislature, and our courts to discern the public policy of this state."

The public policy violated in this case appeared to be based on an Arizona statute that forbids "indecent exposure." Citing the statute, the court noted that indecent exposure occurred if a person "exposes his or her genitals or anus or she exposes the areola or nipple of her breast or breasts and another person is present, and the defendant is reckless about whether such other person, as a reasonable person, would be offended or alarmed by the act." Somewhat problematically, this statute did not seem to be aimed at free speech, political beliefs, or activities typically associated with public life. Nonetheless, the court said, the statute was "enacted to preserve and protect the commonly recognized sense of public privacy and decency. The statute does, therefore, recognize bodily privacy as a 'citizen's social right.'" Making the point clear, the court expressly ruled, "We thus uphold this state's public policy by holding that termination for refusal to commit an act which might violate [the statute] may provide the basis of a claim for wrongful discharge." Wagenseller, consequently, stated a legal cause of action when she alleged that she was terminated for refusing to expose her buttocks before an audience of her coworkers.

Some Questions About the Case

1. The court noted that one reason for creating exceptions to the employment at will rule is that corporations had become large and powerful, and employees had become "relatively immobile" in their opportunity to find other employment. Would that statement be more applicable to a mill hand working at the U.S. Steel plant in Pittsburgh in 1919 or to

an emergency room nurse in Phoenix in 1979? A dissenting judge on the Tennessee Supreme Court observed in 1884 that if employers had absolute power to hire and fire, aggregated capital would subject employees to its "grinding exactions" and threaten their livelihoods.[79] If it was so obvious that employees needed protection against "abusive corporate power," why did it take the judiciary over a century to modify the employment at will rule?

2. This case invites serious thought about the respective roles of courts and legislatures. If the Arizona legislature made indecent exposure a crime, why does the court not defer to the legislature to make wrongful discharge against the law? Along those lines, are elected officials or appointed judges in a better position to decide what rights of citizens should be protected in the workplace? Do judges make general rules that apply to many situations, or are they just ruling on the facts of a particular case? Do the facts here lend themselves logical extension— that is, how often do you think employees are required to take off their clothes and sing and dance? To your knowledge, did Wagenseller have any statutory rights in this situation, such as protections against workplace sexual harassment? Is there any indication that Smith was interested in sexual relations with Wagenseller?[80]

3. In some respects, the court's opinion is an embarrassment for everyone concerned. The statute prohibiting indecent exposure is quite specific, and it precisely delineates the necessary elements to make out an offense. In a footnote, the court tries to avoid an indelicate inquiry with the following caveat:

> We have little expertise in the techniques of mooning. We cannot say as a matter of law, therefore, whether mooning would always violate the statute by revealing the mooner's anus or genitalia. That question could only be determined, we suppose, by an examination of the facts of each case. We deem such an inquiry unseemly and unnecessary in a civil case. Compelled exposure of the bare buttocks, on pain of termination of employment, is a sufficient violation of the *policy* embodied in the statute to support the action, even if there would have been no technical violation of the statute.

Thus, the court admits that the statute might not have been violated by mooning. It then dodges the issue by saying that in any event the policy of the statue was violated. Why does the clear language of the law not define the entire scope of the policy? Moreover, how could this question ever be resolved—by having witnesses moon the trial judge and jury?

(Continued)

(Continued)

4. From the hospital's perspective, consider this argument: emergency room personnel work under conditions demanding trust, cooperation, teamwork, and personal bonding. Wagenseller demonstrated that she would not become a part of the team when she refused to commit herself to the norms of the group. The camaraderie involved in the *Moon River* skit was not much different than an executive taking his employees on a trip to climb a mountain and firing anyone who refused to participate because they exhibited a lack of collective engagement. What would be wrong with this explanation for the firing?

Summary

- The Occupational Safety and Health Act is a comprehensive and controversial scheme of protection against harmful working environments. Its structure follows a plan of standards, inspections, citations, and penalties. The effectiveness of OSHA depends on employers' perception of the costs and benefits of compliance. The law is highly politicized, as illustrated by the ergonomics standard.
- Pensions make up an important part of employment. After World War II, unions negotiated for a system of private retirement to supplement Social Security. Pension plans may be of the defined benefit type, which pays a fixed amount to retirees, or the defined contribution plan (such as the 401(k)), which has no guaranteed stream of income. Defined benefit plans are also insured against company bankruptcy by the Pension Benefit Guaranty Corporation. The Employee Retirement Income Security Act of 1974 is a federal law which regulates pension programs.
- U.S. workers do not have an entitlement to health care insurance. Congress did pass the Consolidated Omnibus Budget Reconciliation Act in 1985 to protect workers who were laid off from a job with health care benefits. Workers can pay to continue their coverage for a period of time. Congress also protected workers who changed jobs by requiring the workers' new employer to extend any health care coverage without regard to preexisting conditions.
- The Family and Medical Leave Act grants covered employees a period of unpaid leave for purposes of dealing with birth, illness, and other family conditions. It is limited in application and only provides a right to return to a previous job. Other countries typically offer some amount of income security for workers on family leave.
- Beginning in the 1980s, courts began to fashion exceptions to the employment at will rule. The two major doctrinal lines rest on tort and contract theory. The exceptions have severely eroded the rule itself and pose serious threats of litigation for employers. The state of Montana enacted a statute that gave employees just cause protection against discharge and preempted common law suits. That statute offers guidance for reforms of our employment system.

Further Analysis

1. The problems with OSHA enforcement are fairly obvious. How might they be corrected? One analogy is to examine other regulatory regimes, such as traffic laws. Motorists routinely break speed limits because they know the likelihood of apprehension is small. In Colorado, some municipalities began using photo radar to catch violators, and the technique worked very well. The state government then imposed severe limitations on a city's right to use the photo equipment. What implications does this example have for OSHA? If general lawbreaking occurs, should we repeal the laws?

2. The OSHA standard dealing with work-related muscular disorders promised to provide protections for a large segment of the working population, but political influence killed the standard. What does that suggest about the nature of safety and health regulation? About the political power of organized labor after the 2000 elections?

3. Pensions will be the socioeconomic issue of the next decade. What should be done to address the problem of retirement security? ERISA does not require any employer to offer a pension plan, and most plans can be terminated without much trouble. What might induce nonunion employers to offer a defined benefit pension plan to workers? Are younger workers adequately informed about the nature of pension programs in this country? How might they be better informed?

4. COBRA represents a compromise about health care coverage. It is the only federal law that imposes a duty on employers to provide insurance, and it is limited to the employer's former employees if they pay the costs of the premium. Does COBRA represent the limit of employers' tolerance for government intrusion in health care insurance? Given the political alignment leading up to the 2004 elections, can Democrats successfully campaign on the issue of health insurance? If not, what environmental factors would ever result in more comprehensive legislation?

5. The Family and Medical Leave Act presents administrative issues for employers. One organization, the FMLA Technical Corrections Coalition, maintains a Web site criticizing the law and offering proposals for change. See http://workingforthefuture.org [visited May 28, 2003]. What weaknesses of the law should be corrected? Should the law be strengthened by providing compensation for workers on leave? California adopted legislation to furnish some income security to workers qualifying for FMLA leave. What effect might this law have on the business environment in the state?

6. The Montana Wrongful Discharge Act develops a comprehensive structure for resolving employment claims. What benefits does the law have for employees? For employers? Why does the Montana law exempt claims of civil rights violations from its coverage? If the federal government considered a similar law, would employers support it? Assume the federal government proposed to do away with the Equal Employment Opportunity Commission and all laws under its jurisdiction and enact a wrongful discharge law that provided the only remedy for employment claims. Would employers support this version of a statute?

Suggested Readings

Burton, John F., Jr., and James R. Chelius. "Workplace Safety and Health Regulations: Rationale and Results," in *Government Regulation of the Employment Relationship*, ed. Bruce Kaufman. Madison, WI: Industrial Relations Research Association, 1997.

Friedman, Sheldon, and David C. Jacobs, eds. *The Future of the Safety Net: Social Insurance and Employee Benefits.* Urbana, IL: Industrial Relations Research Association, 2001.

Rothstein, Mark A. *Occupational Safety and Health Law,* 4th ed. St. Paul, MN: West, 1998.

U.S. Department of Labor. *Health Benefits Under the Consolidated Omnibus Budget Reconciliation Act, COBRA.* Washington, DC: Pension and Welfare Benefits Administration, 2002.

U.S. Department of Labor. *What You Should Know About Your Pension Rights.* Washington, DC: Pension and Welfare Benefits Administration, 2001. Available online at www.pueblo.gsa.gov/cic_text/employ/penrghts/penrghts.txt.

Wisensale, Steven K. *Family Leave Policy: The Political Economy of Work and Family in America.* Armonk, NY: M. E. Sharpe, 2001.

Endnotes

1. 29 U.S.C. §§ 651–678 (1993).

2. For a summary of pre-OSHA legislation, see Mark Rothstein, *Occupational Safety and Health Law,* 4th ed. (St. Paul, MN: West, 1998), § 1.

3. H.R. Report No. 1291, 91st Cong., 2d Sess. (1970); reprinted in Bureau of National Affairs Editorial Staff, *Job Safety and Health Act of 1970: Text, Analysis, Legislative History* (Washington, DC: BNA Books, 1970), 152–153. For another survey of the law and working conditions, see Nicholas A. Ashford and Charles C. Caldart, *Technology, Law, and the Working Environment,* rev. ed. (Washington, DC: Island Press, 1996), Chap. 1.

4. Quoted in Michael McClintock, "Foreword" [Occupational Safety and Health Act Symposium], *Gonzaga Law Review* 9 (1974): 318–319.

5. Bureau of National Affairs, *Job Safety and Health Act,* p. 14.

6. For a comparative analysis, see Bureau of National Affairs, *Job Safety and Health Act,* pp. 280–296. Congressman Perkins presented a summary of the conference report and the changes that had been made in the House and the Senate versions of the bill. Senator Williams told his colleagues in the Senate that the final legislation reflected "to a most unusual degree, the wishes of the Senate" (p. 295).

7. Rothstein, *Occupational Safety,* § 3.

8. See the OSHA fact sheet at www.osha.gov/SLTC/ergonomics/four-pronged_factsheet.html.

9. For a review of state plans, see www.osha.gov/fso/osp/index.html.

10. For a copy of the statement, see OSHA's Web site at www.osha.gov/media/oshnews/mar00/opastmt031300a.html.

11. See House Resolution 79 EH, 107th Congress. The Senate passed its own resolution disapproving the standard. Congress's action was unprecedented.

12. For a discussion of the development of the standard and the text of the final rule, see the *Federal Register,* 52 (August 24, 1987): 31852–31886.

13. The report is available at the following URL: www.osha-slc.gov/SLTC/hazard-communications/wgfinal.html.

14. The regulations pertaining to inspections are set forth in 29 CFR § 1903.7.

15. The Supreme Court ruled in *Marshall v. Barlow's, Inc.*, 436 U.S. 307 (1978), that OSHA inspectors required a search warrant to inspect for safety hazards and violations of the act. The Court permitted the issue of warrants under the relaxed standard of an administrative search.

16. See Rothstein, *Occupational Safety*, §§ 301–308, for relevant case precedent.

17. Rothstein, *Occupational Safety*, § 305.

18. For an analysis of the politics of deregulation during the first Reagan administration, see Charles Noble, *Liberalism at Work: The Rise and Fall of OSHA* (Philadelphia: Temple University, 1986), 99–120.

19. David McCaffrey, "Decentralizing Occupational Health and Safety Regulation: An Evaluation of the Foundation and Prospects," *California Western Law Review* 21 (1984): 101–127.

20. McCaffrey, "Decentralizing Occupational Health and Safety Regulation," p. 101.

21. McCaffrey, "Decentralizing Occupational Health and Safety Regulation," p. 102 and Table I.

22. McCaffrey, "Decentralizing Occupational Health and Safety Regulation," pp. 124–126 and Table V.

23. Arthur Amchan, "The Future of OSHA," *Labor Law Journal* 35 (1984): 547.

24. Amchan, "The Future of OSHA," pp. 548–549.

25. W. Kip Viscusi, "The Structure and Enforcement of Job Safety Regulation," *Law and Contemporary Problems* 49 (1986): 127–150.

26. Viscusi, "The Structure and Enforcement of Job Safety Regulation," p. 144.

27. Viscusi, "The Structure and Enforcement of Job Safety Regulation," p. 139.

28. Ann Bartel and Lacy Thomas, "The Costs and Benefits of OSHA-Induced Investments in Employee Safety and Health," in *Workers' Compensation Benefits: Adequacy, Equity, and Efficiency*, ed. John Worrall and David Appel (Ithaca, NY: ILR Press, 1985), 41–56.

29. Bartel and Thomas, "The Costs and Benefits," pp. 53–54.

30. Richard Lacayo, "Death on the Shop Floor," *Time*, September 16, 1991, pp. 28–29.

31. Statement of Congressman Scott McGinnis, Review of the Occupational Safety and Health Act, *Hearings Before the Subcommittee on Workforce Protections of the Committee on Education and the Workforce*, House of Representatives, March 27 and April 29, 1998, Serial No. 105–84 (Washington, Government Printing Office, 1998), 55.

32. McGinnis, Review of the Occupational Safety and Health Act, pp. 369–370.

33. John F. Burton Jr. and James R. Chelius, "Workplace Safety and Health Regulations: Rationale and Results," in *Government Regulation of the Employment Relationship*, ed. Bruce Kaufman (Madison, WI: Industrial Relations Research Association, 1997), 282.

34. Noble, *Liberalism at Work*, p. 105.

35. An excellent critique of the model is William Dickens, "Occupational Safety and Health and 'Irrational' Behavior: A Preliminary Analysis," in Worrall, *Workers' Compensation Benefits*, pp. 19–40.

36. Noble, *Liberalism at Work*, p. 241.

37. Patrick W. Seburn, "Evolution of Employer-Provided Defined Benefit Pensions," *Monthly Labor Review* (December 1991): 16–23.

38. An insightful study of labor's role in creating the U.S. pension program is Beth Stevens, "Labor Unions and the Privatization of Welfare: The Turning Point in the 1940s," in *The Privatization of Social Policy? Occupational Welfare and the Welfare State in America, Scandinavia and Japan*, ed. Michael Shalev (New York: St. Martin's Press, 1996), 73–103. Stevens argues that a set of unique conditions in the immediate postwar period motivated unions to focus on private benefits obtained through negotiations rather than on political action.

39. *Inland Steel Co.,* 77 NLRB 1 (1948).

40. 29 U.S.C. §§ 1001–1461.

41. 29 U.S.C. § 1001(b) and (c).

42. 29 U.S.C. § 1022.

43. See 29 U.S.C. § 1023.

44. Major changes in the vesting requirements were made in 1986. See 29 U.S.C. § 1053(a)(2), 1988 Cum. Supp.

45. 29 U.S.C. § 1082.

46. 29 U.S.C. §§ 1101–1106.

47. 29 U.S.C. § 1302.

48. 29 U.S.C. § 1306.

49. "Will the Bough Break?" *BusinessWeek,* April 14, 2003, pp. 62–63. One proposal raised the issue of declining stock portfolios and suggested that plans shift out of stocks and into the more stable bond market. See Mary Williams Walsh, "New Rules Urged to Avert Looming Pension Crisis," *New York Times,* July 28, 2003 [online edition].

50. For a critique of ERISA and private pension plans generally, see Merton Bernstein and Jean Bernstein, *Social Security: The System That Works* (New York: Basic Books, 1988), 123–148.

51. One news report stated, "A host of growing problems is deepening the effects of the bear market for the estimated 52 million people with 401(k)s." Among the problems are declining participation, employer cutbacks of the plans, and the use of pension funds for loans. "The result is that the 401(k) is looking increasingly like a tattered promise, and there is growing concern that millions of Americans won't have enough for retirement." Ruth Simon, "Why Even a Rally Won't Save You," *Wall Street Journal,* May 1, 2003, p. D1.

52. "Defined Contribution Retirement Plans Becoming More Prevalent," The Editor's Desk, *Monthly Labor Review,* January 6, 1999.

53. Lawrence Mishel, Jared Bernstein, and Heather Boushey, *The State of Working America, 2002/2003* (Ithaca, NY: Cornell University Press, 2002), 148, Figure 2G.

54. For an excellent introduction and overview, see Sheldon Friedman and David C. Jacobs, eds., *The Future of the Safety Net: Social Insurance and Employee Benefits* (Urbana-Champaign, IL: Industrial Relations Research Association, 2001).

55. 29 U.S.C. §§ 1161 et seq.

56. 100 Stat. 229, § 603.

57. Department of Labor, ERISA Technical Release, No. 86-2, reprinted in Bureau of National Affairs, *Policy and Practice Series: Compensation,* 339:68-69 (Washington, DC: BNA Books, 1987).

58. In *Geissal v. Moore Medical Corp.,* 524 U.S. 74 (1998), the Supreme Court discussed the general purposes of COBRA and the importance of the time of an employee's election of benefits.

59. Public Law 104–191 (1996).

60. H.R. 15 (January 7, 2003).

61. 29 U.S.C. §§ 2601 et seq.

62. 29 U.S.C. at § 2601(a)–(b).

63. Linda Greenhouse, "Supreme Court Ruling Increases Federal Power," *New York Times,* May 28, 2003 [online edition].

64. For the points covered in this paragraph, see 29 U.S.C. §§ 2611–2617.

65. Vicki Lovell, "A Citizenship Perspective on Work-Family Policies" (paper presented at the Industrial Relations Research Association Conference on Work and Family, Washington, DC, June 22, 2000).

66. See www.doleta.gov/wd/finalregbaa.htm for the text of the regulation. The document contains an informative discussion of leave policies and the federal–state unemployment insurance relationship.

67. For the text of the letter, see www.workingforthefuture.org/gregg_letter.html. The sponsoring organization for the Web site offers extensive commentary on the FMLA.

68. 174 Cal. App. 2d 184, 344 P.2d 254 (1959).

69. 344 P.2d at 27.

70. 111 Cal. App. 3d 443, 168 Cal. Rptr. 722 (1980).

71. 168 Cal. Rptr. at 729.

72. "Jury Orders Helmsley to Pay $11M to Gay Man," Associated Press, February 5, 2003.

73. For a thoughtful analysis of the confusing, overlapping, and contradictory protections for employees, see Ann C. McGinley, "Rethinking Civil Rights and Employment At Will: Toward a Coherent National Discharge Policy," *Ohio St. Law Journal* 57 (1996): 1443–1524. Another more recent treatment argues that because common law created the at-will rule, judges should abrogate the doctrine. Edwin Cottone, "Comment: Employee Protection From Unjust Discharge: A Proposal for Judicial Reversal of the Terminable-At-Will Doctrine," *Santa Clara Law Review* 42 (2002): 1259.

74. See Montana Code Annotated, § 39-2-901, et seq.

75. M.C.A., § 39-2-904.

76. M.C.A., § 39-2-905.

77. M.C.A., § 39-2-912.

78. 147 Ariz. 370, 710 P.2d 1025 (1985).

79. *Payne v. Western & Atlantic R. R. Co.* 81 Tenn. 507 (1884) (Freeman, J., dissenting).

80. The U.S. Supreme Court applied the sexual harassment doctrine to cases involving heterosexual males who harassed another man using sexual terminology. See *Oncale v. Sundowner Offshore Services, Inc.,* 523 U.S. 75 (1998). If Wagenseller's claim was just a sexual harassment case, the Arizona courts should have ruled that the matter was properly litigated under Title VII.

PART IV

Rebuilding the Employment Contract

Practices, Policies, and Politics

CHAPTER 8

Contemporary Employment Issues

The preceding chapters of this book dealt with the historical evolution of the U.S. labor relations system, the way the system functions, and the broader context of labor relations. Those chapters make clear that the present employment system lacks coherence, consistency, and efficiency. Some employment claims fall within the purview of common law, with its doctrines of compensation for emotional injuries, economic loss, and punitive damages. Such litigation can be particularly vexatious for employers. Other claims, such as allegations of race or gender discrimination, proceed within an administrative context. Remedies in those cases are more limited and frequently incur extensive delays. The labor relations system of grievance and arbitration functions well as a dispute resolution mechanism for unionized employees, but arbitrators typically issue only "make whole" remedies that restore the employee to his or her previous status and do not punish employers for deliberate wrongdoing. The overlapping, contradictory, and arbitrary outcomes of employment claims lead to confusion and uncertainty for employers, difficult and ambiguous alternatives for employees, and burdens on the judicial and administrative systems (paid for by tax dollars).[1]

Coupled with the administrative shortcomings associated with individual rights, the long-standing practice of linking important social benefits to the workplace has undergone substantial erosion since the 1970s. Americans traditionally acquired health insurance, disability insurance, pensions, and other important protections through their jobs. Because many benefits are discretionary, employers faced with labor cost competition may choose to eliminate or reduce benefits. The tacit or psychological employment contract likewise underwent a renegotiation. Most employees no longer have expectations of long-term careers with one firm, with increases in compensation and benefits based on experience and culminating in a retirement plan that offers genuine security. As a result, workers share the risks and anxieties of a changing economic environment.[2] This chapter explores the possibility of change in important areas of employment. It begins with three prerequisites necessary to a rational scheme of employer–employee relations.

First, the system should be integrated. U.S. labor law emanates from different sources, and different legal authorities can make different rules. Often, those rules conflict with one another because they arise from various policy concerns. For example, if an employer contracts with a worker to arbitrate employment disputes, a court or administrative agency may interfere with that bargain, which disrupts the parties' expectations. In a recent administrative proceeding, the Equal Employment Opportunity Commission (EEOC) pursued a charge against an employer even though the employee had agreed to arbitration over any dispute. The EEOC's position is that it acts to vindicate the rights of all similarly situated employees, and therefore it has sufficient reason to seek its own resolution of the matter to establish legal precedent.

Second, the system should promote the efficient allocation of resources. Legal entanglements impose delays and costs on all parties to the dispute. Lawyers have an incentive to pursue cases under a contingent fee arrangement if the prospects of recovery are sufficiently large. Depending on the nature of the claim, then, an injured employee might or might not be able to obtain independent legal representation. Even questionable claims, however, will be prosecuted if the defendant has substantial resources, because a settlement might be cheaper than responding to a lawsuit.[3] Employees need prompt and effective enforcement of their rights. Employers need protection against abusive litigation. The system needs simplicity, clarity, and balance. Workers' compensation, whatever its perceived weaknesses, offers an excellent example of a compromise scheme that satisfies an acceptable quantum of contending interests.

Third, employment policy requires focus. At present, we promote myriad goals through employment, including political and social ones. Whatever guiding principles apply, they should be clearly described and comprehensible. A well-known authority on the National Labor Relations Act argues forcefully that the national legislation dealing with collective bargaining works at cross-purposes with itself, and the result is haphazard enforcement of workers' rights to engage in concerted activity for their mutual benefit.[4] Unions suffered the consequences of a scheme that permitted courts and administrative officials to choose among competing rationales when deciding cases.

With the foregoing elements as a foundation, this chapter surveys some practical improvements in the employment scheme. The discussion here begins with an analysis of levels, foci, and outcomes of actions. Each level builds on the preceding one, and the outcomes have an increasingly broad reach. Table 8.1 sets forth the main points.

Table 8.1   Strategies for More Effective Employment Relations

Level of Action	Focus of Action	Outcome of Action
Workplace level	Dispute procedures	Reduces employer's risk of employment litigation and excessive damage awards
Institutional level	Representation	Promotes employees' interests in establishing an effective workplace voice
Political level	Coalitions	Aligns diverse interests toward political action, which enhances prospects for meaningful legislative reforms

Organizational Justice as an Alternative to Litigation

Regardless of legalities, employers and employees have explicit and implicit understandings about the nature of their relationship and rely on those understandings to conduct routine dealings with one another. A prominent topic in contemporary industrial–organizational psychology research addresses the matter of employee expectations concerning fair treatment in the workplace and its role in effective management. Recent studies examine how employee perceptions of fairness influence such crucial behaviors as motivation, loyalty, and work effort. Fairness depends not only on the outcomes of employment policies, such as compensation, but also on the presence of clear, effective procedures for resolving disputes and the interpersonal relations between employees and managers in administering the procedures. A number of scholarly contributions demonstrate the importance of justice systems as a key element in employment policies, and their use will undoubtedly continue to grow.[5]

Justice systems have a dual function. They explain managerial decisions to employees, thereby influencing employee perceptions, and they offer employees an opportunity to challenge those decisions.[6] In the latter situation, dispute procedures superficially resemble the grievance procedures in unionized workplaces. The difference is in the final stage of resolution, in which unionized employees may invoke binding arbitration conducted by an outside, impartial decision maker. Increasingly, however, nonunion firms rely on binding arbitration to resolve disputes and avoid litigation. By affording a contractual remedy to the individual employee, the firm aims to preempt legal claims that might lead to judicial action. Supreme Court decisions over the past few years give impetus to the adoption of justice systems, and, in turn, they set a foundation for the further evolution of employment policies.

As discussed in the material on welfare capitalism, employee representation plans—sometimes referred to as the company union—played an important part in the overall development of welfare capitalism. Arbitration appeared very early in the U.S. workplace, and it performed a crucial role in the welfare policies. For example, in the 1870s, the Straiton & Storm cigar company gave employees a right to negotiate with management over wages, hours, working conditions, and other aspects of employment, and, in the event of disagreement, the matter would be submitted to an impartial arbitration board. George Storm, a founding partner in the firm, testified before a congressional committee in September 1883 about the theory and practice of industrial democracy. Storm pointed out that in the United States, "those coming under the head of wage-workers have the same political rights that are accorded to people who are supposed to be capitalists." For that reason, workers deserved a voice in employment matters affecting their livelihood. In Storm's view, the arbitration process derived from essential American values of democratic participation, equality, and civic responsibility. Storm rejected the idea that managers could manipulate the system to their own advantage; rather, it depended on legitimacy to be effective.[7] Justice systems thus have a long and honorable provenance in U.S. labor relations.

With the evolution of civil rights laws, formal justice systems have become commonplace in one area of employment relations—sexual harassment. Most employers subject to coverage of Title VII have implemented formal complaint procedures giving employees an opportunity to protest unlawful sexual harassment in the workplace. The procedures arise from Supreme Court decisions shielding employers from liability for sexual harassment if the employee does not use the procedures to protest harassment. In two 1998 cases, the Court ruled that a complaint procedure provides an affirmative defense to a claim of sexual harassment. Once an employee brings a charge of harassment, the employer can show that it had a procedure and that the employee failed to use the procedure to bring the harassment to management's attention.[8] Empirical evidence shows that such complaint procedures indeed help to deflect employees' propensities to engage in more adversarial behavior, such as litigation or quitting.[9] Building on the basic concepts of justice and its attendant procedures, employers increasingly offer nonunion arbitration to resolve issues of termination.[10]

In *Circuit City v. Adams*, the Supreme Court upheld an individual's contractual obligation to arbitrate before proceeding in another forum. The case involved an employee who was discharged from Circuit City and who then filed suit under a variety of statutory and common law theories. The employer argued that the employee was obligated in the first place to seek a remedy through arbitration. The Court agreed with the employer, ruling that arbitration contracts were valid under relevant federal law and the litigation was precluded until the employee arbitrated his claim.[11] As a result, the employer shielded itself from defending the case before either an administrative tribunal or a court. The Court subsequently ruled, however, that the EEOC had the authority to proceed in a case where it was pursuing its own legal interests, even though the individual who initially made the claim had agreed to arbitrate the dispute.[12]

Legal scholars have commented extensively on the use of nonunion arbitration, particularly when an employee agrees to forego statutory rights. One of the most prominent critics of arbitration argues that contractual processes should not compel workers to surrender important legal protections as a condition of employment.[13] Because statutes typically provide fundamental procedural rights as well as broad remedies, employees may be deprived of valuable safeguards when they submit to an arbitration forum provided by the employer. Other studies assert, to the contrary, that mandatory arbitration confers no significant advantage on employers and that its use is intended to reduce costs rather than to gain strategic leverage over the outcomes of a dispute procedure.[14] The debate helps to illuminate a basic principle concerning internal dispute procedures. To the extent that they displace other legal protections and defend employers from litigation, they should ensure minimal standards of fair procedures and outcomes.

To balance the competing demands of efficiency and equity, an institutional framework is needed to support nonunion arbitration. That framework would provide for full and competent representation in arbitration, review of arbitration awards for compliance with statutory provisions, and standards of finality. Collective representation meets those needs. More specifically, labor organizations have the resources to extend representation services across U.S. workplaces and fill the institutional gaps in nonunion employment arbitration systems.

Bringing Unions Back In

Union decline and its causes were analyzed in Chapter 5. A number of factors, including changes in the nature of firms, the evolution from a manufacturing to a service economy, and global labor markets, provide a broad context for decline. In the United States, however, one of the most widely accepted explanations focuses on managerial hostility to unions. That hostility is manifested in a number of tactical moves, including illegal behavior, to discourage unionization. In trying to defeat unionism, managers act rationally to protect their interests. Unions enable workers to exercise monopoly bargaining power and force employers to pay higher compensation. The proposition that union members enjoy higher wages and benefits is well established; according to a February 2003 news release from the Bureau of Labor Statistics, "In 2002, full-time wage and salary workers who were union members had median usual weekly earnings of $740, compared with a median of $587 for wage and salary workers who were not represented by unions."[15] Other factors influence compensation, but the union differential is one of the most important. Obviously, higher wages will tend to increase the costs of production. Employers may pass those costs on to consumers, accept lower profits, or become more productive. If employers raise the prices of their products, consumers either refuse to buy the products or purchase them at lower prices from nonunion competitors.

Monopoly wage bargaining, however, is not necessarily a zero-sum game. An impressive body of research indicates that unions actually improve productivity within a firm. According to the theory, unions force managers to be more rational and efficient in dealing with employees. Better management usually includes rational workplace policies, more focused attention to labor practices, and intensive training. Because union workers have access to a grievance procedure that gives them a voice at work, they are less likely to quit or reduce their work effort to protest against management. Such ideas are particularly associated with Richard Freeman and James Medoff's influential 1984 book, *What Do Unions Do?*[16] Subsequent studies based on their ideas find that the basic propositions put forward in *What Do Unions Do?* are still valid in the 2000s. In a survey article, Freeman summarized the following conclusions that can be drawn from the economic literature about union impacts on firms.[17]

- Unions reduce turnover among employees and increase the tenure of workers at firms. Long-term attachment is to the advantage of the firm as well as the worker.
- Unions obtain increased fringe benefits for workers; those benefits include health insurance and pensions. Pensions contribute to our national savings and resources available for investment.
- Unions tend to restrict managerial discretion regarding wages, thus reducing wage inequality. They also force employers to promulgate and follow rules governing the workplace.
- Unions do not harm productivity, and in many cases, unions improve productivity by improving the labor relations climate.
- Unionized firms are less profitable. As a result, U.S. managers oppose workers' attempts to unionize. Employer opposition to unions is the most important single factor in declines in union density over the 1970s and 1980s.[18]

On balance, Freeman asserts, unionism is good for the national economy. He goes on to argue that further declines in unionization will weaken workers' protections against arbitrary management, produce more wage inequality, and harm productivity.

Despite the positive economic and social outcomes associated with unions, productivity gains rarely offset the costs of the union wage premium, and unionized firms suffer a competitive disadvantage.[19] Accordingly, if a nonunion firm competes in a heavily unionized environment, as is the case with Wal-Mart and the grocery industry, the nonunion firm enjoys a substantial edge. The unionized firm, among other strategies, will seek concessions from the union or will engage in its own union avoidance tactics. It may even seek relief from union contracts through bankruptcy, as United Airlines did in early 2003.[20] If unions could successfully "take wages out of competition," they would minimize managerial opposition. Alternatively, if government imposed some social costs on all firms—such as health insurance, pensions, and other important protections—a more level playing field would meliorate low-wage strategies and union avoidance. The conditions necessary to such reforms include a broad coalition of citizens, legislators, and institutions.

Several factors impede a program of reform. To start with, if we assume that employer antiunionism arises from strategies designed to offset union effects on profits, legal change to encourage organizing activity will encounter political resistance because unions affect a firm's financial outcomes and therefore investment in those firms. As one study contends, "Evidence of the poor economic performance by union companies supports the proposition that the restructuring in industrial relations and increased resistance to union organizing have been a predictable response on the part of U.S. businesses to increased domestic and foreign competition." The result of this view is that employers must be free to pursue strategies designed to cope with globalization of labor markets. Accordingly, "In the absence of narrowing union-nonunion performance differences, modifications in labor law that substantially enhance union organizing and bargaining power are likely to bring about a reduced competitiveness of U.S. firms."[21] On this argument, regulatory strategies should not foster union expansion, and if unionized firms cannot respond to competitive pressures, they eventually fail. Given the reality of economic pressures, does labor have any viable options for future growth?

Whatever their attitudes toward unions as bargaining monopolies, many U.S. workers demonstrate a strong desire for some form of workplace representation. One industrial relations authority believes that employees lack motivation to join unions because the current system of individual representation satisfies most U.S. workers. Leo Troy, the foremost proponent of this idea, says that the "structural break" that drove the evolution of the current system "was the product of markets rather than government policies." He describes those forces as "the newly emerging labor market [after World War II], its negative impact on the organized system, managerial experience and knowledge about labor relations gained in the aftermath of the New Deal, and significant changes made in public policy by the Labor Management Relations Act of 1947 (the Taft-Hartley Act)."[22] One shortcoming of Troy's perspective, however, is that it overlooks the effectiveness of managers in shaping employee opinions about collective action and the long-term effects of attitudes on individual decision making.[23] If managers perceived some value in a union relation, many employees would most likely accept a collective system of workplace dealings. Organizational justice systems, including nonunion arbitration, offer the possibility of a limited, low-cost, and low-resistance type of representation.

The criticisms of nonunion arbitration typically emphasize a perceived inequality of power in the relationship, which leads to manipulation and abuse of dispute procedures. Arguably, nonunion arbitration could be used for purposes of avoiding unions and eviscerating statutory rights, but in that case, the objectives of providing justice and reducing quit rates and other negative behaviors may fail.[24] Employers have legitimate interests in reducing litigation, providing effective conflict resolution, and administering personnel policies in an efficient way. Employees have interests in ensuring that they are afforded their statutory and administrative rights in any conflict with their employers. The state has an interest in accommodating the interests of the parties as well as its own interests in the best deployment of resources and functioning of labor market institutions. Fitting those pieces together offers an opportunity for unions to create a modified structure of membership and service.

Unions as Justice Facilitators

Using the basic concepts of workers' compensation systems, we can envision a system that attracts the support of workers and employers and allows unions some positive workplace role. The interest of employers is to be free from the risks of idiosyncratic litigation, bureaucratic ineptitude, and unstable legal environments. The interest of employees is in vindication of their statutory rights, fair and expeditious resolution of complaints, and access to competent information, advice, and advocacy. Unions traditionally promoted collective bargaining as their primary objective, but unions now lack the bargaining power to effectively fulfill that role in many workplaces. Rather than negotiating for economic benefits, unions could provide safeguards guaranteeing the efficacious adjudication of complaints. Many commentators propose an innovative form of union association by which employees could gain some benefits of collective action without falling under a labor agreement at the workplace.[25] For a small monthly fee, say, workers could purchase a type of employment insurance that would entitle them to advice and counsel about employment disputes. Such a scheme would enable unions to satisfy employees' needs for expertise and advice, employers' concerns about trustworthy and legitimate procedures, and the public policy interest in fair, objective representation in workplace conflict.

To make employment arbitration viable, employers must be persuaded to provide resolution systems for all employees. The first step in accomplishing this objective is to shield employers from the myriad possibilities of liability arising out of workplace disputes. The process set forth below offers an accommodation similar in nature to the system of workers' compensation. It proposes a mechanism to adjudicate employee complaints in exchange for protections against litigation. Ideally, the system would follow the guidelines prescribed below, and it would also feature a source of independent legal advice for workers through the auspices of organized labor.

As an initial step for the model, the employer must offer and the employee must accept arbitration as the method of resolving any work-related complaint. The arbitration clause will specify that it is the means that the parties have chosen to deal with conflict, and arbitration is a prerequisite to any legal action. The employee explicitly surrenders his or her right to any statutory or common law cause of action until arbitration takes place. This process is consistent with the most recent Supreme Court precedent and with other successful examples of employment arbitration, such as the Montana wrongful discharge statute. Employees should be free to choose arbitration or litigation in a given case rather than as a term of employment, but the choice of arbitration would constitute both a waiver of all common law rights and a condition precedent to administrative remedies.[26]

To illustrate the process, assume an employee is discharged for violating attendance policies, poor performance, and other rule infractions. She claims that the discharge is actually motivated by gender discrimination and submits her case to arbitration. She prevails in that forum and is awarded a remedy consistent with arbitral doctrine. Note that at this point, several options exist for each party. The employee might believe the arbitrator's award did not sufficiently compensate her for her injuries—by ordering reinstatement but not back pay, for example—and she is inclined to pursue her rights under civil rights laws. Likewise, the employer might conclude that the arbitrator's award is flawed or tainted by bias and irrationality and is therefore unacceptable as a resolution of the matter.

In the latter situation, the employer has the choice of implementing the award or not. If the employer chooses not to grant the ordered remedy, the employee should then be legally entitled to any available recourse, including judicial enforcement of the arbitration award, litigation under a common law theory, or administrative action. The arbitrator's award in favor of the employee could be given evidentiary weight in the discretion of the judge or administrative official. Generally, as discussed below, the Supreme Court regards arbitration as a beneficial and trustworthy process entitled to substantial deference. Consequently, the threat of ongoing legal action, backed by the authority of an arbitrator's opinion, would be an effective deterrent against the employer's disregard of the outcome.

On the other hand, assume the employer prevails in arbitration and the employee's claims are rejected. Should the employee have further recourse in an administrative or a judicial forum? Existing rules about arbitration already give a practical answer to this question. The National Labor Relations Board (NLRB) has developed principles to accommodate union grievance procedures and statutory rights under the National Labor Relations Act, and administrative entities such as the EEOC could easily adapt those principles to deal with arbitration and civil rights statutes. A longstanding set of legal rules, which have evolved over years of application, would go far toward ensuring employees' protections against deprivation of rights under any relevant statutes. By incorporating those rules into administrative guidelines, employers and employees would gain a clear understanding of their various courses of action and legal strategies.[27]

Under NLRB rules, arbitrators can adjudicate employees' statutory rights if the awards conform to specific standards that are now well settled. Provided the requisite conditions are met, the board will defer to the arbitration process both at the outset of a claim and after the arbitration award is issued.[28] The same requirements could be applied by other administrative agencies to determine whether a statutory violation occurred and whether the remedy conforms to statutory requirements. Below is brief description of the system's main features. For purposes of describing the system, keep in mind the example of gender discrimination mentioned above, where a claimant challenges a termination decision on various grounds, including disparate treatment. The deferral policy operates according to certain prerequisites that are summarized below. The thrust of the deferral policy is to avoid unnecessary duplication of effort and expenditure of resources; where conditions are satisfied, the agency will require all claimants to submit to arbitration and will decline to take further action after the arbitration.

The Contract to Arbitrate and Arbitrability

The NLRB requires a contractual relationship that recognizes the rights of the parties and the principles underlying the statute. If the nonunion arbitration provision contained specific language acknowledging all employee rights, such as protections against various forms of discrimination, and instructed the arbitrator on the scope of his or her authority to decide claims, that legally binding agreement should constitute an enforceable agreement. The submission to arbitration would explicitly confer the power on the arbitrator to hear evidence about the civil rights claim and to apply the relevant doctrinal rules necessary to resolve the claim. A broad scope of authority ensures that the claim is in fact heard and obviates any question of the arbitrator's power.[29] Like the NLRB, the EEOC could stipulate that as a condition of the deferral of any charge, all relevant claims would be presented in the arbitration forum.

The predicate of any deferral requires that arbitration be available. If the employer raised defenses of timeliness, procedural irregularity, or other incidental matters, then deferral would not be available. The EEOC could take up the charge and deal with it as with any other complaint. Relatedly, the arbitration contract should offer substantial procedural rights, such as access to relevant information, power to compel production of witnesses or documents, and other rights attaching to the administrative claim. Arbitrators routinely deal with such matters, and their orders concerning production of evidence can be judicially enforced. Employees should have a full opportunity to exercise any procedural rights that they would have in the administrative forum. While arbitration is not litigation and is deliberately designed to avoid the delay and obstruction that make up some legal strategies, the forum nonetheless provides rudimentary mechanisms for ensuring adequate compliance with procedural safeguards. For most employers, the opportunity to preclusively arbitrate a dispute is incentive enough to motivate cooperative behavior.

Consideration of Issues and Evidence

The NLRB in its deferral policy requires that the arbitration forum address the statutory issue. As above, the submission agreement can mandate consideration of any statutory and contractual rights presented to the arbitrator. Both sides have substantial motivation to make a full and complete presentation of the case. For the employer, deferral turns on a resolution of the statutory claims, and the employer will therefore try to raise and defeat any relevant issues arising out of the facts. For the employee, arbitration provides an opportunity for a quick adjudication of his or her rights and possible reinstatement instead of protracted administrative and legal proceedings that may or may not result in some remedy. If the employee is forced to waive his or her common law claims in order to gain access to arbitration, that waiver prompts the employee to fully develop any remaining claims. The NLRB precedent sometimes permits an inference that the statutory claim is resolved by arbitration if relevant evidence is presented. Where the parties have an interest in making sure that claims are adjudicated, the likelihood of their doing so can be assumed.

Guarantees of a Fair and Impartial Hearing

The most sustained attacks on arbitration stem from its informality and flexibility. Because it is administered by private individuals rather than judicial officers, critics point out that arbitration lacks the institutional regularity needed to protect workers' rights. The problem is compounded in nonunion schemes where the employer retains substantial control over the process. To overcome the perceived shortcomings of employment arbitration, employers can be prompted to establish the reliability of the process as a condition of deferral. In other words, the EEOC can devise standards for the arbitration hearing that employers must meet as a condition of deferral. Where those standards were not met, the EEOC would reject the arbitration award as insufficiently trustworthy and proceed with the complaint.

A full and fair hearing includes, at a minimum, an adversarial process in which the parties present evidence, cross-examine witnesses, and submit arguments in support of their positions before an impartial adjudicator. The important issue here is the notion of an adversarial process. Where the employee lacks financial resources, expertise, and competent representation, a hearing is not truly adversarial. Nor can the employer correct the deficiency by offering to furnish those elements. An adviser hired by the company does not represent the interests of the employee, and an arbitrator whose entire fee is paid by one party implicitly has a degree of partiality. Independent union participation, however, offers a guarantee of adversarialism. As part of its deferral policy, the EEOC might presume that any hearing where the claimant had outside representation would be deemed to meet the requirement of a full and fair hearing.

Returning to the notion of a union-sponsored employment insurance system, it is clear that such a program would offer advantages to all parties associated with nonunion employment arbitration operating in an environment of agency deferral. Employees benefit from expert advice and representation in the arbitration forum. Employers have assurances that the presence of a union representative would enhance the likelihood of EEOC deferral to a favorable arbitration award. Unions establish a relationship with an individual and create a contractual bond that persists across workplaces and firms. If unions performed to the satisfaction of employees, they would promote a positive image and generate interest in other forms of collective action. Because employers had an interest in furthering this limited type of representation, they would encourage rather than discourage a union presence.

Indeed, employers might negotiate an arbitration-only contract with a labor union, entitling the union to represent employees in a designated work group for purposes of arbitration. Because the union would not be an exclusive representative for purposes of collective bargaining, the arrangement would not fall under NLRB rules about union–management dealings.[30] The union would not *bargain over* the employer's policies, but would merely act as the employee's representative in enforcing the employer's terms of employment as stated in the handbook or made evident through the rules of the workplace. The further contractual understanding between employer and employee would be an agreement to waive any other rights to the full extent permitted by law. Thus, the employer would gain maximum protection against litigation and the employee would gain maximum enforceability of the employment contract offered by the employer.

The foregoing set of procedures requires neither legislative sanction nor judicial acquiescence. The NLRB devised its deferral policy by deciding cases in which it applied the principles and confirmed them in subsequent opinions. The EEOC could accomplish the same end by promulgating guidelines explaining the circumstances in which it would uphold arbitration as a satisfactory resolution of statutory claims. In the past, the EEOC has exercised its authority to interpret legislation through published guidelines, such as mental disabilities under the Americans With Disabilities Act, and it could do so with respect to employment arbitration. While courts do review the propriety of agency action, the Supreme Court decisions in *Waffle House* and *Circuit City* offer ample and authoritative precedent for the EEOC to proactively accommodate arbitration to the existing framework of workplace rights.

The final element in the nonunion employment arbitration setting involves judicial review of an arbitrator's award. Again, definitive labor law precedent already sets out the rules that a court applies in determining whether to uphold or vacate an arbitrator's award. The authority of courts to review labor arbitration awards derived from Section 301 of the National Labor Relations Act, which conferred jurisdiction on federal courts to enforce contracts between unions and employers. In the 1961 *Steelworkers Trilogy,* the Supreme Court laid down the principles by which judges enforce arbitration awards.[31] Those principles have generated a massive body of precedent, but the overriding idea can be simply stated. As Justice Douglas wrote, judges must defer to an arbitrator's decision if it "draws its essence" from the parties' agreement to arbitrate. The policy reasons supporting such deference rest on basic notions of contractual rights and the federal interest in stable labor relations. While cases vary according to their facts, courts uniformly adhere to the basic formulation expressed in the *Trilogy.*[32]

In the context of nonunion arbitration, the same policy considerations obtain. If employers and employees prefer the expedited process of arbitration, their preferences deserve to be given effect as an expression of contractual intent. Arbitration conserves judicial resources and promotes conflict resolution at the most fundamental level; by avoiding involvement with an entrenched bureaucracy having its own interests and goals, the parties stand the best chance of cooperative adjustment of the dispute. Arbitration offers speed, flexibility, and accommodation rather than delay, legal rigidity, and obstruction. It is far less costly than litigation and does not impose financial burdens on taxpayers. For those reasons, courts should favor employment arbitration.

To conclude, representation in the setting of dispute resolution clearly confers benefits on all parties. One important reason is that it offers safeguards against unfair advantages and imbalances of power in the employment relationship. That point also has particular relevance for contemporary workplace design. Just as unions can furnish a crucial ingredient for successful conflict resolution procedures, a collective institutional presence may add to the effectiveness of innovative work systems. Recent trends in economic theory suggest that such intangible factors as trust, mutual obligation, and cooperative attitudes make up an important dimension of efficient workplaces. Sometimes described as social capital, the concept of productive human networks is increasingly used to illustrate the complex interplay between the management of labor and the nature of firms.[33] Those ideas are not entirely new, of course. The basis of welfare capitalism rested on assumptions about human relations and the benefits of mutualism; one of the most convincing examples was the Baltimore and Ohio Railroad's experiment with labor–management cooperation in the 1910s.[34] If unions played a role in sustaining exemplary relations between workers and managers in the past century, it is possible they may do so in this one.

Unions as a Vehicle for Cooperation

The contemporary managerial emphasis on developing effective team structures, employee initiative, and flexibility in labor deployment depends on the willingness of employees to align their efforts with the firm's agenda. The interest in contemporary forms of work design derives from scientific management and its focus on standardized mass production. The United States' rise to industrial dominance in the early part of this century was predicated on Frederick Taylor's ideas of organizing work in the best and most efficient way by breaking work down into routine and repetitive tasks. Industries organized along such lines, such as Ford Motor Company and U.S. Steel, realized tremendous increases in output through economies of scale and standardization of product. After the Great Depression and the rise of organized labor, Taylorism continued to flourish. Managers exercised detailed control over workers, and unions accepted the basic division between the conception and planning of work and its execution. In business downturns, workers could be laid off to protect price structures and profits. Over the 1950s and 1960s, the system created the world's richest middle class. It also created a "rigid segregation between the front-line workers and their social, intellectual, and occupational superiors."[35]

The mass production system, however, proved inadequate to deal with the economic realities of the 1980s and 1990s.[36] The newly industrialized countries emerged as strong competitors in the market for standardized goods; lower wages translated into lower prices for equivalent products. At the same time, consumers began to demand higher quality, diversified products. "Quality, flexibility and responsiveness to changing consumer tastes would rule now in the world's richest markets, not price and the economies of mass production. Countries that chose to compete on the mass-production model would have to match the wages and hours of the less-developed countries."[37] In their efforts to transform the workplace, U.S. employers turned to systems that encouraged the participation and problem-solving capabilities of employees.

Several alternative models exist for transforming production within firms, many of which are drawn from practices in other industrialized countries. While techniques differ from country to country, taken together they offer policy prescriptions for our industrial relations policies and our future successful competition. First, U.S. firms will have to promote employee participation techniques to provide a greater voice for workers. Unions, likewise, will be forced to broaden their traditional role of adversarial bargaining and "play a partnership role in managing the company while continuing to represent workers' interests." Nonunion workers will require an institutionalized voice in workplace matters. Finally, new social institutions will be necessary to ensure labor–management partnerships, worker training, and employment security.[38]

Assuming the high-performance workplace is a suitable goal for our industrial system, it is helpful to know how many firms in fact have achieved a "transformed" organizational structure. Part of the analysis depends on the definition of a high-performance workplace. If the employer's basic approach is a strategy of high wages, high skills, and high participation, only a few enterprises meet those criteria. One study concludes that less than 5 percent of U.S. firms have adopted high performance, high productivity strategies.[39] But another survey indicates that "the proportion of firms with at least one employee-involvement practice somewhere in the company is large and growing and that a significant number of firms have begun to make more extensive use of these practices."[40]

Despite the emphasis on participation, conclusive evidence is lacking about the relationship between participation and productivity. After a detailed review of the literature on participation, one study reached an equivocal conclusion: "Our overall assessment of the empirical literature from economics, industrial relations, organizational behavior, and other social sciences is that participation usually leads to small, short-run improvements in performance and sometimes leads to significant, long-lasting improvements in performance." The success of participation programs, the authors determined, depends on the extent to which decision-making power is dispersed to employees and the degree of security employees experience in the process.[41] Since trust is the crucial ingredient of cooperative efforts, workers must believe that they will benefit from their efforts and that they are protected against any adverse consequences of their participation. If employees developed a means of reducing labor time to produce a particular product, for example, it would be unfair to lay off those employees because they were no longer needed in that job.

If security is necessary for effective participation, it logically follows that unions would be a good vehicle for the implementation of participation programs. Collective bargaining ensures that employees share in the economic improvements realized by participation. Contractual safeguards against layoffs and discharge provide a substantial degree of job security. The union's right to bargain over changes in methods of production gives employees a voice in the process of change. Because unions stabilize employment, unionized workers will have more seniority, more commitment to the job, and presumably, better skills. Thus, unions theoretically will enhance participatory programs. In fact, empirical evidence bears out that theory.

An early and influential study on the relationship between unions, participation, and productivity examined firms in manufacturing industries that use machine tools in their operations. Empirical analysis showed that where the employer introduced a labor–management committee without a union presence, the efficiency outcomes were worse: these plants had lower levels of productivity and job security. The probable explanation is that participation programs are introduced in larger firms to overcome problems of bureaucratic rigidity, but when they are controlled by management, the programs are themselves another bureaucratic layer unsupported by employee commitment. Accordingly, this study concluded that participation in a nonunion context may fail to attain the desired results. "For collaborative problem solving to succeed, it must be possible for employees to achieve outcomes that also empower them. In management-initiated schemes, the narrow focus and limited objectives for which these programs were designed are quite possibly frustrating these aspirations, undermining the trust and commitment so necessary for success."[42]

There are a number of well-known instances of collaborative efforts between unions and management in the contemporary work environment. Those cases include the Xerox Corporation and the Amalgamated Clothing and Textile Workers Union, AT&T and the Communications Workers of America, and the Chevron Corporation and the Oil, Chemical and Atomic Workers.[43] One of the most widely known programs involves the United Auto Workers and General Motors project to produce the Saturn automobile. Saturn began producing automobiles near the end of 1990. In mid-1992, its cars sold at a rate that exceeded GM's production capacity at the Spring Hill, Tennessee, plant. Saturn successfully met competition from such Japanese imports as Honda, Nissan, and Toyota. Customer satisfaction ratings for the Saturn ranked ahead of Acura, Mercedes-Benz, and Toyota and fell behind only Lexus and Infiniti.[44] It is often cited as an example of an imaginative approach to labor–management relations that "embodies innovations that are currently believed to be 'best practices' in high-performance manufacturing, while establishing a process that gives workers a strong voice in enterprise decisions allowing the parties to adopt new ideas more easily than does the traditional collective bargaining system."[45]

The example of the Saturn accord shows that cooperative efforts succeed where both parties have procedures to articulate and effectuate their interests. Unions can serve as guarantors of trust in situations when no other institutional presence ensures the parties will deal fairly with one another and not resort to opportunism, shirking, or appropriation of resources. Empirical evidence suggests that a lack of social capital in communities has a strong correlation with employer hostility to unions and collective action.[46] Thus, unions moderate the consequences of low social capital and workplace antagonism by providing a bridging form of trust. Rather than inducing an adversarial climate in firms, unions may help to alleviate negative work behaviors.[47]

Economic Security for U.S. Workers:
Health Insurance, Pensions, and Employment Stability

The final element of policy analysis moves to the level of political action. Preceding sections of this chapter demonstrated how unions can function to promote the interests of individuals and the interests of the work group as a whole. We now turn to the arena of national politics. As economic conditions continued to deteriorate through early 2003, several workplace issues of urgent concern for U.S. workers came to national prominence, including health care coverage, pension benefits, and income security. Those issues can be effectively addressed only through federal legislation because of the New Deal framework created during the latter part of the 1930s. Social Security laid the groundwork for a national system of retirement. Subsequent expansions of that program led to medical insurance for Social Security recipients, which provided health care for one discrete segment of the U.S. population at the expense of current workers. The future of Social Security depends on the efforts of the next generation of U.S. workers and their ability to sustain a system that needs immediate attention. Only by mobilizing workers on a broad front and across a coalition of political interests will action occur. The organized labor movement will be vital to formation of such a coalition because it stands as the only meaningful voice of all U.S. workers.[48]

Health Care

By the beginning of 2003, media routinely described the health insurance situation as a crisis. Public attention focused particularly on the lack of health insurance for a sizeable number of Americans, and in March, various groups sponsored a "coverage for the uninsured" week designed to bring political pressure for reform.[49] One commentator summarized the predicament with the following assessment: "We spend about $1.2 trillion each year, two to four times per capita what other developed nations spend, yet we can't find a way to provide health insurance for 41 million citizens." Proposed reforms during the first Clinton administration encountered fierce resistance from pressure groups. As a result, current attempts at change "are only nibbling around the edges of the problem," and strong public support for a comprehensive approach to improvements in the quality of health spending is needed rather than increases in its quantity.[50] The obstacle to reform is public perceptions about socialized health care; those perceptions are rooted in the historical connection between work and insurance.

As emphasized throughout this book, the U.S. employment system is exceptional in its reliance on voluntary, private provision of health care protections. Although that approach served citizens well enough during the era of union influence over employment conditions, from roughly the mid-1940s to the mid-1970s, its shortcomings in the absence of collective bargaining have now become painfully obvious. The protracted economic slump of the 1970s and recession of the early

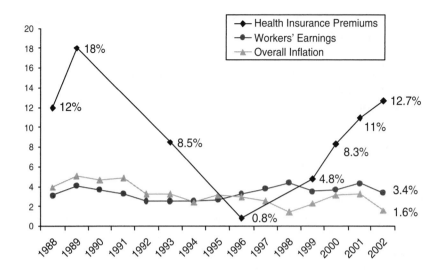

Figure 8.1   Increases in Health Insurance Premiums Compared with Other
Indicators, 1988–2002

1980s generated sharp pressures on employers to reduce labor costs. Overt hostility to collective bargaining caused labor unions to lose membership and bargaining power. The nonunion regime of human resource management assumed control over benefits, and employers engaged in a number of restructuring activities that produced insecurity and flexibility in managerial techniques of compensation containment. Health care costs rose rapidly until the end of the 1980s, declined for nearly a decade, and then escalated at the beginning of the 2000s. The chart shown in Figure 8.1, created by the Kaiser Family Foundation, summarizes those trends.[51]

For nonunion employers, one option to deal with rising costs is simply to curtail or eliminate benefits. No law requires an employer to offer health insurance, and if market conditions discourage rather than encourage such plans, they will decline. In fact, data show that employers have been eliminating plans or passing increasing costs on to employees and that they intend to do so in the future.[52] Various legislative proposals were introduced into Congress in 2003. They varied in scope from modest changes to the more far-reaching National Health Insurance Act (H.R. 15). This bill, introduced by Representative John Dingell in February 2003, would create insurance coverage for every American under a national system. However, political developments abroad—that is, the war and reconstruction of Iraq— overshadowed domestic priorities. And in any event, the large tax cuts enacted in May 2003 will realistically preclude future initiatives that involve discretionary spending.[53]

Congress has no alternative to dealing with Medicare, however. This program features legally enforceable rights for beneficiaries and therefore constitutes a commitment to citizens. Medicare is funded through the same payroll tax mechanism as Social Security and depends on contributions from past and current workers to pay benefits to recipients. Increases in medical costs affect Medicare just as they do private systems. Because of rising costs, Medicare is expected to deplete its surpluses by 2026. The program cannot "go broke" in the same sense that a private company that declares bankruptcy can, but the anticipated shortfalls will necessitate either a decrease in benefits or an increase in contributions, or both. According to the Trustees' Report issued in March 2003,

> In the short range (2003–2012), the financial status of the fund is favorable, with HI [health insurance] assets estimated to increase from 137 percent of annual expenditures in 2002 to 192 percent in 2012. The HI trust fund easily meets the Trustees' test of short range financial adequacy. However, over the next 10 years, the average annual increase in benefit payments is estimated to be 5.9 percent, compared to a growth rate of 5.3 percent for the economy as a whole, as measured by GDP. After 2012, projected HI tax income would fall short of expenditures under present law by a rapidly expanding margin.[54]

If the federal government directs resources to a comprehensive health care program, Medicare would necessarily undergo significant change. But if no national plan emerges, measures must be taken to either supplement the federal system or to curtail its operations.

Health insurance costs also burden pension programs. While Medicare covers workers eligible for Social Security benefits, many retirees depend on private pensions for health protection. For example, workers may take early retirement from a company. If workers do not meet conditions for Social Security, they must obtain insurance through their former employer or purchase their own policy. Many employers made promises to continue health insurance for their retirees, but those promises generally are not enforceable. As a consequence, the employer can terminate health insurance for this group of workers. According to the Bureau of Labor Statistics, fewer employees now have insurance as part of a pension plan.[55] Indeed, pensions themselves are disappearing.

Retirement Security

Like health insurance, pensions make up part of the fringe benefits associated with traditional employment. The Social Security Act created an old-age insurance program, which was conceived at the time as a supplement to individual savings and employer plans. During the zenith of collective bargaining, unions negotiated for the defined benefit type of pension. As discussed earlier, these plans provide a fixed payment to beneficiaries, and the employer has a duty to fund the plan at levels actuarially sufficient to pay benefits. The defined benefit plan offers greater protection for employees because the risk of maintaining the fund falls to the employer. Under a union contract, the employer may also assume the obligation of continuing health care coverage for employees. The defined benefit plan features an

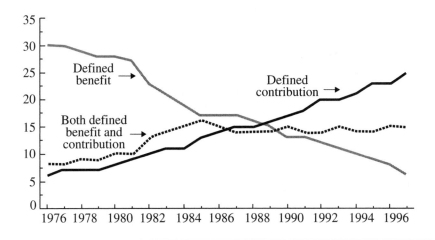

Figure 8.2   Percentage of Workers by Type of Retirement Plan

SOURCE: Pension and Welfare Benefits Administration.

additional safeguard against employer bankruptcy. The Pension Benefit Guaranty Corporation (PBGC), a quasi-public entity described in Chapter 7, operates as an insurer of last resort for defined benefit plans. Using funds collected from employers with defined benefit plans, the PBGC guarantees at least some retirement benefits for persons covered under a plan created by a firm that subsequently becomes bankrupt.

A contrasting type of pension depends on contributions rather than benefits. The defined contribution plans, such as the popular 401(k), are characterized by fixed amounts paid in rather than paid out. Typically, employees contribute a tax-exempt amount deducted from their paycheck, which may or may not be matched by the employer. When employees reach retirement age, they can withdraw money from the plan. The amount will vary according to the amount of contribution and the performance of employees' investments. Defined contribution plans have advantages of portability and flexibility. They also pose greater risks to the individuals. Many employees at Enron, for example, lost their retirement savings when the company collapsed.

Like other fringe benefits, pensions are a source of cost savings for employers. Many employers shifted from the defined benefit plans to defined contribution plans over the period from 1980 to 2000 for obvious reasons. The defined contribution plan does not entail any obligation on the part of the employer to maintain fiscal stability. Those plans are not insured and do not require payment of premiums; in the event of declining investment returns, employees bear the loss. Levels of employer contributions, if any, can be reduced at the employer's discretion. Last, plans are subject to termination without future liability. So long as market conditions permit employers to reduce or eliminate pension programs as a feature of employment, employees have little recourse. The chart shown in Figure 8.2,

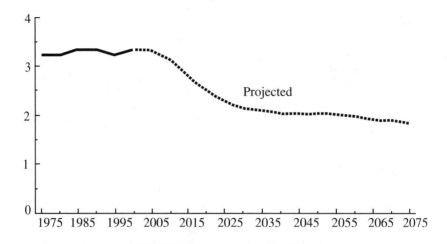

Figure 8.3   Number of Workers Supporting One Beneficiary

SOURCE: Social Security Administration.

prepared by the Bureau of Labor Statistics, shows the changing composition of retirement plans over two decades.[56]

The old-age insurance component of Social Security makes up an economic safety net for the elderly. The genesis of the program was described in Chapter 4; here, the relevant point has to do with the future of the program. Like Medicare, Social Security pension funds face a demographic crisis in only a few decades. The large cohort of citizens in the baby boom generation will have reached retirement age by 2020. The ratio of workers to Social Security recipients will decline from nearly 4 to 1 in the 1960s to 2 to 1 in 2050. The surplus trust funds built up during the baby boomers' peak earning years may be exhausted as early as 2044 using the intermediate economic forecast.[57] But economic conditions will hardly be favorable.

Political and economic developments in early 2003 resulted in projected budget deficits of $60 trillion beginning in 2004. Again, the payment of Social Security benefits will depend on earnings of current workers and their contributions to the trust funds. If there are fewer workers, and those workers have lower earnings, then either benefits will be cut or payroll taxes will be raised, or both. Critics of the Social Security program, including George W. Bush, propose to shift the Social Security program toward a privatized system that would permit workers to make their own investment decisions. Such a shift would necessitate a large infusion of revenues into Social Security for the transition period. Like other domestic matters, Social Security dropped out of the legislative debate in 2003. But it looms as an impending domestic crisis along with health insurance. The demographic problem is illustrated in the chart shown in Figure 8.3.

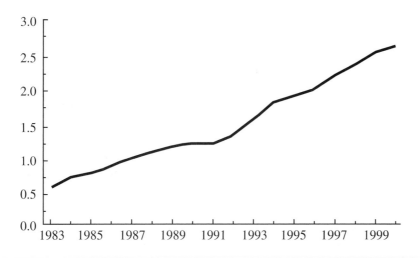

Figure 8.4   Temporary Help as a Percentage of Total Employment

SOURCE: Bureau of Labor Statistics.

Employment Stability

The economic turmoil of the 1980s contributed to the growth of a contingent workforce. The Bureau of Labor Statistics defines a contingent worker as one who has no expectation of continued employment. The bureau also notes that there are a number of persons employed in nonstandard or alternative work arrangements, which are characterized by irregular employment patterns. Independent contractors make up the largest group in the latter category, amounting to 6.4 percent of the workforce. The category also includes on-call workers, temporary help, and company contractors.[58] While the number of contingent and alternative workers has not substantially increased since 1995, it remains considerably higher than in the early 1980s. Detailed studies of nonstandard work arrangements suggest that few general conclusions can be drawn about contemporary trends because those arrangements reflect considerable diversity.[59] Increases in the temporary help industry are clearly substantial, however, as Figure 8.4 indicates.

Typically, workers with irregular employment receive lower wages and fewer fringe benefits than regular employees do.[60] Compensation for independent contractors actually increased during the period, but independent contractors by definition are excluded from job-related benefits such as workers' compensation and Social Security coverage.

Union labor contracts provided job security in various ways. Seniority systems protected long-term employees, job bidding schemes sustained internal labor markets, and just cause provisions eliminated arbitrary and unjustified terminations. Employment security is somewhat broader and consists of two types.

Microeconomic job security has to do with an employee's right to continue work for a given employer. Thus, managers at a firm might be transferred to different departments or different locations and given different job duties, but they enjoyed job security with the company. More broadly, macroeconomic employment security refers to the individual's ability to secure work in the economy as a whole. Last, income security protects the worker against the hazards of unemployment by providing cash supplements during periods without work.[61]

Many complex policy issues are connected with debates about job security. One line of argument suggests that job security in fact leads to higher levels of unemployment. The reasoning is that employers need flexibility to respond to changing economic conditions, including flexibility to separate workers from employment. Any restrictions on the employer's prerogatives increase the costs of hiring and maintaining a labor force. Employers, accordingly, will be reluctant to expand employment. Or alternatively, they will rely on part-time or temporary workers who have no expectation of job security. As a net result, mandated security lowers employment, distorts labor markets, and generally has negative impacts on efficiency. According to a report in March 2003, German chancellor Gerhard Schröder contemplated a drastic restructuring of the German social welfare system, including a reduction in protections for dismissed employees.[62]

Conversely, proponents of security marshal several arguments. Fairness and social equity demand that the state intervene in labor markets to protect individuals from the dynamics of the market. Since workers do not have power equivalent to that of employers, it is necessary to establish that balance by legislation. Employment security, which helps to build a stable and experienced workforce, could lead to gains in economic efficiency.[63] Finally, by compelling employers to provide security, the state will encourage human resource development to a greater extent than would otherwise exist. Rather than allowing imperfect markets to shape labor relations, the state intervenes to implement its superior solutions.[64]

In discussions of employment security, comparisons are often drawn between the United States and other countries having greater protective legislation.[65] The United States is generally regarded as a country with slight formal employment security. The only legislative constraints on layoff and dismissals for all workers— that is, excluding specific laws for the protection of minorities, the disabled, and other protected classes—are the Worker Adjustment and Retraining Notification (WARN) Act of 1988, the common law exceptions to employment at will rule, Montana's wrongful discharge law, and the experience-rating mechanism of unemployment insurance. WARN contains numerous exceptions to its requirements and is not particularly effective either at informing employees of job loss or aiding them in securing new employment.[66] Thus, a formal system of employment security is lacking in this country.[67]

Member nations of the European Union, in contrast, tend to have comprehensive laws regulating individual and mass dismissals. Any dismissal must be justified. Individual dismissals are permissible for reasons of performance or economics, but no economic dismissal occurs before the company considers alternatives such as transfer or reduction of work hours. Dismissals are appealable to the works council or labor court, and possible remedies include reinstatement or compensation. If the dismissal is justified, the employer nevertheless must provide some period of notice before the action is implemented. For collective dismissals involving a significant number of employees, the employer must consult with the works council and notify the state before taking action. Further, the employer in such cases must negotiate with the affected workers over a plan for severance compensation, retraining benefits, and other matters. The government assists employers in dealing with employment security by supplementing short-time work with unemployment insurance benefits and subsidizing early retirement.[68]

Assessing the contrasting approaches in the European Union and the United States involves judgments about values. Economic performance certainly is one value, and the German system, as noted, may create drags on labor market performance. But other countries provide a measure of security and remain globally competitive at the same time. According to rankings by the International Management Development Institute, among the most competitive countries in the world are the United States, Finland, Luxembourg, Netherlands, Singapore, Denmark, Switzerland, Canada, Hong Kong, and Ireland.[69] Most of those countries are social democracies that maintain strong protective networks ensuring universal access to such basic needs as medical care, education, shelter, and employment training. An effective social safety net is not necessarily incompatible with economic competitiveness.

Conclusion

For the foreseeable future, it is unlikely that any meaningful discussion of employment reform in this country will take place. The issues of health care, retirement, and employment security cannot be realistically addressed in light of massive budget deficits caused by the global political situation and domestic fiscal policies. As our financial stability erodes in consequence of declining foreign investment, inflationary pressures, and revenue shortfalls, available resources will be subject to fierce competition. The organized labor movement, workers' voice in the political system, offers one channel of influence. Given the magnitude of the problems, however, that voice is likely to be very muted.

Summary

- Organizational justice plays an important role in human resource policies. The application of justice techniques helps to reduce employee dissatisfaction, turnover, and negative work behaviors.
- Internal dispute procedures, such as nonunion arbitration, are increasingly common in workplaces. The effectiveness of such procedures could be improved by the presence of an outside advocate of the employee's interests; if representation were combined with a system of deferral, both employees and employers would benefit.

- Unions impose costs on employers. They also can improve workplace relations. Federal policy encourages strong and effective labor organizations, but federal law and practice do little to prevent widespread opposition to unions. A better policy approach would assist unions in developing institutional processes to create trust and cooperation in employment relations.
- The crucial issues facing U.S. workers are health care, pensions, and employment security. To deal with those issues, workers need an effective political voice. Whether we can avoid a systemic crisis in these three areas is complicated by ongoing problems in the domestic and global economy.

Further Analysis

1. Assume that in fact unions drive down a firm's profits by raising wages. If union wage premiums lead to employer opposition and eventually to union decline, what legislative policies could be adopted to counteract that progression? Consider the proposition that a collective bargaining contract in a given industry would be extended to other major employers in the industry. Then, for example, Wal-Mart could not compete against Kroger, Safeway, and Albertsons by undercutting labor costs. What arguments could be made for and against the idea?

2. On balance, do you think participation programs provide real benefits for employers and employees, or are they just one more management fad floating to the surface in the business milieu? Would the fact that they encourage democracy in and of itself be a sufficient justification for their adoption? Recall the Rockefeller plan discussed in Chapter 2. What incentives prompted Rockefeller and other employers in the 1920s to provide workplace democracy? If democracy is such an important American value, why does it have so little application in contemporary workplaces?

3. How would you describe a high-performance workplace? If the Saturn plant at Spring Hill is one, what differentiates it from, say, a K-Mart store? Recall that Ford has an auto assembly plant in Hermosilla, Mexico, which produces cars equal in quality to those made in other Ford plants. Does that suggest that high-performance can also be low-wage?

4. Would most Americans now support a national system of health care? Is there a connection between the weaknesses of the U.S. system of job-linked health care benefits and the decline of the U.S. labor movement? If most of us want greater federal involvement in health insurance, why doesn't Congress act on that issue?

5. How does the medical insurance component of Social Security fit into discussions of national health care? Workers and employers now separately contribute 6.2 percent of covered payroll ($87,000 in 2003) to the old-age, survivor, and disability programs and 1.45 percent of all wages to health insurance. Assume Congress decided to extend the health insurance benefits to any worker and to increase the tax rate to 5 percent. Would that be a sound approach to the health care problem?

6. What would be the best approach to employment security? Other countries subsidize retraining, unemployment benefits, family leave, and similar programs. Do European nations provide an appropriate model for the United States in this regard? Why or why not? Would you support a law that requires every employer to offer a standardized contract to employees, which would include a provision requiring proof of a legitimate business reason if the employee is separated from employment?

Suggested Readings

Appelbaum, Eileen, and Rosemary Batt. *The New American Workplace: Transforming Work Systems in the United States.* Ithaca, NY: ILR Press, 1994.

Bluestone, Barry, and Irving Bluestone. *Negotiating the Future: A Labor Perspective on American Business.* New York: Basic Books, 1992.

Buechtemann, Christoph. *Employment Security and Labor Market Behavior: Interdisciplinary Approaches and International Evidence.* Ithaca, NY: ILR Press, 1993.

Cappelli, Peter. *The New Deal at Work.* Boston: Harvard Business School Press, 2000.

Cascio, Wayne. *Responsible Restructuring: Creative and Profitable Alternatives to Layoffs.* San Francisco: Berrett-Koehler, 2002.

Friedman, Sheldon, and David C. Jacobs, eds. *The Future of the Safety Net: Social Insurance and Employee Benefits.* Champaign, IL: Industrial Relations Research Association, 2001.

Hecksher, Charles. *The New Unionism.* New York: Basic Books, 1988.

Herzenberg, Stephen, John A. Alic, and Howard Wial. *New Rules for a New Economy: Employment and Opportunity in Postindustrial America.* Ithaca, NY: Cornell University Press, 1998.

Marshall, Ray, and Marc Tucker. *Thinking for a Living: Education and the Wealth of Nations.* New York: Basic Books, 1992.

Mishel, Lawrence, and Paula Voos. *Unions and Economic Competitiveness.* Armonk, NY: M. E. Sharpe, 1992.

Osterman, Paul, Thomas A. Kochan, Richard Locke, and Michael J. Piore. *Working in America: A Blueprint for the New Labor Market.* Cambridge, MA: MIT Press, 2001.

Weiler, Paul. *Governing the Workplace: The Future of Labor and Employment Law.* Cambridge, MA: Harvard University Press, 1990.

Endnotes

1. Consider, for example, the case of the gay hotel manager whom Leona Helmsley harassed and fired because of his sexual orientation. A jury awarded him more than $11 million in damages for the discharge, including $10 million in punitive and $1.2 million in compensatory damages. An arbitrator's remedy would have been reinstatement to the job and back pay less any interim earnings—hardly $1.2 million. The case is also discussed in the materials on the changing nature of judicial doctrine regarding employment at will in Chapter 7. It demonstrates how changes in common law rules can sometimes go beyond any reasonable boundaries. For a lively polemic against contemporary employment law, see Walter K. Olson, *The Excuse Factory: How Employment Law Is Paralyzing the American Workplace* (New York: Martin Kessler Books, Free Press, 1997).

2. An excellent treatment of changes in work is Paul Osterman, Thomas A. Kochan, Richard Locke, and Michael J. Piore, *Working in America: A Blueprint for the New Labor Market* (Cambridge, MA: MIT Press, 2001).

3. Iowa State University fired its basketball coach, Larry Eustachy, in April 2003 for attending a student party and making advances to a female undergraduate. He publicly apologized for the incident and said that he was an alcoholic whose drinking was out of control that night. He had since attended a rehabilitation program and stopped drinking. The university paid Eustachy $1.2 million to sever the relationship. If Eustachy deserved to be fired, why should the university pay him anything? For the report, see Damon Hack, "Iowa State's Eustachy Quits in Wake of Scandal," *New York Times,* May 6, 2003 [online].

4. James A. Gross, *Broken Promise: The Subversion of U.S. Labor Relations Policy, 1947–1994* (Philadelphia: Temple University Press, 1995).

5. For a good overview of the field, see Russell Cropanzano, ed., *Justice in the Workplace* (Mahwah, NJ: Lawrence Erlbaum Associates, 1993).

6. The theories and techniques associated with workplace justice are analyzed in Jerald Greenberg and Russell C. Cropanzano, eds., *Advances in Organizational Justice* (Stanford, CA: Stanford University Press, 2001).

7. Testimony of George Storm, *Report of the Committee of the Senate Upon the Relations Between Labor and Capital,* vol. 2 (Washington, DC: Government Printing Office, 1885), 803–833. Storm noted that some observers believed the arbitration system favored the company. He said, "I have had employers come to me to inquire about this method of arbitration, and how it worked, and after taking all the trouble to explain it to them, they would say in a sly manner, 'Well, I suppose you have it all your own way, don't you?' These people are unfit to have arbitration—they are tricksters" (p. 806). When asked what Congress might do to improve the condition of labor, Storm replied, "The cardinal object in all legislation should be, I imagine—at least, that would be a beginning in the right direction—to give those who work for wages some consideration in legislation, and to have a care that the laws are not so made that the rich will grow richer and the poor poorer" (p. 832).

8. The cases are *Burlington Industries v. Ellerth,* 524 U.S. 742 (1998), and *Faragher v. City of Boca Raton,* 524 U.S. 775 (1998).

9. See Raymond L. Hogler, Jennifer H. Frame, and George Thornton, "Workplace Sexual Harassment Law: An Empirical Analysis of Organizational Justice and Legal Policy," *Journal of Managerial Issues* 14 (2002): 234–250.

10. For a good analysis of this point, see Alexander J. S. Colvin, "Institutional Pressures, Human Resource Strategies, and the Rise of Nonunion Dispute Resolution Procedures," *Industrial and Labor Relations Review* 56 (2003): 375–392. The study differentiates between arbitration procedures and peer review and concludes that the processes respond to different threats. That is, "Adoption of nonunion arbitration was strongly associated with litigation threats but not associated with unionization threats, whereas adoption of peer review was strongly associated with unionization threats but not with litigation threats" (p. 389).

11. *Circuit City v. Adams,* 532 U.S. 105 (2001).

12. *EEOC v. Waffle House,* 534 U.S. 279 (2002).

13. For a good appraisal of nonunion dispute procedures, see Katherine Van Wezel Stone, "Dispute Resolution in the Boundaryless Workplace," *Ohio State Journal on Dispute Resolution* 16 (2001): 467.

14. Michael Z. Green, "Debunking the Myth of Employer Advantage From Using Mandatory Arbitration for Discrimination Claims," *Rutgers Law Journal* 31 (2000): 399.

15. Bureau of Labor Statistics, Union Member Summary, February 28, 2003. Online at http://stats.bls.gov/news.release/union2.nr0.htm.

16. Richard Freeman and James Medoff, *What Do Unions Do?* (New York: Basic Books, 1984). This book changed the way labor economists viewed unions and initiated an ongoing debate about the effects of unions and collective bargaining.

17. Richard Freeman, "Is Declining Unionization of the U.S. Good, Bad, or Irrelevant?" in *Unions and Economic Competitiveness,* ed. L. Mishel and P. B. Voos (Armonk, NY: M. E. Sharpe, 1992), 143–169.

18. Freeman, "Declining Unionization," in *Unions and Economic Competitiveness,* ed. Mishel and Voos, pp. 145–148.

19. Edward P. Lazear, *Personnel Economics for Managers* (New York: John Wiley, 1998), 521–523.

20. Susan Carey and Scott McCartney, "Long Knives: United's Bid to Cut Labor Costs Could Force Rivals to Follow," *Wall Street Journal,* February 25, 2003, p. A1, col. 5.

21. Barry Hirsch, *Labor Unions and the Economic Performance of Firms* (Kalamazoo, MI: W. E. Upjohn Institute, 1991), 124.

22. Leo Troy, *Beyond Unions and Collective Bargaining* (Armonk, NY: M. E. Sharpe, 1999), 60–61.

23. The leading study on this point is Julius Getman, Stephen B.Goldberg, and Jeanne B. Herman, *Union Representation Elections: Law and Reality* (New York: Russell Sage Foundation, 1976). They conclude that job satisfaction and attitudes toward unions are the main determinants of individual choice.

24. See generally, Colvin, "Institutional Pressures."

25. For a concise overview of contemporary union strategies, see Hoyt N. Wheeler, *The Future of the American Labor Movement* (Cambridge, UK: Cambridge University Press, 2002).

26. The point is analyzed in Arnold M. Zack, "Agreements to Arbitrate and the Waiver of Rights Under Employment Law," in *Employment Dispute Resolution and Worker Rights,* ed. Adrienne E. Eaton and Jeffery H. Keefe (Champaign, IL: Industrial Relations Research Association, 1999), 67–94.

27. In March 2003, the EEOC approved a pilot program involving the use of nonunion dispute resolution. According to the policy, the EEOC will accept the outcome of the employer's dispute process if it satisfies the following criteria:

Participation by its employees is voluntary.
The employer has an established program.
The program has clearly written procedures.
It is free to the employee.
The program addresses all claims and relief under EEOC-enforced statutes.
Settlements obtained must be in writing and enforceable in court.

For the text of the EEOC press release, see www.eeoc.gov/press/3-24-03.html.

28. For a discussion of the rule and supporting case law, see Patrick Hardin, ed., *The Developing Labor Law: The Board, the Courts, and the National Labor Relations Act,* 3d ed. (Washington, DC: Bureau of National Affairs, 1992), 1030–1068.

29. The authority of arbitrators to apply external law occasioned lengthy debates. See Frank Elkouri and Edna Elkouri, *How Arbitration Works,* 5th ed. (Washington, DC: BNA Books, 1997), 516–598.

30. The National Labor Relations Act in Section 8(a)(2) forbids employers from dominating an entity that deals with the employer over wages, hours, and working conditions. The arrangement suggested here does not involve an entity created or dominated by the employer, because it is not a group composed of the employer's employees. Similarly, the relationship would not involve a union illegitimately recognized by the employer, because the employer merely engages the services of a consultant to provide a benefit to employees who wish those services. The union would be in a position similar to that of a health care provider rather than a collective bargaining entity. In any event, the board has held that performance of a merely ministerial function does not violate Section 8(a)(2), *M. K. Morse Co.,* 302 NLRB 924 (1991), and even if the union official negotiated a settlement for an individual worker, the official would not be acting in a representative capacity as to other workers.

31. The trilogy consists of the following cases: *United Steelworkers v. American Manufacturing Co,* 363 U.S. 564 (1960); *United Steelworkers v. Warrior & Gulf Navigation Co.,* 363 U.S. 564 (1960); *United Steelworkers v. Enterprise Wheel & Car Corp.,* 363 U.S. 593 (1960).

32. For a study of judicial review and why courts are poorly suited to interpret labor contracts, see Raymond L. Hogler, "Just Cause, Judicial Review, and Industrial Justice: An Arbitral Critique," *Labor Law Journal* 40 (1989): 281–293.

33. See generally Paul Adler and Seok-Woo Kwon, "Social Capital: Prospects for a New Concept," *Academy of Management Review* 27 (2002): 17–40.

34. O. S. Beyer Jr., "Experiences With Cooperation Between Labor and Management in the Railway Industry," in *Wertheim Lectures on Industrial Relations 1928,* ed. Otto S. Beyer Jr. et al. (Cambridge, MA: Harvard University Press, 1929).

35. The brief account in this paragraph is drawn from the influential study by Ray Marshall and Marc Tucker, *Thinking for a Living: Education and the Wealth of Nations* (New York: Basic Books, 1992), 3–12; quote p. 10. For a similar argument about the problems facing U.S. industry, see Robert Reich, *The Next American Frontier* (New York: Times Books, 1983).

36. For a good treatment of this point, see Michael Piore and Charles Sabel, *The Second Industrial Divide: Possibilities for Prosperity* (New York: Basic Books, 1984).

37. Marshall and Tucker, *Thinking for a Living,* p. 40.

38. Eileen Applebaum and Rosemary Batt, *The New American Workplace: Transforming Work Systems in the United States* (Ithaca, NY: ILR Press, 1993), 54.

39. Marshall and Tucker, *Thinking for a Living,* p. 64.

40. Applebaum and Batt, *New American Workplace,* p. 60.

41. David Levine and Laura Tyson, "Participation, Productivity, and the Firm's Environment," in *Paying for Productivity: A Look at the Evidence,* ed. Alan Blinder (Washington, DC: Brookings Institution, 1990), 183–243; quote p. 204.

42. Maryellen Kelley and Bennett Harrison, "Unions, Technology, and Labor-Management Cooperation," in *Unions and Economic Competitiveness,* ed. Mishel and Voos, pp. 247–277; quote p. 277. For another article reaching similar conclusions, see Adrienne Eaton and Paula Voos, "Unions and Contemporary Innovations in Work Organization, Compensation, and Employee Participation," in the same book, pp. 173–207.

43. These cooperative ventures are described in Peggy Stuart, "Labor Unions Become Business Partners," *Personnel Journal* (August 1993): 54–63.

44. "Saturn," *Business Week,* August 17, 1992, p. 91.

45. Saul Rubinstein, Michael Bennet, and Thomas Kochan, "The Saturn Partnership: Co-management and the Reinvention of the Local Union," in *Employee Representation: Alternatives and Future Directions,* ed. Bruce E. Kaufman and Morris M. Kleiner (Madison, WI: Industrial Relations Research Association, 1993), 339–370; quote p. 368.

46. Robert D. Putnam, *Bowling Alone: The Collapse and Revival of American Community* (New York: Simon & Schuster, 2000).

47. See, for example, Samuel Bowles and Herbert Gintis, "Social Capital and Community Governance," *Economic Journal* 112 (2002): F419–F436; Margaret Levi, "When Good Defenses Make Good Neighbors: A Transaction Cost Approach to Trust, the Absence of Trust and Distrust," in *Institutions, Contracts and Organizations: Perspectives From New Institutional Economics,* ed. Claude Menard (Cheltenham, UK: Edward Elgar, 2000), 158–171.

48. For an excellent study of the role of unions in our political systems, see John Delaney and Marick Masters, "Unions and Political Action," in *The State and the Unions,* ed. George Strauss, Daniel G. Gallagher, and Jack Fiorito (Madison, WI: Industrial Relations Research Association, 1991), 313–346.

49. For materials on the event, see http://covertheuninsured.org/week/ [visited Apri 17, 2003].

50. Shannon Brownlee, "The Overtreated American," *Atlantic Monthly,* January/February 2003, p. 89.

51. For detailed information about health care in the United States, visit the Kaiser Family Foundation Web site at www.kff.org/docs/sections/kcmu/uia2000.html [visited January 18, 2003].

52. During the 1980s, "the share of workers covered by employer-provided health care plans dropped a steep 7.1 percentage points, from 70.2% to 63.1%." Coverage expanded during the economic recovery of the late 1990s, but it never reached levels of 1979. Lawrence Mishel, Jared Bernstein, and Heather Boushey, *The State of Working America, 2002/2003* (Ithaca, NY: Cornell University Press, 2003), 146. For a detailed report, see Kaiser Family Foundation, Trends and Indicators in the Changing Health Care Marketplace, 2002, at www.kff.org/topics.cgi [search terms "trends and indicators"; visited May 29, 2003].

53. Most Americans actually opposed the tax cuts as a method of economic stimulus and preferred that the government use the money to help pay for health care coverage. John Harwood, "Tax-Cut Victory May Prove Costly for Bush," *Wall Street Journal,* May 22, 2003, p. A4. According to this poll, 55 percent of the respondents wanted the government to subsidize health care, and 36 percent wanted tax cuts.

54. Medicare consists of two parts and different trust funds exist for each part. The trustees produced a consolidated report that is available online at the following Web site: http://cms.hhs.gov/publications/trusteesreport/default.asp.

55. The Kaiser Family Foundation surveyed large employers and reported the following findings on retirees and health insurance:

> 95 percent of large employers plan to continue offering health insurance to *current* retirees (those who are already retired under age sixty-five or age sixty-five and older) in the next three years
>
> 22 percent say they are likely to eliminate retiree coverage for *future* retirees (often new or recent hires) within the next three years
>
> 82 percent expect to increase retiree premiums and 85 percent plan to raise prescription drug copayments or coinsurance over the next three years

> 13 percent say they terminated benefits for *future* retirees over the past two years The average retiree contribution rose 19 percent for pre-sixty-five retirees and 20 percent for retirees sixty-five and older between 2001 and 2002

"The Current State of Retiree Health Benefits: Findings From the Kaiser/Hewitt 2002 Retiree Health Survey," at www.kff.org/content/2002/20021205a/.

56. Bureau of Labor Statistics, "Working in the 21st Century," online at www.bls.gov/opub/working/home.htm [March 6, 2003].

57. The trustees' report offers a slightly different perspective on Social Security costs. It notes, "Still another important way to look at Social Security's future is to view its cost as a share of the U.S. economy. [Analysis] shows that Social Security's cost as a percentage of GDP will grow 1.6 times from 4.4 percent in 2002 to 7.0 percent in 2077. Over the same period, the cost of Social Security expressed as a percentage of taxable payroll will grow from 10.95 percent to 19.92 percent." See www.ssa.gov/OACT/TR/.

58. The Bureau of Labor Statistics issued a press release summarizing its findings on contingent labor markets. See "Contingent and Alternative Employment Arrangements, February 2001," at www.bls.gov/rofod/1440.pdf.

59. For an excellent collection of articles, see Françoise Carré, Marianne A. Ferber, Lonnie Golden, and Stephen A. Herzenberg, eds., *Nonstandard Work: The Nature and Challenges of Changing Employment Arrangements* (Champaign, IL: Industrial and Labor Relations Research Association, 2000).

60. For data on nonstandard work, see Mishel, Bernstein, and Boushey, *State of Working America, 2002/2003*, pp. 250–262.

61. See Christoph Buechtemann, "Introduction: Employment Security and Labor Markets," in *Employment Security and Labor Market Behavior: Interdisciplinary Approaches and International Evidence*, ed. Christoph Buechtemann (Ithaca, NY: ILR Press, 1993), 5–7.

62. Christopher Rhoads, "Schröder Faces Germany's Safety Net," *Wall Street Journal*, March 13, 2003, p. A10, col. 3. The German dilemma became more ominous in mid-2003. The high labor costs hobbled gross domestic productivity and led to proposals for massive cuts in the social welfare system. Christopher Rhoads, "In Deep Crisis, Germany Starts to Revamp Vast Welfare State," *Wall Street Journal*, July 10, 2003, p. A1, col. 4. The same strategy of reduced labor costs also became more prevalent in the United States as unemployment levels forced workers to accept lower-paying jobs. Carlos Tejada and Gary McWilliams, "Pay Check—New Recipe for Cost Savings: Replace Expensive Workers," *Wall Street Journal*, June 11, 2003, p. A1, col. 4.

63. A recent book provides compelling evidence to demonstrate that employee retention confers more economic benefit to firms than mass layoffs during downturns. Wayne F. Cascio, *Responsible Restructuring: Creative and Profitable Alternatives to Layoffs* (San Francisco: Berrett-Koehler, 2002).

64. Buechtemann, "Introduction," in *Employment Security*, ed. Buechtemann, pp. 9–14.

65. For an incisive discussion of the point, see "The Trouble With Success," *Economist*, March 12, 1994, p. 78.

66. Ronald Ehrenberg and George Jakubson, "Why WARN? The Impact of Recent Plant-Closing and Layoff Prenotification Legislation in the United States," in *Employment Security*, ed. Buechtemann, pp. 200–214.

67. Firms may follow policies that lead to job security for some workers. The existence of internal labor markets, which refers to the firm's rules for hiring, promotion, compensation, and other personnel issues, offered a measure of employment security. Those

institutional protections tended to break down under the competitive pressures of the 1980s and 1990s. Peter Capelli, *The New Deal at Work: Managing the Market-Driven Workforce* (Boston: Harvard Business School Press, 1999).

68. Katharine Abraham and Susan Houseman, *Job Security in America: Lessons From Germany* (Washington, DC: Brookings Institution, 1993), 11–30.

69. See the International Management Development Institute Web site at www02.imd.ch/wcy/ranking/. The 2003 rankings are categorized in large and small populations.

CHAPTER 9

Conclusions

Back to the Future?

Americans have a fondness for utopian fantasies. From the colonial era to contemporary culture, creative artists have presented a vision of human existence that is sometimes inspiring and sometimes repulsive; always, though, the alternative reality is permeated with themes of good and evil, innocence and experience, and suffering and redemption.[1] One of the most popular and influential books of the late nineteenth century was Edward Bellamy's fictional *Looking Backward, 2000–1887*. The protagonist of the novel, Julian West, is hypnotized one evening in Boston in 1887, and he awakens in the year 2000. Life in the United States in the twenty-first century is idyllic. There are no wars, no poverty, and no social conflict. The elimination of class antagonism has been achieved by transforming work from an experience of demeaning drudgery to a shared, communal activity in which all citizens participate on equitable terms. Labor is regarded as the highest form of social utility, and every type of work is compensated equally.

West contrasts the agreeable life that he finds in 2000 with conditions in Boston at the time of his hypnosis. In one of the most compelling passages in the book, he portrays the environment of the 1880s by analogy to a carriage that masses of humanity are dragging over a difficult road. Some fortunate passengers, he says, ride on the top of the coach, and regardless of the hardships suffered by those hauling the coach, the privileged never descend from their vantage. Even so, the seats on the top of the carriage are insecure and might be lost, in which event the unfortunate victim is then required to pull the carriage with the masses. The passengers do not lack compassion and sympathy for those bearing the burden; however, they are unable to conceive of any different social organization. In West's description, two important facts prevented effective change. First, "it was firmly and sincerely believed that there was no other way in which Society could get along, except the many pulled at the rope and the few rode, and not only this, but that no very radical improvement even was possible, either in the harness, the coach, the roadway, or the distribution of the toil." Second, those riding on the coach suffered from "a singular hallucination" that convinced them "that they were not exactly like their brothers and sisters who pulled at the rope, but of finer clay, in some way belonging to a higher order of beings who might justly expect to be drawn."[2]

Looking Backward seized the public's attention. It quickly became one of the nation's bestselling novels, second only to *Uncle Tom's Cabin,* and influenced millions of Americans. Today, the book has little appeal, and Bellamy's views would likely be rejected by most citizens. The industrial army of production that he proposed resembles the failed Communist experiments in China and the Soviet Union and the regime in North Korea. But one common thread that can be traced through the U.S. employment system, and that is brilliantly realized in *Looking Backward,* is the tension between the rewards attainable through capitalism and the need to restrain competition for the benefit of those who do not fully share in the system. Whatever its practical shortcomings, the book depicts a world without violence, deprivation, and unnecessary suffering.

Moreover, Bellamy emphasizes another important point: work is the linchpin of communal life in our society. It provides psychological as well as economic rewards, and it is the institutional glue holding us together. Indeed, Bellamy's driving insight is the way labor serves communities. When Julian West asks how an economic system can function without the goad of individual self-interest, his host replies, "Does it really seem to you . . . that human nature is insensible to any motives save fear of want and love of luxury, that you should expect security and equality of livelihood to leave them without possible incentives to effort?"[3] Not self-aggrandizement, but honor, patriotism, and duty gave purpose to work. Bellamy viewed labor, leisure, and human fulfillment as a seamless round of human activity. Since Americans now spend more hours at work than do people in any other industrialized country, and produce more consumer goods, it is useful to examine some ongoing prospects for the most powerful economic engine ever known.

The Job Machine in the 2000s

According to a report in the *Wall Street Journal* in May 2003, the beginning of economic recovery has not led to any significant growth of jobs. To the contrary, "Instead of expanding employment, companies are continuing to shed jobs at a furious pace—525,000 nonfarm payroll positions in the past three months alone. Since March 2001, when the recession began, the U.S. economy has lost 2.1 million jobs."[4] The downturn in employment is more protracted than at any time since the Great Depression. Among other reasons for the decline are increased competition from foreign nations, higher levels of productivity as a result of intensified labor, and slow growth. Because the phenomenon involves deep structural change, it has long-term and widespread consequences. Workers who lose jobs remain unemployed for longer periods of time and may not find work in their previous occupations. In addition, the slump affects all segments of the working population, from manual laborers through recent college graduates. Even those fortunate enough to return to work often do so at lower salaries and fewer benefits such as health insurance.

Because social protections in the United States are so tightly enmeshed with employment, the loss of a job usually means the loss of access to medical care and retirement security. This book has described the reasons why the U.S. employment model evolved into its current form, which is heavily dependent on conditions in the labor market. The European model, in contrast, offers citizens basic entitlements regardless of employment status and environmental factors. Those entitlements emanate from a system of national taxation designed to meliorate extremes of wealth. The United States pursues a system of income distribution that has become increasingly unequal over the course of three decades. A leading analyst summarizes the situation as follows:

> Between 1947 and 1973, American families in every income category enjoyed income growth—and the poorest families had the highest rate of all. Then, between 1973 and 1998, income remained close to stagnant (adjusted for inflation) for the bottom 40 percent of families, growing robustly only for the top quarter. Indeed, in 1993, before the boom that followed, the bottom half of families were worse off than in 1973.[5]

After leveling off in the late 1990s, trends in inequality began to rise again in the new century. Looking ahead, the future begins to resemble the past.

Should the U.S. employment system not meet basic social needs, citizens have few realistic alternatives. A move toward the European model, with its levels of taxation and labor market regulation, is improbable. The Bush administration's tax cuts of 2003 preclude any significant governmental expansion of social programs, and a congressional committee concluded that "the positive business investment incentives arising from the tax policy are eventually likely to be outweighed by the reduction in national savings due to increasing Federal government deficits." With regard to employment stimulus, the committee "found the bill would provide no long-term increase in jobs."[6] If job markets remain lackluster and resources are unavailable to support health care and retirement programs, our country begins to move backward toward the pre–New Deal era.

A Final Thought

In many ways, the U.S. employment system stands at a crossroads at the start of the twenty-first century. The historical cycles described in this book illustrate that change occurs in unexpected ways, often in response to crisis. Episodes of labor–management conflict, economic catastrophe, and growth and stability all contributed to today's patterns of employment. As we begin another period of transition, the past may offer insights into possible directions for labor policy. Indeed, another Edward Bellamy might emerge to imagine for us a better world.

Endnotes

1. For a good historical survey of American utopianism, see Krishan Kumar, *Utopia and Anti-Utopia in Modern Times* (Oxford, UK: Blackwell, 1987). The *Matrix* films stand as a contemporary example. Cornel West, a well-known academic, plays a small role in the second and third movies. After meeting with the screenwriters, Larry and Andy Wachowski, West said, "At the core of the *Matrix* trilogy lies the disturbing notion that the world is nothing but perceptions controlled by malevolent forces. While the films repeatedly ask questions about the nature of truth and reality, the possibilities of choice and free will, the meaning of life and love, they offer no answers." Those are common motifs of utopian thinking. Lynn Smith, "The *Matrix* and the Intellectual," *Los Angeles Times,* May 20, 2003 (online).

2. Edward Bellamy, *Looking Backward, 2000–1887,* ed. John L. Thomas (Cambridge, MA: Harvard University Press, 1967 [Ticknor and Company, 1888]), 98.

3. Bellamy, *Looking Backward,* p. 153.

4. Jon E. Hilsenrath, "Looking Longer: Why for Many This Recovery Feels More Like a Recession," *Wall Street Journal,* May 29, 2003, p. A1.

5. Edward N. Wolff, *Top Heavy: The Increasing Inequality of Wealth in American and What Can Be Done About It,* rev. ed. (New York: New Press, 2002), viii.

6. A copy of the report is available from the Center on Budget and Policy Priorities, online at www.cbpp.org/5-13-03tax.htm.

Index

About the Author

Raymond L. Hogler teaches labor relations and human resource management at Colorado State University. He earned Ph.D. and J.D. degrees from the University of Colorado. He attended Emory University as a Woodrow Wilson Fellow and the University of Wales (Swansea) as a Fulbright Scholar. Prior to his employment at Colorado State University, he taught in the Department of Labor Studies and Industrial Relations at Pennsylvania State University, and in 1994, he was a Visiting Scholar at the University of Warwick. He is certified as a labor arbitrator by the Federal Mediation and Conciliation Service. Over the past two decades, he has published a number of books and articles on employment issues, including a study of employee participation programs and labor law in the United States.